SANDRA GUSTAFSON'S

CHEAP
SLEEPS IN
PARIS

EIGHTH EDITION

**A Traveler's Guide to the
Best-Kept Secrets**

SANDRA A. GUSTAFSON

CHRONICLE BOOKS
SAN FRANCISCO

With special thanks to Marv, whose unending patience and good cheer proved that old dogs can learn new tricks, and to Opal, whose detailed knowledge of Paris improved this book immeasurably.

Printed in the United States of America.

EIGHTH EDITION
ISBN 0-8118-1831-4
ISSN 1074-505X

Cover photograph: Ile St. Louis, Paris, France. Charles Nes/Liaison
International
Book design: Words & Deeds
Original maps: Françoise St. Clair

Distributed in Canada by Raincoast Books,
8680 Cambie Street, Vancouver, B.C. V6P 6M9

10 9 8 7 6 5 4 3 2 1

Chronicle Books
85 Second Street
San Francisco, CA 94105

Web Site: www.chroniclebooks.com

Contents

To the Reader

You, who have ever been to Paris know;
And you who have not been to Paris—go.
—*John Ruskin,* A Tour through France, *1835*

La Belle France continues to beckon us no matter what. Paris is one of the most popular travel destinations in the world. Each year Parisians play host to more than 20 million visitors, which is nearly ten times the city's population. The American passion for Paris has now entered its third century: it has continued through wars, riots, occupations, and the rise and fall of hemlines and the dollar. Whether seen for the first or the tenth time, Paris is a never-ending love affair for most of us. Walk a block, turn a corner—in Paris there is always something interesting, something beautiful and new, or something that has been there forever that you never noticed until now. No matter what time of year you visit, it is impossible to keep from falling in love with the city, its grand boulevards, the beautiful men and women, the breathtaking monuments and museums, the glorious food, the famous art, and the sweeping views—from place de la Concorde up the Champs-Élysées, from the steps of the Sacré-Coeur over the entire city, or standing at Trocadéro, looking across the fountains to the Eiffel Tower.

The first priority for visitors to Paris is a roof over their heads. In Paris, despite its reputation for high prices, there is an abundance of hotels in all price ranges, so even travelers on very tight budgets can enjoy a stay in the city.

The essence of any Parisian hotel is its individuality, and no two are alike. They vary from the most luxurious pleasure palaces in the world to those few people would even consider. It is always possible to check in to the Hilton or any other big-name chain hotel, but only in Paris can you sleep in a romantic hideaway in Montmartre and be served breakfast in bed while looking out the window and seeing all of Paris below you, rent a houseboat docked along the banks of the Seine, or check into a suite in a renovated hotel a block from the Ritz, but light-years away in price.

It is certainly true that a trip to Paris will cost more today than it did a few years ago, but what doesn't? Europe—or Paris—on five or ten dollars a day no longer exists for any traveler. Most of those romantically threadbare hotels of our youth are gone for good. More and more smaller hotels are being renovated—adding bathrooms, fluffy towels, fax machines, and buffet breakfasts served in sixteenth-century stone-walled basements. This, of course, means higher prices. Yet, there are still many ways to save money and maximize the buying strength of the dollar without feeling *nouveau pauvre* in the process.

If you are looking for a book about the cheapest beds in Paris, *Cheap Sleeps in Paris* is not for you. What you will find here is a highly selective guide to the hotels that I have discovered to be the best value in their category, be it a no-star with the shower and toilet down the hall or an antique-filled, three-star Left Bank hotel with a Jacuzzi in the marble bathroom. The purpose of this book is to offer fail-safe advice for first-time visitors, as well as for Paris veterans, on accommodations that will keep within their daily needs, tastes, and budgets. The selections include hotels—from the center of Paris to the fringes—for lovers and honeymooners, nostalgia buffs, backpackers, and families. Other options include camping, renting an apartment, or living in a student dorm or hostel. Each listing has been included because I feel it has something special to offer. Some represent a particular style or era; others have been beautifully restored. Some are in nontourist neighborhoods where people like you and I live and work, send their children to school, get their cars repaired, eat lunch, shop, and go to the dentist. Some accommodations are basic, many are charming, and a few are starkly modern. Many are cheap, others not so cheap, and a few fall into the Big Splurge category for those with more flexible budgets and demanding tastes. All have one vital feature in common: the potential for providing a memorable stay that will make you feel you have discovered your own part of Paris.

It is important for readers to know that no hotel can purchase a listing or ask to be included in this book. I pay my own way and I do all the research and writing for *Cheap Sleeps in Paris* myself; the buck stops right here. In reviewing the hotels, I pull no punches and call the shots as I see them . . . including telling you the pluses and minuses of every place, so that you will have the best idea of what to expect when you check in to your room during your Parisian holiday.

What are the guidelines I use for selecting a hotel? The two primary concerns are value for money and cleanliness, followed by location, pleasant surroundings in the room, and management attitude and service. On my visits to the hotels, which are always unannounced, I wipe my fingers across the door tops, check closets, turn on the showers, look for mold, flush toilets, spot thin towels and waxed or sandy toilet paper, open and close windows, bounce on the beds, look under them for dust, and visit the dining room where breakfast is served. I have stumbled along dimly lit corridors, climbed endless flights of stairs, and been squeezed into minuscule cage elevators that seem to have been in operation since the fall of the Bastille.

In addition to giving the value-conscious traveler the inside track to the best hotel prices in Paris, *Cheap Sleeps in Paris* offers insider information on shopping. If you are like I am and believe the eighth deadly sin is paying full retail price for anything, then you will love the Cheap Chic shopping section, which begins on page 258. There you will learn where to find everything from designer discount shops and big-name cosmetics to the latest models of shoes—all sold for less than their regular retail cost.

On my last trip to Paris for this eighth edition of *Cheap Sleeps in Paris,* I inspected every hotel and shop listed in the seventh edition, along with scores of others that did not make the final cut for one reason or another. In so doing, I walked 503.7 miles and wore out my walking shoes and two umbrellas, all in the name of research. And yet, no matter what the weather, how long the day, or the personalities and moods of the people I met along the way, it never seemed like work. I loved every minute of it. My goals in *Cheap Sleeps in Paris* are to show you how to cut corners with style, so that traveling on a budget will not make you give up the good life by lowering your standards, and to give you enough information on the hotels listed to help you select the one that will make your stay in Paris truly special and set the stage for many return visits. If I have been able to do this, I will have done my job well. I wish you *bonne chance* and *bon voyage.*

General Information

Tips for Cheap Sleeps in Paris

1. Unless you enjoy standing in long lines in French government tourist offices or rail stations, or wandering the streets looking for a hotel, never arrive in Paris without confirmed hotel reservations *in writing*.

2. Dealing directly with the hotel almost always insures the best rate. However, if a hotel has a toll-free 800-number to call from the United States and Canada, do call and ask about special package deals for senior citizens, weekends, families, and so on. Then call the hotel directly and see if you can better the price. Chances are good that you can.

3. The two weeks in mid-January and mid-February and the months of May, June, September, and October are the hardest times to find a hotel room in Paris. Try to go during the off-season, especially in July and August, when rates and airfares are at their lowest.

4. Twin beds cost more than a double, and any room with a private shower will be less than one with a bathtub.

5. Back rooms often face blank walls or dreary courtyards and are usually smaller, but they cost less and are quieter.

6. Inquire about the hotel's refund policy in case you send a deposit and then have to cancel at the last minute. Some smaller hotels have draconian ideas about refunds.

7. If you have booked an apartment and paid a chunk of money in advance, are flying charter, or have a nonrefundable and nonchangeable airline ticket, seriously consider purchasing trip insurance. If you have to change dates, interrupt travel, or cancel altogether, you will be grateful for it. The Automobile Club of America has a list of carriers. Some are Access America, Inc., 800-284-8300; Carefree Travel Insurance, 800-323-3149; and Travel Guard International, 800-782-5151.

8. Always check out the room before you check in. Confirm the rate and discuss the cost of any extras (such as telephone calls, both local and long distance) ahead of time, not when paying the bill. All hotels must clearly post their rates by the reception desk, but they are not required to list "hidden" charges they may add on later.

9. Avoid eating breakfast at your hotel if you want to save money. Instead, join the Parisians standing at the bar at the corner café. Be

sure to tell the hotel when reserving, and again at the beginning of the stay, that you will not be eating breakfast, and see that the cost is deducted per person, per day, from your hotel bill if it is included in the original room rate. Only a few hotels refuse to deduct breakfast, but you must ask; it is never done voluntarily.

10. Do not drink the beverages from the minibar. Remove them and put in your own, purchased from the corner grocery store.

11. Do major laundries at the local laundromat and take your cleaning to the neighborhood dry cleaner yourself. Laundry and dry cleaning sent from the hotel can blow a budget to shreds. If you do wash out a few things, be sure they do not drip over carpeting or fabric. And please, do not hang things in the windows!

12. Notify the hotel if you expect to arrive after 6 P.M. Even if you paid the room deposit, the hotel can technically resell your room to someone else if they do not know your arrival time.

13. Change money at a bank, *never* at a hotel.

14. In France, the ground floor (*rez-de-chaussée*) is what Americans call the first floor; the French first floor (*premier étage*) is our second floor.

15. Paris is a very noisy city both day and night, making it heaven for night owls and a nightmare for insomniacs. Traffic, sirens, motor scooters, and voices magnify on the narrow streets, echoing throughout the night. Street-cleaning crews and trash trucks start their rounds at zero-dark-hundred, which provide many a rude awakening for those still sleeping, or wishing they could. If noise is a problem, ask for a room away from the street, in the back of the hotel, or facing an inner courtyard. For added insurance, buy or bring earplugs (*boules de quiess*).

16. Savvy travelers always check with airlines or their travel agents for package deals that include airfare coupled with a car rental and/or a hotel at a fraction of the cost if paid for separately. If you are willing to take a chance and really lock yourself into a ticket that cannot be changed without an act of Congress, investigate discount air ticketers who advertise on Sunday in most major metropolitan newspaper travel sections. The fares are low, but the restrictions are many, so be sure you understand all the fine print and are able to live with it. Another great deal is to fly as a courier.

17. Traveler: Know thyself. It has often been said that all a person needs for adventure is the desire to have one. Your trip to Paris (or any other destination) should be an adventure, filled with treasured memories that last a lifetime. In any adventure, there will always be surprises. If you aren't willing to risk some unexpected turns in your plans, but insist on absolute predictability, especially with your accommodations, then I recommend you do one of

two things: reserve a room at the Hôtel Ritz (tel: 01-43-16-30-30, fax: 01-43-16-36-68/69), or invest your travel money elsewhere and stay home.

When to Go

If you don't travel when you can, your heirs probably will.
—Anonymous

High and Low Seasons

How wonderful it would be to be able to drop everything and fly to Paris whenever the spirit moved us! If such romantic impulses do not quite fit into your schedule or budget, then the high and low seasons must be taken into consideration. These times of the year affect not only the availability of hotel rooms and the rates but airline fares as well. The best time to go to Paris is in the early spring or late autumn, when most of the other tourists have gone home and everything is easier to come by, including métro seats, café tables, and good-natured waiters.

For about two weeks in mid-January and mid-February, fashion shows fill the city to the bursting point, and many hotels charge their highest rates. Dates vary slightly from year to year, so the best bet is to check with the French Government Tourist Office in New York or Los Angeles for the latest information. During most of July and all of August, you will be sharing your Parisian holiday with many other tourists and very few French. Despite government pleadings and tourist demands, August is still the traditional vacation month for most Parisians, and many restaurants and shops are closed for at least a week or two. The good news is that hotels are always open, and during August they may be willing to negotiate lower rates, especially for longer stays.

French Holidays

Holidays (*les jours fériés*) are vital dates to bear in mind when planning any trip to Paris. Banks and stores are all closed, and museums that are open may run on different time schedules. In addition, banks may be closed a half day before each holiday as well as the day after in some instances. The traffic is horrendous, especially if the holiday falls on a Tuesday or Thursday, since many French will take off Monday or Friday to make it a long weekend. Restaurant holiday policies vary with the rise and fall of the economy. *Always* call ahead to make sure—even if they say they are open, they may change their mind and be closed. Skeleton or third-string crews man the hotel desks, and there is often a laid-back attitude during a holiday period, resulting in quick excuses for things not working. It can all add up to some very frustrating times for a traveler.

New Year's Day (January 1)	*Jour de l'An*
Easter Sunday and Monday	*Pâques et Lundi de Pâques*
Ascension Day (40 days after Easter)	*Ascension*

Pentecost (seventh Sunday after Easter and Pentecost Monday)	*Pentecôte et Lundi de Pentecôte*
Labor Day (May 1)	*Fête du Travail*
VE Day (May 8)	*Armistice 1945*
Bastille Day (July 14)	*Quatorze Juillet/Fête Nationale*
Assumption Day (August 15)	*Assomption*
All Saints' Day (November 1)	*Toussaint*
Armistice Day (November 11)	*Armistice 1918*
Christmas Day (December 25)	*Noël*

For motorists, the time to avoid is the last weekend in August, when Parisians return en masse via the *autoroutes*. This *grand rentrée* creates traffic snarls of world-class proportions.

Reservations

People ask me, "Do I need advance hotel reservations in Paris?" The answer is yes, positively! In order to be assured of a room, you *must* reserve as far in advance as possible. Paris can be one of the worst hotel bottle-necks in Europe, and a confirmed reservation, even on the slowest day in the low season, will save you frantic hours spent searching for a room after arrival. It will also save you money, since without advance reservations you will probably be forced to take something beyond your budget, perhaps in a part of the city that you do not like. Do not reserve for more nights than you think you will need. If you decide to leave before you intended, or if you want to switch hotels, you may not get back any money you have paid ahead.

The easiest way to reserve is to let your travel agent do all the work. However, it is not hard to do it yourself, and frankly, with the ease and speed of the telephone, faxes, and e-mail, it is not only easy but better because you will be able to ask questions, inquire about exact rates, and arrange just what you want without going through a middle person. In addition, the hotel may pass along to you their savings of the travel agent's commission. After reserving by one of these methods, you will be asked to guarantee your booking with a major credit card, an international money order, or in a few cases, a money order in French francs.

No matter how you decide to make your reservation, the following points should be covered:

1. Dates of stay, time of arrival, and number of persons in the party.

2. Size and type of room (double or twin beds, extra beds, adjoining rooms, suite, etc.).

3. Facilities needed: private toilet, shower and/or bathtub, or hall facilities if acceptable.

4. Location of room: view, on the street, on the courtyard, or in the back of the hotel.

5. Rates. Determine what the nightly rate will be, including the per person City of Paris tourist tax, called the *taxe de séjour*, which runs 1 to 7 francs per person, per night, depending on how many stars the hotel has (see page 35 for details on this tax). Be sure to state whether or not you will be eating breakfast at the hotel, and remember you will save money if you do not.

6. Deposit required and form of payment.

7. Refund policy if you should have to cancel.

8. Request a written confirmation and take it with you to the registration desk.

E-mail

Fascination with the internet and e-mail has not swept the imagination of the French hotel industry in the magnitude it has in the States. Whenever applicable, the hotel's e-mail and/or internet address has been given. In many cases the hotels subscribe to a general service rather than have their own. Because it is all quite new, please be understanding and patient and expect some snafus.

Fax

All but the smallest budget hotels in Paris have joined the electronic age and have a fax machine. Faxing is the best way to secure a confirmed booking. To fax a hotel in Paris, dial 011-33-1, and then the fax number in Paris.

Telephone

Always call Paris during regular, local weekday business hours to avoid talking to a hotel night clerk who has no authority to make price negotiations. Before calling, write down all your requests and questions. Ask the hotel to send you a written confirmation (or fax), and send them a letter (or fax) confirming your telephone reservation in turn. Send your letter by certified mail and keep a copy. In your letter (or fax) to the hotel, cite the details of the conversation, the name of the person with whom you spoke, and the date and time of the call. You should also enclose a deposit if they do not accept a credit card as a room guarantee. To dial direct to Paris from the United States, dial 011-33-1, and then the number of the hotel.

NOTE: When telephoning or faxing a Paris number from outside France, you drop the 0 at the beginning of the 10 digit phone or fax number (see Telephones, page 20).

Letter

Transatlantic mail can take more than two weeks each way. If there is a strike, who knows how long mail will take to reach its destination. When you consider the entire cost of your trip to Paris against the cost of a fax or a telephone call made when the rates are low, it amounts to a *very* small percentage . . . and never mind the convenience. Now with the speed and ease of e-mail, a letter makes almost no sense; in fact, in today's world, writing for reservations is about as *au courant* as the bustle. If you do insist on reserving by mail, allow sufficient time for the hotel to respond (and that means weeks) and then to make alternative plans when they tell you they are fully booked. The following letter should cover the bases for any written inquiry.

Dear Sir or Madam:

I would like to reserve ____ room(s) that is/are quiet (on the garden/ the street/the courtyard) with two beds (one big bed/one regular-size bed) with bath and toilet (with shower and toilet/without shower/bath and toilet) for ____ night(s) beginning on ____ to ____. I would like to have the room(s) include (without) breakfast. You will find attached ____F (my credit card number and expiration date) as a first night deposit.

Would you please be kind enough to confirm this reservation as soon as possible? Thank you for your assistance.

Yours sincerely,

If you want to write it in French:

Monsieur/Madame:

Je voudrais réserver ____ chambre(s) (tranquille) qui donne sur le (jardin/la rue/la cour) à deux lits (avec un grant lit/à un lit) avec salle de bains et WC (avec douche et WC/sans douche ou bain et WC) pour ____ nuit(s) à partir du ____ au ____. Je voudrais prendre la chambre(s) avec (sans) le petit déjeuner. Vous trouvez ci-joint ____f (mon carte de crédit) à titre d'arrhes.

Auriez-vous le bonté de bien vouloir me confirmer cette réservation dès que possible? Je vous remercie de votre obligeance, et je vous prie de croire, Monsier, à l'assurance de mes sentiments distingués.

With your letter, be sure to enclose an international reply coupon sold at the post office, so the hotel will not have to worry about international postage. It is a courtesy on your part and appreciated on the other side.

Deposits

After making a reservation, most hotels will require at least a one-night deposit, even if you have been a guest there before. This is smart insurance for both sides. The easiest way to handle a deposit is with a credit card. If the hotel does not take credit cards, there are other options. You can sometimes send your own personal check, which the hotel will only cash if you are a no-show. They will return it to you upon arrival. The next best option is to send the hotel an international money order in

U.S. dollars. This can be converted into French francs by the hotel, and it saves you from having to secure a deposit in French francs on this side of the Atlantic. While this option is more convenient for you, it is added work for the hotel, and some, especially in the lower price ranges, simply refuse. If your hotel insists on a deposit in French francs, you will have to purchase them in the form of a money order through your bank.

Money Matters

There are few certainties when you travel. One of them is that the moment you arrive in a foreign country, the American dollar will fall like a stone.

—Erma Bombeck

If you charge big items on your credit card, carry traveler's checks, convert francs as you go, and use ATMs, you will do fine. Also, remember to carry a few of your own personal checks. If you suddenly run out of money, you can use them to get cash advances, provided the credit card you have allows this. Try to have a few francs on hand when you arrive. This gets you out of the airport faster and keeps you from having to wait in line to get enough francs to get into Paris. True, you may pay more for this convenience, but if you change $200 or so before you leave home, you will never miss the few cents extra it may cost. If you cannot get francs locally, you can order them by telephone, and they will be Federal Expressed to you within two days. Please contact Thomas Cook Currency Service, 630 Fifth Avenue, New York, NY 10101; telephone 800-287-7362. Hours are Monday to Friday, 8:30 A.M. to 9 P.M., Eastern Standard Time.

Automatic Teller Machines—ATMs

Automatic Teller Machines are all over Paris. You can use your bank ATM card, American Express, or a Visa or MasterCard (known abroad as Carte Bleu and Eurocard, respectively). There will be fees involved, but you will be getting a wholesale conversion rate that is better than you would get at a bank or currency exchange office. Naturally you are limited to the amount you can withdraw by the type of account you have and your cash advance balance. Please—and I cannot stress this enough—do not think your ATM card or credit card pin numbers will work *as is* in Paris. They might, but chances are great that you will have to have a special pin (personal identification number) or enroll in a special program. Contact the card issuer for the steps you need to take, and allow plenty of time. Setting up an account takes several weeks but costs the cardholder nothing. For the Paris Cirrus locations and details you will need to use your card there, call 800-4-CIRRUS (424-7787). For foreign Plus locations and information, check the Plus directory at your bank. To enroll in the American Express foreign ATM program, call 800-CASH-NOW (227-4669).

Currency Exchange

The worst exchange rates are at the airport. The second-worst rates are at hotels, restaurants, and shops. These places should be avoided at all costs when it comes to money changing. Banking hours are Monday through Friday, 9:30 A.M. to 4:30 P.M. Many banks close at noon the day before a public holiday, and all remain closed on holidays and the day after Christmas, Easter, and Pentecost.

Estimate your needs carefully. If you overbuy francs, you will lose twice, buying and then selling. Every time you change money, someone is making a profit, and, I assure you, it is not you. Your best currency exchange rate will always be at a bank. You will get a better rate for traveler's checks than for cash, but the real cost lies in what you spent to get the traveler's checks in the first place and the commission cost to convert them. If your bank gives free American Express traveler's checks, by all means try to get them in French francs. This eliminates your exchange problems, including reading one word further in this section about currency exchange. If you are unable to get your traveler's checks in francs, you can cash them commission-free at the American Express office in Paris. The drawbacks here are that the exchange rates are not always the best, and the lines are slow and oh, so long. The office is at 11, rue Scribe (9th); telephone 01-47-77-70-07. Take the métro to Opéra; it's open Monday to Saturday from 9 A.M. to 6:30 P.M. Another bank with a multitude of services is Citibank, which has regular banking services plus currency exchange, traveler's checks, and cash advance with Visa cards. They accept Cirrus and most other ATM cards. They also have English-speaking representatives. There are two locations at 30 and 125, avenue Champs-Élysées (8th); telephone 01-49-05-49-05. It's open twenty-four hours, Monday to Saturday. The following banks either give commission-free rates or have longer hours:

Commission-free Rates

Banque Libanaise, 7, rue Auber (9th), around the corner from American Express; métro: Opéra; telephone 01-47-42-33-89; open Monday–Friday 9 A.M.–5 P.M.

Comptoir de Change Opéra, 9, rue Scribe (9th); métro: Opéra; telephone 01-47-42-20-96; open Monday–Friday 9 A.M.–5:15 P.M., Saturday 9:45 A.M.–4:15 P.M.

Later Hours—*Not* Necessarily Commission-free

Chequepoint, 150, avenue des Champs-Élysées (8th); métro: Charles de-Gaulle-Étoile; telephone 01-49-53-02-51; open twenty-four hours daily.

You can also exchange money at scores of authorized money-changers' offices, which are thick around tourist areas, especially along rue de Rivoli, the Champs-Élysées, and the Centre Pompideau (Beaubourg). Sometimes they advertise "commission-free" exchanges, but often you have to change large amounts, and usually the rates are lower than at a bank, or even at American Express. Your best bet with these is to use them only when all else fails, and then shop around for the best deal.

Credit Cards

For the most part, I recommend using a credit card whenever possible. The benefits are many. It is the safest way because it eliminates the need for carrying large sums of cash, which you must purchase by standing in line at a bank or at another money-changing facility. The credit card company gives the rate of exchange on the day the receipt from the expenditure is submitted, and this can also work to your advantage if the dollar is rising. It also provides you with a written record of your purchases, and best of all, you often get delayed billing of up to four to six weeks after you have returned home. If you pay in cash, the money is gone immediately. With a credit card, the money stays in your bank account drawing interest until you need it to pay the final bill. Emergency personal check cashing and access to ATM machines are benefits, as is free travel insurance. Check with your issuing bank to determine the benefits you have . . . you may be pleasantly surprised. Finally, remember, in Europe a MasterCard is Eurocard, and Visa is Carte Bleu. Every listing in *Cheap Sleeps in Paris* tells you whether or not plastic money is accepted. Thankfully, most two- and three-star hotels, and many more one-stars, accept at least one credit card. If, heaven forbid, your cards are lost or stolen, call one of these twenty-four-hour hotlines in Paris, or call collect in the United States to report the loss as soon as possible.

In Paris:

American Express	01-47-77-72-00
Diners Club	01-47-62-75-75
MasterCard (Eurocard)	01-45-67-84-84
Visa (Carte Bleu)	01-42-77-11-90

From Paris, you can call the following U.S. numbers collect to report a theft or loss of your cards:

American Express	919-668-5271
American Express Optima	904-565-7875
MasterCard	314-275-6690
Visa	410-581-9994

Sending Money to Paris from the United States

When your money is history in Paris before you are, and you have exhausted (or preferred not to use) any of the above discussed ways to increase your cash flow, there is one recourse left: Call home for money. The fastest way to refill your wallet is to have the money wired from someone in the States using a moneygram. The transfer is accomplished in minutes and the sender pays the fees, which are based on the amount sent. Here is what to do:

Contact the sender in the States, who in turn will send the money to you in either of two ways: by going to an office located in his or her city or via a credit card given over the telephone. Note, if you decide to send by credit card, there is a five-hundred-dollar limit. To send the money in person, the sender must call 800-926-9400 (twenty-four hours a day, 365 days a year). This is an information line that will provide the sender with the location of agents nearest his or her home and any other particulars for sending the money. To send money by credit card, call 800-945-2244, Monday to Friday from 6 A.M. to 4:30 P.M., Mountain Standard Time. This enables the sender to send up to five hundred dollars and charge it to a MasterCard or Visa credit card. No matter which way the money is sent, the cash-strapped person in Paris will be notified of the transaction and given a confirmation number and an address to go to in Paris to pick up the money (using a photo ID).

Tipping

How much is too much, and what is enough? Here are a few guidelines.

By law, in France, a service charge of 15 percent has already been added to hotel and restaurant bills. This service charge *is* the tip. While this eliminates the need for tips in general, there are certain times when an additional tip is appropriate.

Bars, cafés, restaurants	Leave a few extra francs in a bar or café, and up to 10 percent if the waiter in a restaurant has gone to extra lengths for you.
Hotels	Bellboy 6F per bag; chambermaid about 20F for a three-day stay; room service 10F.
Hairdressers	10–15 percent; shampoo girls 10–15F.
Taxi drivers	10–15 percent.
Theater usher	2–3F for seating two people.

NOTE: *Beware of the tipping scam.* There is an increasingly common practice in restaurants of putting the entire amount of the bill, to which a 15 percent service has *already* been added, in the top box of the charge slip, leaving the boxes marked "tip" and "total" empty. Do not be intimidated. Draw a line from the top figure to the total at the bottom and then write in the total figure yourself. If you are leaving a tip on top of this total (and remember you do not have to), leave it in cash. Often tips left on credit cards are not properly distributed.

The bottom line on tipping in Paris is the same as in anyplace else in the world: It is a matter of personal choice. If you liked the service, reward it; if not, do not feel guilty about not leaving an additional *sou*.

Safety and Security

General Tips

In comparison to other cities, Paris is not a dangerous place. It is still important, however, to take the same sensible precautions you would in any major metropolitan city in the world. Be aware of your surroundings and do not go down dark streets at night, especially alone. Wear a money belt or a neck pouch *inside* your clothing and carry in it *only* what you need with you: passport, some money, and so on. Do not carry any valuables in your wallet, purse, or carry-bag. Thread a safety pin from the zipper on your backpack to pin it closed, and don't wear your fanny pack there . . . wear it in front of you. Keep a close eye on your possessions, and do not leave packages or suitcases unattended on the métro or when making a phone call or hailing a taxi. Be careful of your camera and don't wear flashy jewelry. Lock up important papers, airline tickets, traveler's checks, extra money, and so on in the hotel safe. Even if there is a charge for this, it is nothing when you consider the cost, inconvenience, and hassle of a theft.

Beware of pickpockets, especially on the métro and in tourist areas. Watch out for the bands of gypsy children who will surround you and distract your attention by fluttering papers in your face, and then strip you of your valuables before you can think to say, "Stop thief!" Thieves in métro stations lurk around the turnstiles and try to grab your bag as you go through, or they reach for it as the train door closes. Always avoid métro stations late at night, and when traveling, sit in the first car near the conductor. If you are alone, don't say so to a wide audience. Also, make sure someone at home knows your itinerary, and arrange times to call to check in, just to let them know all is well.

Before leaving home, make two photocopies of every document that is crucial to the successful completion of your trip (passport, airline tickets, hotel vouchers, list of credit card numbers, or the number of your credit card registry). Leave one copy at home with someone you can always contact, and take the other copy with you. In the horrible case that your documents are lost or stolen, you have a record, and the process of replacing everything will be easier. Also, take at least four passport-size color photos. These are handy if you have to replace a passport or purchase a weekly or monthly métro pass.

The U.S. Department of State publishes a pamphlet called *A Safe Trip Abroad*. For a copy, write the Superintendent of Documents, U.S. Government Printing Office, Washington, D.C. 20402.

Hotel Tips

Hotel liability tends to be limited and often provides slim protection for the traveler. If an item is stolen from your room, you may have little recourse, unless you can prove negligence. Here are some points to consider:

1. Avoid rooms on the ground floor.

2. Do not leave any valuables exposed in your room, even when you are sleeping.

3. When you leave your room, close and lock the windows and do not leave (or hide) any valuables. Lock them up in the hotel safe. There isn't a hiding place a thief doesn't know about.

4. Valuables include more than money and jewelry. Consider camcorders, cameras, computers, personal and travel documents, tape recorders, and so on.

5. If you leave luggage at the hotel after you check out, be sure the storage area is secure, and do not leave any bag containing valuables.

6. If you are a victim of a theft, insist on filing a complete report with the local police immediately. The more documentation you have, the better your chances are for compensation.

7. Most Important: If you don't need to take it with you, don't.

Telephones

French telephone numbers have ten digits. Paris numbers begin with 01, the rest of France is divided into four regional zones with prefixes 01 to 05. If you are calling France from abroad, leave off the 0 at the beginning of the ten-digit number. International dialing codes start with 00. Free telephone numbers begin 0800.

Making a call from a public telephone is not as simple as dropping a franc into the pay telephone, dialing 0, and requesting connection. Most public phones in Paris now require a prepaid phone card (*télécarte*), which you buy in increments, or units (*unités*). To make a call, insert the card into a slot on the phone, wait for the dial tone, then start dialing the number. The amount of your call is automatically deducted from the remaining value. These cards offer several advantages: you do not need a pocketful of francs; calling from a public phone eliminates the surcharges in hotels, cafés, and restaurants; and the card has no expiration date, so you can use what is left on your card on your next trip. Where to buy the *télécarte*? Post offices, *tabacs*, and cafés all sell them.

Avoid going through your hotel switchboard when calling home. Even if you reverse the charges and use USA DIRECT, you will be charged a surcharge, sometimes up to 100 percent of the call. Check with the hotel operator about your hotel's policy, as they all differ. To avoid the surcharge, go to a pay telephone booth, use your *télécarte*, and dial USA DIRECT, which puts you in touch with an English-speaking AT&T operator. Tell the operator if you want to call collect or pay for the call using your AT&T calling card number. This is simple, painless, and definitely the least expensive way to stay in touch.

For further savings, call when the rates are low. Within France, call on Monday through Friday, 10:30 P.M. to 8 A.M., and from Saturday at 2 P.M. to 8 A.M. Monday. From anyplace in Europe, call Monday to Friday between 9:30 P.M. and 8 A.M., and Saturday after 2 P.M., all day Sunday, and public holidays. There are two cheap rates to the United States and Canada. The lowest rates are Monday through Friday, 2 A.M. to noon. The next cheapest rate is Monday to Saturday from noon to 2 P.M. and 8 P.M. to 2 A.M., and Sunday and public holidays from noon to 2 A.M. Remember, when calling the United States, Paris is six hours ahead of Eastern Standard Time and nine hours ahead of Pacific Standard Time.

Some Numbers You Might Need

To call Paris from the United States   011-33-1 + number. Remember to eliminate the 0 at the beginning of the ten-digit number.

To call the United States from Paris (you will reach an English-speaking operator):

AT&T   0800-99-00-11

MCI   0800-99-00-19

Sprint   0800-99-00-87

Making long-distance calls within France   Dial the ten-digit number

Making calls abroad   00+country code+city code+number

Directory information   12

Operator   10

International information   00-33-12 + country code (1 for U.S.)

America Online   0800-90-39-10

AT&T information (from the U.S.)   1-800-874-4000

NOTE: Every time a French person dials a call, they pay for it, even if it is just next door. You will be charged for every call you make from your hotel or apartment telephone.

Transportation

Getting into Paris from the Airports

Roissy-Charles de Gaulle Airport: General information in English, twenty-four hours daily, 01-48-62-22-80.

A taxi is the easiest and most comfortable way to go, but it is expensive. The ride into central Paris takes about fifty minutes on a good day; during rush hours add at least thirty minutes. Taxis will take no more than three people and charge a 6F surcharge for every piece of luggage. Fares range around 200F to 250F during the day and are more from 8 P.M. to 7 A.M. A 15-percent tip is expected.

A more economical way is by the direct RER-B3 train to Paris. There is direct access from Terminal 2. A free shuttle bus (look for the word *navette*) runs from Terminal 1 and takes passengers to the Roissy train station, where you board the Roissy Rail (RER B3) into the city, with stops at Gare du Nord, Châtelet-Les Halles, Luxembourg, Port Royal, and Denfert-Rochereau. The train leaves every twenty-five minutes between 5 A.M. and 11 P.M. and costs under ten dollars. The train trip takes thirty minutes, and the shuttle to the airport station fifteen minutes.

Air France Buses (to use them, you do not have to be a passenger on one of their flights) leave from both terminals and run to the Arc de Triomphe (métro: Charles-de-Gaulle-Étoile) at avenue Carnot every fifteen minutes from 5:30 A.M. to 11 P.M. It takes about forty minutes and runs around 60F. The buses also stop at the place de la Porte de Maillot/Palais des Congrès (métro: Port de Maillot) and near the Gare Montparnasse at 113, boulevard Vaugirard. For recorded information, call 01-43-23-82-20.

The RATP-run Roissybus runs every twenty-five minutes between the airport and rue Scribe, near place de l'Opéra, and takes about forty-five minutes. Cost is 60F.

Orly Airport: English-speaking information, daily 6 A.M.–11:30 P.M., 01-49-75-15-15.

The easiest way to get into Paris is on the RER-C line, on the métro. The high-speed Orlyval shuttle train runs every five to eight minutes to RER station Antony, costs 50F, and takes thirty minutes.

There is the courtesy bus Orlyrail to RER station Pont de Rungis, where you get a train to Paris for 30F. Trains run daily every fifteen to twenty minutes from 6:30 A.M. to 11:30 P.M. and take fifty minutes.

Air France buses run daily every twelve minutes between 5:50 A.M. and 11 P.M. to the Air France air terminal at Les Invalides, or Montparnasse. The fare is around 40F, and the trip takes between thirty and sixty minutes, depending on traffic. Another bus option is the Orlybus, which leaves daily every ten minutes between 6 A.M. and 11:30 P.M., going to and from the Denfert-Rochereau métro station. Cost is 30F.

Taxis to and from Orly cost at least 150F during the day and up to 200F at night, plus 6F for each piece of luggage. Allow forty-five minutes.

Le Bourget: Information 01-48-62-12-12.

This is where Charles Lindbergh landed after his transatlantic flight. Now the airport is used mainly for charter flights within France. If you land here, take bus No. 350, which leaves every fifteen minutes from

6 A.M. to 11:45 P.M. and costs two métro tickets, to Gare du Nord or Gare de l'Est, where you can get the métro to your Paris destination. You can also catch the No. 152 bus, which also makes these two stops and also goes to Porte de la Villette, if this is better. Hours of operation and costs are the same.

Public Transportation

The public transportation system in Paris is made up of the métro (underground subway), buses, and the RER suburban railway. All three services are run by the RATP, the local transport authority. For twenty-four-hour recorded information in French, call 01-43-46-14-14, or call daily between 6 A.M. and 9 P.M. when a human will answer your questions.

Métro

The Paris métro system, with 370 stations, is one of the most efficient in the world. It can take you within walking distance of almost everything you want to see and do in the city. Trains run from 5:30 A.M. until 12:45 A.M. You can buy individual tickets, but a *carnet* of ten is much more practical and cheaper by 40 percent. There is a special *Paris Visite* card that is *not* a good deal. If you are staying in Paris more than a few days, buy the weekly *Coupon Hebdomadire* or the monthly *Carte Orange.* Both allow unlimited travel on the métro and buses. To buy either, you must have a passport-size photo (there are photo booths in some larger métro stations, but it is better to bring an extra photo from home). Always hold on to your ticket. If you are caught without it, you will be fined. You may buy métro tickets at the cashier window in almost any métro station, or from the RATP offices: place de la Madeleine, 75008 (8th); telephone 01-40-06-71-45; métro: Madeleine; open May to September, Monday to Friday from 8:30 A.M. to noon, 1 to 4:30 P.M., Saturday from 8:30 A.M. to noon, 2 to 4:30 P.M. The other office is at 53, bis quai des Grands Augustins, 75006 (6th); telephone 01-40-46-44-50; métro: St-Michel; open year-round Monday to Saturday at the same hours. These offices have métro maps. For the most detailed bus and métro routes, consult the *Plan de Paris par Arrondissement* (see page 39). Métros are generally safe. Just use common sense and do not leave a wallet in a back pocket or your purse unzipped. Late at night, the following stations should be avoided: Barbes-Rochechouart, Pigalle, Châtelet, Les Halles, Trocadéro, and Anvers.

Bus

Because the métro is so fast and efficient, visitors often overlook the buses in Paris. The routes of each bus line are generally posted at each stop. They are also listed in the back of the *Plan de Paris par Arrondissement* (see page 39), or you can pick up a free bus map, *Autobus Paris-Plan de Reseau,* at tourist offices and in some métro stations. If you have a métro ticket, or a weekly or monthly métro pass, these will all work on the bus; just show your pass to the driver. Warning: Do not punch your weekly ticket when you board the bus, just show it. Punching it will render it unusable. You can punch your individual ticket, which, if you don't already have one, you can purchase from the bus driver. Always hold on to your ticket until you get off the bus. If caught without it, you will be fined. All buses run Monday to Saturday from 6:30 A.M. to 8:30 P.M. Some continue until 12:30 A.M., and some run on Sunday. The *Noctambus* runs all night, but the routes are fewer. The pamphlet printed by the RATP—*Paris Bus, Métro, RER Routes*—lists several scenic bus routes and gives directions to major museums and monuments.

IMPORTANT WARNING: Buy your métro or bus tickets and passes from cashiers inside métro stations, or from one of the RATP offices listed above. Do not, under any circumstances whatsoever, buy from independent shysters who work the train stations claiming to be authorized RATP employees, which they are not. They are cheats out to steal your money through their scam.

Taxis

The challenge of finding a taxi in Paris often rivals that of New York City on a busy Friday afternoon. Add rain to that and you are better off riding public transportation or walking. Hailing a cab on a corner is difficult. It is smarter to go to a taxi stand; they are located on most major thoroughfares and at all the railroad stations. Taxis are required by law to stop for you if the large white light on top is on (unless it is the driver's last half hour on duty or the passenger is less than fifty meters from a taxi stand). A glowing orange light means the taxi is not available. The driver will take you anywhere you want to go in Paris or to either airport, follow a route of your choosing, accept all handicapped passengers, and give you a receipt. They are *not* required to take animals (even though they may have their own dog riding with them in the front seat), take more than three persons, or accept an unreasonable amount of luggage. They might do any of these things, but there will be a supplemental charge. Normal taxi fares are based on area and time of day. Beneath the taxi light are three little lights—a, b, and c. One of these will light up according to what tariff applies. The tariff is also shown on the meter display inside the taxi. A 15-percent tip is customary. If you want an early-morning taxi to take you to the airport, book it the night before. If you need a taxi at a specific time and don't want to chance not finding one, call ahead. If you do call a taxi, the fare starts when the driver gets the call, not when you get in.

Alpha	01-45-85-85-85
Taxi Bleu	01-49-36-10-10
Taxi G7 (to reserve in English and pay with any credit card)	01-41-27-66-99

Paris taxi drivers are quite honest and above-board, and they provide receipts upon request. Ask for *un reçu, s'il vous plaît*. If you have problems, note the cab number and company name and write to the Service des Taxis, Préfecture de Police, 36, rue des Morillons, 75732, Paris Cedex 15; telephone 01-45-31-14-80.

Train

The SNCF is the name of the French national train system. There are six train stations in Paris: Gare de Lyon for trains going to the southeast of France and Italy; Gare d'Austerlitz for trains going to the southwest of France and Spain; Gare de l'Est for trains to the east; Gare Saint-Lazare for the northwest and Normandy; Gare du Nord for trains to Brussels, London via the Chunnel, and other destinations to the north; and Gare Montparnasse for trains to the west and Brittany. At each station is a métro stop with the same name. For information go to 16, boulevard des Capucines, 75002 (2nd), métro: Opéra, or call 01-45-82-50-50 daily from 7 A.M. to 7 P.M.

The RER is the suburban train system with an express line and stops in Paris. These stops are clearly marked on the métro maps.

Car

What for? Parking is impossible, traffic is from hell, gasoline is expensive, and the one-way streets will drive you crazy. Did you know that Paris has 988 miles of streets, of which 435 miles are one way?! Is this a vacation? Behind the wheel, the Parisian driver is a kamikaze pilot taking no prisoners. They think nothing of driving and parking on the sidewalk, blocking traffic on narrow streets, cutting in and out with inches to spare, and flashing their lights to indicate displeasure (honking the horn is forbidden until the moment of impact). Then there is the *priorité à droite* to get used to: this gives the right of way to the car approaching from the right, regardless of the size of the street, the traffic on it, or the safety hazard of the moment. The best reason to drive a car in Paris is to get out of town and head for the provinces.

Limousines and Motorcycles

You can hire a chauffeured limousine with a bilingual driver from Carey Limousine (01-42-65-54-20).

Frustrated thrill-seekers will want to call SP2, a chauffeured-motorcycle service for people who find darting in and out of Paris traffic at high rates of speed fun. I know what I am talking about because I have done it. Trust me, it is definitely not for the faint of heart. Reservations must be made in advance for the chauffeur-driven BMW motorcycles, equipped with helmets and telephones, to pick you up and take you to your destination, including the airports. If this is your mode of transport to and from the airport, you better be traveling *very* light. For further details, call 01-55-65-19-19.

What to Wear

Naturally, you will leave your heavy wool coat and long johns at home when you visit Paris in August. But what kind of coat makes sense in May or June? Knowing the monthly average temperatures will help: January 45.5°F (7.5°C); February 44.8°F (7.1°C); March 50°F (10.2°C); April 60.3°F (15.7°C); May 61–62°F (16.6°C); June 75°F (23°C); July 77°F (25.1°C); August 78°F (25.6°C); September 69–70°F (20.9°C); October 61.7°F (16.5°C); November 53°F (11.7°C); December 46°F (7.8°C).

If you follow only one piece of advice in *Cheap Sleeps in Paris,* let it be this: *travel light.* Porters are no longer roaming airports or train stations, and bellboys are almost relics of the past for most hotels in the Cheap Sleep category. Therefore, *you* are going to have to carry your own luggage, and believe me, after the first ten minutes, less is definitely best. Take twice as much money as you think you will need and half as much clothing. Keep it simple, color coordinate your outfits, and remember, this is Paris, not Mars, so you can go out and buy something wonderful if you need to fill a gap in your travel wardrobe.

One of the favorite pastimes of Parisians and their expatriate friends is to sit in a café along a busy boulevard and pick out the tourists. You can spot them a mile away, in their summer tank tops and shorts, and bundled up in parkas in the winter, as if the ski slopes were just around the corner. Of course, they all wear jogging shoes and the men have baseball caps . . . often turned backward.

Parisians are some of the most stylish people on earth. They are also some of the most conservative in their dress. Yes, you will see some off-the-wall outfits on bionic, buffed bodies, but you will never see short shorts on any well-groomed Parisian man or woman. Big-city clothes are the call of the day, no matter what the weather may be. Jeans are universal and certainly acceptable for sightseeing and casual dining. However, they are not considered *in vogue* at more expensive restaurants or if you are invited to someone's home. Men will feel comfortable wearing slacks and a nice shirt or turtleneck, and a jacket if it is cool. Women will feel best in simple, well-tailored outfits. Gauzy, lime-green jumpsuits with sequined Eiffel Tower T-shirts, along with jogging shoes for every occasion, spell *tourist.*

Senior Citizen Discounts

Carte Vermeil   If you have reached your sixtieth birthday, in France you are a member of the *troisième age* (third age) and eligible for a Carte Vermeil (CV).

This card entitles you to a number of significant discounts, including reductions on air and rail travel as well as on the bus and métro in Paris. The French domestic airline, Air Inter, honors "third agers" by giving 25- to 50-percent reductions on regular nonexcursion ticket prices. On French trains, you can save between 25 and 50 percent of the cost of a first- or second-class compartment and 10 percent of an excursion ticket.

These air and rail reductions are not available during all times of the year, and restrictions do apply. However, if you can cash in on the savings, they can be significant. Other benefits include reduced entrance rates for theaters, museums, and cinemas. Wherever you go in France, ask if there are special rates for senior citizens; the answer will often be yes.

The Carte Vermeil is valid for one year from June 1 to May 31 of the following year. The card cannot be purchased in the United States, but it is available at any major railway station in France. Do not expect clerks to speak English, but you won't need much French to communicate your wishes, as most of them are used to dealing with foreigners who are privy to this super deal. When you go to purchase your card, you will have to show your passport as proof of age. For more information, contact the French National Railroads, 610 Fifth Avenue, New York, NY 10012; telephone 212-582-2816.

Other Senior Citizen Discounts Members of the AARP are entitled to discounts on air tickets, rooms in selected major chain hotels, and some train and car rentals. Always inquire when booking a reservation.

Elderhostel operates programs throughout Europe, and many are in France. Contact them at 75 Federal Street, Boston, MA 02110-1941; telephone 617-426-7788.

Disabled Travelers

Paris is not known for being easy for the handicapped traveler. Many hotels in *Cheap Sleeps in Paris* do have rooms that have been somewhat refitted for handicapped guests, but the facilities are often meager, consisting only of a wide door, a grab-bar by the tub, or just the fact that the room is on the *rez-de-chaussée* (ground floor). The French Tourist Office (127, avenue des Champs-Élysées, 75008; telephone 49-52-53-54; métro: Charles-de-Gaulle-Étoile) has copies of *Paris: Guide des Musées, Bibliothèques, Centres et Ateliers Culturels . . . A l'Usage des Personnes Présentant un Handicap.* This gives information on disabled access. They also have a free guide in English called *Touristes Quand Même: Paris.* Not all the métros or the buses are suitable for wheelchair use. Call RATP (01-43-46-14-14) for a list of the most accessible. Theoretically, taxis are obliged to pick up passengers in wheelchairs, but don't count on it. It is better to reserve with one of the following companies who specialize in service for the handicapped.

Aihrop specializes in trips to and from the airport: 4, passage Saint-Antoine, 92504, Rueil-Malmaison; telephone 01-40-24-34-76; open Monday to Friday from 10 A.M. to 3 P.M. GiHp, geared more for trips in and around Paris, is at 98, rue de la Porte Jaune, 92210, St Cloud; telephone 01-47-72-74-90; open Monday to Thursday from 8:30 A.M. to noon and 2 to 6 P.M., Friday 2 to 5 P.M.

The Association des Paralysés de France publishes a guide, *Où ferons-nous étape?* (Where Will We Stop Off?), which lists hotels in France with facilities for the disabled. Write to 22, rue du Père-Guérain, 75013;

telephone 01-44-16-83-83; métro: Place d'Italy; open Monday to Friday from 9 A.M. to 12:30 P.M. and 2 to 6 P.M.

Auxiliaire des Aveugles (01-43-06-39-68) has a bilingual staff that provides information on services in Paris for the visually impaired.

Neuf Orthopedio (9, rue Léopold Bellan, 75002; telephone 01-42-33-83-46; métro: Sentier) is a store selling wheelchairs, canes, and other accessories for the handicapped.

Practical Information

Emergency Numbers

The American Hospital	63, boulevard Victor Hugo, Neuilly; Tel: 01-46-41-25-25; métro: Porte Maillot + bus No. 82
The British Hospital	3, rue Barbès, 92300, Levallois-Peret (a suburb of Paris); Tel: 01-47-58-13-12; métro: Anatole-France
Search for hospitalized persons	01-40-27-30-81; 8:45 A.M.–5:50 P.M.
AIDS Information Hotline	01-42-70-03-00, daily 9 A.M.–7 P.M.
Burns (24 hours)	Hôpital St-Antoine, 184, rue du Faubourg St-Antoine, 75012; Tel: 01-49-28-20-00
Children	Hôpital Necker, 149, rue de Sèvres, 75015; Tel: 01-44-49-40-94; métro: Duroc
Fire	Dial 18
Homeopathic doctor	01-43-87-60-33, 01-45-55-12-15. Many pharmacies also sell homeopathic medicines.
Poison (24 hours)	01-42-05-63-29, 01-40-37-04-04
Police	Dial 17
SAMU Ambulance	Dial 15 or 01-45-67-50-50
SOS Cardiac	01-45-45-41-00, 01-47-07-50-50
SOS Dentist	01-43-37-51-00
SOS Depression (24 hours)	01-44-08-78-78
SOS Doctor (24 hours)	01-43-37-77-77, 01-47-07-77-77
SOS Drug Crisis	01-45-81-11-20

SOS Eye	01-40-92-93-94
SOS Handicap (medical assistance for the handicapped)	01- 47-41-32-33
SOS Help (Bilingual crisis hotline, 3–11 P.M.)	01-47-23-80-80, 01-47-20-89-98
SOS Lawyer	01-43-29-33-00; Mon–Fri 7–11 P.M.
SOS Nurse	01-43-43-25-45
SOS Pediatric Emergency pediatric doctors will make house calls Mon–Fri, Sun and holidays, 7 A.M.– midnight; Sat 2 P.M.–midnight.	01-42-93-19-99
24-hour pharmacy	Pharmacie Dhèry, 84, avenue des Champs-Élysées (8th); Tel: 01-45-62-02-41; métro: Franklin D. Roosevelt; open 365 days a year
American Pharmacy	Pharmacie Anglo-Américaine, 6, rue Castiglione (1st); Tel: 01-42-60-72-96; métro: Tuileries; open Mon–Sat 9 A.M.–7:30 P.M.
To find the pharmacy open at night (on a rotating basis) nearest you	01-45-62-02-41

Useful Numbers

Alcoholics Anonymous	01-46-34-59-65
American Consulate	2, rue St-Florentin, 75001; Tel: 01-43-12-22-22; 01-43-96-14-88; métro: Concorde
American Embassy	2, avenue Gabriel, 75008; Tel: 01-42-96-12-02; métro: Condorde
American Express	11, rue Scribe, 75009; Tel: 01-47-77-77-00; métro: Opera; open Mon–Fri 9 A.M.–6 P.M., Sat 9 A.M.– noon
Complaints about a hotel	Direction du Tourisme, 2, rue Linois (15th); métro: Charles-Michels
Consumer complaints	Direction Départmentale de la Concurrence, de la Consommation,

Write to this office in the Ministry of Finance with any consumer complaints. Be sure to include an explanation, copies of your receipt, and any correspondence you have had with the seller.

et la Répression des Fraudes, 8, rue Froissart, 75153 Paris; Tel: 01-40-27-16-00

Emergency car repair

01-42-57-33-44

Internet: AOL Customer Service

Toll free: 0800-90-39-10

Lost and Found

Bureau des Objects Trouvés, 36, rue des Morillons (15th); Tel: 01-45-31-14-80, ext. 4208; métro: Convention; Mon–Fri 8:30 A.M.– 5 P.M. No information given over the phone.

Lost object in street openings

01-44-66-49-25
A sewer worker will try to rescue that key or diamond earring that fell through the sewer grate.

Post Office (24 hours)
This is where you go to pick up *Poste Restante* (General Delivery) mail. You must show your passport and pay a small fee for each letter you receive. You can also receive mail c/o American Express, 11, rue Scribe (9th); Tel: 01-47-77-77-07; métro: Opéra; Mon–Fri 9 A.M.–5 P.M., Sat 9 A.M.–noon

Hôtel des Postes, 52, rue du Louvre (1st); Tel: 01-40-28-20-00; métro: Louvre

Time

01-36-99-84-00

Traffic

01-48-94-33-33

Tourist Information

Main office of French Government Tourist Office, 127, avenue des Champs-Élysées, 75008 (8th); Tel: 01-49-52-53-54, 01-49-52-53-56; métro: Charles-de-Gaulle-Étoile; summer hours: 9 A.M.–9 P.M. daily; winter hours: 9 A.M.–6 P.M. daily; Tel: 01-47-23-61-72

French Government Tourist Offices in the U.S.	444 Madison Avenue, New York, NY 10020; Tel: 212-838-7300; and 9450 Wilshire Blvd., Beverly Hills, CA 90212; Tel: 320-271-6665
Weather	Paris: 01-36-65-00-00 France: 01-36-65-01-01

Glossary of Hotel Terms

a room for one/two persons	*une chambre pour une/deux personnes*
a double bed	*un lit double*
twin beds	*deux lits*
a room with an extra bed	*une chambre avec un lit supplémentaire*
a room with running water and bidet	*une chambre avec cabinet de toilette*
a room with shower and toilet	*une chambre avec douche et WC*
a room with bath and toilet	*une chambre avec salle de bain et WC*
for one/two/three nights	*pour une/deux/troix nuits*
suite	*appartment*
two-level suite	*duplex*
a room on the courtyard	*une chambre sur la cour*
a room over the street	*une chambre sur la rue*
ground floor	*rez-de-chaussée*
first floor	*premier étage*
second floor	*deuxième étage*
sixth floor	*seizième étage*
with a view	*avec vue*
quiet	*calme*
noisy	*bruyant*
I would like breakfast	*Je voudrais prendre le petit déjeuner*
I do not want breakfast	*Je ne veux pas de petit déjeuner*
air-conditioning	*climatisé*
blankets	*couvertures*
elevator, lift	*asenseur*
heat	*chauffage*
key	*clef*
to do laundry	*faire la lessive*
to iron	*repasser*
pillow	*oreiller*
sheets	*draps*

A Few Last-Minute Tips

1. What's happening in Paris while you are there? The two best sources of events in Paris are the weekly magazines *Pariscope: Une Semaine de Paris* and *l'Officiel des Spectacles*. They come out on

Wednesday, cost 3 to 4 francs, and are sold at every kiosk in the city. In these magazines you will find listings for the opera, theater, films, concerts, art exhibitions, special events, naughty nightlife, weekly TV programs, swimming pool hours, and interesting guided tours. Although the magazines are printed in French (with the exception of a small English-language section in *Pariscope* devoted to weekly highlights), a non-French speaker can quickly decipher the information given.

2. It is important to know that a *hôtel* is not always a hotel. The word *hôtel* has more than one meaning in French. Of course it means a lodging place for travelers. It also means a mansion or townhouse, like the Hôtel Lambert, or a large private home (a *hôtel particulier*). The city hall is the Hôtel de Ville; auctions are held at the Hôtel des Ventes; Hôtel des Postes refers to the general post office; and the Hôtel des Invalides, once a home for disabled war veterans, is now the most famous military museum in the world and the final resting place for Napoléon Bonaparte. Finally, if you are in the hospital, you are in a *Hôtel-Dieu.*

3. For avid museum-goers, there are now one-, three-, and five-day French passes that provide direct access to more than sixty museums, including the Louvre and Musée d'Orsay, Musée Picasso, Versailles, and other famous sights. The pass, called *La Carte,* covers your admission for each museum and allows you go to the head of any line without waiting. You can also revisit your favorites as many times as you want, at no extra charge. Entry is free for children under eighteen in most museums, and on Sunday, entrance to museums is free to anyone, but the crowds can be frightening. If you have the museum pass, you will at least avoid standing in the lines to get in, and that is worth something. The passes are on sale in the museums, major métro stations, and tourism offices in Paris, including the one at 127, Champs-Élysées. *La Carte* passes can also be purchased before leaving the United States through Challenges International, Inc., 10 East 21st Street, Suite 600, New York, NY 10010; telephone 212-529-8484, fax 212-529-4833; open Monday to Friday from 8:30 A.M. to 5:30 P.M. Challenges International, Inc., also sells *télécartes* (phone cards), transportation passes, and more.

4. Standards of Measure. France uses the metric system. Here are the conversions:

1 inch = 2.54 centimeters	1 centimeter = 0.4 inch
1 mile = 1.61 kilometers	1 kilometer = 0.62 miles
1 ounce = 28 grams	1 gram = 0.04 ounces
1 pound = 0.45 kilograms	1 kilogram = 2.2 pounds
1 quart = 0.95 liter	1 liter = 1.06 quarts
1 gallon = 3.8 liters	

How much is that in miles, feet, pounds, or degrees? Here is how to do the conversions:

Kilometers/miles: To change kilometers to miles, multiply the kilometers by .621. To change miles to kilometers, multiply the miles by 1.61.

Meters/feet: To change meters to feet, multiply the meters by 3.28. To change feet to meters, multiply the feet by .305.

Kilograms/pounds: To change kilograms to pounds, multiply the kilograms by 2.20. To change pounds to kilograms, multiply the pounds by .453.

Celsius/Fahrenheit: Double the Celsius figure and add 30. If the Celsius figure is below zero, double the sub-zero number and subtract it from 32.

5. French electrical circuits are wired at 220 volts. You will need a transformer and an adapter plug for appliances you bring that operate on 110 volts. Things such as hair dryers and hair curling irons may have switches that convert the appliance from one voltage to another. This only eliminates the need for a transformer, *not* for the adapter plug. If you are planning on using a computer, be sure you have a transformer with enough power, otherwise you could end up damaging your machine. Don't worry if you find yourself without the proper adapters or transformers. Go to the basement of BHV department store (5, rue de Rivoli, 75004; métro: Hôtel-de-Ville; see Cheap Chic, page 265) and take the appliance with you. If they don't have it, chances are it doesn't exist.

How to Use Cheap Sleeps
in Paris

Abbreviations

The following abbreviations are used to denote which credit cards a hotel will accept:

American Express	AE
Diners Club	DC
MasterCard	MC
Visa	V

Stars

Hotels throughout France are controlled by a government rating system that ranks them from no stars to four-star deluxe. Every hotel must display prominently the number of stars it has.

A no-star hotel is mighty basic, with few, if any, private bathrooms and little in the way of English. Many of them, however, are spotlessly clean, well located, and excellent budget values. A one-star hotel has minimum facilities, but again, it may be well located and very clean. Two stars means a comfortable hotel with direct-dial phones in all rooms and an elevator in buildings of four or more stories. Three stars means a very comfortable hotel where all rooms have direct-dial phones, a majority have private plumbing, and there is an elevator. A four-star hotel is first class all the way, usually with a restaurant, and a four-star deluxe is a virtual palace, with every service you could dream of.

Because the number of stars has nothing to do with the level of cleanliness, attitude of management or personnel, location, or value for money, you cannot always judge the quality of a hotel by its stars.

Accommodations: Checking In

The lobby is usually one of the most attractive parts of a hotel, both because first impressions are important and because it is where the owner and manager spend their day. When you arrive at your hotel, ask to see your room. This is a normal and expected practice in all hotels in France. If you are dissatisfied, ask to see another room. After approving the room, reconfirm the rate and whether or not you will be eating breakfast at the hotel. This advance work prevents any unpleasant surprises at checkout time.

In Paris, the hotel day begins and ends at noon. If you overstay, you can be charged the price of an extra day. If you are arriving before noon after a long international flight, the room might not be ready if the hotel is fully booked. If you *must* have your room at 8 or 9 A.M., you might have to book (and pay) for it the night before. If you think you might arrive after 6 P.M., be sure to notify the hotel; otherwise your room could be given away, even if you have a deposit.

In most hotels, you pay for the room, not for the number of persons occupying it. Thus, if you are alone and occupy a triple, you will pay the triple price, unless negotiated otherwise. Watch out! Most rooms are set up for two, and the few singles tend to be tiny and located on a top floor without much view or along the back side facing a blank wall. Most hotels have two kinds of double rooms: those with a double bed (*un grand lit*) and those with twin beds (*deux lits*). If you ask for a *double,* you will get a room with a double bed, so when reserving, be sure to be specific about exactly what type of bed arrangement suits you.

Rates: Paying the Bill

Just like French restaurant menus, hotel rates and their number of stars must be posted.

The city of Paris levies a visitors' tax on persons not liable for the resident tax (a tax raised on habitual residents of the City of Paris). This visitors' tax, called *taxe de séjour,* applies to all forms of paying accommodations: hotels and tourist residences, furnished flats, holiday campsites, and RV parking. The tax is charged per person, per night. Some hotels charge it over and above the quoted rate; others include it in the total hotel rate. All *Cheap Sleeps in Paris* listings state whether or not this tax is included or extra. However, policies on this tax change, so to avoid confusion, be sure to inquire at time of booking whether or not the *taxe de séjour* is included or extra. The following categories apply:

Type of accommodation	Price per person, per day
4-star hotels and other equivalent establishments	7 francs
3-star hotels and other equivalent establishments	6 francs
2-star hotels and other equivalent establishments	5 francs
1-star hotels and other equivalent establishments	3 francs
No-star hotels and other equivalent establishments	1 franc
Camping and RV areas	1 franc

The proceeds of the *taxe de séjour* are allocated for the development and promotion of tourism in Paris.

The French government no longer tightly controls hotel prices, but they do give special authorization for hotels to increase prices by a certain percentage twice a year. Many hotels do this; others have held steady for two and three years at a time. It usually depends on the economy. Many hotels offer different rates at different times of the year, getting what they can when they can, based on the law of supply and demand.

All rates listed in *Cheap Sleeps in Paris* are for full price and do not reflect any special deals. The rates tell whether or not breakfast is extra or included and, if included, whether or not the hotel will allow you to deduct it if not taken. While I have made every effort to be accurate on the rates, I cannot control changes or fluctuations of the dollar against the franc, so please be fully prepared to have the prices vary (unfortunately, usually upward). All listings state which credit cards are accepted. In most Cheap Sleeps, payment is required one night in advance. Some low-priced hotels, youth hostels, and student accommodations do not accept credit cards. It is cash up front in French francs *only*. I have yet to see one of these hotels bend on this important point, so be prepared.

Hotel exchange rates are terrible. If you plan to pay your bill in francs, convert your money at a bank before checkout time (see Currency Exchange, page 16). Before leaving the hotel, go over your bill carefully, question anything you do not understand, and get a receipt marked *paid* before leaving.

Breakfast

Almost every Parisian hotel serves a continental breakfast consisting of coffee, tea, hot chocolate, bread, croissants or other rolls, butter, and jam. Some throw in a glass of juice or a piece of cheese. Hotels stand to make as much as a 200-percent profit on this meal, so they naturally encourage their guests to take it at the hotel. If you want anything extra, it will cost dearly and is usually not worth the extra expenditure. Many better hotels are now offering a buffet downstairs for the same price (or for a little more than the continental, which they will serve in your room). An all-you-can-eat buffet with cereals, yogurt, hard-boiled eggs, and fruit added to the standard continental fare can sometimes be worth the price, especially if you plan to skip lunch.

Unless otherwise noted, none of the hotels listed serve meals other than breakfast.

English Spoken

All the hotel listings in this book state whether or not English is spoken. If you can dust off a few French phrases, smile, and display good will, you will find that the hotel staff will prove to be friendly and go out of their way to help you. If you do not speak any French and want to avoid the stress of trying to communicate without it, make sure you know whether someone at the hotel speaks English. While it is fun to practice your high-school French, it is not fun to try to deal with a problem while struggling to speak it.

Parking

Very few hotels have private parking. If a hotel does have it, it is stated in the *Cheap Sleep* listing, and so is the price per day. Public parking is well situated in Paris, and finding a facility close to your hotel should not be hard. The hotel will be able to advise you on the closest one. However, you should know that parking in Paris is not cheap.

Smoking/Nonsmoking Rooms (*Fumer/Non-Fumer*)

Bonne chance on this one! There is only one hotel group in Paris that devotes an entire floor of rooms to its nonsmoking guests. This is Libertel, of which several are listed in *Cheap Sleeps in Paris*. Many other hotels will say they have nonsmoking rooms, but what they really mean is that the maid will open the window and spray air freshener on the day you arrive. If the hotel provides nonsmoking rooms, it is definitely noted under Facilities and Services. Fortunately, many of the hotel breakfast dining rooms are nonsmoking.

Facilities and Services

A brief summary at the end of each hotel listing states which facilities and services are offered by the hotel. Of course, the better the hotel, the more offerings there will be.

Nearest Tourist Attractions

Each hotel listing tells you if the hotel is on the Right or Left Bank and gives you the nearest tourist attractions within a reasonable walking distance.

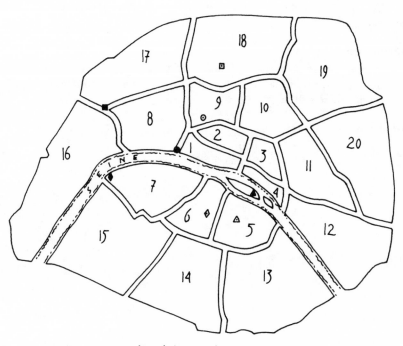

- ● Place de la concorde
- ■ Arc de Triomphe
- ▲ Notre Dame
- ◆ Tour Eiffel
- ⊙ Opéra
- ▣ Sacré-Coeur
- △ Panthéon
- ◇ Jardin du Luxembourg

Hotel Listings by Arrondissement

Paris has more than nine million inhabitants occupying 432 square miles. Despite these numbers, it is a very compact city, bound by a ring road known as the *périphérique* and divided into twenty districts called *arrondissements*. Anything outside the *périphérique* is the *banlieu* and is considered the suburbs. In the late nineteenth century, Paris was reorganized and modernized by Baron Haussmann, the farsighted planner who gave the city its wide boulevards, beautiful parks, and system of arrondissements that make up the city today. Each arrondissement has a character all its own, as well as its own mayor, city hall, police station, and central post office. Knowing which arrondissement is which is the key to understanding Paris and quickly finding your way around.

Starting with the first arrondissement, which is the district around the Louvre, the numbering of the districts goes clockwise in a rough spiral. From a visitor's standpoint, the arrondissements of greatest interest are the first through the eighth, although there are interesting things to see and do in the others, too. For instance, Montmartre occupies most of the eighteenth, and to attend a performance at the Opéra Bastille, you will journey to the eleventh. The River Seine divides Paris into the Right Bank (*Rive Droite*) and the Left Bank (*Rive Gauche*). Right Bank arrondissements are one, two, three, four, eight, nine, ten, eleven, twelve, sixteen, seventeen, eighteen, nineteen, and twenty. Left Bank arrondissements are five, six, seven, thirteen, fourteen, and fifteen. For mailing purposes, the Paris zip code is 750 followed by a two-digit number indicating the arrondissement: 75001 is the first, 75002 is the second, and so on. For every address in *Cheap Sleeps in Paris*, both the postal zip code and the arrondissement are given. For example, 75005 (5th).

The maps in the book are here to help you choose a hotel in relation to major landmarks and your particular interests in Paris. They are not intended as detailed streetmaps to guide you about the city. If you plan to be in Paris for more than a day, a necessary investment, and one that will last forever, is a copy of the *Plan de Paris par Arrondissement*. This Parisian "bible" offers a detailed map of each arrondissement, with a completely keyed street index, métro and bus routes, tourist sites, churches, and other valuable information. It is available at major newsstands and bookstores. All Parisians have a copy, and so should you.

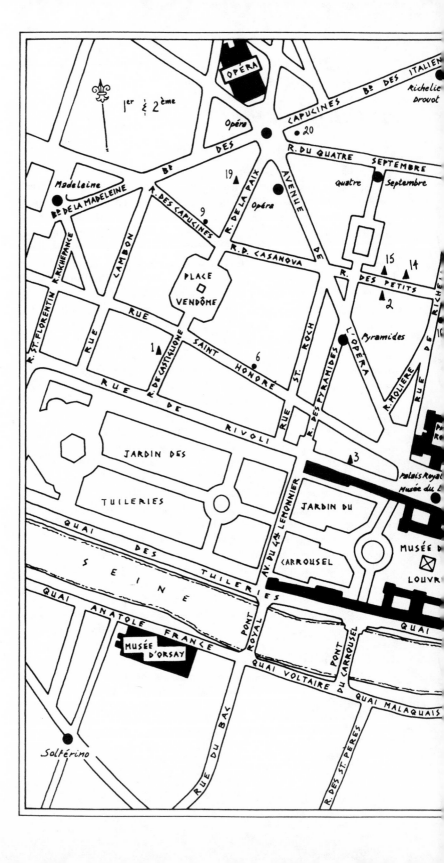

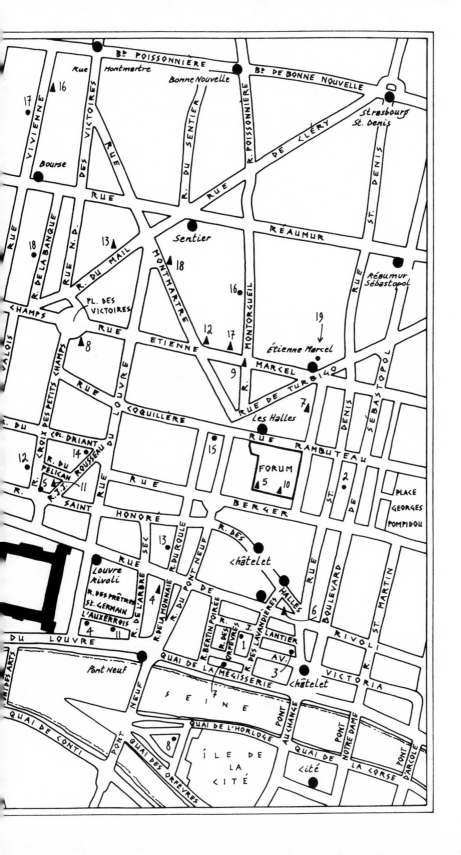

First Arrondissement

RIGHT BANK
Conciergerie, Île de la Cité, Pont Neuf, Les Halles, Louvre, Palais de Justice, Palais Royal, place Vendôme, Ste-Chapelle, St-Eustache, Notre Dame Cathedral

Paris began on the Île de la Cité, and Parisians still regard it as the center not only of their city but of all France. The Tuileries Gardens and Louvre Museum are the cornerstone of this regal *quartier* and the center from which the arrondissement begins. Here you will find the rejuvenated Les Halles, with Forum des Halles housing two hundred or more boutiques along with movie theaters, fast-food joints, several museums, and a métro station, which has the reputation of being unsafe after dark. Ste-Chapelle, with its magnificent red and blue stained-glass windows, and St-Eustache, the largest Gothic Renaissance church in Paris, are here. The palaces surrounding the moneyed place Vendôme include the famed Cartier jewelry store, Ministry of Justice, and the world-renowned Ritz Hôtel, where room prices are within the budget of any average emir or Texas oil mogul.

HOTELS IN THE FIRST ARRONDISSEMENT

OTHER OPTIONS
Student Accommodations

*Indicates a Big Splurge

(1) GRAND HÔTEL DE CHAMPAGNE ★★★
Angle 17, rue Jean-Lantier and 13, rue des Orfèvres, 75001 (1st)
43 rooms, all with shower or bath and toilet

Hidden on a small corner near the River Seine and the Châtelet métro stop, the family-owned hotel appeals to travelers who are looking for an A+ location for exploring the Louvre, the Islands, St-Michel, and St-Germain-des-Prés.

If you look carefully in the sitting area off the reception, you will see the date 1562 carved on one of the original wooden pillars. This tells you when the building was built, but it doesn't tell you that it is the oldest structure on rue Jean-Lantier, and that before its present charmed transformation, it served as a residence for members of tailor and shoemaker guilds and housed a Christian girls' school.

Different themes are carried out in each of the forty-three rooms and suites, with interiors running the gamut from masculine-modern to frankly feminine. Many of the rooms have hand-painted murals done by artists over the years (perhaps in lieu of a final payment?). Room 304 has a fanciful scene of Venice on the bathroom wall, and no. 302, one of my favorites, shows a pretty girl peeking through a cloud-filled sky. No. 205, a twin-bedded room with exposed stone walls and a double mirrored closet, has a pink marbled bath, excellent space, and good light. The viewless no. 308 reminds me of a chapel, with its stone walls, high beamed ceilings, and extra-quiet location. No. 301, in bright turquoise, with black and white accents, has a divided sitting area and a fantasy bathroom with double sinks. Rooms 502 and 504 have terraces. The unusual two-room suites are large. If you like sunken bathtubs, platform beds, conversation pits, and lots of open space splashed with color, these will undoubtedly please you.

Management is justifiably proud of its buffet breakfast served downstairs. Designed to appeal to lumberjack appetites, it includes fresh fruit, juices, a variety of breads and rolls, several selections of meat, cheese and pâté, eggs, and cereals. After this meal, you won't need to eat until dinnertime.

ENGLISH SPOKEN: Yes

FACILITIES AND SERVICES: Bar; direct-dial phone; elevator to fifth floor, stairs to three rooms on sixth floor; laundry service; minibar in suites; TV with international reception; safe in office, no charge

TELEPHONE
01-42-36-60-00; toll-free from U.S., 1-800-44-UTELL

FAX
01-45-08-43-33

MÉTRO
Châtelet (use rue de Rivoli, *nos impairs*—odd numbers, or Bertin Poirée exit)

CREDIT CARDS
AE, DC, MC, V

RATES
Single 600–725F, double 650–830F, suites 1,150–1,300F
Taxe de séjour: 6F extra per person, per day

BREAKFAST
55F extra per person; buffet downstairs or continental in room

NEAREST TOURIST ATTRACTIONS (RIGHT BANK): Forum des Halles, Beaubourg, Louvre, Île de la Cité, Île St-Louis, St-Michel, St-Germain-des-Prés, shopping at BHV department store (which has the finest hardware department in France and is a do-it-yourselfer's heaven)

(2) HÔTEL AGORA ★★
7, rue de la Cossonnerie, off rue Pierre Lescot, 75001 (1st)
29 rooms, all with shower or bath and toilet

TELEPHONE	01-42-33-46-02
FAX	01-42-33-80-99
MÉTRO	Les Halles, Châtelet
CREDIT CARDS	MC, V
RATES	Single 315–500F, double 510–530F
Taxe de séjour:	5F extra per person, per day
BREAKFAST	40F extra per person

The decor at the Hôtel Agora is an eclectic pastiche of flea market nostalgia that gives new meaning to the phrases frou-frou and hand-me-downs. The rooms are not large, and neither are the bathrooms, but if you want something different in an active, animated section of Paris, read on.

The location, in the midst of a block of shops selling tourist kitsch, is hardly inspiring. Guests walk up a short flight of stairs and enter a rather formally outfitted reception room with living plants draped all over the windows. A mirrored breakfast room has two covered tables and a sitting area to one side with several antique pieces and a photo of an Italian film star, who stayed here in leaner times.

The rooms are whimsically individual, mixing the old with the new in a way that comes together. No. 31, a twin, features an armchair covered in a leopard print, a fireplace, and a gold-framed headboard with hand-painted flowers on it. In no. 64 you will have a rooftop view of St-Eustache Church, sleep in a double bed, and use a small bathroom with a mini–corner shower and wash basin. In Room 52, colored hearts on cotton bedspreads add a feminine touch to a room with gold bas-reliefs over twin beds. The mirrored armoire and two side tables fit in with the blue Laura Ashley–style wall covering and matching blue tiled bath with one of the better showers. Room 61 is the biggest and will hold three, but I think it is better for two. The room is dominated by a nineteenth-century painting of a woman and a mixture of similar-era art scattered on the walls. A Tunisian wood sculpture looms over the twin beds.

ENGLISH SPOKEN: Yes

FACILITIES AND SERVICES: Direct-dial phone; elevator from first floor; TV with international reception; room safe, no charge

NEAREST TOURIST ATTRACTIONS (RIGHT BANK): Heart of Les Halles, Centre Georges-Pompidou (Beaubourg), Île de la Cité, Île St-Louis, Louvre

(3) HÔTEL BRITANNIQUE ★★★
20, avenue Victoria, 75001 (1st)
40 rooms, all with shower or bath and toilet

The history of this hotel goes way back. In 1870–71, it was run by a Quaker mission to aid war victims. During World War I, it was where war casualties recuperated. Today it is a gracefully restored, sound choice between Châtelet and Hôtel de Ville. In the refashioning of the hotel several years ago, the owners wisely kept many original parts. The winding stairway with polished banister and the carved reception counter are two examples of how the old can blend beautifully with the new. Granite hallways lined with red print carpet lead guests to their rooms, which are behind eggplant-purple doors. Best choices are on the top three floors, just high enough to escape the brunt of the street noise and to avoid blank-wall views on the back. The rooms, though small, are professionally decorated in soft colors with tone-on-tone wallpaper, faux marble accents, and coordinated print fabrics. Classical music soothes early morning diners in the pretty breakfast room, which overlooks a small interior garden. A buffet is laid out here, or you can have a continental breakfast sent to your room for the same price. The sunken lounge, with eye-level windows on the street, is accented with some lovely old heirlooms. Be sure to notice the bird cage, the early record player, and the intricately detailed model of an old sailing vessel.

ENGLISH SPOKEN: Yes

FACILITIES AND SERVICES: Bar; direct-dial phone; hair dryer; elevator; minibar; TV with international reception; room safe, no charge

NEAREST TOURIST ATTRACTIONS (RIGHT BANK): Louvre, Tuileries, Beaubourg and Forum des Halles, Île de la Cité, Île St-Louis, St-Michel, Seine

TELEPHONE
01-42-33-74-59

FAX
01-42-33-82-65

E-MAIL
mailbox@hotel-britannique.fr

MÉTRO
Châtelet

CREDIT CARDS
AE, DC, MC, V

RATES
Single 660F, double 800–900F; extra bed 100F
Taxe de séjour: 6F extra per person, per day

BREAKFAST
60F extra per person

(4) HÔTEL DE LA PLACE DU LOUVRE ★★★
21, rue des Prêtres Saint-Germain l'Auxerrois, 75001 (1st)
20 rooms, all with shower or bath and toilet

The name of the hotel gives you a hint. From the front door the Louvre is only a five-minute stroll, the

TELEPHONE
01-42-33-78-68

FAX
01-42-33-09-95

MÉTRO
Louvre, Pont Neuf

CREDIT CARDS
DC, MC, V

RATES
Single 510–725F, double 695–825F, triple 775–825F, suite 850F
Taxe de séjour: included

BREAKFAST
45F extra per person

quays along the Seine a block away, and all the Left Bank has to offer is just a few minutes across the Pont Neuf to St-Michel. The hotel is imaginatively done from start to finish. Portions of the original stone walls are artistically exposed to the dramatically modern entry. Murals on curving walls lead to a tented sitting area with a purple chamois wall covering highlighted by black and tangerine leather and chrome furniture. A multicolored curtain hangs above the front window, which faces the St-Germain l'Auxerrois Church across the street. All of the imaginatively done rooms are named for famous artists whose work hangs in the Louvre. The brilliant pink, third-floor Picasso suite has a view of the church, marble-topped bedside tables, a corner desk, mirrored wardrobes, and a wonderful upstairs bathroom with a skylight. If you check into the green-and-white Kandinsky double, you will have good luggage space and a salmon tiled bath with gray monogrammed towels and plenty of shelf space. Breakfast is served in the original fourteenth-century stone-walled *cave* in the basement.

NOTE: Same management and owners as Hôtel Parc Saint-Séverin (see page 89) and Hôtel Mansart (see page 49).

ENGLISH SPOKEN: Yes

FACILITIES AND SERVICES: Bar; direct-dial phone; hair dryer; elevator; minibar; radio; TV with international reception; room safe, no charge

NEAREST TOURIST ATTRACTIONS (RIGHT BANK): Louvre, Beaubourg, Seine, St-Michel, Île de la Cité, Île St-Louis

(5) HÔTEL DE LILLE (NO STARS)
8, rue du Pelican, 75001 (1st)
14 rooms, 6 with shower, none with bath and toilet

TELEPHONE
01-42-33-33-42

FAX
None

MÉTRO
Palais-Royal, Louvre

CREDIT CARDS
None, cash only

No private toilets, no closets (only hooks), no English spoken, no breakfast served, and no elevator in a five-floor hotel (housed in a thirteenth-century building). Who needs this? Seekers of a very Cheap Sleep near the Louvre do, and believe me, they stay here in droves. If you do decide to stay here, don't expect thick towels, a particularly helpful staff, minibars (but there is a drink machine between the second and third floors), TVs, or other services or amenities. This is a Cheap Sleep thrill all right, but also a safe and clean one you can count on if all you need is a place to hang your hat and rest your weary head after a long day in Paris.

ENGLISH SPOKEN: None

FACILITIES AND SERVICES: None

NEAREST TOURIST ATTRACTIONS (RIGHT BANK): Louvre, Palais-Royal, Les Halles, Tuileries, shopping on rue St-Honoré, Seine, Île de la Cité, Île St-Louis

RATES
Single 200F, double 240–290F; coin-operated shower 30F
Taxe de séjour: included

BREAKFAST
None served

(6) HÔTEL DES TUILERIES* ★★★
10, rue Saint-Hycinthe, angle place du Marché St-Honoré, 75001 (1st)
26 rooms, all with shower or bath and toilet

If there is a better example of that wonderful, small, romantic antique-filled hotel in a great location equidistant from the Louvre and place de la Concorde, nobody is telling. The Hôtel des Tuileries, a converted eighteenth-century mansion listed as a historical landmark, is also a member of the Relais du Silence Hotels, which insures guests peace and quiet.

All twenty-six rooms have obviously been done by someone with a sense of style and enough money to carry it out. Room 8, a deluxe on the front, has lavender blue carpet leading from a small entryway to a room with two comfortable armchairs, two sunny windows, a crystal chandelier, and a seven-drawer dresser. The queen-size bed is covered in a white polished cotton spread, and the excellent bathroom offers a separate toilet, double sinks, a tub and shower, and the best-quality toiletries. Room 2, done in metallic floral wallpaper, is on the back and smaller. It has a little porch opening onto an interior garden and a well-lit marble bathroom with its own telephone. It is a perfect selection for the solo traveler. In no. 1, which faces front, the wrought-iron double bed, Chinese red print wallpaper, and matching deep red carpet add drama. After a long day you can stretch out in the Jacuzzi bath and figure out how to extend your Parisian stay in this delightful hotel.

ENGLISH SPOKEN: Yes

FACILITIES AND SERVICES: Air-conditioning in all rooms; bar; direct-dial phone; hair dryer; elevator; minibar; radio; TV with international reception; room safe, no charge; trouser presses; Jacuzzi in one room

NEAREST TOURIST ATTRACTIONS (RIGHT BANK): Louvre, Palais Royal, Opéra, shopping

TELEPHONE
01-42-61-04-17

FAX
01-49-27-91-56

MÉTRO
Tuileries, Pyramides

CREDIT CARDS
AE, DC, MC, V

RATES
Single 700–1,000F, double 800–1,300F
Taxe de séjour: 6F extra per person, per day

BREAKFAST
60F extra; American breakfast with bacon and eggs

(7) HÔTEL DU PALAIS ★
2, quai de la Mégisserie, 75001 (1st)
19 rooms, 14 with shower or bath and toilet

TELEPHONE
01-42-36-98-25

FAX
01-42-21-41-67

MÉTRO
Châtelet (exit Place du Châtelet)

CREDIT CARDS
MC, V

RATES
Single 200–275F, double 245–480F, triple 400–575F; extra bed 75F; 10 percent reduction between December 1 and March 31; free hall showers
Taxe de séjour: 3F extra per person, per day

BREAKFAST
35F extra per person

While the location is dynamite and the views from most rooms spectacular, the hotel in general is a true fixer-upper. No elevator services any of the floors; dim-watt bulbs sway from high-pitched ceilings; exposed pipes wrap themselves around the rooms; and the double beds roll to the middle. In addition, if you open the windows or forget your industrial-strength earplugs, it can be hopelessly noisy twenty-four hours a day. However, for the budgeteer who can sleep through anything, the Hôtel du Palais has prices it's hard to refuse. If you land in one of the fourteen rooms with their million-dollar views across the Seine to Nôtre Dame and the Left Bank—and you don't mind the attic school of decorating or a *laissez faire* approach to cleaning—this is a Cheap Sleep in Paris that won't disappoint.

NOTE: All the view rooms have their own bathrooms.

ENGLISH SPOKEN: Yes

FACILITIES AND SERVICES: Direct-dial phone; no safe or elevator

NEAREST TOURIST ATTRACTIONS (RIGHT BANK): Louvre, Beaubourg and Forum des Halles, Île de la Cité, Île St-Louis, St-Michel

(8) HÔTEL HENRI IV (NO STARS)
25, place Dauphine, 75001 (1st)
21 rooms, 2 with shower, none bath and toilet

TELEPHONE
01-45-54-44-53

FAX
None

MÉTRO
Pont Neuf, St-Michel, Cité

CREDIT CARDS
None, cash only

RATES
Single 125–165F, double 185–255F; extra bed 30F; shower 15F
Taxe de séjour: included

BREAKFAST
Included (bread and butter)

Four hundred years ago, King Henri IV's printing presses occupied this narrow townhouse on Île de la Cité's pretty place Dauphine. Today, it is a twenty-one-room hotel that has been touted in every budget guide to Paris and has become a mecca for hard-core Cheap Sleepers and anyone else eager to experience a romantically threadbare hotel adventure in Paris. Despite recent improvements, such as new hall linoleum, new floral wallpaper in Room 2, and showers installed in two rooms, all guests must continue to be philosophical about both the accommodations and the plumbing. The rooms, which passed their prime decades ago, could be a shock to some: the furniture looks like leftovers from a garage sale; the lighting is dim; the mattresses are spongy; most of the wallpaper has seen better days; and the exposed peeling pipes gurgle and sputter all day—and all night—long. Only a bidet and basin come with each room, and the communal shower and toilets are reached via a steep, winding staircase in a dark and freezing-cold airshaft. On the other hand, it is so cheap, so perfectly located, so quiet, and the owners—M. and Mme. Balitrand and their son, François, who now runs it—are so friendly that thousands of young-at-heart guests continue to flock here from around the world and reserve many months in advance.

ENGLISH SPOKEN: Yes

FACILITIES AND SERVICES: None. Office open for reservations from 8 A.M.–7 P.M.

NEAREST TOURIST ATTRACTIONS (LOCATED ON ÎLE DE LA CITÉ): Île St-Louis, St-Michel, St-Germain-des-Prés, Latin Quarter, Left Bank, Louvre, Musée d'Orsay, place Dauphine

(9) HÔTEL MANSART* ★★★
5, rue des Capucines (place Vendôme, angle rue de la Paix), 75001 (1st)
57 rooms, all with shower or bath and toilet

To be close to the Ritz, except in price—because your budget does not allow spending upwards of $700 per night for a double (breakfast extra)—consider staying at Hôtel Mansart, named after the architect of Louis XIV, who designed the place Vendôme, Versailles, and the dome on Les Invalides. The hotel used to be the Hôtel Calais, a rambling wreck totally devoid of style, with labyrinth halls, creaking floors, and turn-of-the-century plumbing. Not anymore! What a stunning transformation the owners of the Hôtel Parc Saint-Séverin (see page 89) have achieved.

By not making any structural changes other than adding spectacular new bathrooms, the owners kept the spirit of the building intact. You will still find long hallways, high ceilings, marble fireplaces, stained-glass windows, well-loved period furnishings, and, in some cases, slightly sloping floors. No two rooms are alike, but all reflect the same high level of style and good taste. Some favorites include no. 603, a top-floor choice done in blue and gray with a mirrored armoire, marble bedside tables, and a tiled bathroom with double sinks. No. 505, a sunny, rear twin room, has a separate stall shower in addition to a stretch-out bathtub that is perfect for luxurious bubble baths. Rooms 506, 507, and 508 have their own terraces. No. 502, facing the street, is enormous, with a fireplace, built-in armoire, large round

TELEPHONE
01-42-61-50-28

FAX
01-49-27-97-44

E-MAIL
espfranc@micronet.fr

MÉTRO
Opéra, Madeleine, Tuileries

CREDIT CARDS
AE, DC, MC, V

RATES
1–2 persons 600–990F, suite 1,300–1,600F; extra bed 110F
Taxe de séjour: included

BREAKFAST
55F extra

table with chairs, and a writing desk. A showcase room is no. 204 overlooking the place Vendôme. This room is done in royal blue with gold carpeting, and its high ceilings, collectable furniture, and lovely oil painting over the marble dresser are reminiscent of hotels on the Grand Tour of Europe that our grandmothers stayed in decades ago.

The stark simplicity of the lobby is created by an interesting mixture of geometric wall designs based on the gardens at Versailles. Antique chairs and love seats and tiny glowing ceiling lights complete the room. A continental breakfast is served in a red carpeted, formal room with arched stained-glass windows and suede-cloth-covered chairs placed around tables covered with yellow damask cloths. Everything works together throughout this impressive hotel and adds up to a smart address in a fine location.

ENGLISH SPOKEN: Yes

FACILITIES AND SERVICES: Air-conditioning in some rooms; bar; direct-dial phone; hair dryer; elevator to fifth floor only; minibar; TV with international reception; room safe, no charge

NEAREST TOURIST ATTRACTIONS (RIGHT BANK): Place Vendôme, place de la Concorde, Opéra, Madeleine, Louvre, shopping on rue St-Honoré

(10)   HÔTEL RICHELIEU-MAZARIN ★
51, rue de Richelieu, 75001 (1st)
14 rooms, 12 with shower or bath and toilet

TELEPHONE
01-42-97-46-20

FAX
01-47-03-97-13

MÉTRO
Pyramides, Palais-Royal

CREDIT CARDS
MC, V

RATES
Single 220–325F, double 240–350F, triple 400F; extra bed 60F; shower 10F
Taxe de séjour: 3F extra per person, per day

BREAKFAST
30F extra downstairs; 35F served in room

The tiny Richelieu-Mazarin can be recommended for budgeteers looking for a good value but not in the market for anything fancy. The entrance off the street is along a stone-walled, well-lit hallway and up some steep steps to a reception area, which doubles as the breakfast room and lounge. Some of the simply done rooms are dark, most have open closets, and only a stool or two for seating, but all have a bouquet of fake flowers to add a note of cheer and are clean enough to please your mother-in-law. If noise keeps you awake, avoid a berth on the front facing the street. No. 29 has a private flight of stairs, its own bath and toilet, and a ceiling window with a tip-toe view of neighboring rooftops. To some the hotel is cozy and cute; for others it is stuffy and claustrophobic. Definitely claustrophobic is no. 20, a closet-sized room with no window at all, only a ceiling vent.

Long lines of regulars know this hotel and book it way in advance, so if you want a central Parisian address for not much money, please do the same.

ENGLISH SPOKEN: Yes

FACILITIES AND SERVICES: Direct-dial phone; radio; safe in office, no charge; no elevator

NEAREST TOURIST ATTRACTIONS (RIGHT BANK): Palais-Royal, Louvre, Tuileries, shopping on rue St-Honoré, place Vendôme, Opéra, place de la Concorde

(11)   LE RELAIS DU LOUVRE* ★★★
19, rue des Prêtres Saint-Germain l'Auxerrois, 75001 (1st)
20 rooms, all with shower or bath and toilet

Just down the street from the Hôtel de la Place du Louvre is Le Relais du Louvre, another top three-star pick hard by the Musée du Louvre. The small lobby, draped in dark red watermarked linen, offers comfortable seating. A massive fresh floral spray sitting atop an antique bureau adds color. The rooms live up to the elegant promise of the lobby. All are attractively furnished with designer fabrics and have good closet space and marble bathrooms with fluffy towels. No. 35, a standard twin-bedded room, offers an armchair covered in a quilted pink hydrangea pattern and a writing desk overlooking the church across the street. Appealing prints of Victorian ladies hang on the walls. If you need a little more space, consider no. 32, a quiet room on the back with a sitting area off the bedroom area. Even larger is no. 52, a suite with a direct view of the gargoyles on the St-Germain l'Auxerrois Church across the street. Rooms 24 and 25 connect, and can be closed off together to form a nice family suite. The singles are small and are on the back, but the interior view is not depressing. An added bonus of this hotel is the English-speaking staff.

ENGLISH SPOKEN: Yes

FACILITIES AND SERVICES: Direct-dial phone; hair dryer; elevator; minibar; TV with international reception; room safe, no charge

NEAREST TOURIST ATTRACTIONS (RIGHT BANK): Louvre, Beaubourg, Seine, St-Michel, Île de la Cité, Île St-Louis

TELEPHONE
01-40-41-96-42

FAX
01-40-41-96-44

MÉTRO
Louvre, Pont Neuf

CREDIT CARDS
AE, DC, MC, V

RATES
Single 625–785F, double 850–950F, suite 1,300–1,975F
Taxe de séjour: 6F extra per person, per day

BREAKFAST
50F extra

(12) TIMHÔTEL LOUVRE ★★
4, rue Croix des Petits Champs, 75001 (1st)
56 rooms, all with shower or bath and toilet

TELEPHONE
01-42-60-34-86
FAX
01-42-60-10-39
MÉTRO
Palais-Royal
CREDIT CARDS
AE, DC, MC, V
RATES
Single 475F, double 570F,
triple 725F
Taxe de séjour: included
BREAKFAST
55F extra

Thanks to the Timhôtel chain, modern, moderately priced two-star hotels are flourishing in Paris. However, some of the locations appeal more to French business travelers than they do to tourists, and others are in Mars from a tourist's standpoint. Those listed here are in the general mainstream of things. This is the French version of Budget Inn, so old-world charm, individual attention, and fine furnishings are not part of the program, but you can expect clean rooms with private bathrooms and value for your money. As an added bonus, the eleventh night is free in any of the chain's hotels throughout France, and the ten nights leading up to it do not have to be consecutive or spent in any one particular Timhôtel. Children under twelve are free if they occupy their parents' room. Some of the hotels have rooms for the handicapped, saunas, and conference rooms. For ease in booking a reservation at any Timhôtel, contact the central reservations center at 01-44-15-81-15 (telephone) or 01-44-15-95-26 (fax).

If you prefer, you may deal directly with each hotel. Check the index in the back of the book for other locations.

ENGLISH SPOKEN: Yes

FACILITIES AND SERVICES: Bar; conference room; direct-dial phone; hair dryer available; elevator; radio; TV with international reception; office safe, 20F per day, 90F per week

NEAREST TOURIST ATTRACTIONS (RIGHT BANK): Tuileries, Louvre, Palais-Royal, place de la Concorde, Beaubourg

(13) TONIC HÔTEL LOUVRE ★★
12–14, rue de Roule, 75001 (1st)
34 rooms, all with shower or bath and toilet

TELEPHONE
01-42-33-00-71
FAX
01-40-26-06-86
MÉTRO
Louvre, Châtelet
CREDIT CARDS
AE, DC, MC, V

Physical fitness buffs who stay at this central budget address can keep themselves in top shape. If you are a morning jogger or walker, it is only a hop, skip, and a jump to join fellow exercisers in the Tuileries or along the banks of the Seine. The hotel is also located well from a sight-seeing standpoint, and there are many good restaurants within easy walking distance (see *Cheap Eats in Paris*).

The hotel consists of two parts: the main building and the new annex next door. In the main part, the simple, pastel rooms include luggage racks, mirrored wardrobes, and double-paned windows to keep out street noise. The bathrooms have either a built-in steam bath, a Jacuzzi in the bathtub, or a pulsating shower massage to ease away the aches and pains of daily tourist safaris through Paris.

In the annex, Rooms 106, 306, and 406 are winners. The dark wood furniture in each goes well with the exposed stone walls, beams, and double floor-to-ceiling windows. The booby prize is shared between Room 207, a dark space on the back facing a wall, and no. 505, a two-level arrangement with steep steps leading upstairs to a pitched roofed room with no view and no air circulation.

ENGLISH SPOKEN: Yes

FACILITIES AND SERVICES: Bar; direct-dial phone; elevator to fourth floor in main building, no elevator in annex; hair dryer; minibar; TV with international reception; shower massage or steam bath in most rooms, Jacuzzis in some; safe in office, no charge

NEAREST TOURIST ATTRACTIONS (RIGHT BANK): Louvre, Tuileries, Seine, Palais-Royal, Île de la Cité, Île St-Louis, St-Michel

RATES
Single 520–720F, double 620–900F, triple 720F, quad 1,000F; extra bed 100F
Taxe de séjour: 5F extra per person, per day

BREAKFAST
40F extra

Second Arrondissement

(See map pages 40–41.)

RIGHT BANK
Bibliotèque Nationale, Bourse,
Cognacq-Jay Museum, *passages,*
place des Victoires

The second arrondissement is known as the area of finance (around the stock exchange, or Bourse), the press, and the rag trade (around place du Caire). It makes up for its small size with the beautiful Victorian shopping *passages* and the boutiques around place des Victoires. The second is within walking distance to the Marais, Centre Georges-Pompidou (Beaubourg), and the Louvre Museum. The southern half around rue Montorgueil has some of the best food markets in Paris. The seedy northern half around rue d'Aboukir should definitely be avoided, and so should rue St-Denis, home of Paris hookers.

HOTELS IN THE SECOND ARRONDISSEMENT

(16) GRAND HÔTEL DE BESANÇON ★★★
56, rue Montorgueil, 75002 (2nd)
20 rooms, all with shower or bath and toilet

TELEPHONE
01-42-36-41-08
FAX
01-45-08-08-79
MÉTRO
Étienne-Marcel, Sentier
CREDIT CARDS
AE, DC, MC, V
RATES
Single 570F, double 590F, suite 630–670F; extra bed 150F
Taxe de séjour: 6F extra per person, per day
BREAKFAST
40F extra downstairs, 60F served in room

Years ago when Les Halles was the wholesale food market for Paris, Rue Montorgueil was one of the main streets. Today, not much has changed, except that in 1992, most of the street was transformed into a pedestrian-only walkway where you can still find everything from the butcher and baker to the candlestick seller. Many of the side streets have received the same pedestrian-only designation and are filled with an eccentric mix of straight and gay all-night restaurants, bars, dives, and shops.

The Grand Hôtel de Besançon stands smack in the middle of it all. For the price, the renovated, look-alike rooms are well supplied with Louis Philippe furnishings, coordinated fabrics, and the required list of perks. The suites are the best deals, especially if space is an issue. Ask for no. 50, which has a courtyard view, or no. 43, which overlooks the street. You don't want no. 34, a viewless double with a tiny stall shower. Breakfast, as usual is extra, and too much so if it is served in your room. A better Cheap Eat for breakfast is across the street at Stohrer, 51, rue Montorgueil, a historic *pâtissèrie* founded in 1730 by Louis XV's chief *pâtissier* and considered one of the best in Paris.

ENGLISH SPOKEN: Yes

FACILITIES AND SERVICES: Direct-dial phone; elevator from first floor; hair dryer; radio; TV with international reception; office safe, no charge

NEAREST TOURIST ATTRACTIONS (RIGHT BANK): Centre Georges-Pompidou (Beaubourg), Les Halles, place des Victoires

(17) HÔTEL VIVIENNE ★★
40, rue Vivienne, 75002 (2nd)
44 rooms, 30 with toilet, all with shower or bath

The picture on the reception desk was taken at the hotel in 1917. The little girl in the photo was born in this hotel, which her parents owned along with a restaurant next door. The present owner, Claudine Haycraft, bought the hotel from the family almost twenty-five years ago. Since then, she has slowly redone it, making it a popular budget destination in this part of Paris. The rooms are kept spotlessly clean by a team of career maids. Room decor falls into the typical two-star category: mix and match furniture, some chenille here and there, and industrial-strength carpeting. Bathrooms are adequate, if somewhat questionable in color schemes. Best room in the house? I think it is no. 14, which faces the street and is large enough to feel at home in for more than overnight.

ENGLISH SPOKEN: Yes

FACILITIES AND SERVICES: Direct-dial phone; elevator to fifth floor; hair dryer in most rooms; TV; safe in office, no charge

NEAREST TOURIST ATTRACTIONS (RIGHT BANK): Bourse, Opéra

TELEPHONE
01-42-33-13-26
FAX
01-40-41-98-19
MÉTRO
Bourse, Richelieu Drouot
CREDIT CARDS
MC, V
RATES
Single 285–455F, double 360–505F; extra bed is 30% of room rate; children under 10 are free
Taxe de séjour: included
BREAKFAST
40F extra

(18) TIMHÔTEL BOURSE ★★
3, rue de la Banque, 75002 (2nd)
46 rooms, all with shower or bath and toilet

Next to Galerie Vivienne (see Cheap Chic, page 288). Please see page 52 for general information about Timhôtels.

ENGLISH SPOKEN: Yes

FACILITIES AND SERVICES: Direct-dial phone; conference room; elevator; hair dryer available; TV with

TELEPHONE
01-42-61-53-90
FAX
01-42-60-05-39
MÉTRO
Bourse, Palais-Royal
CREDIT CARDS
AE, DC, MC, V

RATES
Single 460F, double 575F, triple 725F; children under 12 free. *Taxe de séjour*: included
BREAKFAST
55F extra per person

international reception; office safe, 20F per day, 90F per week

NEAREST TOURIST ATTRACTIONS (RIGHT BANK): Opéra, Louvre, Tuileries, Palais-Royal, place de la Concorde

(19) TIQUETONNE HÔTEL ★
6, rue Tiquetonne, 75002 (2nd)
40 rooms, 30 with shower or bath and toilet

TELEPHONE
01-42-36-94-58
FAX
01-42-36-02-94
MÉTRO
Étienne-Marcel, Reaumur-Sebastopol
CREDIT CARDS
MC, V
RATES
Single 145–225F, double 250F (double beds *only*); shower 25F *Taxe de séjour*: included
BREAKFAST
25F extra (no croissants)

Cheap Sleepers in Paris looking for an old-fashioned, budget-minded family hotel that offers basic, clean rooms in central Paris have hit pay dirt here. The hotel has been run for half a century by Mme. Sirvain, her niece Marie-Jo, and the hotel dog, a strapping German shepherd who surveys the scene from a command post in the lobby.

If you don't mind the hike to the top floor, there is nothing wrong with no. 20, provided you can live in a room with an orange chenille bedspread, red curtains, and floral wallpaper in peach, pink, and green. There is a small table, with a laminated top displaying sailing ships, and two hard chairs. The bathroom has a shelf over the sink and a curtain shielding the enclosed tile shower. Room 24 is a simple, sunny single with only a sink and bidet.

Rock-bottom prices insure popularity, so book early, but don't plan on a room in August or during the week between Christmas and New Year's when the family shuts the hotel and goes on their own vacation.

ENGLISH SPOKEN: Yes

FACILITIES AND SERVICES: Elevator

NEAREST TOURIST ATTRACTIONS (RIGHT BANK): Centre Georges-Pompidou (Beaubourg), Forum les Halles

(20) TULIP INN-OPÉRA DE NOAILLES ★★★
9, rue de La Michodière, 75002 (2nd)
58 rooms, all with shower or bath and toilet

TELEPHONE
01-47-42-92-90; toll-free in the U.S., 800-344-1212 (Golden Tulip Hotels)
FAX
01-49-24-92-71
E-MAIL
Tulip.Inn.de.Noailles@wanadoo.fr

If you are allergic to gilt and cherubs, you will appreciate this smart, hard-edge hotel. Owner Martine Falck took an old hotel and turned it into a sleek, Art Deco–inspired site where different bold color schemes of gray, black, midnight blue, and yellow distinguish each floor. The street entrance leads into a wide-spaced reception room with an atrium garden to one side. All fifty-eight rooms and suites can be recommended, even the smallest, no. 507, done in gray and black with green accents. Room 601 is a step up in size and has a terrace, built-in desk, and comfortable reading chair. Consider the masculine suites if you are in Paris for business. Each has a separate sitting room with a sofa, TV, large working desk, and halogen lighting. There is another remote-controlled TV in the bedroom, and in one room, you can walk onto a wooden planked terrace equipped with a table and chairs for *al fresco* dining . . . or working. The attractive weekend and off-season rates make this a contender if this is your area of choice in Paris.

ENGLISH SPOKEN: Yes

FACILITIES AND SERVICES: Air-conditioning in half the rooms; bar; direct-dial phone; elevator; hair dryer; TV with international reception; safe in office, no charge; laundry service; room service

NEAREST TOURIST ATTRACTIONS (RIGHT BANK): Opéra, shopping at Galeries Lafayette and Au Printemps, Louvre

MÉTRO
Opéra, 4-Septembre

CREDIT CARDS
AE, DC, MC, V

RATES
Single 600–920F, double 750–980F, suites 1,200F; ask about any promotional rates
Taxe de séjour: included

BREAKFAST
Included if you book directly with the hotel; 50F extra if you book through the 800-number

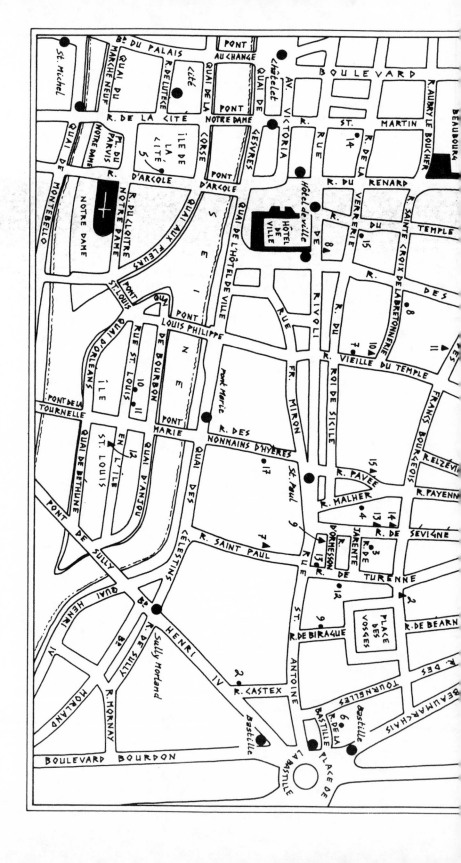

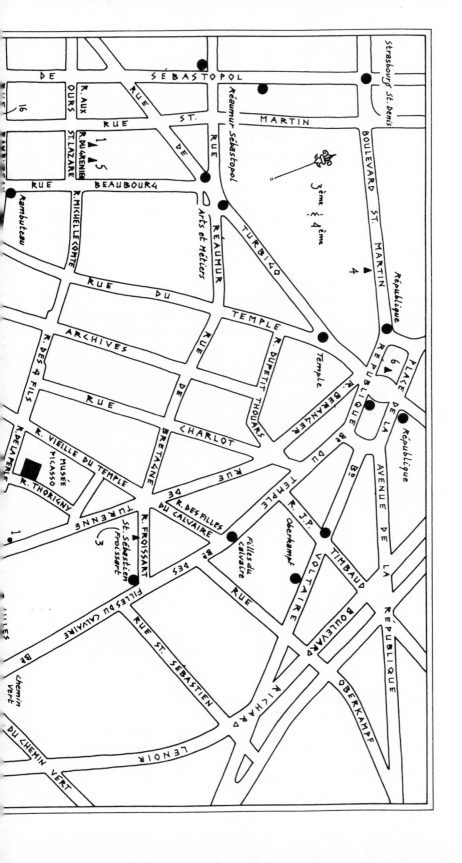

Third Arrondissement

This area includes the northern parts of the revitalized Marais, which until it was rescued by Minister of Culture André Malraux in the 1960s was the worst slum in Paris. Today the magnificent seventeenth-century *hôtel particuliers* (private mansions) have been turned into museums, the most famous of which is the Picasso Museum in the Hôtel Salé.

HOTELS IN THE THIRD ARRONDISSEMENT

(1)	Hôtel des Chevaliers ★★★	60

(1) HÔTEL DES CHEVALIERS ★★★
30, rue de Turenne, 75003 (3rd)
24 rooms, all with shower or bath and toilet

TELEPHONE
01-42-72-73-47
FAX
01-42-72-54-10
MÉTRO
Bastille, Chemin-Vert, St-Paul
CREDIT CARDS
AE, MC, V
RATES
1–2 persons 610–670F
Taxe de séjour: included
BREAKFAST
50F extra for continental, 80F
extra for buffet

The location near the Picasso Museum and on the edge of the vibrant Marais puts the Hôtel des Chevaliers on the list of desirable Cheap Sleeps in Paris. The smartly done rooms are not large, but they are sound-proofed by double-paned windows and brightened by either a welcome fruit basket or bouquet of flowers upon the guest's arrival. I think those on the top floors are the most desirable. The five facing the inner courtyard, and no. 16, a dark twin with no sky view, are the least pleasant. The only other drawback I found was the location of the room safes—on the floor in either the closet or the bathroom, forcing one into a prone position to gain access.

Sixteenth-century exposed supports line the stairway leading to the downstairs breakfast room, fashioned from an old *cave,* with the original water well still in one corner. Nicely upholstered chairs are placed around well-lit tables, where breakfast is served on individual trays. Changing art exhibits line the reception area, and all the art work is available for purchase. Management, headed by owner Mme. Truffaut, is very outgoing and friendly, and repeat guests are many.

ENGLISH SPOKEN: Yes

FACILITIES AND SERVICES: Bar; direct-dial phone; elevator to third floor; hair dryer; minibar; TV with international reception; room safe, no charge

NEAREST TOURIST ATTRACTIONS (RIGHT BANK): Marais, place des Vosges, Picasso Museum, Bastille Opéra

Fourth Arrondissement

The fourth arrondissement stretches from the Marais through the ancient Jewish quarter on the rue des Rosiers to the Île St-Louis in the middle of the Seine. It is an area perfectly suited to exploring on foot, lending itself to discovery at almost every turn. Its immense charm comes from a wonderful mixture of past and present.

Notre-Dame Cathedral, the geographical and spiritual heart of France, sits majestically on the tip of Île de la Cité. Place des Vosges, with its historic pink-brick townhouses set above wide arcade walkways, is the oldest square in Paris and one of the most beautiful. The Île St-Louis is one of the most desirable, and admittedly expensive, places to reside in Paris. The island is a capsule of all that is Paris, with interesting shops, art galleries, boutiques, baroque mansions, lines for the famous Berthillon ice cream, and lovely views along the romantic *quais*. Not to be missed is the controversial (from an architectural standpoint) Centre Georges-Pompidou (Beaubourg), the modern art museum, which logs more visitors each year than the Eiffel Tower.

RIGHT BANK
Centre Georges-Pompidou (Beaubourg), Hôtel-de-Ville (City Hall), Île St-Louis, Jewish Quarter, Notre-Dame Cathedral, place des Vosges, Maison de Victor Hugo, continuation of the Marais

HOTELS IN THE FOURTH ARRONDISSEMENT

(2)	Castex Hôtel ★★	**62**
(3)	Grand Hôtel Jeanne d'Arc ★★	**62**
(4)	Grand Hôtel Malher ★★	**63**
(5)	Hospitel: l'Hôtel à l'Hôpital ★★★	**64**
(6)	Hôtel Bastille Speria ★★★	**64**
(7)	Hôtel Caron de Beaumarchais ★★★	**65**
(8)	Hôtel de la Bretonnerie ★★★	**66**
(9)	Hôtel de la Place des Vosges ★★	**67**
(10)	Hôtel de Lutèce* ★★★	**68**
(11)	Hôtel des Deux-Îles* ★★★	**69**
(12)	Hôtel du Grand Turenne* ★★★	**69**
(13)	Hôtel Practic ★	**70**
(14)	Hôtel Saint-Merry ★★★	**71**
(15)	Hôtel Sansonnet ★★	**72**

OTHER OPTIONS
Apartment Rentals
(†)	RothRay	**239**

Student Accommodations
(16)	Acceuil des Jeunes en France (AJF)	**253**
(17)	Maison Internationale de la Jeunesse et des Étudiants (MIJE)	**256**

*Indicates a Big Splurge
(†) Indicates listing not shown on map

(2) CASTEX HÔTEL ★★
5, rue Castex, 75004 (4th)
27 rooms, 19 with shower or bath and toilet, 8 with shower and no toilet

TELEPHONE
01-42-72-31-52
FAX
01-42-72-57-91
MÉTRO
Bastille
CREDIT CARDS
MC, V
RATES
Single 220–275F, double 300–360F, triple 450F; extra bed for child 70F
Taxe de séjour: 5F extra per person, per day
BREAKFAST
30F extra per person

The friendly Bouchand family has been at the helm of the Castex since 1929. Virtually nothing changed at the hotel until a few years ago when Blaise Bouchand took over as manager and modernized the place. In tossing out the old, the hotel lost some of its funky charm, as it became a neat-as-a-pin, very clean Cheap Sleep done in French Motel Moderne. The generic rooms have open closets, no drawers, and no televisions. The new bathrooms, however, with enclosed showers, rival some three-star numbers in the neighborhood. To watch television, guests must sit at one of the tables in the dining room. Also in this room is a life-size cutout of President Bill Clinton, obviously put there by a Republican prankster. The words on the cutout read: "Thanks for staying at the American administration's official hotel in Paris." While it may not quite live up to such a statement, it does live up to being one of the best Cheap Sleeps in the arrondissement.

ENGLISH SPOKEN: Yes

FACILITIES AND SERVICES: Direct-dial phone; no elevator; safe in office, no charge

NEAREST TOURIST ATTRACTIONS (RIGHT BANK): Bastille Opéra, Marais, Île de la Cité, Île St-Louis, St-Germain-des-Prés

(3) GRAND HÔTEL JEANNE D'ARC ★★
3, rue de Jarente, 75004 (4th)
36 rooms, all with shower or bath and toilet

TELEPHONE
01-48-87-62-11
FAX
01-48-87-37-31
E-MAIL
www.paris-hotel.tm.fr
MÉTRO
St-Paul, Bastille
CREDIT CARDS
MC, V

The Grand Hôtel Jeanne d'Arc sits on a quiet street leading into the Marais. Discovered long ago by astute Cheap Sleepers, the hotel offers spotless rooms with a minimum of snags and tears. Sometimes it is hard to account for different types of decorating tastes, and I will admit to being baffled about a few of the choices in the public areas of this hotel. My prize for the most bizarre mirror on the Continent goes to the one done by a local artist that hangs near the reception and defies rational description. The strange taste in art carries to the bright primary-colored fish painted on the first- and second-floor stairways. Fortunately, the rooms do not keep pace with the unusual decoration elsewhere, and they are actually quite acceptable.

Rooms 11 or 12 are good bets if there are two of you, and if there are four, no. 15 is a good choice. If you are alone, request no. 51, a small top-floor room with a desk, open closet, sunny view, and a compact bathroom with a stall shower. If bathroom floor space is needed, ask for no. 63, with two double beds, a huge blue bathroom, and a rooftop view. Repeat customers comprise the bulk of the clientele, so book early if this one appeals to you.

ENGLISH SPOKEN: Yes

FACILITIES AND SERVICES: Direct-dial phone; elevator; TV with international reception; safe in office, no charge

NEAREST TOURIST ATTRACTIONS (RIGHT BANK): Picasso Museum, Marais, place des Vosges, Bastille Opéra, rue des Rosiers (Jewish Quarter)

(4) GRAND HÔTEL MALHER ★★
5, rue Malher, 75004 (4th)
31 rooms, all with shower or bath and toilet

The Grand Hôtel Malher is a winning two-star with many three-star features. The lobby is dominated by a lovely gold mirror and blue velvet chairs attractively arranged against a backdrop of centuries-old stone walls. Fresh flowers and bowls of potpourri soften the setting. Coordinated bedrooms with tiled bathrooms are welcoming retreats. Best choices are on the sunny top floors in rooms with balconies. Room 55, a light lavender twin with a little balcony, faces front. No. 64, a suite, is ideal for a couple with one child. It has a double and a twin bed, an extra-large sink area in the gray tiled bathroom, and two oil paintings over the bed. Pamela and Didier Fossiez will be your gracious hosts, and your stay with them should be delightful.

ENGLISH SPOKEN: Yes

FACILITIES AND SERVICES: Conference room; direct-dial phone; hair dryer; elevator; minibar; TV with international reception; safe in office, no charge

NEAREST TOURIST ATTRACTIONS (RIGHT BANK): Marais, place des Vosges, Bastille Opéra, Picasso Museum, rue des Rosiers (Jewish Quarter), Île de la Cité, Île St-Louis, St-Germain-des-Prés

RATES
1–2 persons 350–475F, triple 550F, quad 600F; extra bed 75F
Taxe de séjour: included

BREAKFAST
35F extra

TELEPHONE
01-42-72-60-92

FAX
01-42-72-25-37

E-MAIL
www.paris-hotel.tm.fr/gb/
bastille.09/malher.html

MÉTRO
St-Paul

CREDIT CARDS
MC, V

RATES
Single 595–650F, double 700–750F, junior suite 1,000F
Taxe de séjour: 5F extra per person, per day

BREAKFAST
45F extra

(5) HOSPITEL: L'HÔTEL À L'HÔPITAL ★★★
1, place du Parvis Notre-Dame de Paris, 75004 (4th)
The hotel is located on the sixth floor of Building 2
(*au 6ème étage du batiment B2*); see note below
14 rooms, all with shower or bath and toilet

TELEPHONE
01-44-32-01-00
FAX
01-44-32-01-16
MÉTRO
Cité
CREDIT CARDS
AE, DC, MC, V
RATES
Single 445F, double 520F
Taxe de séjour: included
BREAKFAST
40F extra

Wanted: A quiet hotel room on the doorstep of Notre-Dame Cathedral, only seconds away from all the fun and frolic going on around place St-Michel and the Left Bank. Impossible? *Mais non!* Not if you check into Hospitel: l'Hôtel à l'Hôpital, located within the walls of Paris's most prominent hospital: L'Hôtel Dieu de Paris. Originally opened to serve relatives of patients, the fourteen rooms are now open to anyone. Frankly, I had my doubts when I first heard about it. I could just imagine the depressing rooms with linoleum floors and institutional furnishings, all smelling like Lysol. How wrong I was. Actually, the hotel has a great deal going for it. In addition to the dynamite location, its contemporary rooms, done with Art Deco overtones and in vibrant primary colors, are blissfully quiet and air-conditioned. The tiled baths are above average; it is, of course, absolutely spotless; and above all, the low prices are amazing for this expensive, touristy sector of Paris. The only downside to the hotel is its location on the sixth floor under a mansard roof. There are no real windows, only skylights—but they are ample and let in plenty of light and sunshine. The closet and drawer space is not geared to long stays, and you might see a few hospital patients in bathrobes *en route* to your elevator. If you can live with this, it is a Cheap Sleep find.

NOTE: To find the hotel within the hospital, enter directly through the door just beside the main door. The entrance is marked.

ENGLISH SPOKEN: Yes

FACILITIES AND SERVICES: Air-conditioning in all rooms; direct-dial phone; elevator; TV; room service; office safe, no charge; rooms for the handicapped

NEAREST TOURIST ATTRACTIONS (RIGHT BANK): Notre-Dame, Île de la Cité, Île St-Louis, St-Michel, St-Germain-des-Prés

(6) HÔTEL BASTILLE SPERIA ★★★
1, rue de la Bastille, 75004 (4th)
42 rooms, all with shower or bath and toilet

TELEPHONE
01-42-72-04-01

With the opening of the new Bastille Opéra, along with many galleries, new wave boutiques, trendy restaurants, and hot night spots throughout the *quartier,* the Bastille is one of the most popular places in Paris today. Visitors longing to be in the center of all this action can stay at the Bastille Speria, which is next to the famed brasserie Bofinger (see *Cheap Eats in Paris*) and only a few yards from the place de la Bastille. The interior of the hotel was renovated in the late 1980s and continues to be well maintained. The nicely decorated rooms have uncluttered lines and contemporary furnishings. The modern breakfast area and lounge have the same trim lines and feature a small garden and large aquarium with colorful fish.

ENGLISH SPOKEN: Yes

FACILITIES AND SERVICES: Direct-dial phone; elevator; hair dryer; minibar; TV with international reception; room safe, 15F per day; trouser press

NEAREST TOURIST ATTRACTIONS (RIGHT BANK): Bastille Opéra, Marais, place des Vosges, Picasso Museum; typical outdoor market, Thursday and Sunday mornings, 8 A.M.–noon, on boulevard Richard Lenoir

FAX
01-42-72-56-38

MÉTRO
Bastille

CREDIT CARDS
AE, DC, MC, V

RATES
Single 530–575F, double 570–650F, triple 780F
Taxe de séjour: included

BREAKFAST
50F extra

(7) HÔTEL CARON DE BEAUMARCHAIS ★★★
12, rue Vieille-du-Temple, 75004 (4th)
19 rooms, all with shower or bath and toilet

Named after the boisterous author of the *Marriage of Figaro,* the Caron de Beaumarchais is close to interesting shopping in the Marais, the Jewish Quarter, and the Bastille Opéra. The beautifully restored hotel opened for business in June 1993, and is run by father and son owners Etienne and Alain Bigeard. Between them they have all the credentials necessary to run a fine, small hotel. Service and attention to guests' needs is a dwindling commodity in today's hotel market, but not here. When I was at the hotel, guests could not say enough about the care and consideration extended to them during their stay, and this is backed up by the many glowing letters I have received from contented readers who have stayed here.

The downstairs lobby features a Louis XVI fireplace, copies of eighteenth-century murals, an antique game table laid out with authentic old playing cards, and an atrium garden off to one side. A brunch with freshly squeezed orange juice, assorted pastries, fresh fruit, and yogurt is served in a comfortable room that lends itself to lingering while thumbing through the collection of guide books left here for everyone's use. If guests prefer,

TELEPHONE
01-42-72-34-12

FAX
01-42-72-34-63

MÉTRO
Hôtel-de-Ville, St-Paul

CREDIT CARDS
AE, DC, MC, V

RATES
1–2 persons 660–750F; extra bed 100F
Taxe de séjour: included

BREAKFAST
Continental 50F extra; brunch 80F extra

a continental breakfast will be brought on a tray to their rooms.

The nineteen bedrooms are small, but effective design and elegant eighteenth-century decor overcome this. No detail has been overlooked in providing a coordinated look. The Gustavian III–style furniture was made especially for the hotel. Original pages from the *Marriage of Figaro* are framed and hang in each room. Hand-painted and signed ceramic tiles highlight the bathrooms, where even the color of the soap in the soap dish has been taken into consideration. All rooms are air-conditioned and soundproofed; and six have balconies with tables and chairs. In operating the hotel, the family strives to re-create a typically French atmosphere where guests feel at home and want to return. They achieve their goal with great success.

ENGLISH SPOKEN: Yes

FACILITIES AND SERVICES: Air-conditioned and sound-proofed rooms; bathrobes; direct-dial phone; hair dryer; elevator; minibar; TV with international reception; safe in office, no charge

NEAREST TOURIST ATTRACTIONS (RIGHT BANK): Place des Vosges, Marais, Jewish Quarter, Île St-Louis, Île de la Cité, Picasso Museum, Bastille Opéra

(8) HÔTEL DE LA BRETONNERIE ★★★
22, rue Sainte-Croix-de-la-Bretonnerie, 75004 (4th)
31 rooms, all with shower or bath and toilet

TELEPHONE
01-48-87-77-63

FAX
01-42-77-26-78

MÉTRO
Hôtel-de-Ville

CREDIT CARDS
MC, V

RATES
1–2 persons 680–825F,
suites 755F
Taxe de séjour: 6F extra per
person, per day

BREAKFAST
50F extra

A stay in this captivating hotel will make you feel like an inhabitant of old-world Paris. Set in a restored seventeenth-century townhouse in the heart of the picturesque Marais, it is just minutes from Beaubourg, place des Vosges, the Picasso Museum, the banks of the Seine, and Notre-Dame. High praise goes to long-time owners M. and Mme. Sagot and their daughter for providing a warm welcome to their many returning guests, who rightfully consider this to be one of the best small hotels in Paris.

Quality and taste are evident from the minute you enter the comfortable lobby and sitting room, which has a bar to one side. The rooms are individually decorated and all are recommended. For a special treat, reserve no. 25 with modern British colonial wicker and a four-poster metal bed. Bathroom touches include fabric wall coverings, a deep tub, and an inset sink with plenty of space for all the cosmetics one could possibly need. A special favorite is no. 28, a two-room suite with a double bathroom to die for . . . just wait until you sink into the massive oval tub. No. 35 is wonderful. Magnificently done in soft mauve tones with enviable antiques, it consists of a bedroom, a separate sitting room, and one of the most beautiful three-star marble baths in Paris. For something smaller, but just as appealing, try Room 12, imaginatively decorated in blue with a small sitting area and an adobe tiled bathroom.

ENGLISH SPOKEN: Yes

FACILITIES AND SERVICES: Bar; direct-dial phone; elevator; laundry service; TV with international reception; room safe, no charge

NEAREST TOURIST ATTRACTIONS (RIGHT BANK): Place des Vosges, Bastille Opéra, Beaubourg, Marais, Picasso Museum, Seine, Île de la Cité, Île St-Louis, rue des Rosiers (Jewish Quarter)

(9) HÔTEL DE LA PLACE DES VOSGES ★★
12, rue de Birague, 75004 (4th)
16 rooms, all with shower or bath and toilet

A vigorous transformation project more than a decade ago turned this ancient little hotel into one of the top choices of many American visitors to Paris. It is located on the outside edge of the beautiful place des Vosges, the oldest square in Paris and one that is steeped in the history of the city. Victor Hugo, Cardinal Richelieu, and Madame de Sévigné all lived on the square, and the present inhabitants of the area are no less influential, wealthy, and powerful. The setting puts you in the heart of the Marais and within easy walking distance to the Picasso Museum and the fashionable area around the Bastille Opéra. It is also close to all types of night spots and a host of Cheap Eats in Paris.

In restoring the hotel, the owners displayed faithful attention to detail and maintained the architectural past of the building by keeping the original beamed ceilings, wood-paneled walls, large tapestries, and antique furnishings displayed in the lobby. Like the hotel, the prices are small, and so are most of the sixteen rooms, which thankfully have been redone since my last visit. Minuscule bathrooms and closets complement the luggage space, which is almost nil. The best room, and naturally the most popular, is no. 60 on the top floor with a view of the rooftops and the Bastille Opéra. If you are alone, Rooms 40 or 50 are the best picks; the worst is

TELEPHONE
01-42-72-60-46

FAX
01-42-72-02-64

MÉTRO
St-Paul, Bastille

CREDIT CARDS
AE, DC, MC, V

RATES
Single 345–460F, double 480–500F
Taxe de séjour: included

BREAKFAST
40F extra per person

no. 20 facing a depressing gray wall. If you don't mind tiny, this is a popular hotel in a fascinating part of Paris. Please note the hotel is booked months in advance; in fact, one guest has already booked and *paid for* the entire hotel, where he and his friends will stay while welcoming the New Year 2000.

ENGLISH SPOKEN: Yes

FACILITIES AND SERVICES: Direct-dial phone; elevator from the second floor; TV with international reception; safe in office, no charge

NEAREST TOURIST ATTRACTIONS (RIGHT BANK): Place des Vosges, Marais, Bastille Opéra, Picasso Museum, Seine, Île de la Cité, Île St-Louis

(10) HÔTEL DE LUTÈCE* ★★★
65, rue Saint-Louis-en-l'Île, 75004 (4th)
23 rooms, all with shower or bath and toilet

TELEPHONE
01-43-26-23-52

FAX
01-43-29-60-25

MÉTRO
Pont-Marie

CREDIT CARDS
AE, V

RATES
1–2 persons 720–875F, triple 1,000F
Taxe de séjour: 6F extra per person, per day

BREAKFAST
45F extra per person

The Île St-Louis is a small island in the middle of the Seine, six blocks long and two blocks wide. Every day and night, and especially on the weekends, crowds of tourists and Parisians surge down the main street, browsing through the boutiques and art galleries or stopping for an ice cream at the famed Berthillon. Lovers of this unique part of Paris check into either the Lutèce or the Deux-Îles (see below), both owned by husband-and-wife team Roland and Elisabeth Buffat. Stepping inside the Hôtel de Lutèce from the island's main street, you are welcomed by bouquets of fresh flowers and a large stone fireplace surrounded by soft couches and armchairs. The rooms at the Lutèce are not large by any standards, but they are nicely decorated and have the requisite exposed beams, provincial prints, and pretty rooftop views (if you are lucky and secure a top-floor room, particularly nos. 51, 52, 53, or 62). Because the hotel exudes charm from top to bottom, it is booked months ahead, so you should reserve as far in advance as possible.

ENGLISH SPOKEN: Yes

FACILITIES AND SERVICES: Air-conditioning in all rooms; direct-dial phone; elevator; hair dryer; TV with international reception; safe in room, no charge

NEAREST TOURIST ATTRACTIONS (RIGHT BANK): Île St-Louis, Île de la Cité, St-Germain-des-Prés, Latin Quarter, St-Michel, Bastille, place des Vosges, Picasso Museum, Marais

(11) HÔTEL DES DEUX-ÎLES* ★★★
59, rue Saint-Louis-en-l'Île, 75004 (4th)
17 rooms, all with shower or bath and toilet

To capture the enchantment of Paris, stay on the Île St-Louis. But be forewarned—you may never want to leave!

Many people like being on the island because they are steps from the cluster of Notre-Dame Cathedral, Ste-Chapelle, and the Conciergerie; within walking distance to the Marais; and close to the Bastille Opéra and all the excitement this popular area generates. Only a few feel isolated and frustrated by its narrow streets, weekend crowds, and lack of easy parking. Personally, I love it, but I am biased because this is where I lived the first year I spent in Paris.

The Hôtel des Deux-Îles is a beautiful seventeenth-century mansion, owned by decorator Roland Buffat and his wife, Elisabeth (see Hôtel de Lutèce, above). This hotel shows their touches at every turn, from the lobby with its atrium garden to the Louis XIV–tiled bathrooms. The snug hotel breakfast area downstairs has a big fireplace and several secluded nooks with soft overstuffed sofas, making it a perfect place to start your Paris day. The rooms, where the very essence of Paris can be viewed from the top-floor windows, are very small, but they are well done with provincial prints, fabric wall covering, bamboo furniture, and tiled baths.

ENGLISH SPOKEN: Yes

FACILITIES AND SERVICES: Air-conditioning in all rooms; direct-dial phone; elevator; hair dryer; TV with international reception; room safe, no charge

NEAREST TOURIST ATTRACTIONS (RIGHT BANK): Île St-Louis, Île de la Cité, Latin Quarter, St-Michel, St-Germain-des-Prés, Marais, Picasso Museum, place des Vosges, Bastille Opéra

TELEPHONE
01-43-26-13-35
FAX
01-43-29-60-25
MÉTRO
Pont-Marie
CREDIT CARDS
AE, V
RATES
Single 770F, double 890F
Taxe de séjour: 6F extra per person, per day
BREAKFAST
50F extra per person

(12) HÔTEL DU GRAND TURENNE* ★★★
6, rue de Turenne, 75004 (4th)
41 rooms, all with shower or bath and toilet

The Libertel hotel group has more than twenty smart lodgings in Paris. All are beautifully done from top to bottom with coordinated colors and furnishings. Hôtel du Grand Turenne offers forty-one charming rooms done in blues, greens, or soft reds. The first floor is devoted entirely to nonsmokers. There are several categories of rooms, and for the slight increase in price, I recommend

TELEPHONE
01-42-78-43-25; central reservation number, 01-44-70-24-24
FAX
01-42-74-10-72; central fax number, 01-44-70-24-51

MÉTRO
St-Paul

CREDIT CARDS
AE, DC, MC, V

RATES
Single 780F, double 850–900F,
suite 1000F
Taxe de séjour: included

BREAKFAST
80F extra (buffet)

the Superior rooms because they offer more space, especially for a double. There is one exception, however, and that is no. 603, a top-floor Superior double. The big bathroom with windows and a tub is nicely appointed, but the slanted wall makes it awkward for a tall person. Full room service is available from the morning until 2 P.M., and again from 6 to 11 P.M. This is a lifesaver if you have children or are just arriving with a case of jet lag and need something to eat at an off hour. The hotel location, only a five-minute walk from place des Vosges, offers visitors a solid base for exploring one of the most interesting *quartiers* in Paris. From here it is an easy walk to the Picasso Museum, Île de la Cité, Île St-Louis, the Bastille Opéra, and all the wild and woolly nighttime fun in the burgeoning eleventh arrondissement. In addition, many restaurants listed in *Cheap Eats in Paris* are close by.

ENGLISH SPOKEN: Yes

FACILITIES AND SERVICES: Bar; direct-dial phone; hair dryer; elevator; laundry service; minibar; room service; TV with international reception; safe in office, no charge; first floor is all nonsmoking

NEAREST TOURIST ATTRACTIONS (RIGHT BANK): Place des Vosges, Picasso Museum, Bastille Opéra, Île St-Louis, Île de la Cité

(13) HÔTEL PRACTIC ★
9, rue d'Ormesson, 75004 (4th)
24 rooms, 15 with shower or bath and toilet

TELEPHONE
01-48-87-80-47

FAX
01-48-87-40-04

MÉTRO
St-Paul, Bastille

CREDIT CARDS
MC, V

RATES
Single 195–325F, double 260–
375F; free shower
Taxe de séjour: 1F extra per
person, per day

BREAKFAST
30F extra per person

A good choice for a thrifty stay in the Marais near place des Vosges is the Hôtel Practic. When making reservations, avoid room no. 15 unless you don't mind facing a blank wall. Better choices would be either no. 25, a light top-floor location affording a view over neighboring rooftops or no. 8, also with a view. Don't lament the lack of any style whatsoever in the rooms, or the absence of ruffles and flourishes in the service department. Focus instead on the cleanliness of the hotel, its nice location on the pretty place Marché Sainte-Catherine, and the easy-on-the-wallet prices.

ENGLISH SPOKEN: Yes

FACILITIES AND SERVICES: Direct-dial phone; no elevator or TV; safe in office, no charge

NEAREST TOURIST ATTRACTIONS (RIGHT BANK): Place des Vosges, Marais, Picasso Museum, Bastille Opéra, Île St-Louis, Île de la Cité

(14) HÔTEL SAINT-MERRY ★★★
78, rue de la Verrerie, 75004 (4th)
**11 rooms, 9 with shower or bath and toilet; 1 suite
with shower, bath, and toilet**

The former presbytery of the seventeenth-century Gothic church of St-Merry is now the most unusual hotel in Paris. It is the labor of love of owner M. Crabbe, who for more than thirty-five years has been working to create a true Gothic masterpiece. His immense pride in his achievement is well deserved, and the results are spectacular.

The entrance to the hotel is through a short hallway with exposed beams and stone steps leading up to the lobby and reception area. Each room in the hotel is different and showcases a wonderful collection of authentic Gothic church and castle memorabilia, mixed with custom-made pieces. All the back rooms share a common wall with the church, and wherever possible this stone wall has been kept visible. One room contains a carved-stone flying buttress, flowing from the floor to the ceiling over the bed. Others have rough red tiles from the Chateau de l'Angeres in the Loire Valley, hand-carved mahogany pews, converted confessionals serving as headboards, and impressive eight-lamp chandeliers. All of the windows in the hotel are stained glass, and the balcony rails still bear the St-Merry Church crest. Since each room is unique, room rates vary accordingly, depending on the plumbing and the level of the Gothic detailing.

For years M. Crabbe has been working on Room 20, the Gothic Suite, and it is finally completed. It isn't just a Gothic hotel suite, it is an experience! The approach is through an entry hall and up seventeen steps into a huge, pitched-roof room with cross beams, a baronial dining table seating six, sky lights, a ten-foot clock, a fireplace, a wall of carved wooden shelves, and a large sofa bed where you can view the large-screen television. The bedroom is equally as dramatic, with a view of the Church of St-Merry. Even the bathroom is fabulous, with an ornately carved door depicting the three wise men, Mary, Joseph, and baby Jesus.

Warning: The hotel is located on a pedestrian walkway, making it accessible by car or taxi *only* to the determined.

ENGLISH SPOKEN: Yes

TELEPHONE
01-42-78-14-15

FAX
01-40-29-06-82

MÉTRO
Châtelet, Hôtel-de-Ville

CREDIT CARDS
None, cash only

RATES
1–2 persons 500–1,200F (prices vary; no two rooms alike); suite for 2 persons 1700F, 4 persons 2300F
Taxe de séjour: included

BREAKFAST
65F extra per person

FACILITIES AND SERVICES: Direct-dial phone; no elevator; TV in suite; office safe, no charge

NEAREST TOURIST ATTRACTIONS (RIGHT BANK): Beaubourg, Marais, Seine, Île de la Cité, Île St-Louis, St-Germain-des-Prés. Don't miss the St-Merry Church adjoining the hotel. It has a beautiful choir and the oldest church bell in Paris, cast in 1331.

(15) HÔTEL SANSONNET ★★
48, rue de la Verrerie, 75004 (4th)
26 rooms, 22 with shower or bath and toilet

TELEPHONE
01-48-87-96-14
FAX
01-48-87-30-46
MÉTRO
Hôtel-de-Ville, Châtelet
CREDIT CARDS
MC, V
RATES
Single 250–375F, double 370–400F; shower 20F
Taxe de séjour: included
BREAKFAST
35F extra per person

The family-owned Sansonnet offers better two-star values than most of its competitors in the neighborhood. The hotel is clean, reasonably modern, and has been managed for twenty-five years by M. and Mme. Neau. A colorful aquarium sits at the lobby entrance, which is up an easy flight of stairs from the street. Several of the singles without facilities are minuscule, but if you have only a small suitcase and plan to just sleep in your room, these are buys. The doubles are good sized, with uniform color schemes and blended fabrics. The closets have shelves and most of the showers have doors. From this address you won't find a better Paris location for exploring the area around Beaubourg and the Forum des Halles. For sightseeing and shopping farther afield, it is a ten-minute walk to the islands, St-Michel, the big department stores on rue de Rivoli, and a number of good Cheap Eats in Paris.

ENGLISH SPOKEN: Yes

FACILITIES AND SERVICES: Direct-dial phone; hair dryer in rooms with full facilities; no elevator; TV with international reception; safe in office, no charge

NEAREST TOURIST ATTRACTIONS (RIGHT BANK): Beaubourg, Forum des Halles, BHV and La Samaritaine department stores, Île de la Cité, Île St-Louis

Fifth Arrondissement

The fifth is known as the Latin Quarter. *Latin* refers to the language heard here until 1798. The arrondissement stretches from the colorful street *marché* on rue Mouffetard to the dome of the Panthéon, through the botanical wonders of the Jardin des Plantes to the Sorbonne. This ancient, interesting, and exhilarating part of Paris is crisscrossed with networks of narrow, curved streets lined on both sides with bookshops, restaurants, and cafés that surge with action twenty-four hours a day. It is youthful, cosmopolitan, bohemian, and fun. Even though St-Michel has lost its penniless chic, it is still the soul of the Latin Quarter. Crowds of all ages and types gather daily around the St-Michel fountain to flirt, eat, drink, argue, and watch the sidewalk entertainment. The area around place de la Contrescarpe is where Hemingway lived when he was a starving writer first in Paris. You can see two of his addresses: 39, rue Descartes, a studio; and 74, rue de Cardinal-Lemoine, where he lived with his wife, Hadley.

LEFT BANK
Cluny Museum, Jardin des Plantes, Latin Quarter, rue Mouffetard, Panthéon, Sorbonne, place de la Contrescarpe

HOTELS IN THE FIFTH ARRONDISSEMENT

(1)	Degrés de Notre-Dame Hôtel (NO STARS)	**76**
(2)	Familia Hôtel ★★	**77**
(3)	Hôtel Agora St-Germain ★★★	**78**
(4)	Hôtel Claude Bernard ★★★	**78**
(5)	Hôtel d'Albe ★★★	**79**
(6)	Hôtel de l'Esperance ★★	**80**
(7)	Hôtel des Allies ★	**80**
(8)	Hôtel des Grandes Écoles ★★	**81**
(9)	Hôtel des Grands Hommes ★★★	**82**
(10)	Hôtel des Jardins du Luxembourg* ★★★	**83**
(11)	Hôtel des Mines ★★	**83**
(12)	Hôtel des 3 Collèges ★★	**84**
(13)	Hôtel du Collège de France ★★	**85**
(14)	Hôtel du Panthéon ★★★	**85**
(15)	Hôtel Esmeralda ★	**86**
(16)	Hôtel Flatters ★	**87**
(17)	Hôtel le Colbert* ★★★	**88**
(18)	Hôtel Marignan ★	**88**
(19)	Hôtel Parc Saint-Séverin* ★★★	**89**
(20)	Hôtel Résidence Henri IV* ★★★	**90**
(21)	Hôtel Résidence Monge ★★	**91**
(22)	Hôtel Résidence Saint-Christophe ★★★	**91**
(23)	Le Jardin de Cluny ★★★	**92**

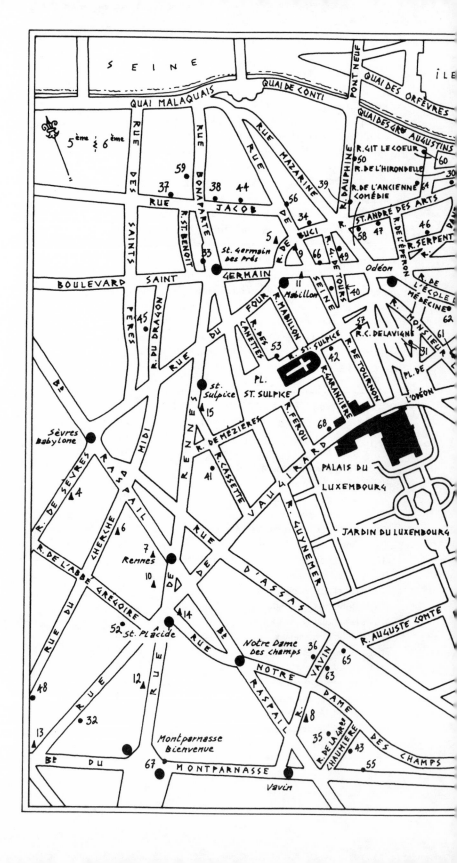

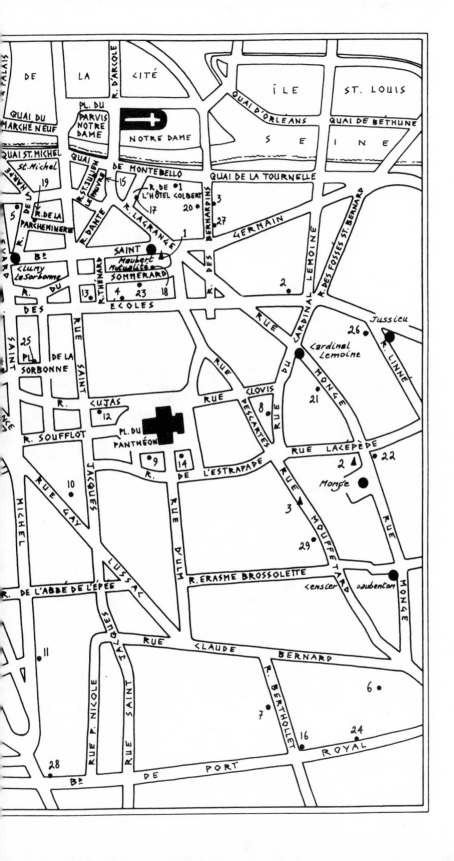

OTHER OPTIONS

Student Accommodations

Private Hostel

*Indicates a Big Splurge

(1) DEGRÉS DE NOTRE-DAME HÔTEL (NO STARS)
10, rue des Grands-Degrés, 75005 (5th)
10 rooms, all with shower or bath and toilet

TELEPHONE
01-43-25-88-38

FAX
01-40-46-95-34

MÉTRO
Maubert-Mutualité

CREDIT CARDS
MC, V

RATES
Single 400–480F, double 450–520F; extra bed 130F
Taxe de séjour: 6F extra per person, per day

BREAKFAST
Included, not deductible

What to expect here? Ten rooms, all located up narrow, winding stairs; the required beams and views of the Left Bank from most rooms; a top-drawer location; quasi-antiques here and there; portable heaters; bare wood floors; and some odd closets. True, there is an upside as well as a downside to the Degrés de Notre-Dame Hôtel, but for the young in both body and spirit, its low prices, superior location within earshot of the chimes of Notre-Dame, and overall rustic charm make it one to consider, especially if you get either Room 47, 48, or 51, all of which have views of Notre-Dame. No. 23 also has a good view, some drawer space, a serviceable bathroom, and small closet. The hotel is above a restaurant of the same name that serves mundane French food you can find anyplace in Paris. Consult *Cheap Eats in Paris* for better alternatives. However, you should probably consider at least having a drink at the bar, where you can pet the house tabby cat named Mimosa; on a wall next to the kitchen is a painting of Mimosa and the cook.

ENGLISH SPOKEN: Yes

FACILITIES AND SERVICES: Bar; direct-dial phone; no elevator; TV; safe in office, no charge

NEAREST TOURIST ATTRACTIONS (LEFT BANK): Notre-Dame Cathedral, Île de la Cité, Île St-Louis, St-Michel, Latin Quarter

(2) FAMILIA HÔTEL ★★
11, rue des Écoles, 75005 (5th)
30 rooms, all with shower or bath and toilet

Many hotels on rue des Écoles are run by foreign managers for absentee owners in the Middle East. As a result, service, cleanliness, and upkeep are often drastically reduced because no one at the hotel has any stake in it or really cares. You will find none of this at the Familia Hôtel. M. and Mme. Gaucheron, along with their son Eric, have owned the hotel for more than a decade, live on site, and take pride in being on top of things every minute. They also go out of their way to insure that all guests are looked after, especially Eric, who speaks rapid-fire English and Spanish. They are always looking for ways to improve their hotel, and on my last visit, the list of new achievements was long. Fourteen rooms now have frescoes of famous Parisian landmarks. Room 62 has the Canal St-Martin painted over the twin beds; no. 43 has the famed Pont Neuf in sepia tones. I like no. 52, with the Pont Alexandre III and the Eiffel Tower gracing one wall and its little outdoor terrace with a view of Notre-Dame. Other improvements include thick, double-glazed windows to ease the traffic noise along the front of the hotel; a revamped entry with an attractive mural of old Paris painted by a friend of Eric Gaucheron; and a new breakfast room featuring Eric's grandmother's glass bookcase filled with his personal collection of antique English and French leather-bound books.

The bedrooms are on a rotating schedule for maintenance and improvements. Some rooms will have new mattresses one year, others a new bathroom, while still others will have new furniture. The size does not change, and they are still a tight fit for some, since they have limited space for bulky luggage or shopping purchases. But guests can always count on clean, snag- and tear-free accommodations. If you want a bird's-eye view of Notre-Dame Cathedral, ask for a front room on the fifth or sixth floor. For a room with a balcony, you want something on the second or fifth floors, facing the street. Staying at the Familia puts guests only a few minutes from St-Germain-des-Prés, the islands, and all the famous cafés in the Latin Quarter. Métro connections are good, and so is the bus transportation.

ENGLISH SPOKEN: Yes, and Spanish

TELEPHONE
01-43-54-55-27

FAX
01-43-29-61-77

MÉTRO
Jussieu, Cardinal-Lemoine, Maubert-Mutualité

CREDIT CARDS
MC, V

RATES
Single 380–530F, double 430–550F, triple 600–630F, quad 700F
Taxe de séjour: 5F extra per person, per day

BREAKFAST
35F extra

FACILITIES AND SERVICES: Direct-dial phone; hair dryer; elevator; minibar; TV with international reception; safe in office, no charge

NEAREST TOURIST ATTRACTIONS (LEFT BANK): Latin Quarter, St-Germain-des-Prés, Île de la Cité, Île St-Louis

(3) HÔTEL AGORA ST-GERMAIN ★★★
42, rue des Bernardins, 75005 (5th)
39 rooms, all with shower or bath and toilet

TELEPHONE
01-46-34-13-00

FAX
01-46-34-75-05

MÉTRO
Maubert-Mutualité

CREDIT CARDS
AE, DC, MC, V

RATES
Single 540–590F, double 690F, triple 900F
Taxe de séjour: 6F extra per person, per day

BREAKFAST
50F extra

The Agora St-Germain continues to represent a success story for both owners and guests. It reopened in 1987 after undergoing a face-lift of remarkable proportions and has been popular ever since. The small, customized rooms with pretty silk wall coverings, ample space, and marble tiled bathrooms are beautifully maintained. A continental breakfast is served in a stone-walled dining room with baskets of fresh flowers and linen napkins on each table. The friendly owners, Pascale and Michèle Sahuc, and their staff see to the wishes of every guest. Firmly recommended by all who have stayed here, this haven for weary travelers is less than five minutes away from good restaurants (see *Cheap Eats in Paris*) and close to all the charm and excitement of this part of the Left Bank.

NOTE: At the corner of rue des Bernardins and boulevard St-Germain is the church St-Nicholas du Chardonnet, the only church in Paris with all services conducted in Latin.

ENGLISH SPOKEN: Yes

FACILITIES AND SERVICES: Direct-dial phone; elevator; hair dryer; minibar; TV with international reception; room safe, no charge

NEAREST TOURIST ATTRACTIONS (LEFT BANK): Latin Quarter, St-Michel, St-Germain-des-Prés, Île de la Cité, Île St-Louis

(4) HÔTEL CLAUDE BERNARD ★★★
43, rue des Écoles, 75005 (5th)
30 rooms, all with shower or bath and toilet

TELEPHONE
01-43-26-32-52

FAX
01-43-26-80-56

MÉTRO
Maubert-Mutualité

The Claude Bernard continues to be a Latin Quarter favorite, thanks to its friendly atmosphere and key location as a base for exploring St-Michel, St-Germain-des-Prés, and the islands in the Seine. After a remodeling project in 1996, things have picked up considerably. With the exception of a restaurant and tearoom next to the lobby and a meeting room, the downstairs is basically the same and the sauna is still free for hotel guests. Upstairs, the rooms combine English country pine furniture with French provincial fabrics, but color coordination has improved and so have most of the bathrooms. During the remodeling, the intricately carved moldings and doors were kept, along with the double French windows overlooking the street. The tremendous triple rooms are good for families, but these rooms face the noisy street, so heavy-duty earplugs would be a must for light sleepers. In fact, all the rooms facing the street should be considered off-limits for all but comatose sleepers.

ENGLISH SPOKEN: Yes

FACILITIES AND SERVICES: Air-conditioning, 100F per day, fans free; direct-dial phone; elevator; hair dryer; minibar; restaurant and tearoom; free sauna; TV with international reception; safe in office, 10F per day

NEAREST TOURIST ATTRACTIONS (LEFT BANK): St-Michel, St-Germain-des-Prés, Île de la Cité, Île St-Louis, Latin Quarter

CREDIT CARDS
AE, DC, MC, V

RATES
Single 500–630F, double 630–730F; suite 1–2 persons 930F, 3 persons 1,130F, 4 persons 1,250F
Taxe de séjour: included

BREAKFAST
55F extra per person

(5) HÔTEL D'ALBE ★★★
1, rue de la Harpe, 75005 (5th)
45 rooms, all with shower or bath and toilet

This is the perfect site for Latin Quarter night owls and other urbanites who consider 11 P.M. the shank of the evening and the crack of dawn bedtime. Rue de la Harpe is just off place St-Michel, the twenty-four-hour, nonstop, pulsating hub of this *quartier.* The street itself is lined with restaurants and cafés geared to tourists out for a good time. So, I must warn you, while this hotel has a good location and is the best on the street, it *is* going to be very noisy unless you use earplugs, sleep with the double-glazed windows tightly shut, and opt for the air-conditioning. Good closet space and new bathrooms complement well-maintained rooms with quilted bedspreads, salmon-colored walls, and green carpets. Best choices are the corner rooms with three windows, but, remember they will be noisy. If there are four of you, look elsewhere, the quad here is too small. The bright modern breakfast room faces the street and plays relaxing classical music while you enjoy a morning croissant and *café au lait.*

ENGLISH SPOKEN: Yes

FACILITIES AND SERVICES: Air-conditioning in half the rooms, 50F supplement per day; bar; direct-dial phone;

TELEPHONE
01-46-34-09-70

FAX
01-40-46-85-70

MÉTRO
St-Michel

CREDIT CARDS
AE, DC, MC, V

RATES
Single 570F, double 750F, triple 760F, quad 800F
Taxe de séjour: included

BREAKFAST
50F extra per person

hair dryer; elevator; TV with international reception; room safe, no charge

NEAREST TOURIST ATTRACTIONS (LEFT BANK): Notre-Dame, Île de la Cité, Île St-Louis, St-Michel, Latin Quarter

(6) HÔTEL DE L'ESPERANCE ★★
15, rue Pascal, 75005 (5th)
28 rooms, all with shower or bath and toilet

<table>
<tr><td>TELEPHONE
01-47-07-10-99</td></tr>
<tr><td>FAX
01-43-37-56-19</td></tr>
<tr><td>MÉTRO
Censier-Daubenton, Gobelins</td></tr>
<tr><td>CREDIT CARDS
V</td></tr>
<tr><td>RATES
1–2 people 370–450F, triple 525F; extra bed 75F
Taxe de séjour: included</td></tr>
<tr><td>BREAKFAST
40F extra per person</td></tr>
</table>

Baubles, bangles, and beads . . . and then some are the significant words to describe the over-the-top frilly decor awaiting you at this hotel. Fortunately, you are not sleeping in the downstairs lobby, which is loaded with fake flowers, Yugoslavian colored crystal, and an extensive array of hand-crocheted pillow covers, doilies, and lamp throws. Add to this a gurgling fountain and reproduction eighteenth-century furniture and some might need blinders to get to their rooms, which are all quite nice and tame by comparison. Room 11 is a double with a private garden and a large bathroom suitable for the handicapped. If you want quiet, book no. 21, a yellow-and-rose double on the back with its own balcony. The location is an interesting one, close to rue Mouffetard and within easy access to most Left Bank, Latin Quarter points of interest.

ENGLISH SPOKEN: Yes

FACILITIES AND SERVICES: Bar; direct-dial phone; elevator; hair dryer; minibar; TV with international reception; safe in office, no charge

NEAREST TOURIST ATTRACTIONS (LEFT BANK): Rue Mouffetard

(7) HÔTEL DES ALLIES ★
20, rue Berthollet, 75005 (5th)
43 rooms, 10 with shower or bath and toilet

<table>
<tr><td>TELEPHONE
01-43-31-47-52</td></tr>
<tr><td>FAX
01-45-35-13-92</td></tr>
<tr><td>MÉTRO
Censier-Daubenton</td></tr>
<tr><td>CREDIT CARDS
MC, V</td></tr>
</table>

Three generations of contented clientele continue to reserve rooms in this pristine Cheap Sleep at the bottom of the fifth arrondissement. The location is not central by any means, but it is within walking distance to all the action and color around rue Mouffetard. It is obvious that money has not been spent on fancy decorating touches, but all the rooms are spotless, with few rips, tears, or dents in sight. The best part is that the rooms come with price tags no serious Cheap Sleeper in Paris can ignore. Room 22 is a steal, with a huge bathroom, twin beds, and nice wallpaper. It is, however, next to the hall shower. No. 2 is also across from a hall shower, and like most of the other rooms, is hose-down simple in every respect. It does have its own bathroom with orange sorbet-colored fixtures and a window. If you are single and feel like climbing 109 steps up to the sixth floor, no. 51 has a view of the dome of *l'eglise du Val de Grace* located on the grounds of a nearby military hospital. No. 5, on the street, has space to spare, a double bed, new wallpaper, and a bathroom with a stall shower. Avoid no. 19 unless the carpet has been changed.

ENGLISH SPOKEN: Yes

FACILITIES AND SERVICES: No elevator or TV; safe in office, no charge

NEAREST TOURIST ATTRACTIONS (LEFT BANK): Rue Mouffetard

RATES
Single 165–175F, double 210–340F, triple 275–420F; public shower 15F (bath towel 4F extra)
Taxe de séjour: included

BREAKFAST
35F extra per person

(8) HÔTEL DES GRANDES ÉCOLES ★★
75, rue du Cardinal-Lemoine, 75005 (5th)
48 rooms, 39 with shower or bath and toilet

Once found, this hotel address is one that its loyal followers whisper only to a select few. Nestled in a beautiful garden and hidden from the world behind towering wooden doors opening off the street, it is definitely one of the most romantic havens of peace and quiet in Paris. The grandmotherly owner, Leonore LeFloch, and her receptionist, Marie, treat their guests like family members. As you can imagine, reservations for this very special hotel are essential months in advance.

Two facing houses make up the hotel. In both, the rooms are decorated with a feminine touch, sparing no ruffle or pretty flowered fabric from the Laura Ashley school of decorating. Almost all of the rooms in both buildings look out onto the large tree-shaded garden with trellised roses, singing birds, spring daffodils, and summer wildflowers. Tables and chairs are placed here, making it a lovely spot for reading and sipping a cool drink. When you look out of your window, you will imagine you are in a French country village, not in the middle of Paris.

The hotel is an uphill climb from the métro, but once there you are close to the place de la Contrescarpe, which played such an important part in Hemingway's Paris. You can also walk to rue Mouffetard, famous for its

TELEPHONE
01-43-26-79-23

FAX
01-43-25-28-15

MÉTRO
Cardinal-Lemoine, Monge

CREDIT CARDS
MC, V

RATES
1–2 people 490–580F, triple 620–680F, quad 680F
Taxe de séjour: included

BREAKFAST
45F extra per person

colorful, daily street *marché,* some good places to eat (see *Cheap Eats in Paris*), and inexpensive clothing stores geared to cute young things.

ENGLISH SPOKEN: Yes

FACILITIES AND SERVICES: Direct-dial phone; elevator; hair dryer; office safe, no charge; no TV

NEAREST TOURIST ATTRACTIONS (LEFT BANK): Rue Mouffetard, place de Contrescarpe, Panthéon, Latin Quarter

(9) HÔTEL DES GRANDS HOMMES ★★★
17, place du Panthéon, 75005 (5th)
32 rooms, all with shower or bath and toilet

TELEPHONE
01-46-34-19-60
FAX
01-43-26-67-32
MÉTRO
St-Michel, RER Luxembourg
CREDIT CARDS
AE, DC, MC, V
RATES
Single 685F, double 795F; 6th-floor suite 880F, ground-floor suite 1,200F; extra bed 100F
Taxe de séjour: included
BREAKFAST
50F extra per person

The Hôtel des Grands Hommes is one of the most stylish three-star hotels in Paris, thanks to the personal management of Corinne Brethous, who is young, energetic, and full of wonderful ideas. In restoring the eighteenth-century building, she spared no effort to create a personal and comfortable hotel. The engaging bedrooms heighten the feeling that one is a guest in a lovely Parisian home rather than in an anonymous hotel room. Rooms with a view are the same price as those without. When reserving, request one of the front rooms with a balcony, where you can have breakfast and gaze onto the Panthéon across the street and see Sacré-Coeur gleaming in the distance. Honeymooners will want to stay in no. 22, with a canopied brass bed and two view balconies, or in no. 32, with a white metal-and-brass bed and a lovely marble bathroom filled with pink towels. Another good choice is no. 60, a two-room suite with a balcony facing the place du Pantheon. The bedroom has pitched beams, twin brass beds and pink Venetian wall lights. There is also a sitting room with a sofa bed and a bathroom with a tub and hand-held shower. The gracious formal lobby is decorated in peach colors with faux marble finishes and outfitted with plenty of soft seating, a small corner bar, and an atrium garden filled with blooming plants.

NOTE: Also under the same ownership is the Hôtel du Pantheon next door (see page 85) and the Hôtel Résidence Henri IV on rue des Bernardins (see page 90).

ENGLISH SPOKEN: Yes

FACILITIES AND SERVICES: Air-conditioning in all rooms; bar; direct-dial phone; hair dryer; elevator; minibar; TV with international reception; safe in office, no charge

NEAREST TOURIST ATTRACTIONS (LEFT BANK): Panthéon, Sorbonne, St-Michel, Jardin du Luxembourg

(10) HÔTEL DES JARDINS DU LUXEMBOURG* ★★★
5, impasse Royer Collard, 75005 (5th)
25 rooms, all with shower or bath and toilet

The Hôtel des Jardins du Luxembourg is a gem located on a narrow, quiet street a short distance from the Luxembourg Gardens. Before its recent renovation it was a down-and-out way station that once housed Sigmund Freud. Now, it is impossible not to be impressed with this completely transformed and charming choice—from the captivating entry with its polished oak floors to the twenty-five rooms displaying the type of refined taste and attention to detail that seasoned travelers demand. The overall theme of the hotel is Oriental with modern overtones. The small lobby is set off by a corner fireplace with two armchairs and a Japanese hibachi used as a bar. A bamboo hat rack adds a whimsical note. Bold colors of burnt sienna, royal blue, gold, and green work together to set off the rooms, which are economical in space, but not in style. No. 14, on the first floor with its own balcony, is a good example; it's the perfect arrangement of a wrought-iron bed, drop-leaf table, folding leather chair and armoire fitted with drawers, hanging space, and a safe. The well-lit bathroom has inset tiles carrying out the same color scheme of the room. On the top floor, Rooms 24 and 25 have glimpses of the Eiffel Tower and are slightly larger. While both are nice, no. 24 has the edge thanks to its bathroom with a stretch tub, extra sink space, and heated towel rack.

ENGLISH SPOKEN: Yes

FACILITIES AND SERVICES: Air-conditioning in all rooms; bar; direct-dial phone; elevator; hair dryer; minibar; TV with international reception; room safe, no charge; handicapped-accessible rooms

NEAREST TOURIST ATTRACTIONS (LEFT BANK): Latin Quarter, St-Michel, Luxembourg Gardens, Panthéon

TELEPHONE
01-40-46-08-88

FAX
01-40-46-02-28

MÉTRO
RER Luxembourg

CREDIT CARDS
MC, V

RATES
1–2 persons 840–900F
Taxe de séjour: included

BREAKFAST
50F extra per person

(11) HÔTEL DES MINES ★★
125, boulevard St-Michel, 75005 (5th)
51 rooms, all with shower or bath and toilet

Charge reasonable prices for sensible, well-kept rooms and you also will enjoy the longevity of this Cheap Sleep in Paris. Owner Laurent Cuypers attributes the decorating to his mother, who personally made the curtains and bedspreads in all the rooms.

TELEPHONE
01-43-54-32-78

FAX
01-46-33-72-52

MÉTRO
RER Luxembourg

CREDIT CARDS
AE, DC, MC, V

RATES
Single 430F, double 430–500F,
triple 590F, quad 680F
Taxe de séjour: included

BREAKFAST
40F extra per person

Boulevard St-Michel is a major thoroughfare through this part of Paris. If peace and quiet is high on your list of requirements, I recommend a courtside room on a higher floor. If you don't mind some noise or can sleep with earplugs, no. 502 is a beamed twin-bedded room with dark blue carpeting and white stuccoed walls. There is luggage space, an open closet, and a blue tiled bath. Even though it faces the street, it has double-paned windows to help diffuse the noise. Salmon is the color of choice in no. 305, which has a new bathroom and an interior view. American guests who value space should book Room 509, which is large enough to sleep four.

ENGLISH SPOKEN: Yes

FACILITIES AND SERVICES: Bar; direct-dial phone; hair dryer in most rooms; elevator to 5th floor; TV; office safe, 10F per day

NEAREST TOURIST ATTRACTIONS (LEFT BANK): Jardin du Luxembourg, St-Michel, Panthéon

(12) HÔTEL DES 3 COLLÈGES ★★
16, rue Cujas, 75005 (5th)
44 rooms, all with shower or bath and toilet

TELEPHONE
01-43-54-67-30

FAX
01-46-34-02-99

MÉTRO
RER Luxembourg, St-Michel,
Cluny

CREDIT CARDS
AE, DC, MC, V

RATES
Single 400–630F, double 500–680F, triple 785F; extra bed 100F
Taxe de séjour: included

BREAKFAST
45F extra per person

If you want a modern room with a reasonable price tag in a good Left Bank neighborhood between the Sorbonne and the Panthéon, this is the place to go. The operative word here is *simple.* The small, off-white lobby has a California look, with modern chairs, large green plants, and bleached wooden floors. The pocket-size rooms have all the necessities: luggage racks, desks and chairs, full-length mirrors, wall-mounted television sets, and fitted bathrooms. Rooms 62, 63, and 64 are best from a size standpoint, and no. 46 is a nice selection for the single traveler. The glass-roof breakfast room off the lobby showcases a large tree in the center, with white bistro tables and rattan chairs placed around it. Management and staff are pleasant and helpful in giving directions, making reservations, and confirming flights.

ENGLISH SPOKEN: Yes

FACILITIES AND SERVICES: Direct-dial phone; elevator; hair dryer; laundry service; TV; safe in office, no charge; tearoom with a section for nonsmokers

NEAREST TOURIST ATTRACTIONS (LEFT BANK): Panthéon, Sorbonne, St-Michel

(13) HÔTEL DU COLLÈGE DE FRANCE ★★
7, rue Thénard, 75005 (5th)
29 rooms, all with shower or bath and toilet

Well placed in the heart of the Latin Quarter and across the street from the Collège de France, this is an outstanding value for a two-star hotel. The owner, M. Georges, is on hand daily to ensure that all runs smoothly. The immaculate rooms are plainly, yet uniformly done. The best ones are on the top floors and have wooden beams and paneling, glimpses of Notre-Dame Cathedral, and in summer are equipped with portable fans. No. 62 is the largest and most requested, probably due to the two floor-to-ceiling windows opening onto a small balcony where you can see the Collège de France. The bathrooms are modern enough, with hair dryers, large towels, and space for more than just a toothbrush. The lobby and breakfast room have been redone with a rusty red fabric covering the sectional seating. There's a nice collection of healthy green plants, and a statue of Joan of Arc guards the entryway. The popularity of this little hotel is reflected in its guest register, which is almost filled months ahead, so plan accordingly.

ENGLISH SPOKEN: Yes

FACILITIES AND SERVICES: Direct-dial phone; fans; elevator to fifth floor; hair dryer; TV with international reception; safe in office, 30F per week

NEAREST TOURIST ATTRACTIONS (LEFT BANK): Latin Quarter, St-Michel, St-Germain-des-Prés, Sorbonne, Panthéon, Luxembourg Gardens, Île de la Cité, Île St-Louis

TELEPHONE
01-43-26-78-36
FAX
01-46-34-58-29
MÉTRO
Maubert-Mutualité, St-Michel, Cluny-Sorbonne
CREDIT CARDS
AE, MC, V
RATES
Single 480F, double 500–580F; extra bed 100F
Taxe de séjour: 5F extra per person, per day
BREAKFAST
35F extra per person

(14) HÔTEL DU PANTHÉON ★★★
19, place du Panthéon, 75005 (5th)
34 rooms, all with shower or bath and toilet

The Hôtel du Panthéon, an elegantly converted townhouse, faces the imposing place du Panthéon in the fifth arrondissement. The métro is about five blocks away, but if you love this part of Paris, you know that almost everything is within walking distance.

From the ground up, the hotel benefits from the impeccable taste and preservationist sensibilities of the gracious owner, Corinne Brethous, who also owns Hôtel des Grands Hommes next door (see page 82) and the Hôtel Résidence Henri IV on rue des Bernardins (see page 90).

TELEPHONE
01-43-54-32-95
FAX
01-43-26-64-65
MÉTRO
St-Michel, RER Luxembourg
CREDIT CARDS
AE, DC, MC, V
RATES
Single 680, double 790F; extra bed 100F
Taxe de séjour: included

The entry leads to the attractive lounge, with a corner coffee bar and a small atrium garden to one side. The continental breakfast is served under the stone arches in the house's original cellar, or in the privacy of your own room. Guests will feel at home immediately in any one of the thirty-four rooms, decorated with antique furniture, textile-covered walls, and floor-length curtains hanging from fourteen-foot ceilings. The front rooms facing the Panthéon are naturally in demand, but if you need absolute silence and calm, the viewless back rooms will guarantee this.

ENGLISH SPOKEN: Yes

FACILITIES AND SERVICES: Air-conditioning in all rooms; conference room; direct-dial phone; elevator; hair dryer; minibar; TV with international reception; safe in office, no charge

NEAREST TOURIST ATTRACTIONS (LEFT BANK): Panthéon, Sorbonne, Latin Quarter, Luxembourg Gardens

(15) HÔTEL ESMERALDA ★
4, rue Saint-Julien-le-Pauvre, 75005 (5th)
19 rooms, 16 with shower or bath and toilet;
4 apartments next door, all with shower or bath and toilet

TELEPHONE
01-43-54-19-20
FAX
01-40-51-00-68
MÉTRO
St-Michel
CREDIT CARDS
None, cash only
RATES
Very small single 175F, 1–2 persons 350–525F, triple 585F, quad 650F
Taxe de séjour: included
BREAKFAST
45F extra per person

Warning: This hotel is not for perfectionists!

The Esmeralda is an unconventional hideaway directly across the Seine from Notre-Dame Cathedral. It is a hotel people either love or absolutely hate. Maybe it does not have the most modern accommodations in town, but it does have one of the best Left Bank locations and some of the most interesting guests. The lack of embellishments, which might disappoint some, is the lure that brings others back again and again. This is a hotel with character for people with character.

No two rooms are alike, and they definitely are far from modern. Just like the unique owner, they flaunt convention and are eccentric to the core. Some are the size of a walk-in closet; others have chandeliers, marble fireplaces, and picture-perfect postcard views of Notre-Dame Cathedral over the gardens of St-Julien-le-Pauvre, Paris's oldest church. All the rooms are reached by passing through a stone-walled lobby (complete with Mona, the house cat, occupying the most comfortable chair) and climbing up a winding flight of ancient stairs. Some of the floors slant, a few areas need more than just a paint brush, and others have only a nodding acquaintance with the housekeeper. It is also *noisy.* But its many cult followers do not care because just being at the Esmeralda spells Paris for them. Be sure to bring ear plugs and reserve way in advance.

NOTE: Insiders here for longer stays know to ask for one of the four apartments next door. These are, however, not for everyone. Reached via a dark, winding, wooden staircase right out of a Victor Hugo novel, the apartments offer Paris without apologies. Yes, they are *very* old and dusty, and not everything works all the time. But for some, this faded charm with a definite past has a great appeal, especially when sitting by one of the large windows and looking across the Seine to Notre-Dame bathed in moonlight.

ENGLISH SPOKEN: Yes

FACILITIES AND SERVICES: Direct-dial phone; no elevator or TV; safe in office, no charge

NEAREST TOURIST ATTRACTIONS (LEFT BANK): Notre-Dame, Île de la Cité, Île St-Louis, St-Michel, St-Germain-des-Prés, Latin Quarter

(16) HÔTEL FLATTERS ★
3, rue Flatters, 75005 (5th)
22 rooms, 16 with bath or shower and toilet

If you want to splurge on dinner or a new outfit rather than on a night's sleep, this one-star in the bottom of the fifth may be just the hotel you need.

For years I've wanted to include it, but could not get past the mean-spirited owner, who was never taught the value of a smile or a kind word. New owners, thank goodness, have taken over. Nineteen of the rooms have been redone, and all rooms on the first floor have private facilities. The location is quiet for Paris and back room vistas are okay. Some rooms have carpeting; others bare wood floors. No. 2 has hardwood floors, but the black marble fireplace, peach walls, and newly tiled bathroom with a stall shower and good light (but no shelf space) compensate. Breakfast is served in a cozy room with three marble bistro tables and the only TV set in the hotel. Management is friendly. They know the value of a smile and a kind word.

ENGLISH SPOKEN: Yes

FACILITIES AND SERVICES: No elevator; TV in breakfast room

NEAREST TOURIST ATTRACTIONS (LEFT BANK): Rue Mouffetard, Jardin des Plantes

TELEPHONE
01-43-31-74-21

FAX
None

MÉTRO
Censier-Daubenton, Gobelins

CREDIT CARDS
None

RATES
Single 170–290F, double 230–320F, triple 380F; shower 15F
Taxe de séjour: included

BREAKFAST
25F extra (bread, no croissants)

(17)   HÔTEL LE COLBERT* ★★★
7, rue de l'Hôtel-Colbert, 75005 (5th)
36 rooms, all with shower or bath and toilet

TELEPHONE
01-43-25-85-65,
01-40-46-79-50
FAX
01-43-25-80-19
MÉTRO
Maubert-Mutualité, St-Michel
CREDIT CARDS
AE, MC, V
RATES
Single 875F, double 1,025F,
suite 1650F, apartment 1,950–
2,000F
Taxe de séjour: included
BREAKFAST
70F extra per person

For a memorable stay in Paris, you simply cannot miss at this hotel. The location is fantastic. Built around a courtyard on a tranquil, almost traffic-free street, the centuries-old townhouse is one minute from the Seine and two from Notre-Dame. It is the perfect address for anyone who likes to wander through the winding streets around St-Michel and be within easy walking distance of the many wonderful restaurants (see *Cheap Eats in Paris*).

Polished professionalism and good old-fashioned service underscore Le Colbert's many assets, making it one of the most sought-after small hotels in Paris. The rooms and suites are models of space and uncluttered decor, with slipper-style comfort and refined good taste. Windows in eight of the rooms frame Notre-Dame Cathedral; others look over the peaked rooftops of this ancient part of Paris; and some overlook the courtyard entrance. A favorite of mine is no. 21. A small entry gives a feeling of more space in the pretty blue-and-white twin room. The closet space is adequate, and the bathroom very light with a glass-enclosed shower over a stretch tub. For more space and a Notre-Dame view, the suite or apartment makes an excellent choice. All of this does not come at bargain prices, but as anyone who has ever stayed at Le Colbert will tell you, it is well worth the extra francs for the Big Splurge.

ENGLISH SPOKEN: Yes

FACILITIES AND SERVICES: Bar; direct-dial phone; hair dryer; elevator; minibar; TV with international reception; safe in room, no charge; terry robes; laundry service

NEAREST TOURIST ATTRACTIONS (LEFT BANK): St-Michel, St-Germain-des-Prés, Latin Quarter, Notre-Dame Cathedral, Île de la Cité, Île St-Louis

(18)   HÔTEL MARIGNAN ★
13, rue de Sommerard, 75005 (5th)
30 rooms, none with shower or bath and toilet

TELEPHONE
01-43-54-63-81
FAX
None
MÉTRO
Maubert-Mutualité

The Marignan lives up to the three C's of all Cheap Sleepers: it is clean, convenient, and cheap, especially in November and December, when rooms for two, three, or four people are 15 percent less than the published prices. The hotel is usually jammed year round with a frugal crowd of students, backpackers, and professors. A spirit of camaraderie prevails in this busy spot, making it impossible to feel lonely for long. To their credit, long-term owners/managers Paul and Linda Keniger have provided guests with a wealth of information on Paris, including a large detailed map of the *quartier* showing the métro stops, banks, pharmacies, money-changing offices, bakeries, and tourist sites. The management also clearly states the rules of the hotel, and guests are expected to abide by them or move out. They are listed in plain sight at the check-in desk, so no one can claim "I didn't know" not to put my suitcase on the bed; to eat or leave empty bottles or cans in the room; to turn off the light when leaving; and to never go barefoot in public areas or on the stairs. Between March and September, reservations for singles are not taken; during this time, reservations are only for two for a stay of two nights or more. All reservations are payable in advance, and no refunds are made if cancellation is less than one week before arrival. Last but not least in the rule department is the management's parsimonious breakfast philosophy. I quote Mr. Keniger: "If we give more, it encourages people to stay and eat, and then we won't have room to feed other guests." Since the breakfast, which is generous by one-star standards—including cheese along with bread and jam, but no croissant—is included in the rate and cannot be deducted, guests are stuck with an attitude that must reflect hard times for the owners.

ENGLISH SPOKEN: Yes

FACILITIES AND SERVICES: Basement laundry and ironing area (no room laundry allowed); dining area where guests can eat food they bring in, boil water for a cup of tea, or use the refrigerator, microwave and dishes; no elevator or TV; safe in office, no charge

NEAREST TOURIST ATTRACTIONS (LEFT BANK): Cluny Museum, Latin Quarter, St-Michel, St-Germain-des-Prés, Île de la Cité, Île St-Louis

CREDIT CARDS
None, cash only

RATES
Single 210F, double 310–410F, triple 390–460F, quad 490–680F; extra bed 50F; showers free
Taxe de séjour: included

BREAKFAST
Included, cannot be deducted

(19)   HÔTEL PARC SAINT-SÉVERIN* ★★★
22, rue de la Parcheminerie, 75005 (5th)
27 rooms, all with shower or bath and toilet

Dyed-in-the-wool aficionados of life around St-Michel, who also like elegantly understated surroundings, will love this hotel. The owners are to be applauded for turning a rundown building into an alluring, modern establishment that is serene, serious, and pleasing to the eye. For someone very, very special, reserve no. 70, the private penthouse suite with its own elevator

TELEPHONE
01-43-54-32-17

FAX
01-43-54-70-71

MÉTRO
St-Michel

CREDIT CARDS
AE, MC, V

RATES
Single 530–1,050F, double
650–1,100F, suite 1,100–
1,700F; children under 12 free
Taxe de séjour: included

BREAKFAST
50F extra per person

entrance. The wraparound terrace provides unequaled views of Notre-Dame, St-Séverin Church (which is one of the most popular in Paris for weddings), the Panthéon, Collège de France, Tour Montparnasse, and, in the distance, the Eiffel Tower and the Sacré-Coeur on Montmartre. The interior of this dream suite glows with a blend of antiques and contemporary furnishings. The other rooms in the hotel display the same standards of excellence, and many have impressive views. The management and staff are exceptional in their attention and service for all of their guests. For those who want up-to-the-minute convenience and luxury in the heart of old Paris, the Parc Saint-Séverin is a favorite choice of many discriminating *Cheap Sleeps in Paris* readers.

NOTE: For other hotels under the same ownership, see Hôtel de la Place du Louvre (page 45) and Hôtel Mansart (page 49).

ENGLISH SPOKEN: Yes

FACILITIES AND SERVICES: Air-conditioning in some rooms; direct-dial phone; hair dryer; elevator; minibar; TV with international reception; room safe, no charge

NEAREST TOURIST ATTRACTIONS (LEFT BANK): St-Michel, Latin Quarter, Cluny Museum, St-Germain-des-Prés, Île de la Cité, Île St-Louis

(20) HÔTEL RÉSIDENCE HENRI IV* ★★★
50, rue des Bernardins, 75005 (5th)
14 rooms, all with shower or bath and toilet and fully fitted kitchenette

TELEPHONE
01-44-41-31-81

FAX
01-46-33-93-22

MÉTRO
Maubert-Mutualité

CREDIT CARDS
AE, MC, V

RATES
1–2 persons 950–1,300F
Taxe de séjour: 6F extra per
person, per day

BREAKFAST
45F extra per person

Fifteen years ago, when I began writing *Cheap Sleeps in Paris*, this hotel had another name and an image of faded respectability. Several years ago it was taken over by Corinne Brethous, who owns Hôtel des Grand Hommes (see page 82) and Hôtel du Panthéon (see page 85). Whatever Mme. Brethous touches speaks of style and distinction, and her latest renovated endeavor is certainly no exception. Quietly situated opposite the leafy square Paul-Langevin, at the end of rue des Bernardins, the hotel offers fourteen spacious rooms, each with the added plus of fully fitted kitchenettes, as well as all the hotel services and facilities a guest could want. I think the best buys are the beautiful two-room suites done in soft yellow, blue, green, or ochre. These offer separate sitting areas, marble fireplaces, and just enough extra space to make a long stay very comfortable. No. 22, in blue, has a magnificent gold-framed mirror over its fireplace. Hand-painted moldings and the original ceiling are carried through to the bedroom, which has a large armoire and a corner fireplace to add to its charm. No. 42 is large enough to accommodate a family and has a bonus of two fireplaces. No. 10, on the ground floor, has no fireplace and needs to be redone before you book it. The hotel is peaceful and calm, yet it is minutes away from almost everything on a visitor's A-list of things to see and do in the Latin Quarter and St-Germain-des-Prés.

ENGLISH SPOKEN: Yes

FACILITIES AND SERVICES: Two air-conditioned rooms; direct-dial phone; elevator; hair dryer; TV with international reception; safe in room, no charge

NEAREST TOURIST ATTRACTIONS (LEFT BANK): Latin Quarter, St-Michel, St-Germain-des-Prés, Île de la Cité, Île St-Louis, Cluny Museum

(21) HÔTEL RÉSIDENCE MONGE ★★
55, rue Monge, 75005 (5th)
36 rooms, all with bath, shower, or toilet

It isn't posh by any means, just a modest hotel run by a delightful owner, Mme. Chatillon. Rooms are generally small by American standards, but they're the norm in this sector of Paris. If you book no. 31, you will have one of the best in the house. It is a quiet room done in salmon and blue colors with two windows overlooking a playground and a bathroom with both a tub and shower. You can expect some noise in both Rooms 1 and 15 because they face the street. Imitation flowers and plants abound, especially in the breakfast room, which is overflowing with many bright varieties sitting in floral trimmed pots.

ENGLISH SPOKEN: Yes

FACILITIES AND SERVICES: Direct-dial phone; elevator; hair dryer; minibar; TV with international reception; office safe, no charge

NEAREST TOURIST ATTRACTIONS (LEFT BANK): Rue Mouffetard, Jardin des Plantes

TELEPHONE
01-43-266-87-90

FAX
01-43-54-47-25

E-MAIL
www.paris-hotel.tm.fr/
RESIDENCE_MONGE
www.paris.hotel.com/
RESIDENCE_MONGE

MÉTRO
Place Monge, Cardinal-Lemoine

CREDIT CARDS
MC, V

RATES
Single 350–450F, double 380–500F; extra bed 100F
Taxe de séjour: 5F extra per person, per day

BREAKFAST
35F extra per person

(22) HÔTEL RÉSIDENCE SAINT-CHRISTOPHE ★★★
17, rue Lacépède, 75005 (5th)
31 rooms, all with shower or bath and toilet

At the Résidence Saint-Christophe, you will find compact rooms with burnished orange-tufted bedspreads, a desk, two upholstered chairs, and good luggage and

TELEPHONE
01-43-31-81-54

FAX
01-43-31-12-54
MÉTRO
Monge
CREDIT CARDS
AE, DC, MC, V
RATES
1–2 persons 675–725F
Taxe de séjour: 6F extra per person, per day
BREAKFAST
Included, not deductible

closet space. The rooms also have nice bathrooms and no backside views onto blank walls. Skillfully run by Michele Verrechia, the hotel is located near rue Mouffetard, famous for its animated outdoor market, and place Monge, where a jewel of a Sunday market is held. Lower rates in July and August and the friendliness of management and staff more than make up for the location, which is slightly south of Tourist Central.

ENGLISH SPOKEN: Yes

FACILITIES AND SERVICES: Direct-dial phone; hair dryer; elevator; minibar; radio and TV with international reception; safe in office and in room, no charge

NEAREST TOURIST ATTRACTIONS (LEFT BANK): Rue Mouffetard, Jardin des Plantes

(23)   LE JARDIN DE CLUNY ★★★
9, rue du Sommerard, 75005 (5th)
40 rooms, all with shower or bath and toilet

TELEPHONE
01-40-54-22-66; toll-free from U.S. and Canada, 800-528-1234
FAX
01-40-51-03-36
MÉTRO
Maubert-Mutualité, St-Michel
CREDIT CARDS
AE, DC, MC, V
RATES
Single 630–690F, double 695–835F, suite 1,100F
Taxe de séjour: 6F extra per person, per day
BREAKFAST
50F extra per person

Occupying a key Left Bank location between boulevard St-Michel and boulevard St-Germain, the Jardin de Cluny is close to all the fun, glamour, and bright lights this animated *quartier* offers. The uniformly designed rooms, with black wicker furnishings, are larger than most others in the neighborhood. I like no. 601, a combination bedroom and sitting room with large closets and a view of the spires of Notre-Dame. Also nice is the large top-floor family suite that boasts a view of the cathedral from the bathroom. Breakfast is served on Villeroy and Bosch china in a stone-walled dining room. Nicely upholstered chairs arranged around large, lighted tables make this a pleasant place to start the day with a Continental breakfast or just a glass of orange juice.

ENGLISH SPOKEN: Yes

FACILITIES AND SERVICES: Air-conditioning in half the rooms; bar; direct-dial phone; hair dryer; elevator; minibar; TV with international reception; trouser press in some rooms; safe in room, no charge

NEAREST TOURIST ATTRACTIONS (LEFT BANK): Latin Quarter, St-Michel, St-Germain-des-Prés, Cluny Museum, Île de la Cité, Île St-Louis

(24)   PORT-ROYAL HÔTEL ★
8, boulevard Port-Royal, 75005 (5th)
48 rooms, 20 with shower or bath and toilet

Cheap Sleepers looking for maximum value without sacrificing quality of surroundings or services will find the Port-Royal Hôtel impossible to beat. In fact, it is so far ahead of most other one-star hotels in Paris (and many two- and three-star hotels for that matter) that there simply is no contest. I will admit that I had my doubts at first, as I trudged along the long boulevard Port-Royal in a driving rainstorm looking for the hotel. Once inside, however, I forgot all about feeling banished to the boonies by the location and found the hotel to be nothing short of amazing. It is obvious that the Giraud family, who has owned the hotel for seventy years, is paying close attention to every detail. On top of being an absolute steal for the money, it is spotless and exceptionally well decorated. The usual one-star dimestore taste—dusty plastic floral arrangements, mismatched colors, and exhausted, sagging furniture—is nowhere in sight. Instead, everything is in perfect order, from the red carpeted stairs and hallways with security and fire doors to the well-coordinated rooms, many with new wallpaper and carpeting. Those on the front have double-paned windows to let you sleep peacefully. Even the showers have doors, a rare find in Paris and almost a curiosity in one-star hotels. Those selecting the smallest rooms need not feel like Cinderella after midnight. These rooms have all the nice touches of their more expensive neighbors, including a piece of candy on the pillow at night.

The facade has been repainted, enhancing the Art Deco glass gracefully curving over the front door. The inviting streetside sitting room, with its comfortable chairs, bubbling aquarium, and beautiful live tropical plants, belies the hotel's budget category. So does the breakfast room, overlooking a neatly manicured interior garden. Real flowers on the tables, caned chairs with upholstered seats, and an interesting collection of the family's antique woodworking tools displayed on the walls add to the appeal.

The hotel is easily accessible to St-Michel, the Louvre, Musée d'Orsay, and the Champs-Élysées by bus. It connects to Orly by direct bus from the métro stop. Close by is a huge shopping complex with 150 boutiques and a branch of Au Printemps department store. Also near are cinemas, a selection of restaurants and cafés (see *Cheap Eats in Paris*) and public parking. All in all it adds up to one of the best Cheap Sleeps in Paris.

ENGLISH SPOKEN: Yes

FACILITIES AND SERVICES: Direct-dial phone; elevator; TV in sitting room; safe in office, no charge

TELEPHONE
01-43-31-70-06 (reservations accepted by phone 7 A.M.–7 P.M. only)

FAX
01-43-31-33-67

MÉTRO
Gobelins

CREDIT CARDS
None, cash only

RATES
Single 170–310F, double 210–310F; shower 15F
Taxe de séjour: included

BREAKFAST
30F extra per person

(25) SELECT HÔTEL ★★★
1, place de la Sorbonne, 75005 (5th)
68 rooms, all with shower or bath and toilet

TELEPHONE
01-46-34-14-80

FAX
01-46-34-51-79

MÉTRO
St-Michel, RER Luxembourg

CREDIT CARDS
AE, DC, MC, V

RATES
Single 550–790F, double 670–800F, triple 900F, duplex 1,350F; extra bed 30% of room rate; children under 10 free during low season; honeymooners receive complimentary champagne and breakfast during low season
Taxe de séjour: 6F extra per person, per day

BREAKFAST
35F extra per person

In 1937 Eric Sevareid paid 50¢ a night at the Select. Things have changed . . . considerably.

Dramatically renovated in late 1987, the hotel now has one of the most spectacular interior garden courts in Paris, complete with blooming tropical plants, a waterfall, and singing birds. The lobby and reception area are studies in ultramodern design, with chrome and black leather furniture highlighted by posters of Paris. This sleek approach is carried into the intimate bar, breakfast room, and seating alcoves tucked around the skylit garden.

Most of the rooms have as much appeal as the public areas, especially those overlooking the garden court or the place de la Sorbonne in front. Those on the backside and in the annex have all the perks but are dark, viewless, and done in some hideous wallpapers and colors. No. 41, a duplex, is also one to avoid due to the treacherous spiral staircase leading to the cavelike downstairs bedroom. Two of the nicest are nos. 33 and 53, which display the original stone wall of the hotel and centuries-old oak beams. Two large floor-to-ceiling windows open onto the *place* below. Comfortable armchairs, good reading lights, a large working desk, hidden storage space, and a split bathroom make these favorites for longer stays. No. 65 is a good-looking double with a wraparound desk, two leather chairs, and a nice bath with good mirrors and space. An ideal Latin Quarter location, lower off-season rates and three-star creature comforts make the Select Hôtel a front runner in the *quartier*. Unfortunately, it no longer costs only 50¢ a night.

ENGLISH SPOKEN: Yes

FACILITIES AND SERVICES: Air-conditioning in some rooms; bar with light snacks; conference room; direct-dial phone; elevator; hair dryer; radio; TV with international reception; safe in office, no charge

NEAREST TOURIST ATTRACTIONS (LEFT BANK): Latin Quarter, Sorbonne, St-Germain-des-Prés, Île de la Cité, Île St-Louis

(26) TIMHÔTEL JARDIN DES PLANTES ★★
5, rue Linné, 75005 (5th)
33 rooms, all with bath or shower and toilet

Letters . . . do I ever get letters! I am glad readers write to tell me about what they like and what they don't. For many years, this hotel was a *Cheap Sleeps in Paris* reader favorite, one of the top five in its price category. Everyone who stayed here liked it and always went back. Then, all of a sudden, new owners appeared and everything went to seed. The hotel went downhill fast, people stayed away in droves, and the letters started arriving. Because the hotel had been such a favorite, I always went back on every trip just in case things had improved. On my last visit, success at last—new owners have arrived and restored it to its original charm and friendliness. The hotel is now part of the Timhôtel chain in Paris.

The location across from the Jardin des Plantes is great if you are a walker or jogger. The rooms are now in white with bamboo and cane furniture and green carpets. A floral tile insert in the new bathrooms is the only remnant of the flower theme that dominated the hotel in earlier times. Not all rooms are equal in size, shape, or view. I like the rooms on the fifth floor, where no. 50 opens onto the hotel terrace and nos. 51 and 52 overlook the street. I don't like no. 42, an unappealing small space designed for two. No. 40 has both good and bad points: it is spacious enough for two and has a nice marble sink in the bathroom, but it is on the back, which means quiet, but no view.

NOTE: Remember, if you stay ten nights in any Timhôtel, the eleventh night is free.

ENGLISH SPOKEN: Yes

FACILITIES AND SERVICES: Bar; direct-dial phone; elevator; hair dryer; TV with international reception; office safe, 25F per day

NEAREST TOURIST ATTRACTIONS (LEFT BANK): Jardin des Plantes, rue Mouffetard, Latin Quarter, Panthéon

TELEPHONE
01-47-07-06-20

FAX
01-47-07-62-74

MÉTRO
Jussieu

CREDIT CARDS
AE, DC, MC, V

RATES
Single 490F, double 590F, 5th-floor rooms 675F
Taxe de séjour: included

BREAKFAST
50F extra per person

Sixth Arrondissement

(See map pages 74–75.)

LEFT BANK
École des Beaux-Arts, Luxembourg Gardens, Odéon National Theater, St-Germain-des-Prés Church, St-Sulpice Church

Literary and artistic Paris *is* the heart of the sixth . . . a continuation of the Latin Quarter and one of the most stimulating parts of the city. Intellectual, elegant, and very appealing, it has tiny side streets, old buildings, antique shops, a thriving café life, and more atmosphere block for block than anyone could ever soak up. The square by the St-Germain Church is the main focus of the district. Les Deux Magots and Café de Flore, the two most celebrated cafés in Paris, were the hangouts of Hemingway, Sartre, Simone de Beauvoir, and James Joyce. Today they are jammed with Parisians and tourists alike engaged in some of the best people-watching in the universe.

HOTELS IN THE SIXTH ARRONDISSEMENT

OTHER OPTIONS

Residence Hotels

Student Accommodations

*Indicates a Big Splurge

(30) DHELY'S HÔTEL ★
22, rue de l'Hirondelle, 75006 (6th)
21 rooms, none with toilet or bathtub, 7 with shower

For the quintessential budget hotel, steps from the Seine and place St-Michel, Dhely's is the place. Many Left Bank hotels in this neighborhood are severely lacking in housekeeping, but not this one. Everything is shipshape, from the hall toilets and showers to the rooms, most of which have pretty floral wallpaper and window boxes with real flowers. The larger rooms have carpeting; the smaller ones have linoleum floors. Of course, the higher you climb, the better it gets in price and view. While the hotel *is* basic, it does have some redeeming architectural details, such as the original sixteenth-century tiled entryway and classical stairway, open beams, and exposed stone walls. In its most infamous moment, it was the home of King François Premier's favorite mistress. For the last eighteen years, the hotel has been owned by Mme. Kenniche.

ENGLISH SPOKEN: Some

FACILITIES AND SERVICES: Direct-dial phone; elevator to the fifth floor; TV; safe in office, no charge

NEAREST TOURIST ATTRACTIONS (LEFT BANK): St-Michel, Île de la Cité, Île St-Louis, St-Germain-des-Prés

TELEPHONE
01-43-26-58-25

FAX
01-43-26-51-06

MÉTRO
St-Michel

CREDIT CARDS
AE, DC, MC, V

RATES
Single 200F, double 290–370F, triple 480F; extra bed 100F; shower 25F
Taxe de séjour: 5F extra per person, per day

BREAKFAST
35F extra per person

(31) GRAND HÔTEL DES BALCONS ★★
3, rue Casimir-Delavigne, 75006 (6th)
55 rooms, all with shower or bath and toilet

TELEPHONE
01-46-34-78-50
FAX
01-46-34-06-27
MÉTRO
Odéon
CREDIT CARDS
MC, V
RATES
Single 350–400F, double 450–
520F, triple 570F
Taxe de Séjour: 5F extra per
person, per day
BREAKFAST
50F extra per person

The Grand Hôtel des Balcons is one of the most dignified low-budget hotels in this part of the Left Bank, and it's a perennial favorite with older, cost-conscious budgeteers who have found that it is a much better value than the other three-star hotels on the same block.

The impressive lobby is a masterpiece of Art Nouveau design, with glorious stained-glass windows and masterfully turned wood. There are always beautiful fresh-flower displays, arranged by the manager's wife, who is a recognized ikebana expert. On the reception desk is a tin of biscuits, which you are invited to enjoy along with afternoon tea. Uniformed maids are relentless in keeping everything dust free. To management's credit, the halls have been freshened with yellow paint and new gray carpeting, and most rooms have been redecorated with nice wallpaper and good reading lights. Vintage baths tend to be small, but are spotless. The location is tops, close to loads of budget restaurants (see *Cheap Eats in Paris*) and near place de l'Odéon, boulevard St-Michel, St-Germain-des-Prés, and one of the city's most popular parks, the Jardin du Luxembourg.

ENGLISH SPOKEN: Yes

FACILITIES AND SERVICES: Direct-dial phone; elevator; radio; TV; office safe, no charge

NEAREST TOURIST ATTRACTIONS (LEFT BANK): St-Germain-des-Prés, St-Michel, Luxembourg Gardens, Île de la Cité, Île St-Louis

(32) HÔTEL AVIATIC ★★★
105, rue de Vaugirard, 75006 (6th)
43 rooms, all with shower or bath and toilet

TELEPHONE
01-45-44-38-21; toll-free from
the U.S., 800-845-6636
FAX
01-45-49-35-83
MÉTRO
Falguière, St-Placide,
Montparnasse (also 10 bus lines
at Montparnasse)
CREDIT CARDS
AE, DC, MC, V

The hotel is named after the aviators who came here to have drinks around the turn of the century. Today the Art Deco glass and the black wrought-iron awning over the door—flanked by two brass-and-copper lamps—set the welcoming stage for this warm and inviting family-run hotel. The lobby has faux marble columns and small groupings of velvet chairs and antique marble chests topped with bouquets of fresh flowers. To one side is the breakfast room, papered with vintage Parisian art posters. A wide, winding stairway with overhead skylights leads guests up to forest-green carpeted hallways and the forty-three rooms in two buildings. There is more than just a touch of class in these well-thought-out chambers, which all have built-in luggage racks, good space to spread out, armchair seating, and ample closets. The rooms in the front building are bright and airy, with pretty views of the surrounding Montparnasse neighborhood. Those in the back are sunny, but they don't have much of a view.

ENGLISH SPOKEN: Yes

FACILITIES AND SERVICES: Bar; direct-dial phone; hair dryer; elevator; minibar; parking, 90F per day; TV with international reception; office safe, no charge

NEAREST TOURIST ATTRACTIONS (LEFT BANK): Montparnasse

RATES
Single 650F, double 750F, triple 950F (lower rates in Jan, Feb, Aug)
Taxe de séjour: included

BREAKFAST
Included, cannot be deducted

(33) HÔTEL BONAPARTE ★★
61, rue Bonaparte, 75006 (6th)
29 rooms, all with shower or bath and toilet

The Hôtel Bonaparte is a thrifty two-star a whisper away from some of the best this Left Bank *quartier* has to offer. Not only are you in shopping heaven, but you'll be close to scores of restaurants and famous cafés (see *Cheap Eats in Paris*), the Luxembourg Gardens, and the lovely St-Sulpice Church. Transportation to other parts of Paris is a snap either by bus or métro.

Most of the rooms have been refreshed, and for the price, they are well supplied with a hair dryer, minibar, television, room safe, and a fan if the weather demands it. An added plus is that the nice owner, Mme. Dumas, speaks English well. If it is twin beds you want, ask for no. 27 with two windows on the street, one on the front, and a black marble fireplace; or ask for no. 16, with a large marble bath and white wicker furniture. I would avoid both no. 26, unless the peeling paint has been redone, and no. 28, which needs new wallpaper.

ENGLISH SPOKEN: Yes

FACILITIES AND SERVICES: Direct-dial phone; elevator; hair dryer; minibar; TV; room safe, no charge

NEAREST TOURIST ATTRACTIONS (LEFT BANK): St-Germain-des-Prés, shopping, Seine, Île de la Cité

TELEPHONE
01-43-26-97-37,
01-43-26-54-10

FAX
01-46-33-57-67

MÉTRO
St-Sulpice, St-Germain-des-Prés, Mabillon

CREDIT CARDS
AE, MC, V

RATES
Single 440–650F, double 570–680F, triple 760F
Taxe de séjour: included

BREAKFAST
Included, cannot be deducted

(34)   HÔTEL BUCI LATIN* ★★★
34, rue de Buci, 75006 (6th)
27 rooms, all with shower or bath and toilet

TELEPHONE
01-43-29-07-20
FAX
01-43-29-67-44
MÉTRO
St-Germain-des-Prés
CREDIT CARDS
AE, DC, MC, V
RATES
1–2 persons 900–1,700F,
duplex 1,600F, junior suite
1,700F
Taxe de séjour: 6F extra per
person, per day
BREAKFAST
Included, cannot be deducted

Down the street from the picturesque Buci street *marché* is the Hôtel Buci Latin. To say the hotel is different is the understatement of the year. Owners Ronald MacLeod and Laurence Raymond have mixed an aggressively imaginative interior with an old period French building, and the results are nothing short of spectacular. The entrance announces immediately that this is a hotel where creativity and pure whimsy are raised to new levels. A wooden-planked walkway leads guests to the reception desk, where three clocks display local time. To one side is a full-size race car, painted and polished within an inch of its life. On the other side is a collection of airplanes and automobiles made out of soft drink cans. Photos of all twenty-seven guest-room doors, which were crafted and hand painted by nine local artists, hang in the lobby. You have to see them . . . they defy description. If you take the elevator to your room, you will miss the graffiti-covered stairway, authentically done by a knowledgeable New York artist. The rooms are simple, yet extremely well planned. Orange walls offset crisp white duvet covers on electric beds with built-in headboards hiding closets. Long, blond wall desks with halogen lights and a fabric-draped chair complement open-slat wooden armoires. What rooms are best? I can recommend them all, but no. 162, a top-floor junior suite with a circular Jacuzzi bath and a balcony with two chaise lounges, wins by a nose. A close second is no. 140, a duplex with a huge upstairs bathroom housing skylight views of St-Germain Church, an old-fashioned, claw-foot bathtub (and a modern stall shower for diehards), a beautiful antique sink, and an adobe tiled floor with an Indian rug under a marvelous wicker *coiffeuse* (dressing table).

We are not through yet! The downstairs coffee shop is no less unusual, with its row of theater seats and chairs covered in pink, turquoise, and purple velvet. A collection of vegetable graters decorates a steamer trunk that doubles as a buffet displaying teatime pastries. A mirror made from beer caps set in cement, a collection of ceramic whiskey bottles, and a fish pond round out the experience. Even if you do not stay here, please stop by for a look. The coffee shop is open for Saturday, Sunday, and holiday brunch, and Tuesday through Sunday for lunch and afternoon tea. Hours are Tuesday to Sunday from noon to 6:00 P.M. with continuous service. Lunch is served from noon to 4:00 P.M. Closed a week between Christmas and New Year's, all of August, and Monday.

ENGLISH SPOKEN: Yes

FACILITIES AND SERVICES: Air-conditioning; bar; direct-dial phone; elevator; minibar; room service; TV with international reception; safe in office, no charge

NEAREST TOURIST ATTRACTIONS (LEFT BANK): St-Germain-des-Prés, St-Michel, Île de la Cité, Île St-Louis

(35) HÔTEL CHAPLAIN ★★
11, bis rue Jules-Chaplain, 75006 (6th)
25 rooms, all with shower or bath and toilet

The lobby mural of Monet's lily pond at Giverny and a breakfast area opening onto a plant-filled patio make for a pleasing beginning at this attractive Montparnasse hotel. On the ground floor, five rooms open onto this little courtyard. Throughout the hotel, the coordinated rooms display simple good taste and have nice bathrooms. Within five minutes' walking distance of the hotel are scores of restaurants in all price categories (see *Cheap Eats in Paris*), a dozen movie theaters, and the Luxembourg Gardens. For farther sight-seeing jaunts, it's easy to catch a bus or the métro and be almost anywhere in Paris in fifteen minutes.

ENGLISH SPOKEN: Yes

FACILITIES AND SERVICES: Direct-dial phone; elevator; hair dryer; TV with international reception; room safe, 10F per day

NEAREST TOURIST ATTRACTIONS (LEFT BANK): Montparnasse, Luxembourg Gardens

TELEPHONE
01-43-26-47-64

FAX
01-40-51-79-75

MÉTRO
Vavin, Notre-Dame-des-Champs

CREDIT CARDS
AE, DC, MC, V

RATES
Single 425F, double 475F, triple 625F, quad 725F
Taxe de séjour: included

BREAKFAST
40F extra per person

(36) HÔTEL DANEMARK ★★★
21, rue Vavin, 75006 (6th)
15 rooms, all with shower or bath and toilet

For the Nurit family, nothing seems to be too much trouble when it comes to pleasing their guests. They have a special fondness for Americans, many of whom have been repeat guests for years, even before the hotel was what it is today. The Nurits are proud of their fifteen-room hotel in Montparnasse, and they should be. It is an imaginative lesson in how to take an old student-style hotel and turn it into an eye-catching spot on the cutting edge of hotel chic.

TELEPHONE
01-43-26-93-78

FAX
01-46-34-66-06

MÉTRO
Vavin, Notre-Dame-des-Champs

CREDIT CARDS
AE, DC, MC, V

RATES
1–2 people 690–890F
Taxe de séjour: 6F extra per
person, per day
BREAKFAST
55F extra per person

Cool blues and grays dominate the downstairs color scheme, with artist-inspired furnishings that look like exhibits from New York's Museum of Modern Art. The walls are dotted with a collection of dramatic posters of Parisian landmarks and famous race cars, along with a collection of bold paintings done by an architect friend of the family. The rooms, done in soft yellows, green, lavender, or cocoa brown, are constantly being upgraded. While compact, everything is provided for a comfortable stay. All rooms have their own Italian marble bathroom with heated towel racks, good make-up lighting, and, in a few, a Jacuzzi. The rooms from the third floor up have no interior views. Those on the front face a pretty, white-brick apartment building with terrace gardens, and those on the top floor are under sloping, beamed ceilings with skylights.

ENGLISH SPOKEN: Yes

FACILITIES AND SERVICES: Direct-dial phone; hair dryer; elevator; some Jacuzzis; minibar; TV with international reception; office safe, no charge

NEAREST TOURIST ATTRACTIONS (LEFT BANK): Montparnasse

(37) HÔTEL D'ANGLETERRE* ★★★
44, rue Jacob, 75006 (6th)
27 rooms, all with shower or bath and toilet

TELEPHONE
01-42-60-34-72
FAX
01-42-60-16-93
MÉTRO
St-Germain-des-Prés
CREDIT CARDS
AE, DC, MC, V
RATES
Single 650F, double 825–
1,000F, suite (2 persons)
1,100–1,200F; extra
person 275F
Taxe de séjour: 6F extra per
person, per day
BREAKFAST
50F extra per person

Benjamin Franklin refused to enter this building to sign the Treaty of Paris because it was the British Embassy and considered British soil. Ernest Hemingway had no qualms about it when he occupied Room 14, describing it to his friends as "good and cheap." Today the Angleterre is no longer "cheap," but it is a declared national monument and a well-known classic hotel with a long list of guests clamoring to get in.

With the exception of no. 24, which needs redecorating, I can recommend all of the traditional rooms and suites, which are each different and appointed with a high ceiling, exposed beams, large bed, exceptional closet space, and fabulous double-sink bathroom. Room 5 on the back has a Venetian chandelier, a wicker armchair, and a great bathroom with an antique marble sink. In Room 38, a ground-floor favorite that opens onto a terrace, you will have a Parisian beamed ceiling, a sitting room, and a stone wall in back of a curved wooden bed. The large closet with shelves allows for spreading out and settling in. The lobby offers a bar and an intimate piano lounge. A plant-filled interior patio is a lovely spot to spend an hour or two in the afternoon, after a morning of browsing through all the interesting shops in the neighborhood. Breakfast is served in a sunny dining room with well-spaced tables and good lighting for reading the morning papers. The rates are on the high side, but the hotel is included for those seeking a distinguished location in one of the most popular tourist *quartiers* in Paris. When reserving, be sure to specify either a standard or a deluxe room, or a suite (only two of which are serviced by an elevator), and get written confirmation. While the accommodations are all lovely, the standard rooms probably will be too small for two people with bulky luggage.

ENGLISH SPOKEN: Yes

FACILITIES AND SERVICES: Bar; direct-dial phone; hair dryer; two rooms with Jacuzzi; elevator to most floors; TV with international reception; room safe, no charge

NEAREST TOURIST ATTRACTIONS (LEFT BANK): Superb shopping and browsing, St-Germain-des-Prés, St-Michel, Île de la Cité, Île St-Louis

(38)   HÔTEL DANUBE* ★★★
58, rue Jacob, 75006 (6th)
40 rooms, all with shower or bath and toilet

The building has an interesting history. The American Treaty of Independence from Britain was signed here on September 3, 1783. David Hartley represented the King of England and Benjamin Franklin, John Jay, and John Adams were the American representatives. During World War II, from September 1939 to June 1940, it was the home of General Sikorsky, head of the Polish government in exile. Today it is the Hôtel Danube, a St-Germain charmer with forty rooms offering good value for many Cheap Sleepers in Paris who have more flexible budgets.

A red floral wallpapered entry flows along a multicolored tile floor. To one side is an inviting sitting room with a fireplace flanked by two wing-back chairs. Just beyond an interior courtyard is a breakfast room displaying a collection of blue-and-white Oriental porcelain.

The large bedrooms are individually done with a mixture of styles that range from colonial Chinese and Indian to mid-Victorian. Double windows in Room 15 open onto the street. Seating is provided by two cane chairs positioned around a glass-topped table. Other

TELEPHONE
01-42-60-94-07 (reservations), 01-42-60-34-70

FAX
01-42-60-81-18

MÉTRO
St-Germain-des-Prés, Rue du Bac

CREDIT CARDS
AE, MC, V

RATES
1–2 persons 625–925F, apartment (2-4 persons) 1,300F *Taxe de séjour*: 6F extra per person, per day

BREAKFAST
50F extra per person

appointments include a marble-topped chest of drawers, lighted closet, and gray monogrammed towels in the bathroom. No. 10 is the same in size, and it has a beautiful double brass bed, but the bathroom is in an older style of tile. For what Room 40 on the courtyard may lack in view, it more than makes up for in space. No. 41, a two-room apartment in pink and blue, is another large choice. It has an antique double bed in one room and two regular doubles in the second. The new marble tile bathroom has a tub with a hand-held shower over it and sink space for toiletries.

ENGLISH SPOKEN: Yes

FACILITIES AND SERVICES: Direct-dial phones; elevator; hair dryer available; TV with international reception; office safe, no charge

NEAREST TOURIST ATTRACTIONS (LEFT BANK): Excellent shopping, St-Germain-des-Prés, St-Michel, Île de la Cité, Île St. Louis, Seine

(39) HÔTEL DAUPHINE SAINT-GERMAIN-DES-PRÉS* ★★★
36, rue Dauphine, 75006 (6th)
30 rooms, all with shower or bath and toilet

TELEPHONE
01-43-26-74-34, toll-free from the U.S., 800-448-8355

FAX
01-43-26-49-09

E-MAIL
dauphine22@ saintgermain.francenet.fr

INTERNET
www.123france.com/europe/ france/paris/hotels/ hodaupus.htm

MÉTRO
Odéon

CREDIT CARDS
AE, DC, MC, V

RATES
1–2 persons 825F; suite 1–2 persons 1,020F, 3-4 persons 1,180F; lower rates in off-season
Taxe de séjour: included

BREAKFAST
65F extra per person

In the early days, the first and second floors of Parisian townhomes were for the nobility, the higher floors for the servants. This explains the larger rooms and higher ceilings you will encounter in this sixteenth-century building. Unfortunately, the rooms on the back (except on the top floor) and those ending in the number 4 face an uninspiring back view. However, they are quiet and certainly have the same three-star decorating standards and benefits found in the rest of the hotel. Otherwise, there is plenty to choose from, including nos. 55, 56, 65, and 66, which are exclusively reserved for non-smoking guests, and no. 52, decorated in a rose salmon provincial print, with a recessed double bed and view of the neighboring rooftops. No. 61 is a blue-and-white sloped-roof suite that can accommodate up to four. The mansard windows let in plenty of light and offer a view of Notre-Dame Cathedral and the dome of the Panthéon.

A special feature of your morning routine here is the American-style breakfast buffet, which includes all the usual pastries, breads, fresh fruit, and cereals, as well as such extras as ham, pâté, Brie cheese, and for a little extra, the option of bacon and eggs.

ENGLISH SPOKEN: Yes

FACILITIES AND SERVICES: Air-conditioned rooms; bar; direct-dial phone with fax connections in each room; elevator; hair dryer; minibar; radio; TV with international reception; room safe, no charge; several nonsmoking rooms

NEAREST TOURIST ATTRACTIONS (LEFT BANK): St-Germain-des-Prés, St-Michel, Île de la Cité, Île St-Louis, Seine, shopping

(40) HÔTEL DE FLEURIE* ★★★
32–34, rue Grégoire-de-Tours, 75006 (6th)
29 rooms, all with shower or bath and toilet

If you enjoy the colorful, round-the-clock atmosphere of St-Germain-des-Prés, then the dynamic Hôtel de Fleurie is for you. This exceptional hotel is owned and managed by the Marolleau family, who for two generations owned Brasserie Balzar (see *Cheap Eats in Paris*). When they sold the brasserie, they bought this down-and-out hotel, and with a year of hard work, they completely transformed it into the delightful hotel it is today.

The facade of the hotel has been restored to its former glory and is embellished with statues that are lighted at night. The lobby and sitting rooms are models of gracious comfort and charm, showcasing some of Mme. Marolleau's stunning collection of Art Nouveau plant and flower containers. A spiral staircase leads from the reception desk down to a stone-walled *cave,* where a full buffet is served. Continental breakfasts, which include fresh orange juice, pound cake, and cheese in addition to the usual croissants and fresh bread, are served only in the rooms. Almost all of the rooms have modern marble bathrooms and a good layout of space. All come equipped with a minibar, remote-controlled television with CNN reception, international hookups for computers, and in the deluxe rooms, terry robes, and all are air-conditioned . . . a welcome relief during the dog days of summer in Paris. Room 60, on the top floor with no elevator access, overlooks a beautiful mosaic-tiled building across the street. Other deluxe choices include nos. 11, 14, 24, and 34. Room 54, a standard double, has a writing table, white cane headboard, lighted mirrored closet in the entry, and heated towel racks in the bathroom. No. 50, with a double bed, has a small window with a view and a pink marble bathroom. It would be nice for a single visitor.

TELEPHONE
Information 01-53-73-70-00; reservations 01-53-73-70-10

FAX
01-53-73-70-20

E-MAIL
bonjour@hotel-de-fleurie.tm.fr

INTERNET
www.hotel-de-fleurie.tm.fr

MÉTRO
St-Germain-des-Prés, Odéon

CREDIT CARDS
AE, DC, MC, V

RATES
Single 680–880F, double 890F, deluxe room 1,400–1,600F; extra bed 150F (only in deluxe rooms); children under 12 free
Taxe de séjour: included

BREAKFAST
55F extra (for either continental or buffet)

ENGLISH SPOKEN: Yes

FACILITIES AND SERVICES: Air-conditioning; bar; direct-dial phone; international computer hookup in each room; elevator to all but top floor; hair dryer; minibar; TV with international reception; room safe, no charge

NEAREST TOURIST ATTRACTIONS (LEFT BANK): St-Germain-des-Prés, St-Michel, Île de la Cité, Île St-Louis

(41)   HOTEL DE L'ABBAYE* ★★★
10, rue Cassette, 75006 (6th)
46 rooms, all with shower or bath and toilet

TELEPHONE
01-45-44-38-11
FAX
01-45-48-07-86
MÉTRO
St-Sulpice
CREDIT CARDS
AE, MC, V
RATES
1–2 persons 1,050–1,700F, suite 1,950–2,050
Taxe de séjour: included
BREAKFAST
Included, cannot be deducted

In the sixteenth and seventeenth centuries, the Abbaye Saint-Germain was a Catholic convent. Today it is a very special hotel for those who love its quiet location near Saint-Sulpice, discreet staff, and commendable service. The entrance is off the street through fifteen-foot-high green doors that open onto a plant-filled, cobblestone courtyard, where the nuns once gathered before going to chapel for daily prayers. The central reception room is handsomely furnished with magnificent antiques and comfortable sofas centered around a marble fireplace. Behind this is an exquisite garden salon with intimate seating, a profusion of flowers, and a nice bar with big wicker armchairs.

Returnees clamor for the top-floor terrace suites, with their arched ceilings and rooftop views, or the two ground-floor rooms with private gardens. I like no. 302, a two-level suite with a downstairs sitting room done in warm reds, and no. 303, another two-level Oriental suite with a wonderful terrace and huge marble bath with plenty of shelf space. Other favorites are no. 11B, a standard twin on the back with brass beds and two windows overlooking ivy-covered walls, and no. 4, a twin with its own patio.

Because the l'Abbaye is so special, it is higher in price and included for those whose budgets allow for more flexibility.

ENGLISH SPOKEN: Yes

FACILITIES AND SERVICES: Air-conditioning in all rooms and suites; bar; direct-dial phone; hair dryer; elevator; minibar; TV; room service for light snacks; safe in office, no charge

NEAREST TOURIST ATTRACTIONS (LEFT BANK): Latin Quarter, Luxembourg Gardens, St-Germain-des-Prés, St-Sulpice, good shopping

(42) HÔTEL DE L'ODÉON* ★★★
13, rue Saint-Sulpice, 75006 (6th)
29 rooms, all with shower or bath and toilet

Hôtel de l'Odéon has become a popular Paris destination for travelers who want luxury and impeccable service in a distinguished hotel that is still small enough to maintain a personal touch.

The interior is in the style of a seventeenth-century inn, beautifully blending antique charm and atmosphere with all the modern conveniences one expects in a top three-star hotel. In the charm department, the Odéon has it all: high beamed ceilings, stunning furniture, massive tapestries, intricately scrolled brass-and-metal beds with hand-crocheted coverlets, skylights, blooming flower boxes under the windows, lovely oil and watercolor paintings hanging throughout, and a manicured atrium garden sitting to one side of the breakfast area. On the convenience side, the baths are large and the bedside lighting is good. Double-paned windows keep street noise to a minimum, air-conditioning allows warm-weather comfort, and the closets are large enough for more than the contents of an overnight bag.

ENGLISH SPOKEN: Yes

FACILITIES AND SERVICES: Air-conditioning in all rooms; bar; direct-dial phone; hair dryer; elevator; TV with international reception; room safe, no charge

NEAREST TOURIST ATTRACTIONS (LEFT BANK): St-Germain-des-Prés, Latin Quarter, St-Sulpice, St-Michel, Île de la Cité, Île St-Louis, Luxembourg Gardens

TELEPHONE
01-43-25-70-11
FAX
01-43-29-97-34
MÉTRO
Odéon
CREDIT CARDS
AE, DC, MC, V
RATES
Single 670–880F, double 770–960F, triple 1,120–1,150F, family room 1,120F
Taxe de séjour: included
BREAKFAST
55F extra per person

(43) HÔTEL DES ACADÉMIES ★
15, rue de la Grande Chaumiére, 75006 (6th)
21 rooms, 17 with shower or bath and toilet

When planning your trip to Paris, you may begin to wonder where all the non-millionaires sleep. Many of them have been sleeping at Hôtel des Académies for years because they do not have to dig too deeply into their pockets to pay the final bill. The owner, Mme. Charles, who was born in the hotel more than eighty years ago and still lives there, runs it with a firm hand, not standing for a *soupçon* of hanky-panky. Assisting her with the welcoming formalities is her dog, Diavolo, which she described as "sort of a griffon." She is a devoted dog lover and welcomes guests who arrive with their own well-behaved dogs.

TELEPHONE
01-43-26-66-44
FAX
01-43-26-03-72
MÉTRO
Vavin
CREDIT CARDS
MC, V
RATES
Single 210–340F, double 285–340F; shower 40F; dogs free, no cats
Taxe de séjour: included

BREAKFAST
35F extra per person (only bread and jam); served in rooms only

Her plain, little, upstairs Montparnasse location delivers small but spotless rooms at unheard-of rates to a band of devoted regulars, who keep in touch by sending her postcards and souvenirs that she proudly displays in her tiny reception room. There are no extras here, and the rooms mix 1950s chrome and plastic with varying color and pattern schemes. But with these breathtakingly low prices, who cares? Certainly not the generations of families who return year after year making it their home base in Paris.

ENGLISH SPOKEN: None

FACILITIES AND SERVICES: None

NEAREST TOURIST ATTRACTIONS (LEFT BANK): Montparnasse, Luxembourg Gardens

(44) HÔTEL DES MARRONNIERS ★★★
21, rue Jacob, 75006 (6th)
37 rooms, all with shower or bath and toilet

TELEPHONE
01-43-25-30-60
FAX
01-40-46-83-56
MÉTRO
St-Germain-des-Prés
CREDIT CARDS
MC, V
RATES
Single 530–875F, double 725–875F, triple 950–1,050F; extra bed 180F
Taxe de séjour: included
BREAKFAST
50F extra per person

Hôtel des Marronniers is hidden away from rue Jacob in a sunny garden filled with the towering chestnut trees that give the hotel its name. Throughout the flower-filled hotel, which has been declared a French national monument, themes of nature predominate. Breakfast and afternoon drinks are served on a beguiling glassed-in verandah or, when the weather permits, on the lawn beyond. Downstairs, the vaulted cellars have been turned into two comfortable lounges and a conference room.

Most of the small, quaint rooms have interesting views. The attic rooms overlook the rooftops of Paris, and the rooms on the lower floors look onto St-Germain-des-Prés Church. During the spring, the rooms facing the garden in full bloom are especially appealing. Every room is quiet, and this is a rarity in this bustling *quartier*.

The hotel is what most of us think a romantic small hotel in Paris should be. It does have one flaw, however, and that is the attitude of the desk personnel, which can sometimes be *very* frosty. Management has promised to remedy this, and I hope that when you arrive, you will not experience it.

ENGLISH SPOKEN: Yes

FACILITIES AND SERVICES: Air-conditioning in all rooms; bar; conference room; direct-dial phone; elevator; TV; office safe, no charge

NEAREST TOURIST ATTRACTIONS (LEFT BANK): St-Germain-des-Prés, Latin Quarter, Île de la Cité, Île St-Louis, excellent shopping

(45) HÔTEL DU DRAGON (NO STARS)
36, rue du Dragon, 75006 (6th)
28 rooms, all with shower, 19 also with toilet

Despite its no-star status and typical industrial car-peting, plastic plants, and calendar art, the Hôtel du Dragon is one of the last outposts for decent budget anchorage in the heart of the Left Bank. This genuine cheapie displays untouched, prewar furnishings—some of which belonged to the owner's grandparents—in spot-less rooms bedecked in flowered or striped wallpaper. Of course there is no elevator, and the air-conditioning consists of opening the window. However, you do get orange juice with your morning baguette and jam (served in your room only), a television in your room, and a warm welcome from the Rabier-Roy family, who have owned the hotel since the 1920s. The bottom line for Cheap Sleepers in Paris is this: you get a good deal for your money, and today, that is not always easy to do.

ENGLISH SPOKEN: Yes

FACILITIES AND SERVICES: Direct-dial phone; TV; safe in office, no charge; no elevator

NEAREST TOURIST ATTRACTIONS (LEFT BANK): St-Germain-des-Prés, St-Michel, wonderful shopping and browsing

TELEPHONE
01-45-48-51-05

FAX
01-42-22-51-62

MÉTRO
St-Sulpice, St-Germain-des-Prés, Sèvres-Babylone

CREDIT CARDS
AE, MC, V

RATES
Single 275–325F, double 390–450F, triple 450F; extra bed 30% of room rate
Taxe de séjour: included

BREAKFAST
30F extra per person

(46) HÔTEL DU LYS ★★
23, rue Serpente, 75006 (6th)
22 rooms, all with shower or bath and toilet

For many Cheap Sleepers in Paris, the Hôtel du Lys has more French charm and romantic appeal than many three-star hotels in the area that charge almost twice as much. Other readers have written to me complaining about the dark back rooms (which no one can remedy) and the need for housekeeping to get busy with the Lysol in the bathrooms (which is definitely a quick fix). Quite frankly, I am on the fence with this hotel, and I find the no credit card policy in a two-star hotel very out of date. However, the location is dynamite, the prices in line, and if you hit the right room, the stay should be pleasant.

The owner, Marie-Hélène Decharne, who took over when her father retired after running the hotel for fifty years, made some welcome cosmetic improvements and added bathrooms to all the rooms that were with-out. The rooms are done in a cozy *vielle*, shabby chic, French style with beams, a stone wall here and there, and

TELEPHONE
01-43-26-97-57

FAX
01-44-07-34-90

MÉTRO
St-Michel, Odéon

CREDIT CARDS
None, cash only

RATES
Single 380–450F, double 480F, triple 580F
Taxe de séjour: included

BREAKFAST
Included, cannot be deducted

matching bedspreads and curtains. If you are reserving by telephone, please bear in mind that Mme. Decharne is usually at the hotel only on weekday mornings from 9 A.M. to noon. Otherwise, you will probably be dealing with a desk clerk with limited English and authority. When reserving, I would request no. 11, one of the better twin-bedded rooms with a beamed ceiling and stone wall. Two windows opening onto flowerboxes let plenty of light in the room, with its orange-and-blue color scheme carried out in the wall covering, bedspreads, and curtains. A blue tiled bath with a nice tub, two chairs, and a large armoire complete the picture. No. 6 is a brightly done double with a cabbage-rose print dominating. I would not request no. 14 because of its strange WC perched on a platform, or no. 10, whose only window is in the bathroom.

ENGLISH SPOKEN: Yes, if Mme. Decharne is there; otherwise, limited

FACILITIES AND SERVICES: Direct-dial phone; hair dryer; no elevator; TV with international reception; safe in office, no charge

NEAREST TOURIST ATTRACTIONS (LEFT BANK): St-Michel, St-Germain-des-Prés, Île de la Cité, Île St-Louis, Latin Quarter

(47) HÔTEL EUGÉNIE ★★
31, St-André-des-Arts, 75006 (6th)
30 rooms, all with shower or bath and toilet

TELEPHONE
01-43-26-29-03

FAX
01-43-29-75-60

MÉTRO
St-Michel, Odéon

CREDIT CARDS
AE, DC, MC, V

RATES
Single 500–550F, double 600–675F, triple 725F
Taxe de séjour: 5F extra per person, per day

BREAKFAST
40F extra per person

Situated on one of the busiest pedestrian streets in the very core of old Paris, the Eugénie offers good value for your hotel franc, while giving you pulsating, round-the-clock atmosphere in the bargain. The upbeat little rooms in blues, grays, and maroon have double-paned windows and remote-controlled TVs, and they are big enough to turn around in. They are, however, short on luggage, closet, and seating space. The baths have the extras that tend to make a difference: hair dryers, absorbent towels, and the latest fixtures. As you can see, there will be few surprises, but it is a useful Cheap Sleep in a popular location within easy walking distance to good shopping, good sight-seeing, and good eating (see *Cheap Eats in Paris*).

ENGLISH SPOKEN: Yes

FACILITIES AND SERVICES: Direct-dial phone; elevator; hair dryer; minibar; small safe in room, 20F per day; TV with international reception

(48) HÔTEL FERRANDI ★★★
92, rue du Cherche-Midi, 75006 (6th)
42 rooms, all with shower or bath and toilet

The Hôtel Ferrandi continues to be on everyone's top-ten list of wonderful small hotels on the Left Bank. Thoroughly dignified in every way, the hotel is unusually successful in combining the best in old-world style with modern comforts and expectations. The attractive owner, Mme. La Fond, and her exceptional staff are on top of the details that make a difference in a guest's stay.

The downstairs sitting area is defined by an ornate marble fireplace and a crystal chandelier. Loads of comfortable chairs, fresh flowers, attractive art, and daily papers in French and English create a pleasing place to relax. Stained-glass windows add color to the front hall. The interior hallways, lined with ocher fabric to keep noise to a minimum, are gracefully joined by a winding staircase painted in a faux marble finish. The large rooms are furnished with period antiques, are coordinated in soft shades of blues, browns, and pinks, and have all the comforts of home. Most have extra closet and luggage space and are just the ticket for those of us who do not travel lightly. For longer stays, I like Room 50, a ground-floor, two-room apartment with a roomy pink marble bathroom, or no. 43, with a four-poster bed, ornamental ceiling, plenty of drawer and closet space, good light, and inviting armchairs. Another favorite is no. 23, with a blue-and-white half-canopy bed, marble fireplace, and massive armoire. No. 27, with a brass bed, double closet, and single chair, is the least expensive room; it's perfect for one. Some of the bathrooms, especially in the smaller rooms, tend to be cramped, but most are equipped with heated towel racks, and all have an assortment of soaps and toiletries. Motorists will appreciate the hotel garage, and shoppers will love all the discount shopping stores within easy reach.

ENGLISH SPOKEN: Yes

FACILITIES AND SERVICES: Air-conditioning in all rooms; bar; direct-dial phone; hair dryer; elevator to four floors; some minibars; private parking (125F per day, must reserve ahead); radio; TV with international reception; safe in office, no charge; same-day laundry service

TELEPHONE
01-42-22-97-40

FAX
01-45-44-89-97

INTERNET
www.paris-hotel.tm.fr.gb/gb/montparnasse.07/ferrandi.html

MÉTRO
Sèvres-Babylone

CREDIT CARDS
AE, DC, MC, V

RATES
1–2 people 480–800F, deluxe room 980F, suite 1,280F
Taxe de séjour: 6F extra per person, per day

BREAKFAST
60F extra per person

parnasse, Luxembourg Gardens, Bon Marché department store (all quite a walk); good discount shopping
(close)

(49) HÔTEL LEFT BANK SAINT-GERMAIN* ★★★
9, rue de l'Ancienne Comédie, 75006 (6th)
31 rooms, all with shower or bath and toilet

TELEPHONE
01-43-54-01-70; toll-free in
the U.S. and Canada, 800-528-
1234 (Best Western)

FAX
01-43-26-17-14

MÉTRO
Odéon

CREDIT CARDS
AE, DC, MC, V

RATES
Single 895F, double 990F, suite
1,400F; extra bed 100F
Taxe de séjour: 6F extra per
person, per day

BREAKFAST
50F extra per person (continental in room, buffet downstairs)

It is hard to imagine a small hotel in Paris more
appealing than this one, which is, quite frankly, just the
sort of hotel that will make anyone fall in love with Paris
forever.

Located in the ever-popular St-Germain *quartier* and
convenient to everything, it is run by Claude Teil and
his family, who also operate the Hôtel Lido in the eighth
arrondissement (see page 159). It is therefore no surprise
to find the Hôtel Left Bank Saint-Germain just as beautiful, from the entrance where guests all admire an
adorable antique baby carriage filled with authentically
dressed vintage dolls to the large top-floor suite with
dormer window views onto Notre-Dame, Centre
Georges-Pompidou (Beaubourg), and Sainte-Chapelle.
To add to the overall allure, there are fresh flowers
everywhere, museum-quality tapestries, polished antiques mixed with special handmade furnishings from
Perigord, and excellent eighteenth-century reproduc-
tions, open oak beams, stone walls, and a very helpful,
English-speaking staff. The standard-size rooms are done
in paisley prints with built-in minibars and room safes.
The bathrooms are excellent. For my hotel franc, the
suites and larger doubles are the best choices because
they have alcove seating with soft armchairs, larger baths,
and loads of out-of-sight storage space. As you can see, I
am sold on this hotel as a wonderful choice for those with
more flexible budgets.

ENGLISH SPOKEN: Yes

FACILITIES AND SERVICES: Air-conditioning in all rooms;
bar; direct-dial phone; elevator; hair dryer; minibar;
ratio; TV with international reception; same-day laundry service; room safe, 50F per stay

NEAREST TOURIST ATTRACTIONS (LEFT BANK): St-
Germain-des-Prés, St-Michel, Île de la Cité, Île St-Louis,
wonderful shopping

(50) HÔTEL LE RÉGENT* ★★★
61, rue Dauphine, 75006 (6th)
25 rooms, all with shower or bath and toilet

For Parisian atmosphere in a setting of nonstop activity, it is hard to top Le Régent, which offers guests traditional charm in a renovated eighteenth-century building. Fresh flowers and green plants add soft touches to the stone entry and reception areas, which are decorated with antiques and tapestry-covered chairs. A selection of Deux Magots teas, jams, champagne, and dishes is for sale in a display case. The downstairs breakfast room has pink linen cloths and a fresh bouquet on each table. It is a nice place to read the *International Herald Tribune* or *Le Figaro* while enjoying breakfast.

All the rooms are well maintained and have the creature comforts most deem necessary, with the added bonus of terry robes (which are available upon request) and trouser presses. The bathrooms are modern, but the real showstoppers are in the rooms on the highest floors. For one of the prettiest pink-tiled bathrooms in Paris, request Room 52. No. 41, a large burnt-orange-and-blue twin with three windows, also has an outstanding spacious bathroom with monogrammed towels, a lighted magnifying mirror, and a deep glass-enclosed tub and shower. Room 11, in green and rust, is on the first floor and just like it, but because it faces front, guests should expect some street noise. Room 53 is a wood-paneled twin with a view to the top of Notre-Dame. If I had to pick a favorite room, I would select no. 62, nestled under the eaves on the sixth floor. Gingham bed coverlets complement the blue and white colors in the room and in the bathroom. From the room, you can look out and see Notre-Dame Cathedral. Sitting on the balcony, you will be looking over the rooftops to La Tour Montparnasse.

ENGLISH SPOKEN: Yes

FACILITIES AND SERVICES: Air-conditioning; direct-dial phone; hair dryer; elevator from first floor; minibar; TV with international reception; terry robes upon request; trouser press; room safe, no charge; same-day laundry service

NEAREST TOURIST ATTRACTIONS (LEFT BANK): St-Germain-des-Prés, St-Michel, Île de la Cité, Île St-Louis

TELEPHONE
01-46-34-59-80

FAX
01-40-51-05-07

MÉTRO
Odéon

CREDIT CARDS
AE, DC, MC, V

RATES
1–2 persons 775–1,000F; extra bed 150F; children under 12 free; dogs 40F; lower rates in off-season
Taxe de séjour: 6F extra per person, per day

BREAKFAST
60F extra per person

(51) HÔTEL LE RELAIS MÉDICIS* ★★★
23, rue Racine, 75006 (6th)
16 rooms, all with shower or bath and toilet

TELEPHONE
01-43-26-00-60
FAX
01-40-46-83-39
MÉTRO
Odéon
CREDIT CARDS
AE, DC, MC, V
RATES
Single 930–1,200F, double
995–1,500F, triple 1,615F;
sometimes lower rates off-
season
Taxe de séjour: included
BREAKFAST
Included, cannot be deducted

The jury is still out on whether heaven can be as divine as a stay at Le Relais Médicis. I will admit it was love at first sight the minute I walked into this picture-perfect dream hotel where something artistic and imaginative catches your eye at every turn—it might be a humorous bench with black bears painted on it, two papier-mâché deer heads peering at guests from their wall posts, or the antique metal toys and Italian Majolica spice jars displayed behind the desk. The total look of the hotel is characteristically French, with the mix of patterns, shapes, sizes, and colors all adding up to a stunning visual effect. In the lush salon, lovely oil paintings are set off by deep red fabric-covered walls and antique birdcages, which add a light touch. Garden paintings define the springtime feel of the breakfast room, where even the lights reflect the floral theme. Vintage black-and-white photos displayed throughout the halls of the hotel add notes of interest.

Two lifts take guests to the sixteen bedrooms, all of which I could live in happily for a long Parisian stay. For instance, in no. 22 you will be surrounded by soft greens and corals, with floral dust ruffles complementing the cotton bedspreads. An enviable display of turn-of-the-century colored prints of young women and children complement a solo modern painting. The marble bath has reproduction antique chrome fittings and the mirrored wardrobe is large enough to hold everything you brought with you. If you occupy the quiet and secluded no. 39, the color scheme is a soft orange sorbet, and the view is of the buildings across the way. Frankly feminine, no. 26 is a cheerful, large, beamed room with twin beds, three windows, and an adorable old desk. Colors and fabrics are coordinated in a garden motif; decorative accents include a gold clock and an assortment of old tins. Room 24 is a smaller double with a five-drawer marble-topped dresser. The mirrored wall gives the illusion of more space in this room, which is still big enough to accommodate a round table and two chairs, the perfect place to enjoy a continental breakfast.

ENGLISH SPOKEN: Yes

FACILITIES AND SERVICES: Air-conditioning in all rooms; bar; direct-dial phone; elevator; hair dryer; minibar; TV with international reception; room safe, no charge; *peignoirs* (bathrobes) in all rooms; porter

NEAREST TOURIST ATTRACTIONS (LEFT BANK): St-Germain-des-Prés, St-Michel, Luxembourg Gardens, Île de la Cité, Île St-Louis, shopping

(52) HÔTEL LE SAINT-GRÉGOIRE* ★★★
43, rue de l'Abbé Grégoire, 75006 (6th)
20 rooms, all with shower or bath and toilet

Everyone raves about it because on all counts the Hôtel le Saint-Grégoire is a stunning hotel. Although it is on the high side for a Cheap Sleep, I can assure you many *Cheap Sleeps in Paris* readers believe it is worth every *sou*, not only for the comfort and surroundings, but for the welcome and assistance extended by the staff, skillfully headed by M. François de Béné.

The color scheme is purple, yellow, orange, red, and beige . . . and it works. Decorator David Hicks has created an elegantly intimate atmosphere in this twenty-room hotel by mixing period antiques with handsome modern pieces and sprinkling interesting fabrics and rich silks throughout a garden setting. As a result, the hotel has a feeling of well-being, from the fireplace in the rose-filled lobby to the linen-clad tables in the *cave* dining room, where freshly squeezed orange juice and yogurt are served with the continental breakfast.

Please forward all mail to me care of Room 100, a bright yellow, ground-floor double opening onto a small garden. It has a marble-topped coffee table, a bureau large enough to hold the contents of my suitcase, and two comfortable chairs for lazy late-night reading. The bath has heated towel racks and enough towels to last almost forever. If this room is not available, I would be supremely happy in no. 102, a junior suite, also on a garden, with its own entryway leading to a large room with a sofa, two easy chairs, and a table at one end. No. 14 is a pink double with its own terrace, and just perfect if you are alone. Families can request that Rooms 24 and 26 be combined. No. 24 is a small, peach-colored room with a wall hat rack; no. 26, a larger double with a nice writing table, armoire, and black marble-topped dresser, has a light bath with a separate enclosed toilet.

After one or two nights at this hotel, there will be a problem; you will wish you *never* had to leave Paris.

ENGLISH SPOKEN: Yes

TELEPHONE
01-45-48-23-23
FAX
01-45-48-33-95
MÉTRO
St-Placide, Rennes
CREDIT CARDS
AE, DC, MC, V
RATES
1–2 persons 790–990F, suite and rooms with terrace 1,400F
Taxe de séjour: included
BREAKFAST
60F extra per person

FACILITIES AND SERVICES: Air-conditioning in most rooms; bar; direct-dial phone; hair dryer; TV with international reception; room service from La Marlotte Restaurant (owned by the hotel, see *Cheap Eats in Paris*); safe in office, no charge

NEAREST TOURIST ATTRACTIONS (LEFT BANK): Luxembourg Gardens, discount shopping, Montparnasse, Bon Marché department store

(53) HÔTEL LOUIS II ★★★
2, rue Saint-Sulpice, 75006 (6th)
22 rooms, all with shower or bath and toilet

TELEPHONE
01-46-33-13-80

FAX
01-46-33-17-29

MÉTRO
Odéon

CREDIT CARDS
AE, DC, MC, V

RATES
1–2 persons 550–780F, triple 900F
Taxe de séjour: 6F extra per person, per day

BREAKFAST
45F extra per person

Restored in the style of Louis II, with beams, brocade and damask, red tiled floors, and graceful, hand-rubbed antiques, this hotel is one of the best examples of what a little imagination, taste, and money can do to revive an exhausted Left Bank site. All the old wood alcoves and rooms under the eaves were saved. Flowered wallpaper, lacy bedcovers, and period furnishings have been combined to create the varied bedchambers. If space is a priority, request Room 5, a double with a small bathroom and separate toilet, crocheted bed and pillow covers, and a hand-painted mural that extends from one corner to the door. The two top-floor rooms (nos. 22 and 23) have the advantage of air-conditioning and beamed ceilings. In no. 23, the beams extend into the mirrored bathroom. Equally nice is the bathroom in no. 22, with an oval tub. An elegant salon off the main entrance doubles as the breakfast room and is a place where you can sit in the afternoon with a luscious pastry from the corner *pâtisserie* and order a cup of tea or coffee to go with it. This would truly be the perfect hotel if more of the rooms were just a bit bigger, if any luggage space existed, and if the closets held more. However, if you are traveling by yourself or without piles of suitcases, and you love the charm of this part of Paris, then this hotel is bound to please you.

ENGLISH SPOKEN: Yes

FACILITIES AND SERVICES: Air-conditioning in two rooms on the top floor; direct-dial phone; elevator; hair dryer; minibar; TV; room safe, no charge

NEAREST TOURIST ATTRACTIONS (LEFT BANK): St-Germain-des-Prés, Luxembourg Gardens, St-Michel, Île de la Cité, Île St-Louis, shopping

(54) HÔTEL LUXEMBOURG* ★★★
4, rue de Vaugirard, 75006 (6th)
33 rooms, all with shower or bath and toilet

Over time the building has had several lives, including serving as the lodgings for the grooms of King Louis XIV. For many years, I thought the hotel rested on its past laurels and never made much of an attempt to improve its tired and faded image. However, because of its good location near the Luxembourg Gardens and St-Sulpice, I never gave up on it completely. Now I am happy to say the hotel has been tastefully redone with soft coordinating colors, fabrics, and furnishings. The new look combines the best of the old with the practicality and convenience of the new with its up-to-date bathrooms, good bedside lighting, and double closets with shelves. The attractive lobby has two side salons with comfortable, pillowed armchairs and sofas. The nonsmoking breakfast room is in an arched stone *cave* where the tables are set with Limoges china.

Of interest to many Cheap Sleepers in Paris are the package deals offered throughout the year for both groups and individuals.

ENGLISH SPOKEN: Yes

FACILITIES AND SERVICES: Bar; direct-dial phone; elevator; hair dryer; minibar; TV with international reception; room safe, no charge

NEAREST TOURIST ATTRACTIONS (LEFT BANK): Luxembourg Gardens, St-Sulpice, St-Michel, St-Germain-des-Prés, shopping

TELEPHONE
01-43-25-35-90
FAX
01-43-26-60-84
E-MAIL
luxhotel@luxembourg.grolier.fr
INTERNET
www.grolier.fr/luxembourg
MÉTRO
Odéon, RER Luxembourg, St-Michel
CREDIT CARDS
AE, DC, MC, V
RATES
Single 745F–860F, double 770–865F, triple 1,050F; ask about lower off-season rates and special package offers
Taxe de séjour: included
BREAKFAST
60F extra per person

(55) HÔTEL NOVANOX ★★★
155, boulevard du Montparnasse, 75006 (6th)
27 rooms, all with shower or bath and toilet

From the outside it doesn't inspire. But inside, the future beckons at the Novanox, an impressive example of what a sense of style and a great imagination—with a little money thrown in—can do with an old hotel. Hats off to owner Bertrand Plasmans, who, several years ago, gambled everything on creating a modern hotel with the latest designs and contemporary craftsmanship. The yellow-and-blue lobby, with dangling mobile lights and the faces of Greek gods and goddesses softly painted on the walls and depicted on the upholstered chairs and couches, reminds me of a playful fairyland. At one end of the lobby is a breakfast area overlooking an enclosed sidewalk terrace. Dainty croissants and buttery brioches

TELEPHONE
01-46-33-63-60
FAX
01-43-26-61-72
MÉTRO
Vavin, Raspail
CREDIT CARDS
AE, DC, MC, V
RATES
1–2 people 580–750F; extra bed 150F; ask for special weekend rates
Taxe de séjour: included
BREAKFAST
60F extra per person

fill the breakfast baskets and are accompanied by an assortment of jams and a pot of sweet butter. A portion of cheese and fresh fruit complement the meal.

The rooms upstairs have a pastel color scheme, with contemporary furniture especially built to fit the design of each room. The toiletries are from Roger and Gallet, the fresh flowers from the owner's mother's garden, the lamps from Spain, the carpet imported from Germany, and the ideas all from M. Plasmans. The result? Still *magnifique!*

ENGLISH SPOKEN: Yes

FACILITIES AND SERVICES: Bar; direct-dial phone; some hair dryers; elevator; minibar; TV; room safe, no charge

NEAREST TOURIST ATTRACTIONS: Montparnasse

(56) HÔTEL PRINCE DE CONDÉ* ★★★
39, rue de Seine, 75006 (6th)
12 rooms, all with shower or bath and toilet

TELEPHONE
01-44-07-30-40

FAX
01-44-07-36-34

MÉTRO
Odéon, St-Michel

CREDIT CARDS
AE, DC, MC, V

RATES
Single 790–900F, double 970F, suite 1,630F
Taxe de séjour: included

BREAKFAST
60F extra per person (continental in room, buffet downstairs)

For a discreet, smart St-Germain address, the revamped Prince de Condé is a twelve-room winner. Under the Libertel banner, the hotel displays dignified good taste from top to bottom with the snug rooms all facing the picturesque rue de Seine. They are well coordinated with bold red, green, or yellow prints matching or blending with the wall coverings and bedspreads. The only room with a special view of the St-Germain-des-Prés Church steeple is a suite on the sixth floor. The size of two normal rooms, it offers the benefit of a sitting room with two upholstered chairs, a desk, and a Jacuzzi. The only drawback I could see were the three rather odd-shaped closets under the eaves. The location is picture-postcard Paris . . . just down the street from the animated produce hawkers and outdoor cafés surrounding the Buci *Marché,* close to the Seine, St-Michel, and numerous restaurants (see *Cheap Eats in Paris*), and within a work-out-walk to the Louvre.

ENGLISH SPOKEN: Yes

FACILITIES AND SERVICES: Air-conditioning in all rooms; direct-dial phone; elevator; hair dryer; minibar; TV with international reception; room safe, no charge; room service for light snacks; Jacuzzi in the suite

NEAREST TOURIST ATTRACTIONS (LEFT BANK): St-Germain-des-Prés, St-Michel, Seine, the islands, Louvre, excellent shopping

(57) HÔTEL RÉCAMIER ★★
3, bis place Saint-Sulpice, 75006 (6th)
30 rooms, 22 with shower or bath and toilet

The same owner, Mme. Dauphin, has been here since 1980 and has no plans to change anything. She did break down and bring the office up to speed by adding a fax. Never mind, it is all part of the folksy charm the faithful Cheap Sleepers who stay here love. For Paris, the location overlooking the church on place St-Sulpice is calm. A peaceful night's rest is further assured because the hotel does not appeal to a *branché* crowd of late-night revelers. Breakfast is served in a room papered in a loud burgundy print, with a brass chandelier, an old bistro coat rack and umbrella stand with hooks, and dining chairs covered in a provincial print. Drab brown hallways lead you to the neat and clean, style-free rooms, where you will see egg-yolk yellow chenille set against pink floral wallpaper. You will not, however, find much that is run down or worn to a nub anywhere in this hotel.

ENGLISH SPOKEN: Yes

FACILITIES AND SERVICES: Direct-dial phone; elevator; safe in office, no charge; no TV

NEAREST TOURIST ATTRACTIONS (LEFT BANK): St-Germain-des-Prés, Luxembourg Gardens

TELEPHONE
01-43-26-04-89
FAX
01-46-33-27-73
MÉTRO
St-Sulpice, Mabillon
CREDIT CARDS
MC, V
RATES
1–2 persons 405–605F, large room 910F; shower 20F
Taxe de séjour: 5F extra per person, per day
BREAKFAST
35F extra per person

(58) HÔTEL SAINT-ANDRÉ-DES-ARTS ★
66, rue Saint-André-des-Arts, 75006 (6th)
32 rooms, all with shower or toilet

Since my last visit, this hotel has been redone—well, sort of. Some airless, trainlike bathrooms with hot red toilet seats have been added, and a fresh coat of paint has been slapped on most of the rooms and halls. The carved misericord, which priests used to sit and lean against during long masses, continues to grace the entry, and the manager still stands behind his ruling philosophy, "We are a hotel without extras, including the charges."

The location is strategic; the prices low; and the nonconventional crowd of fashion groupies, hip musicians, budding actors, and starving backpackers is party-loving and carefree. For some, the rooms are so small that cabin fever sets in immediately. Others may object to the unpleasant symphony of noises drifting through the walls at all hours or to the dim-watt lights dangling from the ceilings. For its devoted regulars, this wrinkled hotel still has a tattered charm they love to romanticize

TELEPHONE
01-43-26-96-16
FAX
01-43-29-73-34
MÉTRO
Odéon
CREDIT CARDS
MC, V
RATES
Single 360F, double 460F, triple 570F, quad 620F
Taxe de séjour: included
BREAKFAST
Included, cannot be deducted

and an attitude by the management they eagerly applaud. Now that you know both sides, you probably also know which camp you are in.

ENGLISH SPOKEN: Yes

FACILITIES AND SERVICES: Direct-dial phone; no elevator or TV; office safe, no charge

NEAREST TOURIST ATTRACTIONS (LEFT BANK): St-Germain-des-Prés, St-Michel, Île de la Cité, Île St-Louis

(59) HÔTEL SAINT-GERMAIN-DES-PRÉS* ★★★
36, rue Bonaparte, 75006 (6th)
30 rooms, all with shower or bath and toilet

TELEPHONE
01-42-26-00-19

FAX
01-40-46-83-63

MÉTRO
St-Germain-des-Prés

CREDIT CARDS
AE, MC, V

RATES
1–2 persons 800–1,050F, suite 1,350–1,650F; extra bed 225F
Taxe de séjour: 6F extra per person, per day

BREAKFAST
Included, cannot be deducted

The Saint-Germain-des-Prés is the kind of small hotel everyone hopes to find in Paris. Superbly located in the very *coeur* of St-Germain, only a minute or two from two of the most famous cafés—Les Deux Magots and Café Flore—it has a long history of famous guests. It began in 1778 as a Masonic lodge to which Voltaire, Benjamin Franklin, and U.S. Navy Captain John Paul Jones belonged. After it became a hotel, it housed philosopher Auguste Comte, American playwright Elmer Rice, and authors Henry Miller and Janet Flanner. Ms. Flanner lived here for years and wrote her "Letters from Paris" column for the *New Yorker* from her top-floor suite.

The hotel is known for its lovely displays of fresh flowers, which are massed everywhere, from the entryway with its Venetian glass chandelier and hand-painted celestial ceiling to the antique- and tapestry-filled salon overlooking a walled garden filled with blooming hydrangeas and azaleas. The rooms, which are all different, have hand-painted doors and are done in dark woods, with fabric-covered walls, brass beds, and good lighting. The suites, with their separate sitting rooms, are captivating, especially no. 26, which has Oriental rugs tossed on polished wooden floors, a canopy bed, leaded-glass windows, flower boxes, and a marble bath with Art Nouveau lights and fixtures. Space is well used in no. 25, a double on the back where built-in closets frame the bed and a small desk, chair, and luggage bench offer comfort. Air-conditioning in all the rooms is an added bonus on hot days in this noisy part of Paris.

The hotel's deserved popularity today is due in no small measure to the thoughtfulness of the staff members, who go to great lengths to cater to the needs of their guests. Everyone who stays here agrees that it is definitely worth the Big Splurge.

ENGLISH SPOKEN: Yes

FACILITIES AND SERVICES: Air-conditioning in all rooms; bar; direct-dial phone; hair dryer; elevator; minibar; room service for light meals; TV with international reception; room safe, no charge; terry robes in suites

NEAREST TOURIST ATTRACTIONS (LEFT BANK): St-Germain-des-Prés, Latin Quarter, Île de la Cité, Île St-Louis

(60) HÔTEL SAINT-MICHEL ★
17, rue Gît-le-Coeur, 75006 (6th)
25 rooms, 11 with shower only, 6 with shower and toilet

This down-and-out hotel is for those with slim budgets and romantic notions about bohemian accommodations in Paris. The reception room is textbook one-star: a red loveseat with fringe, assorted fake plants and floral bouquets, a knickknack collection of varying quality, and a display behind the desk of soft drinks and bottled water available for sale. The hotel is included here because the modest prices and super location help to offset the basic rooms—which are beginning to show their age. A few have a private shower and toilet, others just showers, and a third are altogether facility-free. Hooks substitute for closets, and some views can be downright depressing. My advice is to inspect the room before accepting it. Potential guests should also get the rate of the room guaranteed by the hotel in writing, and be aware that the first night is payable *in advance.* Night owls take note: a 100F *caution* (refundable deposit) is collected for a front-door key because management goes to bed at 1 A.M.

ENGLISH SPOKEN: Not much, but Italian, Spanish, and Portuguese

FACILITIES AND SERVICES: No elevator (steep stairs); TV; office safe, no charge

NEAREST TOURIST ATTRACTIONS (LEFT BANK): St-Michel, St-Germain-des-Prés, Latin Quarter, Île de la Cité, Île St-Louis

TELEPHONE
01-43-26-98-70

FAX
None

MÉTRO
St-Michel

CREDIT CARDS
None, cash only

RATES
Single 215–370F, double 250–420F, triple 500–540F; shower 12F
Taxe de séjour: included

BREAKFAST
Included, cannot be deducted (includes a croissant)

(61) HÔTEL SAINT-PAUL ★★★
43, rue Monsieur-le-Prince, 75006 (6th)
31 rooms, all with shower or bath and toilet

TELEPHONE
01-43-26-98-64

FAX
01-46-34-58-60

MÉTRO
Odéon

CREDIT CARDS
AE, DC, MC, V

RATES
Single 700F, double 700–800F,
suite 900–1,020F
Taxe de séjour: included

BREAKFAST
Continental 50F extra;
American with two eggs and
ham 70F extra

In the seventeenth century, this building served as a hostel for Franciscan monks. For the last forty years, it has been a hotel owned by the Hawkins family and is now competently run by their daughter, Marianne, who is ably assisted by an accommodating staff and the house cat, Perkin. The family's collection of antiques, Oriental rugs, and watercolor paintings has been used in the hotel with elegant results. The seasonal fresh flower bouquets that grace the public areas are grown and arranged by one of the housekeepers, who has been with the hotel for two decades. Custom-made curtains, fabric-covered walls, and interesting brass and four-poster beds combine with modern baths to create the pleasing rooms. There are four rooms similar to no. 31, a single overlooking the garden and done in beige grass cloth with a white brass metal bed. No. 14 has a high ceiling that accommodates a four-poster bed with a tapestry-covered headboard and matching canopy. Twin sleigh beds and plenty of sunshine add to the enjoyment of room no. 43, located on the front of the hotel. One of my favorites is no. 51, done in yellow. Situated under the eaves, it has a cozy bedroom with a small sitting room and a bird's-eye view of École de Médecine. For those insisting on total calm, no. 36 on the back is a pretty choice, with its adorable brass bed, big bath, lovely old beams, and open window framing a big tree and rooftop garden across the way.

ENGLISH SPOKEN: Yes

FACILITIES AND SERVICES: Air-conditioning in some rooms; direct-dial phone; elevator; hair dryer; minibar; TV with international reception; room safe, no charge

NEAREST TOURIST ATTRACTIONS (LEFT BANK): Luxembourg Gardens, St-Germain-des-Prés, St-Michel, Panthéon

(62) HÔTEL SAINT-PIERRE ★★
4, rue de l'École de Médecine, 75006 (6th)
50 rooms, 25 with shower or bath and toilet, all with shower and sink

TELEPHONE
01-46-34-78-80

FAX
01-40-51-05-17

If you want a central Latin Quarter location without spending big bucks to get it, the Saint-Pierre, next to the École de Médecine, is a smart Cheap Sleep. Gone are the usual budget two-star sagging mattresses, dull halls, and garage-sale-reject furniture in the lobby. Twin beds are available and so are stall showers *with* doors, double-glazed windows where necessary, and international television reception. The unexceptional bedrooms will continue to inspire you to leave early and return late, spending your time discovering Paris, not snoozing in your room. The rooms pay homage to plain plastics and oddly matched colors, but they are always neat and well-maintained and have decent closet and luggage space. You will probably not want to check into a room ending in the number 5. They are near the noisy elevator with a slamming door. Management keeps a tight lid on loud voices, carry-in food, and nonpaying guests in the rooms.

ENGLISH SPOKEN: Yes

FACILITIES AND SERVICES: Direct-dial phone; elevator; minibar in three rooms; TV with international reception; safe in office, no charge

NEAREST TOURIST ATTRACTIONS (LEFT BANK): Latin Quarter, St-Michel, St-Germain-des-Prés, Île de la Cité, Île St-Louis, Luxembourg Gardens

(63) L'ATELIER MONTPARNASSE HÔTEL ★★★
49, rue Vavin, 75006 (6th)
17 rooms, all with shower or bath and toilet

The present Montparnasse landscape of fast-food stops, blockbuster movie theaters, and urban renewal projects almost makes one forget that this was once the artistic heart of Paris. The Atelier Montparnasse reminds guests of these past times by dedicating each floor of the hotel to the work of a famous Montparnasse artist, including Modigliani, Matisse, Erté, and Picasso. Each of the plain, concise rooms has noise-proof double-paned windows, a minibar, a television, and a modern bathroom with a tiled mosaic work of the artist represented on that floor. The artist Fujita is featured in no. 62, a large, yellow-and-blue accented room with a double bed and two windows facing the street. Unfortunately, even a Matisse painting cannot improve no. 41, an oddly shaped double facing a blank wall. The 1920s-inspired lobby has curved gray and blue walls, Art Deco furniture, and an impressive display of contemporary original paintings selected by young artists whom Marie-José Tible, the hotel owner, has discovered. A floor mosaic—based on a cartoon drawing from the Musée des Arts Decoratifs—as well as the mosaics in the bathrooms were done by Martine Lionel du Pont, the mother of the former owners of the hotel. In addition to being one of the more interesting places to sleep in this area, the hotel

MÉTRO
Odéon

CREDIT CARDS
AE, DC, MC, V

RATES
Single 355–390F, double 400–475F, triple 580F
Taxe de séjour: included

BREAKFAST
35F extra per person

TELEPHONE
01-46-33-60-00

FAX
01-40-51-04-21

MÉTRO
Vavin

CREDIT CARDS
AE, DC, MC, V

RATES
Single 610F, double 720F, triple 975F; extra bed 100F
Taxe de séjour: 6F extra per person, per day

BREAKFAST
45F extra per person

is within an easy walk to the métro and the famous cafés, brasseries, and restaurants of Montparnasse (see *Cheap Eats in Paris*).

ENGLISH SPOKEN: Yes

FACILITIES AND SERVICES: Direct-dial phone; elevator; minibar; TV; office safe, no charge

NEAREST TOURIST ATTRACTIONS (LEFT BANK): Montparnasse, Luxembourg Gardens

(64) LE RELAIS-HÔTEL DU VIEUX PARIS* ★★★
9, rue G't-le-Coeur, 75006 (6th)
20 rooms, all with shower or bath and toilet

TELEPHONE
01-43-54-41-66; toll-free from the U.S., 1-800-44-UTELL

FAX
01-43-26-00-15

E-MAIL
vieuxpar@worldnet.fr

INTERNET
www.travel2000.com/h/Europe/France/Paris/relaispa.fr/l.htm

MÉTRO
St-Michel

CREDIT CARDS
AE, DC, MC, V

RATES
1–2 persons 990–1,180F, suite 1,280–1,380F, apartment 1,480–1,680F
Taxe de séjour: 6F extra per person, per day

BREAKFAST
70F extra per person

In its heyday in the 1950s and early 1960s, this hotel had no proper name, just a street number: 9, rue G't-le-Coeur. It was the haunt of the movers and shakers of the Beat generation: Allen Ginsberg, Harold Norse, William S. Burroughs, Harold Chapman, Thelma Shumsky, and many others. Things were happening in each room. People were painting, writing, talking, and planning, and the inflexible owner, Mme. Rachou, presided over it all while standing on a box behind the little zinc bar by the entrance. There were no carpets, no telephones, and the antiquated nineteenth-century electrical system provided hit-or-miss service to the rooms. Toilet facilities consisted of a hole in the floor on each stair landing, and advance notice was necessary for a shower. Suddenly, in the mid-1960s, Mme. Rachou sold the hotel. The new owners named it, carpeted and painted the rooms, installed phones, and, of all things, even installed private bathrooms in some rooms. The hole-in-the-floor toilets went the way of the zinc bar. Canvases, manuscripts, and sketches that may have been worth millions of dollars were burned in the battle to disinfect the hotel. Art dealers came in later offering to buy any walls with murals, but they had been covered with wild wallpaper or painted, rendering the original artwork underneath worthless. Currently under its third owner, Mme. Claude Odillard, the hotel has been completely redone and bears no resemblance to its earlier days as a fleabag shrine to the Beat generation in Paris. That famous clientele has long since moved on, replaced today by chic, well-traveled guests, many of whom are not aware of the nostalgic history of the hotel. All that remains now are photos, hung in the lobby, of some of the people who lived here in its early days and a piece of the hideous old wallpaper preserved on an outside beam.

On all counts, Mme. Odillard must be praised for her beautiful transformation of this now outstanding three-star hotel, which includes her own collection of French antiques, judiciously placed throughout, creating a feeling of warmth and comfort seldom seen today. All of the rooms have color-coordinated fabrics and top-of-the-line furnishings. They include absorbent terry-cloth robes, oversized towels, ample closet and drawer space, recessed lighting, and piped-in music. The top-floor suites have Jacuzzis, roof-top gardens, or views of Ste-Chapelle or the Palais du Justice. Fresh flowers and candy are welcoming touches everyone enjoys. The hotel is now recommended as the perfect stopover for those who want romance on their doorstep and the best of Paris at their feet.

ENGLISH SPOKEN: Yes

FACILITIES AND SERVICES: Air-conditioning in all rooms; direct-dial phone; fax outlet in rooms; elevator; hair dryer; minibar; radio; TV with international reception; room safe, no charge.

NEAREST TOURIST ATTRACTIONS (LEFT BANK): St-Michel, St-Germain-des-Prés, Île de la Cité, Île St-Louis

(65)   PENSION LES MARRONNIERS (NO STARS)
78, rue des Assas, 1er étage a droite, escalier A (first floor on the right, stairway A), 75006 (6th)
12 rooms, 1 with shower and toilet

The days of family-run pensions in France, and especially in Paris, are numbered, according to a documentary on the subject filmed here. This *incroyable* Cheap Sleep in Paris, across the street from one of the entrances to the Luxembourg Gardens, has been presided over since the turn of the century by members of the Poirier family. At the Pension les Marronniers, the philanthropically low prices include not only a continental breakfast but a three-course dinner with cheese as well. With advance notice, special dietary needs can be catered for. Students, Frenchmen from the provinces doing a work-study program, and smart budgeteers fill this third-floor walk-up home, which has the Laura Ashley decorating seal of approval in the dining and living rooms, complete with Jimi, the house cat asleep in the most comfortable chair or sunniest window ledge, and the two dogs, Gabin, a sheep dog, and Strat, a noisy Yorkie in charge of providing a friendly welcome. The bedrooms might seem primitive to many, but all are cleaned on a

TELEPHONE
01-43-26-37-71

FAX
01-43-26-07-72

MÉTRO
Vavin, Notre-Dame-des-Champs

CREDIT CARDS
None, cash only

RATES
Single 160–395F, double 260–490F; special rates for long stays
Taxe de séjour: 1F extra per person, per day

BREAKFAST
Included; dinner is also included; neither can be deducted

regular basis, and the linens changed weekly. Reservations are absolutely essential months in advance, and guests who stay for a long time are preferred. Meals are part of the program and cannot be deducted for any reason.

ENGLISH SPOKEN: Some, but many guests speak English

FACILITIES AND SERVICES: Some direct-dial phones; TV and video in lounge; office safe, no charge; no elevator

NEAREST TOURIST ATTRACTIONS (LEFT BANK): Montparnasse, Luxembourg Gardens

(66) WELCOME HÔTEL ★★
66, rue de Seine, at the corner of boulevard St-Germain, 75006 (6th)
30 rooms, all with shower or bath and toilet

TELEPHONE
01-46-34-24-80
FAX
01-40-46-81-59
MÉTRO
Odéon, Mabillon, St-Germain-des-Prés
CREDIT CARDS
MC, V
RATES
Single 395–510F, double 510–565F
Taxe de séjour: included
BREAKFAST
45F extra per person

Unpretentious rooms in a fun-filled location are combined with moderate prices to make a stay here more than welcome. Composed of thirty rooms on six floors, this friendly spot on the corner of rue de Seine and boulevard St-Germain is directly across from the picturesque rue de Buci street *marché*. Because many of the rooms are on the small side, it is an especially suitable stopover for singles. Those wanting more spacious accommodations should ask for a corner room with a view (nos. 21, 23, 33, 43, 51, and 53). The best of these is no. 53, done in pink. The plus here is the large bath (for this hotel) with a tub and shower nozzle above. Other popular picks are no. 54, the best single because it has a writing table and a view, and no. 62, an attic nest with beams and a peaked ceiling. The worst is no. 64, with an open closet and windows too high to see out. Despite double windows, quiet is *not* the buzz word here. For the least noisy bunks, request rooms on rue de Seine, not on boulevard St-Germain. Top-floor rooms can get hot and stuffy in warm weather, but they are very desirable otherwise. These drawbacks are overcome for most by the super location. The hotel is within walking distance of more things to see and do than you will finish in a week. The *quartier* has scores of inexpensive eating places (see *Cheap Eats in Paris*), and shoppers will never finish browsing and wishing.

ENGLISH SPOKEN: Yes

FACILITIES AND SERVICES: Direct-dial phone; elevator; TV; safe in office, no charge

NEAREST TOURIST ATTRACTIONS (LEFT BANK): St-Germain-des-Prés, Île de la Cité, Île St-Louis, St-Michel, Luxembourg Gardens, shopping

Seventh Arrondissement

Known affectionately as "Seventh Heaven," this quiet, luxurious residential area is full of stately mansions built before the Revolution and now occupied by embassies, government offices, well-to-do Parisians, and expatriates. The Champ-de-Mars served as the parade ground for the École Militaire and is the backyard of the Eiffel Tower. Les Invalides is the home of four world-famous military museums and is the final resting place of Napoléon Bonaparte.

LEFT BANK
Assemblée Nationale, Champ-de-Mars, École Militaire, Eiffel Tower, Invalides, Musée d'Orsay, Rodin Museum, UNESCO

HOTELS IN THE SEVENTH ARRONDISSEMENT

(1)	Grand Hôtel Lévêque ★	**127**
(2)	Hôtel Bersoly's Saint-Germain ★★★	**130**
(3)	Hôtel Bourgogne & Montana* ★★★	**131**
(4)	Hôtel de l'Académie* ★★★	**132**
(5)	Hôtel de la Tulipe ★★	**133**
(6)	Hôtel de l'Empereur ★★	**133**
(7)	Hôtel de Londres ★★★	**134**
(8)	Hôtel Duc de Saint-Simon* ★★★	**135**
(9)	Hôtel du Champ de Mars ★★	**136**
(10)	Hôtel du Palais Bourbon ★★	**137**
(11)	Hôtel la Bourdonnais ★★★	**138**
(12)	Hôtel Latour-Maubourg ★★★	**139**
(13)	Hôtel les Jardins d'Eiffel ★★★	**140**
(14)	Hôtel Muguet ★★	**141**
(15)	Hôtel Relais Bosquet ★★★	**142**
(16)	Hôtel Saint-Dominique ★★	**143**
(17)	Hôtel Saint-Thomas d'Aquin ★★	**143**
(18)	Hôtel Solférino ★★	**144**
(19)	Hôtel Verneuil Saint-Germain ★★★	**145**
(20)	Libertel Bellechasse* ★★★	**145**
(21)	Splendid Hôtel ★★★	**146**
	*Indicates a Big Splurge	

(1) GRAND HÔTEL LÉVÊQUE ★
29, rue Cler, 75007 (7th)
50 rooms, 45 with shower and toilet

Committed Cheap Sleepers who like the seventh arrondissement love the Lévêque. Located among the colorful food shops that line the rue Cler, it is close to all the things that one often forgets are so important on a trip: banks, a post office, good transportation, do-it-yourself laundries, cleaners, well-priced shops, cafés for a

TELEPHONE
01-47-05-49-15
FAX
01-45-50-49-36
E-MAIL
Grandhôtelléveque@HORECATM-FR

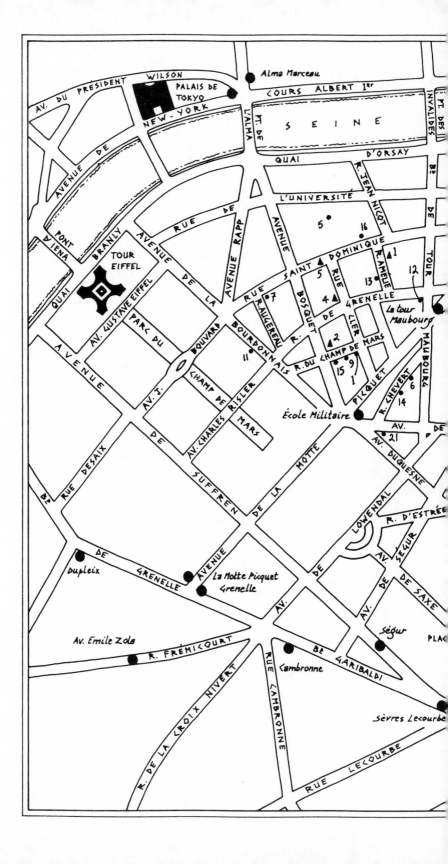

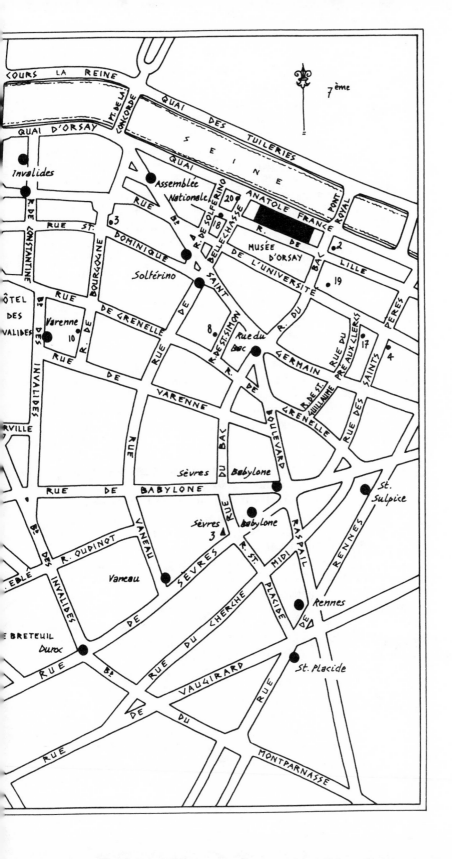

MÉTRO
École Militaire, Latour-
Maubourg

CREDIT CARDS
MC, V

RATES
Single 225F, double 335–380F,
triple 480F; free showers
Taxe de séjour: included

BREAKFAST
30F extra per person

mid-morning cup of hot chocolate, a street *marché,* and several exceptional cheese shops and *charcuteries* to tempt picnickers.

The hotel benefited from a renewal in 1997 and now boasts a glass lift and spiffy, no-nonsense rooms complete with hair dryer, cable TV, an individual safe, and private shower and toilet in all but five singles. Closets and shelves are spacious enough, but drawer space is nonexistent. The owner told me that clients leave behind too many things in drawers, so he just eliminated them altogether. Best rooms definitely face the front. Three on the fifth floor have balconies where you can observe the wonderful street scene below. In nos. 51 and 52, you can lie in bed and see the Eiffel Tower. The hotel is always busy, and I predict it will be even more in demand thanks to the many improvements. So, if you are interested, book ahead at least one month, and more during peak periods.

ENGLISH SPOKEN: Yes

FACILITIES AND SERVICES: Direct-dial phone; elevator; hair dryer; room safe, 10F per stay; TV with international reception

NEAREST TOURIST ATTRACTIONS (LEFT BANK): Champ-de-Mars Park, Eiffel Tower, good shopping, lively street *marché*

(2) HÔTEL BERSOLY'S SAINT-GERMAIN ★★★
28, rue de Lille, 75007 (7th)
16 rooms, all with shower or bath and toilet

TELEPHONE
01-42-60-73-79

FAX
01-49-27-05-55

MÉTRO
Rue du Bac, St-Germain-
des-Prés

CREDIT CARDS
AE, MC, V

RATES
Single 600F, double 650–750F;
two-room, 4-person apartment
850F
Taxe de séjour: included

BREAKFAST
55F extra per person

The old stone walls and floors in the lobby are clean and polished, and the two breakfast rooms downstairs—one in a bistro style and the other in an Oriental motif—are attractive. I must be honest, however, and say that the masses of fake flowers do not add to the character of the hotel. But, gaudy fake flowers don't diminish the *comfort* of the hotel, so it continues to be included as a very good value three-star, which has been owned since the mid-1980s by Mme. Carbonn (who, when I was last here, was two weeks away from delivering her first child, a boy she planned to name Vincent).

Every air-conditioned bedroom has been named for a famous French artist. In each case, a reproduction of one of that artist's paintings hangs in the room, and the mood and color scheme of the room are taken from the painting. If you like bold reds and black, request the ground-floor Picasso room, with its entrance off the atrium. If you prefer pastels, the Seurat or Sisley rooms are the ones to ask for. The Gauguin room can communicate with the Turner to form a family suite. Small bathrooms, low seating in the rooms, and steep steps may discourage some. Others will love the location, only minutes away from the Musée d'Orsay, the Louvre, serious shopping, and equally serious restaurants (see *Cheap Eats in Paris*).

NOTE: The hotel has a two-room, fully fitted apartment in a quiet building about a five-minute walk from the hotel, on rue de Verneuil. It is nicely done with throw rugs on tile floors and furniture from the *rustique* school. The apartment would best serve a couple. The Murphy bed is comfortable, but the sofa bed looked back-breaking to me.

ENGLISH SPOKEN: Yes

FACILITIES AND SERVICES: Air-conditioning in all rooms; bar; direct-dial phone; electric tea pot; elevator; hair dryer; room service; TV with international reception; room safe, no charge

APARTMENT: Direct-dial phone; dishwasher; elevator; hair dryer; fitted kitchen; iron and ironing board; washer and dryer; TV; private safe, no charge; weekly maid service

NEAREST TOURIST ATTRACTIONS (LEFT BANK): Musée d'Orsay, Louvre, Tuileries, shopping

(3) HÔTEL BOURGOGNE & MONTANA* ★★★
3, rue de Bourgogne, 75007 (7th)
34 rooms, all with shower or bath and toilet

The formal Bourgogne & Montana is located in a diplomatic neighborhood between Les Invalides and St-Germain. Combining a taste for tradition with a dignified clientele, the hotel is both regal and efficient, with large reception rooms and a historically classified 1924 elevator with lovely old iron work and open fronts that enable you see the floors pass as you ascend.

If cost is not too much of a factor, book a room on the fifth or sixth floor. I always hope for no. 67, a junior suite with wonderful views of place de la Concorde, the Madeleine Church, the National Assembly building, and the roof of the Grand Palais. When the buildings are illuminated at night, it is pure fairyland. Done in blue and yellow, this twin-bedded room is arranged with antiques a comfortable sofa, large television, built-in closet, luggage space, and a divided bathroom with two

TELEPHONE
01-45-51-20-22, toll-free from U.S., 800-44-UTELL

FAX
01-45-56-11-98

MÉTRO
Invalides, Chambre des Députes

CREDIT CARDS
AE, DC, MC, V

RATES
Single 800–1,025F, double 950–1,125F, suite 1,500–1,575F; extra bed 300F; children under 12 free; lower off-season rates
Taxe de séjour: included

BREAKFAST
Included, cannot be deducted

sinks. If this is not available, ask for no. 61 with a mansard roof line and a round bathtub. Room 54 has a courtyard view and a gleaming tile bathroom with excellent fittings. No. 42 is a standard choice in simple hotel decor, but it does offer space. Special rates in the off-season are offered for the standard-traditional rooms.

ENGLISH SPOKEN: Yes

FACILITIES AND SERVICES: Bar; direct-dial phone; elevator; hair dryer; minibar; free parking on the square if you are lucky; *peignoirs* (bathrobes) in deluxe rooms and suites; minitels in deluxe rooms; TV with international reception; office safe, no charge

NEAREST TOURIST ATTRACTIONS (LEFT BANK): Musée d'Orsay, Rodin Museum, Invalides, Seine, Tuileries, Louvre

(4) HÔTEL DE L'ACADÉMIE* ★★★
32, rue des Saints-Pères, 75007 (7th)
34 rooms, all with shower or bath and toilet

TELEPHONE
01-45-49-80-00, toll-free from the U.S., 800-44-UTELL

FAX
01-45-49-80-10

MÉTRO
St-Germain-des-Prés

CREDIT CARDS
AE, DC, MC, V

RATES
1–2 persons 800–1,300F; lower off-season rates upon request
Taxe de séjour: 6F extra per person, per day

BREAKFAST
60F extra per person

Sheltered in yet another deftly restored seventeenth-century building on the Left Bank, Gerard Chekroun's attractive hotel was once the residence for the private guards of the Duc du Rohan. Intact in the public areas are the original ceilings and stone halls, highlighted by Oriental rugs, country French furniture, and dried floral arrangements. A statue of Diane stands at the entrance to the formal dining room, which is color coordinated down to the last lampshade in green and rose. The small but well-detailed rooms have window treatments and bedspreads in either pink or blue floral print. The bathrooms are nicely tiled and supplied with French toiletries and good towels. None of the suites have views, but the marble baths with gold terra-cotta detailing and whirling Jacuzzis and the lush fabrics—including damask bedspreads—add the needed luxurious touches. The hotel is on the edge of St-Germain-des-Prés and within a brisk walk of the Musée d'Orsay, Notre-Dame, and many restaurants listed in *Cheap Eats in Paris*.

ENGLISH SPOKEN: Yes

FACILITIES AND SERVICES: Air-conditioning in some rooms; bar; direct-dial phone; hair dryer; elevator; Jacuzzi in some suites; minibar; private parking, 150F per night; radio; TV with international reception; room safe, no charge

NEAREST TOURIST ATTRACTIONS (LEFT BANK): St-Germain-des-Prés, Rodin Museum, the islands, within a fitness walk to Musée d'Orsay

(5) HÔTEL DE LA TULIPE ★★
33, rue Malar, 75007 (7th)
22 rooms, all with shower or bath and toilet

For years this was a tired and tattered Cheap Sleep in Paris *sans charme*. Thanks to the efforts of M. Fortuit, a French film actor turned hotelier, it is finally a sweet little Cheap Sleep *avec beaucoup de charme*. The twenty-two rooms are tightly snuggled in around a tree-shaded garden patio. Bright prints, grass-cloth-covered walls, beams galore, ancient stone walls, and the peaceful garden views work nicely together in the small rooms, creating the illusion of being in a country cottage miles away from Paris. If romance is on your itinerary, book no. 24, which once served as the chapel and still has two of the original stone walls and three windows opening onto the patio. From the hotel you are in close range for bargain shopping along rue St-Dominique, soaking up the market atmosphere along rue Cler, and trying many of the favored restaurants in *Cheap Eats in Paris*. For tourist endeavors, the Eiffel Tower is within walking distance for most and so are Invalides, the Seine, and the Musée d'Orsay.

ENGLISH SPOKEN: Yes

FACILITIES AND SERVICES: Direct-dial phone; some hair dryers; minibar; TV with international reception; office safe, no charge; no elevator (only two floors)

NEAREST TOURIST ATTRACTIONS (LEFT BANK): Eiffel Tower, Invalides, Seine, shopping, Musée d'Orsay

TELEPHONE
01-45-51-67-21
FAX
01-47-53-96-37
MÉTRO
Latour-Maubourg, Invalides
CREDIT CARDS
AE, DC, MC, V
RATES
Single 450–500F, double 550F, triple 700F
Taxe de séjour: 5F extra per person, per night
BREAKFAST
45F extra

(6) HÔTEL DE L'EMPEREUR ★★
2, rue Chevert, 75007 (7th)
38 rooms, all with shower or bath and toilet

What a difference a new owner can make. M. and Mme. Bruno are a young couple banking their future on the success of their newly acquired hotel. Already they have made major improvements in its appearance. The rooms, which are redone in shades of green and gold with interesting wrought-iron light fixtures, echo a Napoléonic style. Bathrooms are acceptable, but upgrades are not yet 100 percent. Twin rooms are on the back, singles and doubles on the front, where noise could be an issue, but the view of the Invalides dome is a

TELEPHONE
01-45-55-88-02
FAX
01-45-51-88-54
MÉTRO
Latour-Maubourg, Invalides
CREDIT CARDS
AE, MC, V
RATES
Single 465–470F, double 470–515F, triple 700F, quad 825F
Taxe de séjour: included

BREAKFAST
40F extra

redeeming factor. The ground-floor quad (no. 2) has an elephant-size bathroom with a separate enclosed toilet, but the room view of the trash bin area is hardly pleasing. M. Bruno assured me this would be remedied, so be sure to verify it if requesting this large room. A major benefit for many guests is M. Bruno's fluent English, which he learned during a six-month stay in San Rafael in Marin County, California.

ENGLISH SPOKEN: Yes

FACILITIES AND SERVICES: Direct-dial phone, elevator, hair dryer, minibar, TV with international reception; office safe, no charge

NEAREST TOURIST ATTRACTIONS (LEFT BANK): Invalides, Eiffel Tower, Champ-de-Mars Park, UNESCO

(7) HÔTEL DE LONDRES ★★★
1, rue Augereau, 75007 (7th)
30 rooms, all with shower or bath and toilet

TELEPHONE
01-45-51-63-02
FAX
01-47-05-28-96
MÉTRO
École Militaire
CREDIT CARDS
AE, DC, MC, V
RATES
Single 500F, double 600F, triple 700F; extra bed 140F; lower off-season rates
Taxe de sèjour: included
BREAKFAST
40F extra per person

Realistic prices, a very quiet location in the tony seventh arrondissement, easy walking distance to the Eiffel Tower, colorful shopping, and a good métro connection add up to make this a fine selection. A soothing color scheme of beiges, browns, and soft blues creates a tranquil mood in the exceptionally clean and well-kept bedrooms. Management is ever vigilant, always repainting, recovering, or rewallpapering the minute necessary . . . never waiting until shabbiness sets in. Closet space can be limited, and the tiled baths are functional but on the small side. Rooms 52, 54, 62, and 64 have Eiffel Tower views. Nos. 101, for two, and 103, a triple, are quiet ground-floor choices overlooking the garden. The six larger rooms in the back building are also quiet, but there is no elevator here. Off the reception area is an airy breakfast room, where you will probably see Elza, a Belgian griffon dog, snoozing and dreaming the morning away. The two couples who own the hotel (M. and Mme. Boutet and M. and Mme. DuBois) are sweet and always helpful, and they do their utmost to make your stay here as comfortable and pleasant as possible.

ENGLISH SPOKEN: Yes

FACILITIES AND SERVICES: Direct-dial phone; elevator to most floors (not in the back building); hair dryer; laundry service; minibar; TV with international reception; safe in office, no charge

NEAREST TOURIST ATTRACTIONS (LEFT BANK): Champ-de-Mars Park, Eiffel Tower, Invalides, good shopping

(8) HÔTEL DUC DE SAINT-SIMON* ★★★
14, rue de Saint-Simon, 75007 (7th)
34 rooms, all with shower or bath and toilet

Everyone has their first hotel in Paris, and this was mine. Of course, in those days it bore about as much resemblance to what it is today as the bicycle does to the Rolls Royce. Over the years, and through many changes, my enthusiasm for the hotel has not dimmed, and it still tops my short list of ideal small Parisian hotels.

I am drawn to the Duc de Saint-Simon for many reasons, especially its intimately romantic feeling, wonderful sense of privacy, overall beauty, and high degree of personalized service. Built around a courtyard garden, many of the rooms open onto this green view, while several larger rooms and suites open onto their own private terraces. When I first walked into no. 19, a large suite on the first floor, I thought, This is it—I am never leaving! The antique-filled sitting room has comfortable seating, a lovely writing desk, and good lighting. The quiet bedroom has its own television and a double bed where, in the morning, you are wakened by the birds singing outside your garden window. The older style bathroom has all the nice extras: heated towel racks, a magnifying mirror, a tub with a water shield, and a telephone. I like *all* the other rooms in this very special hotel, but a favorite has always been no. 11, decorated in rich fabrics with a corner sitting area and view windows that open onto the gardens and seem to bring them inside. Another beautiful room is no. 37. It is a soft, feminine room with a floral theme carried out on the wallpaper, curtains, spread, and lamp shades. I also like the two-drawer antique dresser, framed embroideries, and the roomy bathroom with its inset sink, shelf space, and separate stall shower. No. 34 has a double bed framed by lighted closets and a view overlooking the terraces below. It is elegantly decorated with large paisley wall coverings and furnished with a velvet armchair, four-drawer marble dresser, and crystal chandelier.

The owners of the hotel, M. and Mme. Lindqvist, have been antiques collectors of note for many years and have used their handsome collection throughout the hotel, from the beautiful grandfather clock in the lobby to the graceful marble-topped dressers in the bedrooms. The downstairs cellar bar has pillowed niches and quiet corners just big enough for two to sip drinks and talk about life and love.

TELEPHONE
01-44-39-20-20, 01-42-22-07-52 (reservations)

FAX
01-45-48-68-25

MÉTRO
Rue du Bac

CREDIT CARDS
MC, V

RATES
1–2 persons 1,100–1,600F, suite 1,900–1,950F; extra bed 30% of room rate
Taxe de séjour: included

BREAKFAST
75F extra per person

The prices for a stay here are high, no doubt about it. But for those seeking a quietly elegant, discreet stay in Paris, this should be *the* hotel of choice.

ENGLISH SPOKEN: Yes

FACILITIES AND SERVICES: Air-conditioning in some rooms; bar; direct-dial phone; elevator; hair dryer in some rooms; TV with international reception in suites, otherwise on request; robes in suites; room safe, no charge; room service for light snacks

NEAREST TOURIST ATTRACTIONS (LEFT BANK): Musée d'Orsay, Tuileries, St-Germain-des-Prés, Rodin Museum, excellent browsing and shopping

(9) HÔTEL DU CHAMP DE MARS ★★
7, rue du Champ de Mars, 75007 (7th)
25 rooms, all with shower or bath and toilet

TELEPHONE
01-45-51-52-30

FAX
01-45-51-64-36

INTERNET
www.globe.market.com/
h75007hotelchampdemars.htm

MÉTRO
École Militaire

CREDIT CARDS
MC, V

RATES
Single 355–385F, double 360–420F, triple 505F
Taxe de séjour: 5F extra per person, per day

BREAKFAST
40F extra per person

One of the questions I am always asked is "What wonderful, new Cheap Sleep did you discover on your last trip to Paris?" Of course, I always have an answer, and this time, it is the completely redone Hôtel du Champ de Mars. If you are looking for a good Cheap Sleep in Paris, please read on.

The hotel has actually been a regular in this book for years. It was a modest place, well located and clean, in an interesting part of Paris, but totally devoid of charm or personality. Now, under the new ownership of Françoise and Stéphane Gourdal (and their fluffy white dog named Chipie), it is a stylish choice for guests who want to watch their budget but not feel deprived in the process.

The hotel's revamped look reflects the time, talent, enthusiasm, and downright hard work of this delightful couple, who transformed it from stem to stern. The French way with color is often daring. Others might have stopped short of the mix of brightly hued fabrics, but Françoise had both the courage and good taste to pull it off. Her love of flowers is the underlying theme throughout. In the downstairs breakfast room, round tables draped in orange-and-yellow plaid hold bouquets of dried flowers. An old chest with a bowl of potpourri and soft background music create a relaxing place for morning coffee and croissants. White doors with big brass doorknobs lead to the yellow-and-blue rooms, all of which are named after French flowers. Myosotis (no. 55), on the front, is a single with great allure thanks to its small entry, light blue interior, and glimpse of the Eiffel Tower. Mimosa (no. 54) is another pleasant single with a nice view onto the court and rooftops beyond. If it is twin beds you want, ask for Muguet (no. 24). You enter Lilas (no. 4) through a little garden; the striped wallpaper, curtains, bedspreads, and rug are color coordinated in yellow, blue, and white to create a very sweet setting.

Last, but certainly not least, guests will find excellent discount shopping, several banks, a main post office, the métro, a wonderful street *marché* on rue Cler, and lots of favorite Cheap Eats in Paris all close at hand.

ENGLISH SPOKEN: Yes

FACILITIES AND SERVICES: Direct-dial phone; elevator; hair dryer; TV with international reception; office safe, no charge

NEAREST TOURIST ATTRACTIONS (LEFT BANK): Champ-de-Mars Park, Eiffel Tower, Invalides, good discount shopping, interesting daily street *marché*

(10) HÔTEL DU PALAIS BOURBON ★★
49, rue de Bourgogne, 75007 (7th)
32 rooms, 29 with shower, bath, and toilet

The Palais Bourbon has long been a reliable staple for readers of *Cheap Sleeps in Paris* who are looking for a respectable budget hotel suitable for the entire family. Located in a quiet residential area of Paris, only a half block from the Rodin Museum, five minutes from Invalides, and about ten minutes from the Musée d'Orsay, the hotel is just across the Seine from the Tuileries.

The Claudon family has owned, managed, and lived in the hotel for more than fifty years, and they run it with a steely eye out for anything, or anyone, out of line. It may not be the snazziest place to sleep in the *quartier*, but it will be one of the cleanest, thanks to their vigilant housekeeping and ongoing maintenance programs. The brick-floored breakfast room, with its square and oblong tables and one large round one in the center, is softened by a tall green plant in the window and an occasional vase of fresh flowers. Black-and-white prints of the Sorbonne and the Palais Bourbon hang on the white stuccoed walls. Continuing improvements include the addition of more tiled bathrooms, many with bidets. Only a few of the rooms are definitely faded and in need of redoing. To avoid one of these, always ask for a room with a new bathroom. Popular rooms are no. 3, which can connect with the room next door if larger quarters

TELEPHONE
01-44-11-30-70

FAX
01-45-55-20-21

E-MAIL
htlbourbon@aol.com

INTERNET
www.globe-market.com/ h75007palaisbourbon.htm

MÉTRO
Varenne, Invalides, Assemblée Nationale

CREDIT CARDS
MC, V

RATES
Single 290–490F, double 340–580F, triple 700F, quad 790F; extra bed 30% of room rate *Taxe de séjour*: included

BREAKFAST
Included; can be deducted on request (36F per person)

are needed, no. 4, a quiet double, and no. 1, a twin, also on the back.

ENGLISH SPOKEN: Yes

FACILITIES AND SERVICES: Direct-dial phone (on request, private numbers can be given for individual rooms at no charge); elevator; some minibars; TV with international receptions in most rooms; office safe, no charge; room safe in some rooms, no charge

NEAREST TOURIST ATTRACTIONS (LEFT BANK): Rodin Museum, Invalides, Musée d'Orsay, Tuileries

(11) HÔTEL LA BOURDONNAIS ★★★
111, 113, avenue de la Bourdonnais, 75007 (7th)
60 rooms, all with shower or bath and toilet

TELEPHONE
01-47-05-45-42

FAX
01-45-55-75-54

MÉTRO
École Militaire

CREDIT CARDS
AE, DC, MC, V

RATES
Single 520F, double 630–690F, triple 750F, quad 800F, suite 980F
Taxe de séjour: included

BREAKFAST
40F extra per person

Hôtel la Bourdonnais is a personal favorite that over the years has never failed to please. The location could not be better. It is five minutes from the métro and only ten from an RER stop. The area is filled with good shopping, from discount clothing boutiques to a colorful daily street *marché* on rue Cler. There are many inexpensive restaurants within easy walking distance (see *Cheap Eats in Paris*). The beautiful Champ-de-Mars Park, with the Eiffel Tower at one end and the impressive École Militaire at the other, is only two blocks away and a great place for a picnic, people-watching, or a morning jog.

The lobby and reception rooms are accented by velvet-covered furniture, soft lighting, bouquets of flowers, and nice paintings. A small breakfast corner and bar overlook a glassed-in garden where drinks and breakfast are served. The traditional rooms are tastefully decorated with excellent reproduction furnishings and soft fabrics. Some have air-conditioning, others have fans. All have very generous closet and drawer space, comfortable chairs, large writing desks, and hidden combination safes to store valuables. The ample marble bathrooms feature big mirrors, hair dryers, laundry drying racks, and plenty of towels. This outstanding hotel is the choice of many international travelers who seek good value, so to avoid disappointment, book way ahead.

ENGLISH SPOKEN: Yes

FACILITIES AND SERVICES: Air-conditioning in some rooms, fans in others; bar; direct-dial phone; hair dryer; elevator; some minibars; porter; radio; TV with international reception; video; room safe, no charge

(12)   HÔTEL LATOUR-MAUBOURG ★★★
150, rue de Grenelle, 75007 (7th)
10 rooms, all with shower or bath and toilet

The Hôtel Latour-Maubourg is a hotel of character with an exceptional, welcoming spirit of friendliness. I hope you will like it as much as I do. For many years it was an elegant pension-hotel that guests never wanted to leave. In fact, one guest arrived when it first opened and was one of the last to leave when it closed in 1993. Facing Invalides across a small park, this townhouse was in the Klein family for more than 150 years, and it was their home until they opened it to paying guests. Now the Klein family is gone, replaced by young, dynamic new owners, Victor and Maria Orsenne, their three children, and their dog, Faust. Victor is not only a hotelier with an impressive background but a talented gourmet chef. Dog lovers will be interested to know that Faust is 60 percent beagle and a foundling the Orsennes rescued and brought home the day they knew they would have this hotel.

When the Orsennes took over, they closed the hotel in order to totally redo it. They reopened in the spring of 1994, with exceedingly graceful results. They wisely kept the best pieces of furniture, recovering them to give a more up-to-date look. The beautiful wooden staircase has been shined and polished, and the gorgeous high ceilings have been cleaned and repainted. All of the landscape and Anonymous Ancestor paintings have been dusted and rehung. The former dining room, with a large fireplace, now doubles as a sitting room and breakfast area. American guests especially appreciate the fresh orange juice and daily *Herald-Tribune* that come with the generous continental breakfast. The rooms display uniformity and a warm sense of color. The furniture in the bedrooms reflects the 1930s and 1940s and has been custom crafted for the hotel. Soundproof doors have been installed as well as a two-line phone with alarm clock and an outside line for laptops. Some of the bathrooms are new. I wondered about those that seemed to be older. In talking with a guest, she told me that the 1930s-style tubs are long and deep, so you can stretch out and have

TELEPHONE
01-47-05-16-16

FAX
01-47-05-16-14

E-MAIL
victor@worldnet.fr

MÉTRO
Latour-Maubourg

CREDIT CARDS
MC, V

RATES
Single 550–650F, double 700–850F, suite 900–1,400F
Taxe de séjour: in summer, 6F extra per person, per day; otherwise, included

BREAKFAST
Included, cannot be deducted

the bubbles come right up to your chin. She also appreciated the size and shelf space and was glad they had not been changed. The marble fireplaces are still in place and so are the tall, double French windows that open onto the tiny park across the street, where you can watch pensioners in berets feeding the pigeons or discussing the latest political scandal. Beds are covered with pillowy duvets, or blankets . . . it is your choice, just be sure to state your preference.

ENGLISH SPOKEN: Yes, and German

FACILITIES AND SERVICES: Direct-dial phone; fans; fax and computer hookups; hair dryer; no elevator; minibar; TV; safe in office, no charge

NEAREST TOURIST ATTRACTIONS (LEFT BANK): Invalides, Rodin Museum, Musée d'Orsay

(13) HÔTEL LES JARDINS D'EIFFEL ★★★
8, rue Amélie, 75007 (7th)
80 rooms, all with shower or bath and toilet

TELEPHONE
01-47-05-46-21

FAX
01-45-55-28-08

E-MAIL
eiffel@unimedia.fr

MÉTRO
Latour-Maubourg, Invalides

CREDIT CARDS
AE, DC, MC, V

RATES
Single 600–850F, double 660–960F, triple 830–1,080F, quad 1,250–1,700F; ask about lower off-season rates
Taxe de séjour: 6F extra per person, per day

BREAKFAST
Included; can be deducted on request (60F per person)

Les Jardins d'Eiffel has built a solid reputation as a fine small hotel offering many four-star features at three-star prices. The quiet rooms and suites are simply coordinated and well appointed with wooden built-ins and the latest in modern bathrooms, including lighted magnifying mirrors and telephones. Rooms on the third through the fifth floors have views of the Eiffel Tower. In addition, family communicating rooms have private corridor entrances; nonsmokers can reserve anything on the fifth floor; motorists can park in the private hotel garage; and sunbathers can work on their tans at the solarium. A new wing provides garden and executive rooms done in bright primary colors and bold print fabrics. The competent desk staff will book reservations, organize sightseeing trips, rent a car for you—with or without driver—and confirm airline tickets. There is a one-day laundry and cleaning service and a doctor is on call twenty-four hours a day.

NOTE: They have rooms exclusively for nonsmokers and the handicapped.

ENGLISH SPOKEN: Yes

FACILITIES AND SERVICES: Air-conditioning on request; bar; baby-sitting; direct-dial phone; hair dryer; rooms for the handicapped; elevator; laundry and cleaning services; minibar; nonsmoking rooms (fifth floor); private parking (100F per 24-hour period); radio; TV with international reception; room safe, no charge; trouser press; concierge; doctor on 24-hour call

NEAREST TOURIST ATTRACTIONS (LEFT BANK): Champ-de-Mars Park, Invalides, Eiffel Tower, shopping

(14) HÔTEL MUGUET ★★
11, rue Chevert, 75007 (7th)
45 rooms, all with shower or bath and toilet

Hidden on an out-of-the-way, peaceful side street, the Muguet used to be my favorite "vintage" hotel. I knew something had changed a few years ago when a reader wrote to tell me how much she enjoyed the new and modern rooms. At the Muguet? A 1950s-style Cheap Sleep making no pretenses at modernization or *haute* decor? Maybe they just changed one or two rooms, but all forty-five? This I had to see.

Happily, the Muguet had indeed changed . . . all forty-five rooms. When I revisited it for this edition of *Cheap Sleeps in Paris*, I found it still to be one of the smartest, most stylish two-star Cheap Sleep values in Paris. Staying here will make anyone feel like a privileged budget traveler, especially in the suite, with its lovely tiled bathroom. Many of the rooms are air-conditioned . . . a rare extra in a two-star, let me assure you. All are outfitted in country-style furniture with different color schemes in either pink, yellow, or blue. Everything is well coordinated; mirrored wardrobes are generous; and from nos. 61 and 62, on the sixth floor, you can see the Eiffel Tower. From no. 63, your vista is over Invalides. On the fifth floor, ask for no. 51, with a balcony and good Eiffel Tower view. Another room I like is no. 41, a triple with three twin beds. The advantage here is the small sitting room and the large bath with yellow and gray accents.

Thankfully, everything was not thrown away during the renovation. The black and gray-green marble facade is intact, and so is the lovely grandfather clock standing next to the reception desk. No one replaced the colorful flowers and lush green plants in the garden with plastic versions, and, more important, the attractive owners, the Pelettier family and their two poodles, Framboise and Mandarine, live at the hotel and are always ready with their friendly smiles to make their guests feel very special and at home.

The immediate neighborhood could hardly be dubbed "the miracle mile," but it is quiet both day and night. After a nice ten-minute stroll, you can be at Invalides

TELEPHONE
01-47-05-05-93

FAX
01-45-50-25-37

E-MAIL
muguet@easynet.fr

MÉTRO
Latour-Maubourg, École Militaire

CREDIT CARDS
AE, MC, V

RATES
Single 460F, double 480–530F, triple 690F
Taxe de séjour: included

BREAKFAST
47F extra per person

viewing Napoléon's tomb or on a park bench at the Champ-de-Mars Park, admiring the Eiffel Tower while eating a gourmet picnic put together from the food shops that line rue St-Dominique and rue Cler. Good restaurants abound (see *Cheap Eats in Paris*), and so does discount shopping (see Cheap Chic, page 258).

ENGLISH SPOKEN: Yes

FACILITIES AND SERVICES: Air-conditioning on the sixth floor and in all rooms by 1999; direct-dial phone; hair dryer; elevator to five floors; TV with international reception; safe in office, no charge

NEAREST TOURIST ATTRACTIONS (LEFT BANK): Champ-de-Mars Park, Invalides, Eiffel Tower, Rodin Museum

(15) HÔTEL RELAIS BOSQUET ★★★
19, rue du Champ de Mars, 75007 (7th)
40 rooms, all with shower or bath and toilet

TELEPHONE
01-47-05-25-45; toll-free from the U.S., 800-448-8355

FAX
01-45-55-08-24

INTERNET
www.paris-hotel.tm.fr/fr ou gb/invalides.04/bosquet.html

MÉTRO
École Militaire

CREDIT CARDS
AE, DC, MC, V

RATES
Single 680–780F, double 730–830F; extra bed 100F; ask about special promotional rates *Taxe de séjour*: 6F extra per person, per day

BREAKFAST
Continental, 55F extra per person; coffee and juice, 25F extra

The Relais Bosquet offers guests comfort, space, and peacefulness in a renovated forty-room hotel built around a courtyard. Each room has all the three-star perks as well as an iron and ironing board, an electric fan, and an assortment of current periodicals. If you are traveling with an infant, the hotel will provide a free baby bath, chair, food warmer, and bed. Decor is uniform hotel-issue in all the rooms, with creamy wall coverings and nice-quality furnishings. Brass poles, artistically hung with soft pillows covered in the same material as the curtains, are mounted as headboards behind the beds. Baths have three-tiered rolling carts and nice towels. Top room picks are no. 52, a large twin on the back without much personality but with excellent space in both the room and the bathroom, which includes a stretch-out tub and separate enclosed shower; no. 54, which can serve as a small double or generous single; and no. 32, a big room for two with double sinks in the well-lit bathroom. The street is quiet, so consider no. 53 with two windows facing front as a good option. The upscale residential area of the seventh arrondissement offers some of the best Cheap Eats in Paris, casual discount shopping, and easy access by métro or bus to the rest of Paris.

ENGLISH SPOKEN: Yes

FACILITIES AND SERVICES: Direct-dial phone; elevator; hair dryer; electric fan; iron and ironing board; free baby equipment (bed, food warmer, bath, and chair); minibar;

parking; TV with international reception; room safe, no charge

NEAREST TOURIST ATTRACTIONS (LEFT BANK): Eiffel Tower, Invalides, Champ-de-Mars Park

(16)   HÔTEL SAINT-DOMINIQUE ★★
62, rue Saint-Dominique, 75007 (7th)
34 rooms, all with shower or bath and toilet

In the 1700s, this building housed Dominican nuns. Today, it is a quaint hotel on a busy shopping street. An English country theme is carried out from the beamed lobby to the tight rooms, which are furnished in pine and wicker, with soft, billowing curtains dressing the windows. Matching spreads, coordinated wall coverings, and a pretty provincial-style breakfast room, reached via a winding, wooden staircase, are other positive points. My favorite rooms are the two that open onto the terrace, where breakfast is served on warm spring and summer mornings. I also like no. 8, a twin on the back, and although the floors slant a bit, the roomy bedroom and bathroom, with a rolling cart for toiletries, save the day. The rooms do not boast exciting views, the elevator does not service all floors, and not all rooms have a chair . . . only a backless stool. While these may be deterrents for some, many Cheap Sleepers in Paris overlook them in favor of a tranquil stay in a hotel with reasonable rates.

ENGLISH SPOKEN: Yes

FACILITIES AND SERVICES: Direct-dial phone; hair dryer in some rooms; TV with French cable; safe in office and in some rooms, no charge

NEAREST TOURIST ATTRACTIONS (LEFT BANK): Invalides, Champ-de-Mars Park, Eiffel Tower, Rodin Museum, discount shopping

TELEPHONE
01-47-05-51-44

FAX
01-47-05-81-28

MÉTRO
Latour-Maubourg

CREDIT CARDS
AE, DC, MC, V

RATES
Single 430–460F, double 485–610F, triple 705F; extra bed 100F
Taxe de séjour: included

BREAKFAST
40F extra per person

(17)   HÔTEL SAINT-THOMAS D'AQUIN ★★
3, rue du Pré-aux-Clercs, 75007 (7th)
21 rooms, all with shower or bath and toilet

In an area where prices and noise are generally quite high, the Saint-Thomas d'Aquin is a wise Cheap Sleeping choice. An arched entryway leads to the soft salmon-colored lobby and sitting room. The glistening rooms are efficiently arranged and exceptionally well kept. No. 7 is a pleasant site, with its original ceiling, window on a small street, and new bathroom. No. 15 can be made up as a twin or king. It offers good space both in the room

TELEPHONE
01-42-61-01-22

FAX
01-42-61-41-43

MÉTRO
St-Germain-des-Prés, Rue du Bac

CREDIT CARDS
AE, DC, MC, V

RATES
Single 470–550F, double
475–555F
Taxe de séjour: included

BREAKFAST
40F extra per person

and in the closets. The competent English-speaking owners, Christiane and Claude Carcanague, are diligent and friendly, which has encouraged repeat guests who have been loyal to the hotel for many years. The location could not be better. The Musée d'Orsay, Louvre, Tuileries, and all of St-Germain-des-Prés are within a ten- to twenty-minute walk. The shopping is wonderful, and so are many restaurants in the neighborhood (see *Cheap Eats in Paris*).

ENGLISH SPOKEN: Yes

FACILITIES AND SERVICES: Bar; direct-dial phone; elevator; hair dryer in some rooms or available at the desk; fans on request; TV with international reception; office safe, no charge

NEAREST TOURIST ATTRACTIONS (LEFT BANK): Musée d'Orsay, Louvre, St-Germain-des-Prés, shopping

(18) HÔTEL SOLFÉRINO ★★
91, rue de Lille, corner of rue de Solférino, 75007 (7th)
32 rooms, all rooms with shower or bath, 27 also with toilet

TELEPHONE
01-47-05-85-54

FAX
01-45-55-51-16

MÉTRO
Solférino, RER-Musée d'Orsay

CREDIT CARDS
MC, V

RATES
Single 315–515F, double
560–735F
Taxe de séjour: included

BREAKFAST
Included; can be deducted on
request (40F per person)

Cheap Sleepers in search of a sedate location should consider the Hôtel Solférino, delightfully situated just off the Seine and near the Musée d'Orsay. Decorated with an eclectic flair, the hotel mixes antiques, paintings, and curios in a nonconventional way. Dining in the sunny pink-and-green breakfast room, with its skylight, display of hand-painted ceramics, and potted plants and flowers, is like eating in a spring garden. The sitting room reminds me of a maiden auntie's parlor at the turn of the century. A curved, tapestry-covered sofa, complete with fringe, dominates, along with what seems to be a twelve-foot mirror. The large *jardinière* with purple lilacs on it matches the lamp in the window.

The original cage elevator takes guests to the bedrooms. All are adequate, from the tiny top-floor singles to the large doubles equipped with showers and toilets. Avoid anything on the fifth floor and no. 25. Seating in many rooms is limited to a folding metal chair, and age is catching up to the bathrooms and hallways. It is not the Ritz or the George V, but neither are the prices. The long-time owner and her multilingual staff are congenial, and as a result, there are many *Cheap Sleep* readers who return.

ENGLISH SPOKEN: Yes

FACILITIES AND SERVICES: Direct-dial phone; elevator to fourth floor; TV in some rooms; safe in office (access 8 A.M.–3 P.M.), no charge

NEAREST TOURIST ATTRACTIONS (LEFT BANK): Musée d'Orsay, Louvre, Tuileries

(19) HÔTEL VERNEUIL SAINT-GERMAIN ★★★
8, rue de Verneuil, 75007 (7th)
26 rooms, all with shower or bath and toilet

For museumgoers, the Verneuil Saint-Germain is ideally located within walking distance to the Musée d'Orsay, the Louvre, and the Rodin Museum. Antique lovers are in heaven, and so are browsers and shoppers with all the tantalizing shops and boutiques that line this area. Sylvie de Latte is the new owner, and she is full of ideas and plans for her hotel. In the short time she has been here, she has thrown out most of the mishmash of garish statues and paintings that once seemed to cover almost every surface. This is not to say that the decor is now high tech . . . but at least it is thinned out a bit and no longer cluttered and confusing. She has kept the good points: the ornate doors, beamed ceilings, murals of Parisian landmarks in rooms ending in numbers 2 or 4, and the marble bathrooms. The vaulted stone cellar breakfast room, which unfortunately is located down a winding spiral staircase with no elevator access, is still used. Room sizes vary. The biggest is no. 302; the smallest no. 308, which is sold as a double but should be a single.

ENGLISH SPOKEN: Yes

FACILITIES AND SERVICES: Bar; direct-dial phone; elevator; hair dryer; minibar; TV with international reception; office safe, no charge

NEAREST TOURIST ATTRACTIONS (LEFT BANK): Musée d'Orsay, Rodin Museum, Seine, Tuileries, Louvre

TELEPHONE
01-42-60-82-14

FAX
01-42-61-40-38

MÉTRO
RER-Musée d'Orsay, Rue du Bac

CREDIT CARDS
MC, V

RATES
1–2 people 650–950F, suite 1,200F
Taxe de séjour: 6F extra per person, per day

BREAKFAST
Included; can be deducted if requested in advance

(20) LIBERTEL BELLECHASSE* ★★★
8, rue de Bellechasse, 75007 (7th)
41 rooms, all with shower or bath and toilet

Located on an interesting street in one of the nicest areas of Paris, the Libertel Bellechasse allows guests to walk easily to the Musée d'Orsay or across the Seine to the Tuileries and the Louvre. The hotel looks quite basic from the outside, but as soon as you step inside you will be struck by the bold entry done in dark green, blue, and red striped fabrics. The breakfast room is down an

TELEPHONE
01-45-50-22-31; central reservation 01-44-70-24-24

FAX
01-45-51-52-36; central reservation 01-44-70-24-51

MÉTRO
Solférino

CREDIT CARDS
AE, DC, MC, V
RATES
Single 860F, double 920F, suite
1,050F
Taxe de séjour: included
BREAKFAST
75F extra per person (buffet)

impressive, wide stairway with a large mural to one side. Comfortably spaced round tables, dressed in fruit prints, sit under the tentlike ceiling. The small, quiet bedchambers are artfully arranged to take advantage of every inch of space. They have a military-Directoire theme, carried out by using strong colors and hanging a collection of military prints throughout. The suites on the fifth and sixth floors are good, especially no. 508 with a king bed and a view to the trees and houses of the neighborhood. Some of the rooms are done in drab shades of brown and green and tend to be depressing. Better choices would be any of those in red, yellow, or blue.

NOTE: United Airlines frequent flyers can earn miles for their stay.

ENGLISH SPOKEN: Yes

FACILITIES AND SERVICES: Direct-dial phone; elevator; hair dryer; rooms for handicapped; laundry service; minibar; nonsmoking rooms (first floor); room service for light snacks; tea and coffeemakers in suites; TV with international reception; office safe, no charge

NEAREST TOURIST ATTRACTIONS (LEFT BANK): Musée d'Orsay, Tuileries, Louvre

(21) SPLENDID HÔTEL ★★★
29, avenue de Tourville and 1, avenue Duquesne, 75007 (7th)
48 rooms, all with shower or bath and toilet

TELEPHONE
01-45-51-24-77
FAX
01-44-18-94-60
MÉTRO
École Militaire
CREDIT CARDS
AE, DC, MC, V
RATES
Single 600–690F, double 700–
800F, suite 1,000F
Taxe de séjour: included
BREAKFAST
46F extra per person

Before 1992, the Splendid was anything but—now it lives up to its name on almost every count. Done in an Art Deco theme with soft blond wood and pastel wall colorings, the modernized rooms and serviceable baths offer all the comforts three-star sleepers demand. Balconies on the fifth and sixth floors offer views of the École Militaire. While sitting by the window in the suite (no. 507), you will be looking directly at *La Tour Eiffel*. If you would rather work, there is a fax and computer plug. Windows are double glazed to shield against the nonstop traffic at this busy intersection, but on hot nights, better have those ear plugs handy or be prepared to swelter behind shut windows.

A large downstairs bar is a good place to go for a relaxing drink, and don't fret over the purple wall covering, green chairs with black accents, and the chrome bar stools . . . they all work to make the room contemporary in an off-beat way. The hotel is minutes from rue Cler, a pedestrian market street where well-dressed, basket-toting locals shop for their vegetables, flowers, meats, cheeses, and fresh morning croissants. Close to the hotel are several excellent restaurants (see *Cheap Eats in Paris*), and the métro is a two-minute walk.

ENGLISH SPOKEN: Yes

FACILITIES AND SERVICES: Bar, direct-dial phone; elevator; hair dryer; minibar; parking per day, 40F outside, 100F underground; radio; TV with international reception; room safe 16F per day; fax and computer outlet in suites

NEAREST TOURIST ATTRACTIONS (LEFT BANK): Eiffel Tower, Champ-de-Mars Park, discount shopping (see Cheap Chic, page 258)

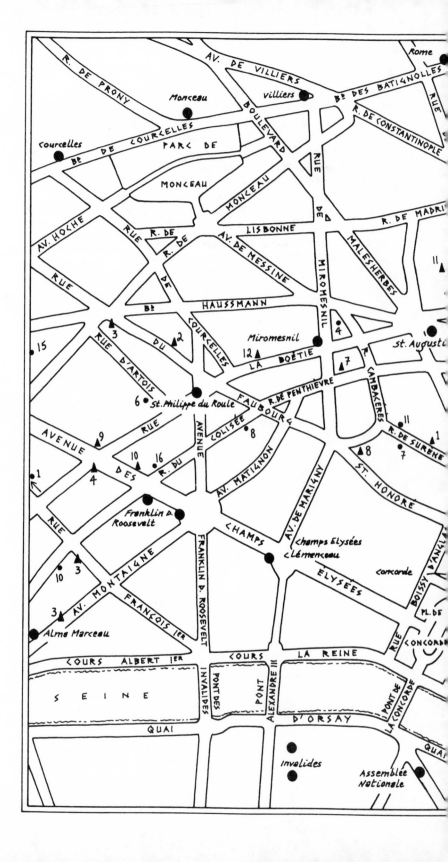

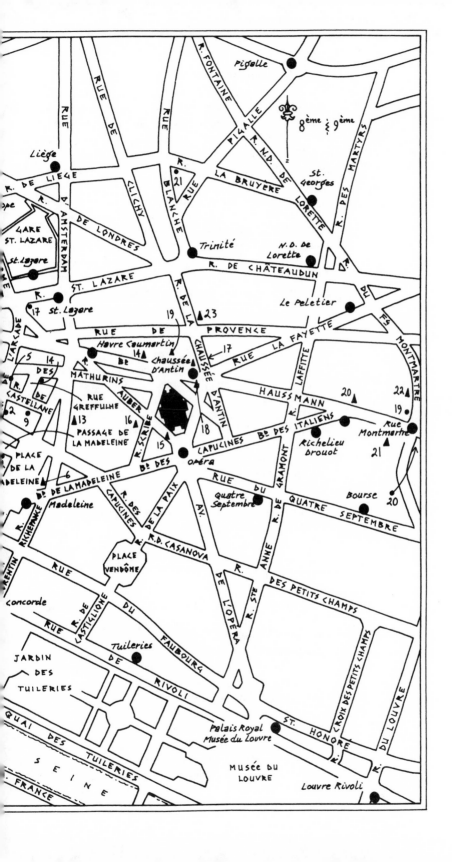

Eighth Arrondissement

RIGHT BANK
American Embassy, Arc de Triomphe, Étoile, Champs-Élysées, elegant shopping on rue du Faubourg St-Honoré, Petit Palais, Grand Palais, place de la Concorde, Madeleine Church

The ten-lane Champs-Élysées, sweeping dramatically from the Arc de Triomphe to the place de la Concorde, is the most famous avenue and parade ground in the world, and it is definitely worth a serious look and stroll. But save the shopping, partying, and eating for less touristy and unspoiled areas. This is the traditional watering hole for show-biz celebrities, glamour girls on the way up and down, tourists in baseball caps, heavy-set men and their young companions, and anyone else who wants to hide behind dark glasses twenty-four hours a day. The flame on the tomb of the unknown soldier burns under the Arc de Triomphe, and the view from the top is inspiring. Twelve avenues radiate from the Arc de Triomphe, forming the world-famous, death-defying traffic circle known as l'Étoile.

The place de la Concorde is the largest square in Paris. Two of its most-famous occupants are the luxurious Hôtel Crillon and the American Embassy. It is thrilling to stand on this strikingly beautiful square and be surrounded by some of the greatest landmarks in the world: the Tuileries Gardens, the Louvre, and the view up the Champs-Élysées to the Arc de Triomphe, across the Seine to the Palais Bourbon, and up the rue Royale to the Madeleine Church. In the evening, when it is all illuminated and the fountains are playing, it is a sight you will never forget.

HOTELS IN THE EIGHTH ARRONDISSEMENT

OTHER OPTIONS

Apartment Rentals

       *Indicates a Big Splurge

(1) GALILEO HÔTEL* ★★★
54, rue Galilée, 75008 (8th)
27 rooms, all with shower or bath and toilet

For years, contented guests with sophisticated, artistic temperaments have flocked to Roland and Elisabeth Buffat's popular hotels on the Île St-Louis: Hôtel de Lutèce and Hôtel des Deux-Îles. Now they have a third option to tempt them, the Galileo. The Buffat's Right Bank hotel re-creates an elegant French townhome in an oasis of calm, only a few steps from the Champs-Élysées.

Like the flowers in the boutique-lobby and garden, guests are beautifully arranged in the elegantly pristine rooms, all fashioned alike in comforting colors of beige, brown, and cocoa. No. 403, a double with two armchairs, a desk, and gray marble bath, has a *Rear Window*–type view onto the life within the nearby apartment building. No. 202, a ground-floor twin with a small sitting area and huge marble bathroom, faces a walled garden. The room jackpot prize is shared by two on the fifth floor (nos. 501 and 502). In addition to being the biggest, their allure comes from their delightful glass-covered, screened verandas with wicker seating that invites year-round usage. Butcher block tables adorn the underground, mirrored dining room, and green plants and posters of familiar Paris landmarks and buildings give it interest.

ENGLISH SPOKEN: Yes

FACILITIES AND SERVICES: Air-conditioning; direct-dial phone; elevator; hair dryer; minibar; radio; TV with international reception; room safe, no charge

NEAREST TOURIST ATTRACTIONS (RIGHT BANK): Champs-Élysées, Arc de Triomphe

TELEPHONE
01-47-20-66-06

FAX
01-47-20-67-17

MÉTRO
George-V, Charles-de-Gaulle-Étoile

CREDIT CARDS
AE, MC, V

RATES
Single 800F, double 950F
Taxe de séjour: 6F extra per person, per day

BREAKFAST
55F extra per person

(2) HÔTEL BEDFORD* ★★★
17, rue de l'Arcade, 75008 (8th)
148 rooms, all with shower or bath and toilet

On last count, I tallied more than eighteen hotels in all price ranges within a three-block radius in this *quartier*. As you can imagine, competition is stiff. The Bedford is an ideal choice for someone looking for a

TELEPHONE
01-44-94-77-77

FAX
01-44-94-77-97

INTERNET
www.123 france.com
MÉTRO
Madeleine, RER-Auber
CREDIT CARDS
AE, MC, V
RATES
Single 810–910F, double 910–980F, triple 1,120F, suite 1,700F; lower off-season rates on request
Taxe de séjour: included
BREAKFAST
70F extra per person

full-service, centrally located hotel that would serve for both business and tourism purposes. The hotel has been stylishly rehabed, rewired, redecorated . . . and repriced. But, sometimes comfort, service, and convenience cost more and are worth it.

The public areas of the hotel are comfortably elegant. Large lounge areas display the owner's valuable art collection, and the restaurant is under a stunning nineteenth-century stained-glass dome. For something less formal, the bar serves light meals throughout the day. Business guests will be able to book one of the four conference rooms for meetings, and later stroll to the Champs-Élysées, the Tuileries, or either Galeries Lafayette or Au Printemps.

Rooms are efficiently done in soft beiges with coordinating fabrics and light wood furnishings. Bathrooms display the latest in fixtures and marble. Suites are great: try no. 423 with two bathrooms and two bedrooms, one with a Murphy bed to allow for more daytime living area. No. 405 has an enormous bathroom with two freestanding sinks, a tub, and a separate enclosed bidet and toilet. This room can be connected with no. 407. The Bedford is listed as a Big Splurge, but in the low season, if you ask, you may be offered much lower rates.

ENGLISH SPOKEN: Yes

FACILITIES AND SERVICES: Air-conditioning in some rooms; bar; direct-dial phones; elevator; some hair dryers; laundry service; meeting rooms; minibar; restaurant; room service; TV with international reception; office safe, no charge; porter

NEAREST TOURIST ATTRACTIONS (RIGHT BANK): Madeleine Church, place de la Concorde, Opéra

(3) HÔTEL CONCORTEL ★★★
19-21, rue Pasquier, 75008 (8th)
46 rooms, all with shower or bath and toilet

TELEPHONE
01-42-65-45-44
FAX
01-42-65-18-33
INTERNET
www.globe-market/
h75008concortel.htm
MÉTRO
Madeleine
CREDIT CARDS
AE, DC, MC, V

For many years, the Concortel has been offering the conveniences and comforts that appeal to many seeking a mid-city location. The hotel consists of two blocks of rooms joined by a courtyard. The color-coordinated bed chambers are well arranged, and most offer the space that travelers desire. The desk staff is exceptional, especially Pierre, who speaks wonderful English and is always ready to help. Lower off-season and corporate rates make this hotel even more attractive.

ENGLISH SPOKEN: Yes

FACILITIES AND SERVICES: Air-conditioning in all rooms; bar; conference room; direct-dial phone; elevator in front building, not in back building (only two floors); hair dryer; laundry service; minibar; radio; TV with international reception; room safe, no charge; porter

NEAREST TOURIST ATTRACTIONS (RIGHT BANK): Place Vendôme, Madeleine Church, place de la Concorde, Opéra, Galeries Lafayette and Au Printemps department stores

RATES
1–2 people 670–900F, triple 1,000F, suite 900–1,000F; ask about special off-season and business rates
Taxe de séjour: included

BREAKFAST
45F extra per person

(4) HÔTEL D'ARGENSON ★★
15, rue d'Argenson, angle 111 boulevard Haussmann, 75008 (8th)
28 rooms, all with shower or bath and toilet

Cheap Sleeping Paris veterans know that the eighth arrondissement is normally Big Splurge territory. Coming to the rescue is this twenty-eight-room, second-floor walk-up, perched above Rene Saint-Ouen, one of the most famous bakeries in Paris. How famous? It was selected to provide all the baguettes to the Élysée Palace, and that is *quite* an honor. Those who are familiar with this part of Paris know that noise is part of the deal, and it won't escape you at this hotel. However, if cost is your guiding light, give this one consideration.

You first enter the small wood-paneled salon with two chairs. Martine, the owner's daughter, is usually behind the desk, along with her black-and-brown cocker spaniel, Flash. Rooms vary from frankly fussy to downright tacky. You may not like the profusion of florals, which in some rooms includes not only the wallpaper, curtains, and bedspread but the ceiling, too. I have trouble with the mustard yellow– and beer brown–colored tiles in the bathrooms and with the plaid towels in others, which fight with all the flowers elsewhere. The hotel is saved because it is cheap, clean, and the rooms are big enough to satisfy almost anyone. Maintenance, performed by Martine's husband, is on top of things. Bottom line: It's a decent Cheap Sleep in Paris, if you can stand the noise.

ENGLISH SPOKEN: Yes

FACILITIES AND SERVICES: Direct-dial phone; elevator; hair dryer at desk; TV on request (35F per day); room safe, no charge

NEAREST TOURIST ATTRACTIONS (RIGHT BANK): Champs Élysées, place de la Concorde, Madeleine Church

TELEPHONE
01-42-65-16-87

FAX
01-47-42-02-06

MÉTRO
St-Augustin, Miromesnil

CREDIT CARDS
MC, V

RATES
Single 310–400F, double 375–435F, triple 500–540F
Taxe de séjour: included

BREAKFAST
Included (served in room), cannot be deducted

(5) HÔTEL DE L'ARCADE* ★★★
9, rue de l'Arcade, 75008 (8th)
41 rooms, all with shower or bath and toilet

TELEPHONE
01-53-30-60-00
FAX
01-40-07-03-07
MÉTRO
Madeleine, RER-Auber
CREDIT CARDS
AE, MC, V
RATES
Single 790–890F, double 970F,
triple 1,175F, duplex 1,170F;
lower off-season rates
Taxe de séjour: included
BREAKFAST
60F extra per person

Good taste is easy to recognize at the Hôtel de l'Arcade, and no wonder when you learn it was decorated by Gerard Gallet, who also did the Orient Express. Thanks to a massive two-year renovation project, the hotel is now one of the smartest three-star addresses in the area. Everything about the hotel is exceptional, and something complimentary can be said about all the soundproofed rooms. The divided lobby, done in celery green and beige, is softened further with fresh flowers and green plants. Wing-back chairs, sofas, and a writing desk are complemented by a decorative stone fireplace. The crowning touch is a beautiful green wrought-iron chandelier with twelve candle lights entwined with white metal flowers. Two banquettes, black-and-white etchings, and windows shaded by white linen café curtains set the stage for the streetside breakfast room. The bedrooms are all in beige with wood built-ins, good closets, and appealing bathrooms. No. 602 is a good choice for two. The corner location with three large windows, two closets, armchair seating, and a lovely, light bathroom make it an inviting choice for a longer stay. No. 605 is a two-story duplex with double televisions and telephones and an upstairs king-size bedroom with a small balcony. Lower summer rates make this hotel an even more exceptional value.

ENGLISH SPOKEN: Yes

FACILITIES AND SERVICES: Air-conditioning in all rooms; direct-dial phone; elevator; hair dryer; minibar; TV with international reception; room safe, no charge

NEAREST TOURIST ATTRACTIONS (RIGHT BANK): Madeleine Church, place de la Concorde, Opéra, shopping on rue St-Honoré or at Au Printemps and Galeries Lafayette department stores

(6) HÔTEL DES CHAMPS-ÉLYSÉES ★★
2, rue d'Artois, 75008 (8th)
36 rooms, all with shower or bath and toilet

TELEPHONE
01-43-59-11-42
FAX
01-45-61-00-61
MÉTRO
St-Philippe-du-Roule

During World War II, this hotel housed Dutch and American soldiers. It now houses savvy Cheap Sleepers in Paris who want a moderate, reliable nest near the Champs-Élysées and the Arc de Triomphe.

Thirty-six attractive rooms and modern baths have coordinated colors, good space usage, and most importantly, provide many three-star amenities for two-star prices. Adding to the hotel's popularity is the warm-toned sitting room with its leather chairs and fresh flowers, a downstairs stone-walled dining room with a lovely old clock, and the hospitality of the staff.

ENGLISH SPOKEN: Yes

FACILITIES AND SERVICES: Bar; direct-dial phone; elevator; hair dryer; minibar; TV with international reception; room safe, no charge

NEAREST TOURIST ATTRACTIONS (RIGHT BANK): Champs-Élysées, Arc de Triomphe, shopping along rue Faubourg du St-Honoré

CREDIT CARDS
MC, V

RATES
1–2 persons 480–550F; extra bed 80F
Taxe de séjour: 5F extra per person, per day

BREAKFAST
45F extra per person

(7) HÔTEL DU MINISTÈRE ★★★
31, rue de Surène, 75008 (8th)
28 rooms, all with shower or bath and toilet

When I'm asked to provide the names of good hotels on the Right Bank near the American Embassy and the Champs-Élysées, the Hôtel du Ministère makes my list. The well-tended rooms, the reasonable prices, and hospitable atmosphere combine to make this an excellent choice, one that is warmly recommended by all who stay here.

Now into its fourth generation of running the hotel, the Blanc family continues to provide their guests with every comfort and convenience. Someone from the family is always available, so you can expect during the course of your stay to meet both M. and Mme. Blanc, and probably their young son and three daughters.

The rooms have been individually decorated by several members of the family, and they combine oak beams, attractive Italian lights, family furnishings, generous closets, beautiful baths, and coordinated colors. A sentimental favorite for me is no. 3 because the furniture M. Blanc's grandmother received as a bride is used, and it is still in mint condition. His father painted the picture in this room, as well as those that hang in many other bedrooms. No. 2 is also nice, thanks its oo-la-la bathtub. Please note there are four rooms like this one. Fortunately, there is only one like no. 18, a tiny, stuffy top-floor room with a dismal bathroom.

ENGLISH SPOKEN: Yes

FACILITIES AND SERVICES: Direct-dial phone; elevator; hair dryer; minibar; TV with international reception; office safe, no charge

TELEPHONE
01-42-66-21-43

FAX
01-42-66-96-04

E-MAIL
hotel-ministere@argia.fr

INTERNET
www.argia.fr/hotel-ministere

MÉTRO
Madeleine, Miromesnil

CREDIT CARDS
AE, MC, V

RATES
Single 410–550F, double 550–610F; extra bed 150F
Taxe de séjour: 6F extra per person, per night

BREAKFAST
35F extra per person

NEAREST TOURIST ATTRACTIONS (RIGHT BANK): Champs-Élysées, place de la Concorde, Madeleine, shopping on rue St-Honoré, Tuileries

(8) HÔTEL ÉLYSÉES MERMOZ* ★★★
30, rue Jean Mermoz, 75008 (8th)
26 rooms, all with shower or bath and toilet

TELEPHONE
01-42-25-75-30; toll-free from U.S. and Canada, 800-44-UTELL

FAX
01-45-62-87-10

INTERNET
www.globe-market.com/h75008elyseesmermoz.htm

MÉTRO
Franklin-D-Roosevelt

CREDIT CARDS
AE, MC, V

RATES
Single 750–815F, double 815–925F, suite 1,250F
Taxe de séjour: included

BREAKFAST
50F extra per person

The focus of the hotel is a glass-roofed garden room flanked by a dining room done in sunny yellows. To one side is a lobby and sitting area, where the garden theme is carried out further by the use of paver tiled floors and lilac upholstery on wicker settees and chairs.

The twenty-one rooms and five suites offer up-to-the-minute amenities every traveler appreciates, and the imaginative use of colors, prints, and furnishings creates visually appealing surroundings in all. No. 204 is my choice for the lone guest. The room is a blend of yellow and blue with a clever fabric backdrop behind the bed. Built-ins allow for more room movement. The *á la mode* bathroom features a light blue enamel sink, mirrored shower, and heated towel racks along with such extras as a drying line and magnifying mirror. For larger parties, or longer stays, book a suite. No. 401 has two rooms divided by a pocket door. The sitting area has a sofa bed; the other room offers twin beds with designer-inspired coverlets. Rich ribbonlike fabric wall coverings and gold watermarked paper give it a slight Oriental cast. The bath is equipped with all the perks, including a mirrored tub and separate shower.

ENGLISH SPOKEN: Yes

FACILITIES AND SERVICES: Air-conditioning in all rooms; direct-dial phone; elevator; hair dryer; laundry service; minibar; TV with international reception; room safe, no charge; one room for the handicapped

NEAREST TOURIST ATTRACTIONS (RIGHT BANK): Champs-Élysées, shopping on rue St-Honoré

(9) HÔTEL FOLKESTONE* ★★★
49, rue Castellane, 75008 (8th)
49 rooms, all with shower or bath and toilet

TELEPHONE
01-42-65-73-09; toll-free from the U.S. and Canada, 800-528-1234

FAX
01-42-65-64-09

The Folkestone is part of the Best Western chain in Paris, and it's definitely one of the better choices in an area where prices are usually over the top. A stay here puts you in the middle of the business, high fashion, and entertainment precinct of the city.

The contemporary bedrooms are decorated in peach, pale gray, and cream, with polished cotton fabrics on the beds and hanging at the windows. The smallest doubles, at the back, have miniature bathrooms and no view. The bright, cheerful rooms on the street have double windowpanes to buffer noise and good general space.

Breakfast is very special here. Every morning, Elvira, one of the housekeepers whose hobby is cooking, rises at dawn to prepare luscious *tartes,* cakes, quiches, and a fresh fruit compote. These are placed on the buffet breakfast table along with yogurt, boiled eggs, hot brioches, *pain au chocolate,* croissants, sweet butter, and assorted jams. English tea, American or French coffee, and hot chocolate are also served. For my money, this sumptuous meal is reason enough to stay at the Folkestone.

ENGLISH SPOKEN: Yes

FACILITIES AND SERVICES: Air-conditioning in all rooms; bar; direct-dial phone; elevator; hair dryer; minibar; radio; TV with international reception; room safe, 30F per stay

NEAREST TOURIST ATTRACTIONS (RIGHT BANK): Madeleine Church, Opéra, shopping on rue Faubourg du St-Honoré and at Au Printemps and Galeries Lafayette department stores

MÉTRO
Madeleine, Havre-Caumartin

CREDIT CARDS
AE, DC, MC, V

RATES
Single 750F, double 850F, triple 950F, quad 1,080F; extra bed 150F
Taxe de séjour: included

BREAKFAST
50F extra per person

(10)   HÔTEL FRANKLIN ROOSEVELT* ★★★
18, rue Clément-Marot, 75008 (8th)
45 rooms, all with shower or bath and toilet

For a fail-safe, upmarket selection near the famous fashion designer shops and fast-track life around the Champs-Élysées, the Franklin Roosevelt is a popular destination.

Mirrored columns give an open feel as you enter the lobby, which is enhanced by the owner's abstract art collection. Fresh flowers and colorful blooming potted plants are everywhere, including all the rooms, and add greatly to the warmth and overall appeal of the hotel, especially in the breakfast room, which is accented with coral seat covers and a floral mural. Light, wide halls lead to large bedrooms and suites, many of which have hand-painted murals setting the theme of the room. No. 59 is Japanese. This motif is reflected in the straw matting covering the closet doors and behind the bed and in the prints over the desk and bed. Sunshine from the tiny top-floor balcony and a huge bathroom with its own

TELEPHONE
01-47-23-61-66; toll-free from the U.S. and Canada, 800-44-UTELL

FAX
01-47-20-44-30

MÉTRO
Franklin-D-Roosevelt

CREDIT CARDS
MC, V

RATES
Single 895F, double 895–945F, suite 1,500F; children under 12 free; lower off-season and corporate rates
Taxe de séjour: included

BREAKFAST
75F extra per person

window complete the picture. Martinique is the mural in no. 23, and in no. 21, a calm, quiet colonial sets the mood.

ENGLISH SPOKEN: Yes

FACILITIES AND SERVICES: Bar; direct-dial phone; elevator; hair dryer; minibar; TV with international reception; room safe, no charge

NEAREST TOURIST ATTRACTIONS (RIGHT BANK): Champs-Élysées, shopping

(11)   HÔTEL LA SANGUINE ★★
6, rue de Surène, 75008 (8th)
31 rooms, all with shower or bath and toilet

TELEPHONE
01-42-65-71-61

FAX
01-42-66-96-77

MÉTRO
Madeleine

CREDIT CARDS
AE, MC, V

RATES
Single 440–450F, double 540F; extra bed 75F
Taxe de séjour: included

BREAKFAST
40F extra per person

The upstairs lobby and reception room promise an intimacy in a rather impersonal business district between the Madeleine Church and the Champs-Élysées. Rooms deliver three- and four-star comforts, such as fax plugs, room safes in most, and telephones in all the bathrooms. Unfortunately, there is no elevator for the four floors, and back views are nothing short of grim. These are *not* reasons to ignore this good-value hotel. The neighborhood is tomblike at night and on the weekends when offices are closed, so an uninterrupted night's rest is assured from a front-facing room. All the rooms have air-conditioning, pleasing colors and fabrics, and most of the showers have curtains. The continental breakfast includes orange juice and homemade croissants along with coffee, tea, or rich hot chocolate. The warm welcome and friendliness extended by assistant manager Claudine Chalande is the reason many return on a regular basis. During the week, when the hotel caters to businesspeople, it is generally full, but when they go home for the weekend, last-minute reservations are possible.

ENGLISH SPOKEN: Yes

FACILITIES AND SERVICES: Air-conditioning in all rooms; direct-dial phone (also in the bathroom); no elevator; hair dryer; minibar; TV with international reception; safe in double rooms, no charge; fax plugs

NEAREST TOURIST ATTRACTIONS (RIGHT BANK): Madeleine Church, shopping on rue St-Honoré, place de la Concorde, Tuileries, Louvre

(12) HÔTEL LIDO* ★★★
4, passage de la Madeleine, 75008 (8th)
32 rooms, all with shower or bath and toilet

For the ultimate center-city location, close to almost everything by foot or métro, the Lido is a stellar choice. Window boxes filled with bright red geraniums set the hotel apart on the little *passage* off place de la Madeleine. An eighteenth-century tapestry dominates the reception and lobby. Exposed beams, magnificent, hand-rubbed antiques, a miniature garden, and masses of fresh flowers complete the charming beginning. Even the smallest, red-linen-lined rooms have enough living space. Minibars are hidden in heavy wooden furniture, and delicate lace spreads cover the large beds. Personalized service by the cordial staff and such extras as free parking in front of the hotel, full-length mirrors, sewing kits, and scented soaps make the Lido one of the top selections in the eighth arrondissement.

NOTE: Also under the same family ownership and management is the Hôtel Left Bank Saint-Germain; see page 112.

ENGLISH SPOKEN: Yes

FACILITIES AND SERVICES: Air-conditioning in all rooms; bar; direct-dial phone; elevator; hair dryer; minibar; free parking in front of the hotel; TV with international reception; room safe, 50F per stay

NEAREST TOURIST ATTRACTIONS (RIGHT BANK): Madeleine Church, Fauchon, place de la Concorde, Tuileries, Louvre, Palais-Royal, Opéra, shopping at Galeries Lafayette and Au Printemps department stores, Champs-Élysées

TELEPHONE
01-42-66-27-37; toll-free from the U.S. and Canada, 800-528-1234

FAX
01-42-66-61-23

MÉTRO
Madeleine

CREDIT CARDS
AE, DC, MC, V

RATES
Single 875F, double 995F, triple 1,100F; extra bed 100F; lower rates in July, Aug, and Dec
Taxe de séjour: 6F extra per person, per day

BREAKFAST
Included, cannot be deducted

(13) HÔTEL MARIGNY ★★
11, rue de l'Arcade, 75008 (8th)
32 rooms, 26 with shower or bath and toilet

Only a few hundreds yards from the Madeleine Church and a bracing ten minutes from Gare St-Lazare and place de la Concorde is this reliable Cheap Sleep owned and aptly run by the Maugars family. The neighborhood is dull as dishwater after 7 P.M. and on weekends, but the prices are right and the métro is close. The spotless rooms are reached by the same antique birdcage elevator that Marcel Proust used when he lived and wrote in the hotel. Most of the rooms are sunny, several connect, and those on the sixth floor, which have double beds only, have balconies where you can step outside and enjoy the view. Renovated rooms are naturally preferred,

TELEPHONE
01-42-66-42-71

FAX
01-47-42-06-76

INTERNET
www.globe-market.com/h75008marigny.htm

MÉTRO
Madeleine, Havre-Caumartin

CREDIT CARDS
MC, V

especially no. 61, a double with a shower. The room is simply decorated in textured white wallpaper, with a matching peach floral fabric on both the bed and curtains. Back rooms are equal in amenities and will be quiet, but you may find yourself in a room with a frosted window, affording absolutely no outlook.

ENGLISH SPOKEN: Yes

FACILITIES AND SERVICES: Direct-dial phone; elevator; minibar; TV; office safe, no charge

NEAREST TOURIST ATTRACTIONS (RIGHT BANK): Madeleine Church, Tuileries, place Vendôme, place de la Concorde, Opéra, shopping at Galeries Lafayette and Au Printemps department stores

(14) HÔTEL QUEEN MARY* ★★★
9, rue Greffulhe, 75008 (8th)
36 rooms, all with shower or bath and toilet

Visitors to Paris who desire a distinguished hotel in the center of the city between the old Opéra and the Madeleine Church will have a hard time doing better than the Queen Mary. The hotel's Scottish owner, David Byrne (who also owns Hôtel du Bois in the sixteenth, see page 202), has spared no effort to improve the creature comforts offered. As a result, everytime I am here, I am impressed all over again.

Beautiful ceiling details and thick moldings soften the rooms, which are uniformly done with English carpeting, rich fabrics, and built-in furniture in pale wood tones. Luxury accessories such as air-conditioning, double-glazed windows, twenty-channel TV, FM radio and alarm clock, two telephones, and beautiful bathrooms add to the appreciation of the rooms. Rooms on the second and fifth floors have balconies. Those looking for extra-special accommodations will do well in the sunny, top-floor, beamed suite with its rooftop view, two televisions, and large gray-tile bathroom with its own window. Breakfast is served in a yellow-and-green basement dining room, where you have your choice of a regular continental repast, one for slimmers, or a no-calorie-barred buffet that includes bacon, eggs, and corn flakes, along with your croissants, butter, and jam.

Many thoughtful touches make the difference here: a decanter of sherry in each room; happy hour from 6 to 8 P.M. in the friendly blue-and-white bar off the entry; afternoon tea served in the salon; room service from nine international restaurants; and drinks served in a tiny fountain garden when weather permits.

Shoppers take serious note: You are in ultra-chic Fashion Country here. The names Lanvin, Yves St-Laurent, Jean-Paul Gaultier, and many more grace boutiques no more than a ten- to fifteen-minute browse from the hotel door.

ENGLISH SPOKEN: Yes

FACILITIES AND SERVICES: Air-conditioning; bar; direct-dial phone; elevator; hair dryer; minibar; room service; radio; TV with international reception; room safe, 10F per day; afternoon tea; happy hour; trouser press; decanter of sherry in room

NEAREST TOURIST ATTRACTIONS (RIGHT BANK): Madeleine Church, Opéra, designer shopping, and shopping at Galeries Lafayette and Au Printemps department stores

(15) HÔTEL RÉSIDENCE LORD BYRON ★★★
5, rue Chateaubriand, 75008 (8th)
30 rooms, all with shower or bath and toilet

The Résidence Lord Byron provides lodgings for half the price of many other hotels in this prestigious, expensive *quartier*. It is on a quiet, winding street less than five minutes from the bright lights and excitement of the Champs-Élysées, and it is so peaceful that it is listed in the *European Guide to Silent Hotels*. Although it has an overall dated and faded feel, the colors are pleasing and the fabrics are coordinated. Most of the larger-than-average rooms overlook a garden courtyard where morning coffee and afternoon tea is served in the summer. The hotel was formerly a *hôtel particulière* (privately owned townhome) and is furnished with a wide range of lovingly worn and near-antiques.

ENGLISH SPOKEN: Yes

FACILITIES AND SERVICES: Direct-dial phone; elevator; hair dryer; minibar; TV; room safe, no charge

NEAREST TOURIST ATTRACTIONS (RIGHT BANK): Arc de Triomphe, Champs-Élysées

TELEPHONE
01-43-59-89-98

FAX
01-42-89-46-04

MÉTRO
George-V

CREDIT CARDS
AE, MC, V

RATES
Single 660–810F, double 670–920F, suite 1,270F; extra bed 150F; children under 12 free
Taxe de séjour: included

BREAKFAST
50F extra per person

(16) ROYAL HÔTEL CHAMPS-ÉLYSÉES ★★
7, rue du Colisee, 75008 (8th)
34 rooms, all with shower or bath and toilet

Surprise! A modest berth only steps from the Champs-Élysées can be yours. In the bargain, you will enjoy two-star decorative touches, such as a tartan blanket tossed

TELEPHONE
01-43-59-32-49

FAX
01-43-59-06-19
MÉTRO
St-Philippe-du-Roule,
Franklin-D-Roosevelt
CREDIT CARDS
AE, MC, V
RATES
Single 500F, double 550–580F,
triple 650F, quad 800F; extra
bed 150F; lower off-season rates
Taxe de séjour: 5F extra per
person, per day
BREAKFAST
30F extra per person

over the chair behind reception, orange wall treatments, a ding or two, and hallways in red floral-print carpeting. Bathrooms have been added and amenities are lean, but there is nothing wrong with no. 5, a single or miniature double. Here you step up to the bathroom, but you will have two chairs in your room and a small terrace facing the street. You get what you pay for, and here that will be a room that is clean, convenient, and a Cheap Sleep in Paris with no apologies.

ENGLISH SPOKEN: Yes

FACILITIES AND SERVICES: Direct-dial phone; elevator; hair dryer; TV; office safe, no charge; room safe, 15F per day

NEAREST TOURIST ATTRACTIONS (RIGHT BANK): Champs-Élysées; Madeleine Church; place de la Concorde

(17) TIMHÔTEL ST-LAZARE ★★
113, rue Saint-Lazare, 75008 (8th)
83 rooms, all with bath or shower and toilet

TELEPHONE
01-43-87-53-53
FAX
01-43-87-66-25
MÉTRO
Saint-Lazare
CREDIT CARDS
AE, DC, MC, V
RATES
1–2 people 550F, triple 690F,
quad 830F
Taxe de séjour: included
BREAKFAST
55F extra per person

This Timhôtel is included for those who feel they must stay near Gare St-Lazare railroad station. Even though it is one of the better in the chain, unless you get a balcony room on the inner courtyard, you will listen to incessant traffic noise twenty-four hours a day. For more information on these hotels, please see page 52.

ENGLISH SPOKEN: Yes

FACILITIES AND SERVICES: Conference room; direct-dial phone; elevator; hair dryer; TV with international reception; office safe, no charge

NEAREST TOURIST ATTRACTIONS (RIGHT BANK): Grand boulevards, shopping at Galeries Lafayette and Au Printemps department stores, Opéra

Ninth Arrondissement

(See map pages 148–149.)

In the southern part of this arrondissement is the beautiful old Opéra with its famous Chagall ceiling, many large banks, and shopping at Galeries Lafayette and Au Printemps. At the northern end is the infamous Pigalle, a sleazy twenty-four-hour neighborhood lined with peep shows, bordellos, "ladies of the night"—anything, generally, that constitutes the seamy side of life. Avoid the métro stops Anvers, Pigalle, and Barbès-Rochechouart after dark.

RIGHT BANK
Grands magazins (Au Printemps and Galeries Lafayette), Opéra, Pigalle

HOTELS IN THE NINTH ARRONDISSEMENT

OTHER OPTIONS
Private Hostel

(19) HÔTEL CHOPIN ★★
10, boulevard Montmartre (46, passage Jouffroy), 75009 (9th)
36 rooms, all with shower or bath and toilet

The Parisians were mall shoppers long before we were. At the turn of the century, Paris had enclosed, skylighted shopping walkways called *passages*. Today these lovely covered areas house a variety of restaurants and shops selling everything from art and antiques to dubious-quality clothing. The Hôtel Chopin is a listed historical monument occupying a unique location at the end of the *passage* Jouffroy. The hotel was opened the same year as the *passage* (1846), so be prepared for some things that may not be totally *au courant*. Fortunately, the hotel has been redone, and now the rooms have bathrooms, the hallways are uniform, and the rooms, which are all quiet, have better than average two-star decorating. Best rooms are on the top floors because they have skyline views and more natural light, but in no. 409, the tub is under a sloping eave making upright shower taking a bit tricky for taller guests.

ENGLISH SPOKEN: Yes

TELEPHONE
01-47-70-58-10

FAX
01-42-47-00-70

MÉTRO
Richelieu Drouot, Montmartre

CREDIT CARDS
AE, MC, V

RATES
Single 430F, double 470–510F, triple 585F
Taxe de séjour: included

BREAKFAST
40F extra per person

FACILITIES AND SERVICES: Direct-dial phone; elevator (but some stairs); TV; office safe, 20F per day, 90F per week.

NEAREST TOURIST ATTRACTIONS (RIGHT BANK): Shopping at Galeries Lafayette and Au Printemps, Opéra

(20) HÔTEL DES ARTS ★★
7, Cité Bergère, entrance at No. 6, rue de Faubourg Montmartre, 75009 (9th)
26 rooms, all with shower or bath and toilet

TELEPHONE
01-42-46-73-30

FAX
01-48-00-94-42

MÉTRO
Rue Montmartre (exit Faubourg Montmartre)

CREDIT CARDS
AE, DC, MC, V

RATES
Single 355–375F, double 375–390F, triple 515F
Taxe de séjour: 5F extra per person, per day

BREAKFAST
30F extra per person

The Cité Bergère is a *passage* in central Paris that has eight hotels offering more than four hundred rooms to weary travelers. I have seen them all, and M. and Mme. Bernard's Hôtel des Arts, filled with plants and flowers, is the best of the bunch by far. While it is nothing fancy, the rooms are spotless and have price tags that appeal to couples on budgets who are happy in a busy city location. The rooms all display a wondrous mixture of period furniture, including some family pieces, such as an old dressing table on the fifth floor that belonged to the owner's *grand'mère.* Flocked and flowered wallpaper, chrome, plastic, fringe, ruffles, and chenille are also used with abandon. There are two small knotty-pine-paneled rooms on the top floor that have mansard windows and are favorites with younger guests. No. 1 is a ground-floor double nicely done in florals with a plain rug, antique bedside tables, and a spotless bathroom that has a stall shower.

A lifetime collection of posters lines the stairs and hallways and now almost reaches the top floor. Postcards and photos sent to the Bernards by their guests cover the top of the reception desk, where Babar, a colorful thirty-year-old parrot, sits in the winter. In the summer he whistles his happy tune in the pretty blue-and-white dining room. While hardly a tourist mecca, the location is within walking distance of the Folies Bergère and a métro stop or two away from Montmartre. Motorists take note: the hotel has four *free* parking spaces. In any part of Paris, that convenience and savings alone are worth double the price of the room.

ENGLISH SPOKEN: Yes

FACILITIES AND SERVICES: Direct-dial phone; elevator; hair dryer; TV; office safe, no charge; four free parking spaces

Folies Bergère, Opéra, shopping at Galeries Lafayette and Au Printemps department stores

(21) HÔTEL MONTEROSA ★★★
30, rue Bruyère, 75009 (9th)
36 rooms, all with shower or bath and toilet

Anyway you look at it, staying in and around Pigalle is a tough call. You either settle for a dump with questionable guests and nonstop street noise or you wind up in a tour-bus hotel filled with revelers in from the sticks for a few laughs. The Hôtel Monterosa, located only a métro stop away from all the earthy activities associated with Pigalle, offers renewed hope to guests who are interested in this part of Paris.

The hotel is a clean, well-priced three-star that packs all the basic comforts and then some. It has been owned for almost twenty years by the Morgans, who have maintained it well. I like the little garden to one side of the lobby area and the small breakfast room lined with paintings of Paris. On the fourth floor, your room might have a balcony, but it will be smaller; on the fifth, you sacrifice the balcony and get beams and more space. On the fifth floor, in no. 501, you can see the date of the construction of the hotel carved on a beam and the sign of the person who built it. All in all, it is a nice hotel in a small enclave that is light-years away in spirit from the seamier neighborhood just next to it.

ENGLISH SPOKEN: Yes

FACILITIES AND SERVICES: Bar; direct-dial phone; elevator; hair dryer; minibar; TV with international reception; room safe, no charge; trouser press

NEAREST TOURIST ATTRACTIONS (RIGHT BANK): Pigalle

TELEPHONE
01-48-74-87-90

FAX
01-42-81-01-12

MÉTRO
St-Georges, Trinite

CREDIT CARDS
AE, DC, MC, V

RATES
Single 400–500F, double 460–600F, triple 600F; lower off-season rates
Taxe de séjour: included

BREAKFAST
35F extra per person

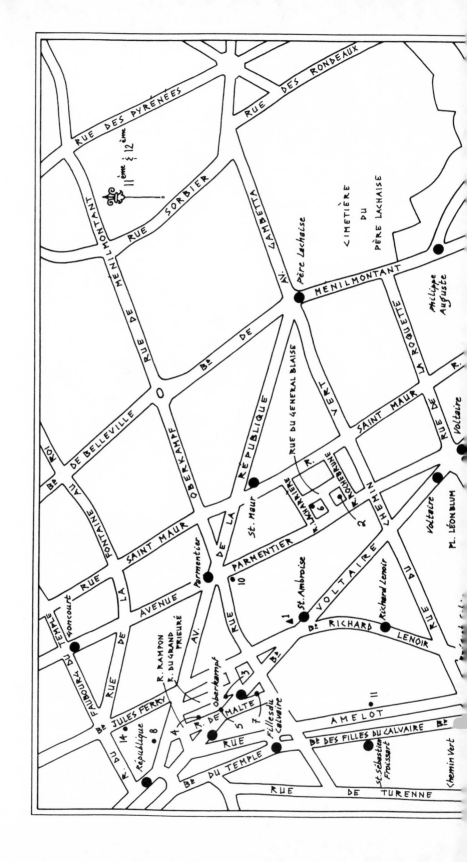

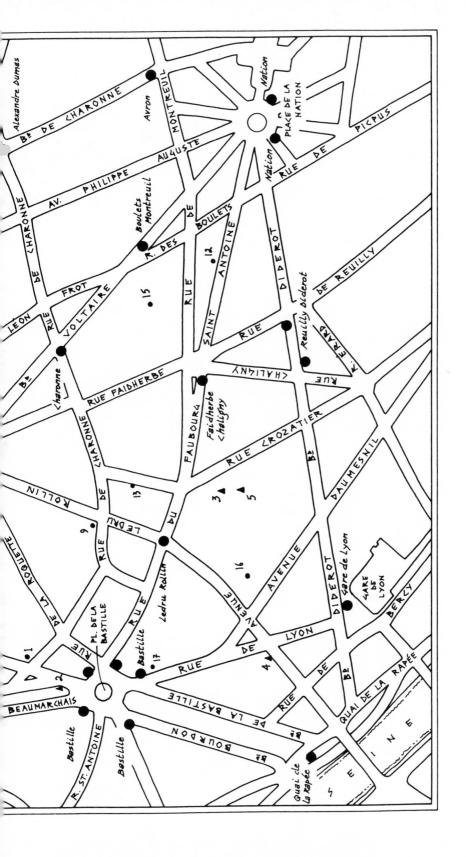

Eleventh Arrondissement

The eleventh and twelfth arrondissements are known as the *quartiers populaires* because they are traditional working-class neighborhoods where many foreigners settle. These are not hotbeds of tourist activity, but they do provide interesting glimpses of both the blue-collar Parisian way of life and the new-wave artists. The neighborhoods around the Bastille and the futuristic new Opéra are the city's new bohemia, full of art galleries, lofts, cafés, night clubs, and boutiques featuring the apparel craze of the moment. This area hums night and day and is definitely the "in" place to see and be seen for anyone who likes to walk on the wild side.

HOTELS IN THE ELEVENTH ARRONDISSEMENT

OTHER OPTIONS
Residence Hotels

Student Accommodations

(1) DAVAL HÔTEL ★★
21, rue Daval, 75011 (11th)
23 rooms, all with shower or bath and toilet

TELEPHONE
01-47-00-51-23
FAX
01-40-21-80-26

M. Gonod and his German shepherd dog, Malko, run this Bastille budget hotel with good sense, good humor, and kindness. Valued mainly for its "in" location and price, the Daval Hôtel occupies a platinum position in the white-hot Bastille area, only a short promenade from the new Opéra and all the cafés, bars, boutiques, and galleries that characterize this increasingly popular *quartier*. The rooms are done in the same minimalistic style: open closets, compact baths, built-in beds and side tables, and no chairs or stools for seating. A few dings and nicks remind you that the rooms have been well lived-in. Mercifully, the walls are thick enough to buffer the neighbor's snoring or late-night television viewing.

ENGLISH SPOKEN: Yes

FACILITIES AND SERVICES Direct-dial phone; elevator; hair dryer; TV with international reception; room safe, no charge

NEAREST TOURIST ATTRACTIONS (RIGHT BANK): Bastille area, new Opéra

MÉTRO
Bastille, Bréguet-Sabin

CREDIT CARDS
AE, MC, V

RATES
Single 320–340F, double 390–490F, triple 490F, quad 560F
Taxe de séjour: 5F extra per person, per day

BREAKFAST
45F extra per person

(2) GARDEN HÔTEL ★★
1, rue du Général-Blaise (facing Square Parmentier), 75011 (11th)
42 rooms, all with shower or bath and toilet

Need a neat, clean, safe, and comfortable Cheap Sleep in Paris in the eleventh arrondissement? If so, reserve one of Mme. Adams's spotless forty-two rooms, many of which face the Square Parmentier, a local, neighborhood gathering place that defines this corner of Paris. The hotel rooms are appointed with light pine built-ins, simple floral wallpaper, and lots of chenille. Color matches do not jar the senses and bathrooms are functional. For breakfast, you can join other guests at a long communal table in a breakfast room accented with a poster of Dutch tulips.

ENGLISH SPOKEN: Limited

FACILITIES AND SERVICES Direct-dial phone; elevator; hair dryer available; TV; office safe, no charge

NEAREST TOURIST ATTRACTIONS (RIGHT BANK): Bastille area, new Opéra

TELEPHONE
01-47-00-57-93

FAX
01-47-00-45-29

MÉTRO
St-Ambroise, St-Maur

CREDIT CARDS
AE, MC, V

RATES
Single 320F, double 370F, triple 470F; extra bed 100F
Taxe de séjour: 5F extra per person, per day

BREAKFAST
35F extra per person

(3) HÔTEL DU GRAND-PRIEURÉ ★★
20, rue du Grand-Prieuré, 75011 (11th)
32 rooms, all with shower or bath and toilet

When people ask for a hotel near place de la République, I now have an answer: the Hôtel du Grand-Prieuré. However, when it came time to decorate, someone had great fun at the fake flower *marché* because plastic blooms are everywhere: outside in window boxes, inside in pots and bouquets, wrapped around standing

TELEPHONE
01-47-00-74-14

FAX
01-49-23-06-64

MÉTRO
République, Oberkampf

CREDIT CARDS
AE, MC, V

RATES
Single 300F, double 310–350F,
triple 380F; extra bed 100F
Taxe de séjour: 5F extra per
person, per day

BREAKFAST
35F extra per person

trees, stuffed in an atrium. Fake floral displays aside, the hotel has merit and value. Each floor sports a different color, and all thirty-two rooms and adjoining baths are acceptable and *très propre*. No. 501, a pink location on the top floor, is a good selection because it has sun, more space, and a bathroom with a bidet, which is hard to find these days in modest two-star hotels. On the same floor, no. 502 has linen-covered walls, a balcony, nice desk, and the toilet apart from the bathroom. Bright red doors greet guests staying in no. 604. A drawback for some might be the low-lying barrel seats designed for supple youngsters, which comprise the lobby seating possibilities. A utilitarian dining room, brightened by red bentwood bistro chairs placed around white square tables, is where they serve a reasonably priced continental breakfast.

ENGLISH SPOKEN: Limited

FACILITIES AND SERVICES Direct-dial phone; elevator; hair dryer; minibar; radio; TV; office safe, no charge

NEAREST TOURIST ATTRACTIONS (RIGHT BANK): None; must use public transportation

(4) HÔTEL NOTRE-DAME ★★
51, rue de Malte, 75011 (11th)
48 rooms, 31 with shower or bath and toilet

TELEPHONE
01-47-00-78-76

FAX
01-43-55-32-31

MÉTRO
Place de la République

CREDIT CARDS
MC, V

RATES
Single 200–350F, double 300–
390F, triple 420–450F;
shower 20F
Taxe de séjour: 5F extra per
person, per day

BREAKFAST
35F extra per person

For those who want to spend time exploring Paris and require only a comfortable bed in a decent hotel close to transportation, this family-run hotel should fill the bill. The working-class neighborhood is made up of shops that supply residents with life's necessities, but it holds little to capture most tourists' attention. However, the place de la République, with a métro station, a taxi stand, and several bus routes crossing it, is only a five-minute walk from the hotel door.

A gray-blue interior extends from the reception on one side to the breakfast room, which doubles as a TV lounge and waiting room. It is simple and a bit sterile, but a clean beginning. All rooms are not created equal and anything that has not been renovated should be avoided. My choices include no. 17, a twin with a built-in open closet, lots of shelf space, and a bathroom with a half tub and a wide sink surface. No. 43 is a double or single (better) with a sunny rooftop view, and no. 45 in soft yellow has a matching fabrics on the bedspread, curtains, and on a backdrop behind the bed.

ENGLISH SPOKEN: Yes

FACILITIES AND SERVICES Direct-dial phone; elevator; TV in two- or three-person rooms with shower and toilet; office safe, no charge

NEAREST TOURIST ATTRACTIONS (RIGHT BANK): Not much, must use public transportation

(5) HÔTEL RÉSIDENCE ALHAMBRA ★★
11 bis & 13, rue de Malte, 75011 (11th)
58 rooms, all with shower or bath and toilet

Here is a textbook example of getting what you pay for. Out of the way? Yes, more than a New York minute to get to what's really happening. Close to the métro? Yes, five major lines serve place de la République. Cheap? Absolutely, even more so if you mention you read about them in *Cheap Sleeps in Paris*—they will provide a free TV set in your room if you do.

The hotel is better than the neighborhood suggests. Automatic doors lead from the street into the leather-clad lobby. Blue or orange colors, open closets, no drawers, a built-in desk, and one chair sum up the rooms. Plumbing is of recent vintage. Eight of the rooms overlook what has to be the prettiest hotel garden on the Right Bank—at least in an out-of-the-way two-star. If you are lucky and secure one of these prime spots, you will overlook rose bushes, seasonal flowers, and trees, all lovingly tended by the owner's sister. Tables and chairs are set outside in the summer, making it an especially nice place to have your morning croissant.

ENGLISH SPOKEN: Yes

FACILITIES AND SERVICES Direct-dial phone; TV in twenty-five rooms, 20F extra per day (free if you mention this book); safe in office, no charge

NEAREST TOURIST ATTRACTIONS (RIGHT BANK): None; must use public transportation

TELEPHONE
01-47-00-35-52

FAX
01-43-57-98-75

MÉTRO
Oberkampf, République

CREDIT CARDS
MC, V

RATES
Single 300–330F, double 320–390F, triple 450–550F
Taxe de séjour: 5F extra per day, per person

BREAKFAST
35F extra per person

(6) HÔTEL RHETIA ★
3, rue du Général Blaise (near avenue Parmentier), 75011 (11th)
24 rooms, 16 with shower or bath and toilet

Keep the prices cheap enough and people will come back again and again, and they do—from Sweden, Belgium, Singapore, Australia, England, the United States, and Canada. As one Sydney, Australia, guest put it, "It is neat, clean, tidy, homey . . . all you need." I agree. Not all the rooms have private bathrooms, but sixteen come with a television. Most are minimally furnished in the

TELEPHONE
01-47-00-47-18

FAX
01-42-61-23-17

MÉTRO
St-Ambroise, St-Maur

CREDIT CARDS
None, cash only

<table>
<tr><td>RATES
1–2 persons 180–240F, triple
250–290F; extra bed 50F;
shower 10F
Taxe de séjour: included</td><td rowspan="2"></td></tr>
</table>

RATES
1–2 persons 180–240F, triple
250–290F; extra bed 50F;
shower 10F
Taxe de séjour: included

BREAKFAST
10F extra per person

usual one-star way, with a well-used collection of furniture. At only 10 francs per person, breakfast can be considered a gift. Grab it! The red hall carpets are worn but clean; the neighborhood is safe and quiet (for Paris); and the rooms along the front face the square Maurice Gardet. You are within reasonable walking distance to all the nightlife the area is known for, and a métro ride to everything else interesting.

ENGLISH SPOKEN: None

FACILITIES AND SERVICES Direct-dial phone; sixteen rooms with a TV; laundromat on the corner

NEAREST TOURIST ATTRACTIONS (RIGHT BANK): Not much other than nightlife about 15-minute walk from the hotel; must use public transportation for everything else

(7) LIBERTEL CROIX DE MALTE ★★
5, rue de Malte, 75011 (11th)
29 rooms, all with bath or shower and toilet

TELEPHONE
01-48-05-09-36

FAX
01-43-57-02-54

MÉTRO
République, Oberkampf

CREDIT CARDS
MC, V

RATES
Single 480F, double 540F;
extra bed 150F
Taxe de séjour: included

BREAKFAST
45F extra per person

A stay at this upgraded two-star near the Bastille can satisfy luxury-loving Right Bank natures as well as those with fun-loving Left Bank streaks. Admittedly it is a few degrees from Tourist Central, but transportation is quick and easy from place de la République.

Rooms are well done, baths are modern, and the staff congenial. The vivid color palate is taken from the reproduction paintings of Wallasse Ting that hang throughout the hotel. An unusual collection of boxed and acrylic art is displayed in the lobby, which flows into a bright glassed-in dining area with gaily upholstered chair cushions. The hotel has two buildings, one of which has an elevator. The other has duplex two-story rooms that are nice for longer stays. The only duplex to definitely avoid is no. 207, where guests will have to contend with a painting of a sprawled nude woman over the bed, and you must take a dangerous, winding fire-escape-style staircase to get to the bathroom, where the low roof will force most people to shower on their knees.

ENGLISH SPOKEN: Yes

FACILITIES AND SERVICES Bar; direct-dial phone; elevator in one building; TV; office safe, no charge

NEAREST TOURIST ATTRACTIONS (RIGHT BANK): None, must use public transportation

(8) MARY'S HÔTEL ★
15, rue de Malte, 75011 (11th)
38 rooms, 25 with shower and toilet

Paris hotel prices for committed Cheap Sleepers in Paris can trigger sticker shock and cause budget catastrophes. Coming to the rescue is Mary's Hôtel, a lean little one-star with simple, clean rooms. The manager told me that a few years ago one guest couldn't pay his bill, so to make up for it, he painted murals on the walls of the breakfast room. The project took a week, and the results aren't bad at all. (I don't suggest trying a similar trick to pay a future bill, and neither does management.) The building dates back to 1870, but there is an elevator and more than half the accommodations have private facilities. If you don't expect the moon, can live with some exposed pipes and one-star plastic, pattern mixes, and plebeian furniture, this is a good value for those wanting a room and not much else.

ENGLISH SPOKEN: Some

FACILITIES AND SERVICES Direct-dial phone; elevator; office safe, no charge

NEAREST TOURIST ATTRACTIONS (RIGHT BANK): Nothing, must use public transportation

TELEPHONE
01-47-00-81-70

FAX
01-47-00-58-06

MÉTRO
Oberkampf, République

CREDIT CARDS
AE, MC, V

RATES
Single 160–190F, double 180–250F, triple 320F; shower 20F
Taxe de séjour: included

BREAKFAST
20F extra per person for first two nights; after two nights, included at no extra charge

(9) PAX HÔTEL ★
12, rue de Charonne, 75011 (11th)
47 rooms, 37 with shower or bath and toilet

If the dark red carpet, orange chenille spreads, and lavender tiled bathroom don't grab you in room no. 204, and neither does the fuzzy beige wall covering in no. 201, surely the bottom-of-the-barrel prices will. Low Cheap Sleeping tabs also prevail in the rest of the hotel, which is unfortunately done in the same "eek" mode. There is no elevator, but you will have a television, and if you are in a bathless roost for more than a week, your shower will be free. On top of that, you couldn't ask for a more *sympa* patron, a kind gentleman who has been here for forty-five years.

Those of you who receive your mail and retirement checks at a Leisure World address, this is not your Paris stomping ground, but for the Cheap Sleeping young and footloose who don't mind street tumult, it's okay. In strolls through the neighborhood, you will undoubtedly run into wine-guzzling *chochards* relaxing in doorways and old ladies in fuzzy slippers tossing baguettes to

TELEPHONE
01-47-00-40-98

FAX
01-43-38-57-81

MÉTRO
Ledru-Rollin, Bastille

CREDIT CARDS
AE, MC, V

RATES
Single 230–240F, double 230–310F, triple 370F, quad 420F; free public shower
Taxe de séjour: 3F extra per person, per day

BREAKFAST
30F extra per person in dining room, 40F in room; free on your first day if you arrive before 10 A.M.

pigeons. However, it is not all residentially challenging . . . not by a long shot. This is the "with-it" *quartier* that boasts everything on the wild side—from late-night disco palaces to cafés and wine bars of the moment. The area is close to the new Opéra Bastille, but a métro ride away from almost everything else, unless you don't mind walking fifteen or twenty minutes to get there.

ENGLISH SPOKEN: Generally

FACILITIES AND SERVICES Direct-dial phone; hair dryer; no elevator; reserved, private parking, 70F per day; TV; no safe

NEAREST TOURIST ATTRACTIONS (RIGHT BANK): Bastille and all the nightlife surrounding it, new Opéra

Twelfth Arrondissement

(See map pages 166–167.)

HOTELS IN THE TWELFTH ARRONDISSEMENT

(16) HÔTEL BELLE ÉPOQUE ★★★
66, rue de Charenton, 75012 (12th)
30 rooms, all with shower or bath and toilet

While not exactly a lodging mecca, quality hotel rooms can be found between the Bastille and Gare de Lyon. The location is especially beneficial for those voyagers taking a train to the south of France, since most leave from the Gare de Lyon. The Hôtel Belle Époque has been thoroughly redone and is now an attractive combination of high tech and late-20s and -30s styles. White walls frame the blue doors and carpets of the rooms, which are functionally furnished with built-ins, mirrored wardrobes, and marble baths. Room numbers correspond to the years Art Deco was in full form, and in each room is a framed newspaper clipping of a noteworthy event of that particular year. With the exception of no. 1929, they have good space and acceptable views.

ENGLISH SPOKEN: Yes

FACILITIES AND SERVICES: Air-conditioning in all rooms; bar; conference rooms; direct-dial phone; elevator; minibar; TV with international reception; office and room safe, no charge

NEAREST TOURIST ATTRACTIONS (RIGHT BANK): Bastille

TELEPHONE
01-43-44-06-66
FAX
01-43-44-10-25
MÉTRO
Ledru-Rollin, Bastille
CREDIT CARDS
MC, V
RATES
Single 670F, double 780F, triple 835F, quad 1,045F; lower off-season rates
Taxe de séjour: included
BREAKFAST
Continental, 55F extra per person; buffet, 70F extra

(17) LE PAVILLON BASTILLE* ★★★
65, rue de Lyon, 75012 (12th)
24 rooms, all with shower or bath and toilet

The Pavillon Bastille is not only a perfect gem of a hotel, smack dab across from the Opéra Bastille, but it is one of the most artistically imaginative hotels in Paris. It also has some of the best package deals going in the city.

The entire hotel is a creative study in blue and yellow by noted architectural designer Jean-Pierre Heim, whose commissions include Christian Lacroix boutiques and the French embassies in New York and Riyadh. His

TELEPHONE
01-43-43-65-65
FAX
01-43-43-96-52; toll-free 800-233-2552
E-MAIL
hotel-pavillon@akaMail.com

INTERNET
www.paris-hotel.com/pavillon-
bastille
MÉTRO
Bastille
CREDIT CARDS
AE, DC, MC, V
RATES
1–2 persons 650–955F, suite
1,400F; ask about special
holiday and weekend packages
throughout the year
Taxe de séjour: 6F extra per
person, per day
BREAKFAST
78F extra per person

work at the hotel received the American magazine *Hotel Restaurant Design International* "Award of Excellence" for the best hotel design under three hundred rooms.

Yellow and blue are used exclusively on everything from the awning hanging over the granite courtyard with a seventeenth-century fountain to the bonbons placed on your pillow at night. Taking his cue from music, Heim wove harmonious details into the design of the hotel: doorknobs shaped like flutes, wall and furniture details adapting the five-line music staff pattern, and rugs with the lines of grand pianos. A mirrored entry ceiling reflects the lounge, which was planned "as a dreamy landscape of light and dark objects floating within space," says Heim. Upon arrival, guests are served refreshments here or escorted to their rooms . . . there is no formal registration area.

I recommend booking a room above the ground floor, otherwise your view and natural daylight will be limited. The twenty-four bedrooms are all slightly different in design, but they have the same custom-made furniture, which make the most of their limited space. A mirrored wall behind the bed reflects the hand-painted Venetian-style yellow walls. Framed prints in each room were gleaned from flea markets. The rooms, either queen or twin bedded, offer all the amenities, including air-conditioning, international TV, and the hotel's written guide to Paris. Bathrooms are beautifully fitted with magnifying mirrors, Porthault robes, and plenty of soft towels. The vaulted cellar is now Le Orchestra, a breakfast room where bleached oak chairs and paneling blend with blue and yellow upholstery and table linens. Hand-painted blue walls complement the dark blue carpeting. A large buffet with yogurt, cereal, fruit, and fresh orange juice is served every morning. During the rest of the day, there is room service for light meals.

Owners Chantal and Michel Arnaud and their English-speaking staff do everything they can to insure guests are happy and cared for. When reserving, check to see what special holiday and summer packages may be offered during your stay. For example, during July, August, and the Christmas school holidays in France, free Disney World Paris passes, which include rides, are given to children under twelve years of age.

ENGLISH SPOKEN: Yes

FACILITIES AND SERVICES: Air-conditioning; bar; direct-dial phone; hair dryer; elevator; minibar; radio; TV with international reception; room safe, no charge; room service for light meals; no charge for ironing guests' clothes; office services; laundry and dry cleaning services

NEAREST TOURIST ATTRACTIONS (RIGHT BANK): Opéra Bastille, Marais

Thirteenth Arrondissement

RIGHT BANK
Gobelins tapestry factory
(Manufacture des Gobelins),
Butte aux Cailles, Bibliothèque
de France

This large, working-class area is generally thought of as a tourist-free zone. It is the sort of place dedicated Parisian visitors see on their seventh or eighth trip, after they have done everything else they thought important. The area does hold some interesting surprises and should not be totally overlooked. There is the still-functioning Gobelins factory, which is open to the public. A stroll around the winding streets of the Butte aux Cailles district provides a delightful look at one of Paris's oldest yet unknown and untouched parts. The arrondissement also has a huge Asian population, which produces some of the best, and certainly the cheapest, Chinese meals to be had. The Bibliothèque de France, designed to replace the Bibliothèque National, is an eight-million-franc project, covering 288,000 square meters along the Seine across from the Ministry of Finance. This new library building has caused as much controversy as the Opéra Bastille did (and still does).

HOTELS IN THE THIRTEENTH ARRONDISSEMENT

Le Vert Gallant ★★   **178**

LE VERT GALLANT ★★
41-43, rue Croulebarbe, 75013 (13th)
15 rooms and studios, all with shower or bath and toilet

TELEPHONE
01-44-08-83-50
FAX
01-44-08-83-69
MÉTRO
Place d'Italie, Corvisart
CREDIT CARDS
AE, MC, V
RATES
Single 400–500F, double 500F;
extra bed 90F
Taxe de séjour: 5F extra per
person, per day
BREAKFAST
40F extra per person

Balzac said it well: "Paris is an ocean in itself, there is always some spot never seen before, some unknown cavern, flower, pearls, delight hitherto unknown . . ."

A stay at the appealing Le Vert Gallant provides that wonderful feeling of discovery, of finding an unknown corner of Paris for your very own. Located in the Gobelins district in the thirteenth arrondissement, this discrete garden hotel is a charming oasis for those who know Paris well and are looking for something a bit beyond the usual hotel room—and who are willing to sacrifice a dead-center location to get it. Across the street from the hotel is the René Le Gall Square, a green park filled with the sound of children's voices, *mamans* pushing prams, and elderly men and women out for a few minutes of gossip or a quiet moment to read the papers. For anything else, you will need the métro, which is a ten-minute walk. Next door to the hotel is its restaurant,

L'Auberge Etchegorry, a Basque retreat that offers hotel guests fantastic prices on *prix fixe* meals. For more on this special restaurant, see L'Auberge Etchegorry in *Cheap Eats in Paris*.

The hotel is made up of fifteen rooms, all of which have windows framing a garden courtyard view. Your morning wake-up call will be the songs of birds in the trees, not the usual rude Parisian awakening from the trash haulers or furious horn-honking motorists. If you want to cook during your stay, reserve a studio on the ground floor. The rooms above also have kitchens, but because of fire regulations, no actual cooking is allowed on the higher floors. All rooms have an uncluttered, modern look. Colors are soft and pleasing, the accessories appropriate, and the fabrics well coordinated. Bathrooms are small but modern. Maïté and Henri Laborde, your hosts here and at their restaurant, attend graciously to their guests, which further contributes to the over-all feeling of well-being one has when staying at this special hotel. A warning is in order: Before arrival, have your affairs in order at home—you may never want to leave.

ENGLISH SPOKEN: Yes

FACILITIES AND SERVICES: Direct-dial phone, each room has its own line; hair dryer; some cook-in kitchenettes; minibar; two parking places, must be reserved ahead, 30F a night (an unheard of bargain!); TV with international reception; office safe, no charge; no elevator (only two floors)

NEAREST TOURIST ATTRACTIONS (LEFT BANK): Nothing, must use public transportation

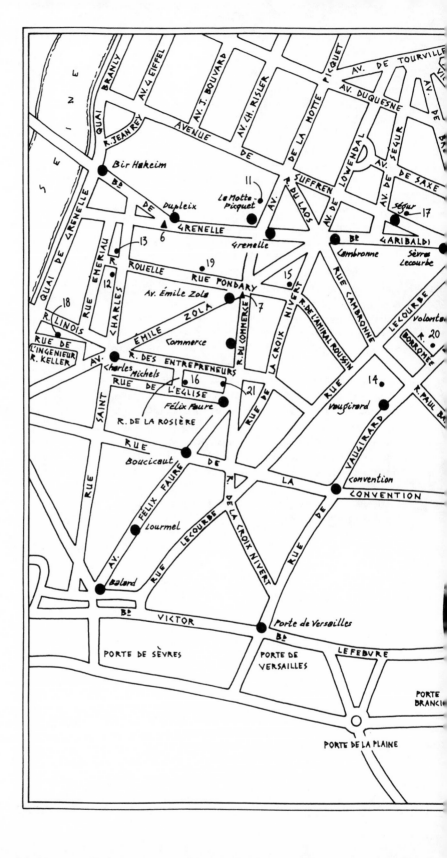

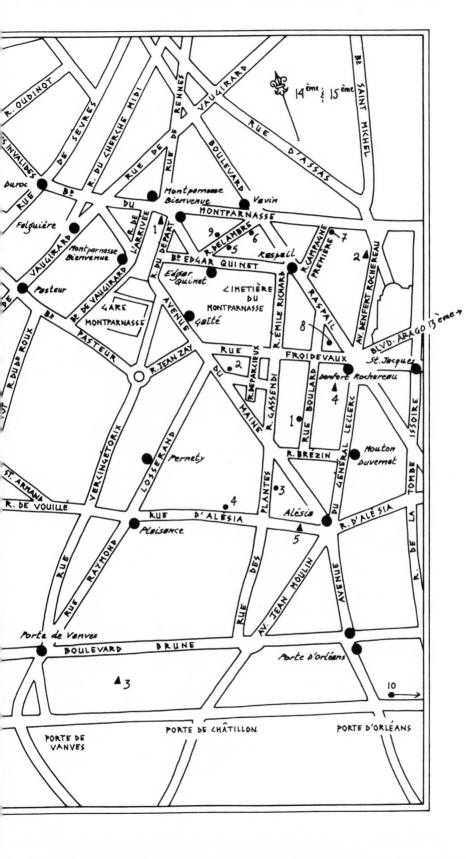

Fourteenth Arrondissement

LEFT BANK
Montparnasse, Les Catecombs

In recent years Montparnasse has become the victim of a tragically insensitive redevelopment policy exemplified by the Tour Montparnasse. During the 1920s and 1930s, the fourteenth was well known as the artistic headquarters of the modern art and literary worlds. Nostalgia buffs return today and head for the historic brasseries Le Dôme and La Coupole to rekindle memories of the famous who ate and drank there, but they find the spirit is just not the same.

HOTELS IN THE FOURTEENTH ARRONDISSEMENT

OTHER OPTIONS
Students Accommodations

(1) GRAND HÔTEL DU SQUARE (NO STARS)
2, rue Boulard, 75014 (14th)
30 rooms, none with shower or bath and toilet

TELEPHONE
01-43-22-50-09

FAX
None

MÉTRO
Denfert-Rochereau

CREDIT CARDS
None, cash only

RATES
Single 135–180F, double 200F; extra bed 60F for child up to 16, otherwise must pay regular rates; shower 10F
Taxe de séjour: included

BREAKFAST
Not served

The Grand Hôtel du Square is certainly *not* grand—in fact, it has not had a face-lift in years, but then neither have the rates, which can be described as almost prehistoric. In addition, its location far from the bright lights and excitement is not what I would call thrilling. But for Cheap Sleepers who find adventure in off-beat, low-budget digs, this could be the right hotel. The bare-bones rooms are done in the attic school of decorating, without carpets or bedside lamps, only an overhead light of questionable wattage. Some rooms have ornate marble fireplaces and sunny views over the nearby square; others display lovely old armoires. Most have chenille spreads that barely fit the slept-in mattresses, none of which are twins. All the rooms are spacious and clean as a whistle. Each floor has a toilet, and there are three showers in the

182

hotel, all of which are clean enough to leave the Lysol in the suitcase. There is no breakfast served, and no one makes any attempt to speak English, unless you happen to run into the owner's daughter, who stops by now and then to visit her mother. The métro stop is not far and bus connections are good.

ENGLISH SPOKEN: None

FACILITIES AND SERVICES: None

NEAREST TOURIST ATTRACTIONS (LEFT BANK): Montparnasse

(2) HÔTEL DAGUERRE ★★
94, rue Daguerre, 75014 (14th)
30 rooms, all with shower or bath and toilet

For a sleek, modern, stay in this neck of the Paris woods, the newly redone Hôtel Daguerre is a safe choice. The standard-issue rooms are comfortable and have more than their share of perks, but they are without much *vielle charme* or inherent French character. The even-numbered rooms face the street and have showers and more noise. The odd-numbered slots have tubs and are quiet. Two rooms are available for the handicapped. No room faces a blank wall. The best feature of no. 501, a cheerful twin, is its wall of windows looking toward Montmartre. If this room is booked, ask for no. 301 with a pleasant view of the garden.

ENGLISH SPOKEN: Yes

FACILITIES AND SERVICES: Direct-dial phone; elevator; hair dryer; minibar; TV with international reception; room safe, no charge

NEAREST TOURIST ATTRACTIONS (LEFT BANK): Montparnasse

TELEPHONE
01-43-22-43-54

FAX
01-43-20-66-84

MÉTRO
Gaîté, Denfert-Rochereau

CREDIT CARDS
AE, DC, MC, V

RATES
Single 400F, double 445F, suite 565F
Taxe de séjour: included

BREAKFAST
40F extra per person

(3) HÔTEL DE BLOIS ★
5, rue des Plantes, 75014 (14th)
25 rooms, 17 with shower or bath and toilet

This was my final hotel stop after a long, rainy day, and as I walked I thought, This place is about two blocks east of nowhere, and it better be very, very good. As you can see, I needed to be impressed, and Mme. Fontange's Hôtel de Blois turned out to be an impressive winner in the one-star *Cheap Sleeps in Paris* sweepstakes. Cozy, clean, and homey are the words that spring to mind when I think of her cheery sitting room with windows overlooking the street. Breakfast is served here in the morning. Around the room, you will see fresh flowers,

TELEPHONE
01-45-40-99-48

FAX
01-45-40-45-62

MÉTRO
Alésia, Mouton-Duvernet

CREDIT CARDS
MC, V

RATES
Single 220–350F, double 220–
275F, triple 260–360F; free
public shower
Taxe de séjour: 3F extra per
person, per day

BREAKFAST
30F extra per person (includes
croissant)

never dusty plastic ones (which, as you know by now, I definitely do not like). Her bedrooms are coordinated—none of this rainbow-color approach with Garage Sale Gothic furniture. Ask for Room 2, with a double bed, polished armoire, tiny floral print wall covering, and a pink tiled bathroom with new fittings and a shower curtain. No. 6 has a shower with doors, a double bed, and no view, but it does have space to live in. Oriental runners on white painted stairs and a different mural on each of the floors make climbing up to your room a pleasant exercise. For those who have been traveling awhile, or are staying more than a few days, a self-service laundromat is right next door. Shopaholics take note: What you save on your room you can spend along rue d'Alésia, the discount-shopping mecca for savvy Parisians. It is about a five-minute walk away. See page 275 in Cheap Chic for details.

ENGLISH SPOKEN: Limited

FACILITIES AND SERVICES: Direct-dial phone; no elevator; hair dryer available; TV with international reception; office safe, no charge

NEAREST TOURIST ATTRACTIONS (LEFT BANK): Discount shopping on rue Alésia; must take public transportation to everything else

(4) HÔTEL DE LA LOIRE ★★
39, bis rue du Moulin-Vert, 75014 (14th)
18 rooms, 15 with shower or bath and toilet

TELEPHONE
01-45-40-66-88

FAX
01-45-40-89-07

MÉTRO
Alésia

CREDIT CARDS
MC, V

RATES
1–2 persons 275–375F,
triple 460F
Taxe de séjour: included

BREAKFAST
35F extra per person; free if you
mention *Cheap Sleeps in Paris*

Those who travel smart by sleeping cheap will find refuge at this family hotel in the depths of the fourteenth. Actually, Cheap Chic shoppers are within bag-toting distance of the discount boutiques along rue d'Alésia, but for most of the bright lights and serious Paris action, a bus or métro ride is required. On the hotel rating scale, the place is zip in the character column and bingo! in the cleanliness section. As for decor, well, if you don't mind pink and can live with chenille, it's a winner. Five rooms on the ground floor open off a little garden. Breakfast is served on a long wooden table, and if you tell the sweet owner, Mme. Noel, you found her in *Cheap Sleeps in Paris,* your breakfast will be free.

ENGLISH SPOKEN: Yes

FACILITIES AND SERVICES: Direct-dial phone; TV; no elevator

shopping on rue d'Alésia; otherwise, must use public
transportation

(5) HÔTEL DELAMBRE ★★★
35, rue Delambre, 75014 (14th)
30 rooms, all with shower or bath and toilet

I am impressed. Patrick Kalmy's Hôtel Delambre has
my vote for the smartest rehab effort in the fourteenth
arrondissement. He took a dog-eared one-star and transformed it from stem to stern into a snazzy three-star
and—this is important for Cheap Sleepers in Paris—still
kept the prices within reason.

In cleaning out the debris from the old hotel,
M. Kalmy found some unlikely treasures he incorpo-
rated nicely in the lobby and breakfast room. In the
streetside dining area, he cleverly displays an old metal
garden gate, and two original regal columns stand by the
elevators.

The rooms are well done in two dominant colors: red
and blue. No. 40, with white walls and enameled doors
with wood detailing, is a double with a built-in curved
desk and an interesting view over a garden to a block of
apartments beyond. No. 50, a minisuite, combines the
charm of sloping ceilings with smaller windows. The
addition of a skylight, good closet space, and a large
bathroom make this a popular choice. For walkers, the
hotel is within reach of the Luxembourg Gardens, St-
Germain-des-Prés, and the best of Montparnasse. Otherwise, public transportation is easy and close by.

ENGLISH SPOKEN: Yes

FACILITIES AND SERVICES: Direct-dial phone; elevator to
fourth floor; fax and computer plugs; hair dryer; minibar
available; TV with international reception; room safe, no
charge

NEAREST TOURIST ATTRACTIONS (LEFT BANK): Montparnasse, Luxembourg Gardens, St-Germain-des-Prés

TELEPHONE
01-43-20-66-31
FAX
01-45-38-91-76
MÉTRO
Montparnasse, Vavin, Edgar-
Quinet
CREDIT CARDS
AE, MC, V
RATES
Single 400–500F, double 450–
500F, suite (1–4 persons) 650F
Taxe de séjour: included
BREAKFAST
40F extra per person

(6) HÔTEL DES BAINS (NO STARS)
33, rue Delambre, 75014 (14th)
41 rooms, all with shower or bath and toilet

For a no-star, the prices seem high, but for what you
get, they are fair. Late risers will appreciate the set-back
location from the street . . . all the rooms are quiet, at
least for this part of Paris. The rooms aren't big on

TELEPHONE
01-43-20-85-27
FAX
01-42-79-82-78

METRO
Vavin, Edgar-Quinet,
Montparnasse

CREDIT CARDS
None, cash only

RATES
1–2 persons 395–450F, suite
(1–2 persons) 475–650F
Taxe de séjour: included

BREAKFAST
45F extra per person (juice,
cereal, yogurt, and cheese)

decorating frills, but they are free from the Day-Glo colors and frayed-at-the-edges furnishings one usually contends with in no-star abodes. They come equipped with a TV, hair dryer, room safe, and the possibility of private parking—all unheard of extras in a no-star hotel. Even the breakfast is worthy of at least two stars. The best deals are the three suites. No. 447 is a two-room selection facing the courtyard. It is open and simply done with hardwood floors, coordinated fabrics, and a corner glass shower in the bathroom. Oddly enough there are no towel racks, and when I asked about their absence, I was told the towels were changed daily. I would hope so. Some of the doubles (nos. 111, 112, and 114) are really too small for two, unless you are staying only a night, have very limited luggage, or enjoy very cozy confines with your traveling companion. A better choice is no. 71, which can be a double or triple. It is decorated in yellow and has a big bathroom with a glassed-in shower.

ENGLISH SPOKEN: Very limited

FACILITIES AND SERVICES: Direct-dial phone; elevator; hair dryer; parking, 70F per day; trouser press; TV; room safe, no charge

NEAREST TOURIST ATTRACTIONS (LEFT BANK): Montparnasse, Luxembourg Gardens, St-Germain-des-Prés

(7)   HÔTEL ISTRIA ★★
29, rue Campagne Première, 75014 (14th)
26 rooms, all with shower or bath and toilet

TELEPHONE
01-43-20-91-82

FAX
01-43-22-48-45

INTERNET
www.paris-hotel.com/istria

METRO
Raspail

CREDIT CARDS
AE, DC, MC, V

RATES
Single 480F, double 540–590F;
extra bed 120F
Taxe de séjour: included

BREAKFAST
40F extra per person

From this address you can wander the tree-lined boulevards and sit in the famous cafés that were the watering holes of Hemingway, Fitzgerald, and Henry Miller when they dominated the Montparnasse literary scene. In the 1920s and 1930s, when this was *the quartier* for artists and writers, the Istria was home to many of them, including Man Ray and his mistress Kiki, Marcel Duchamp, and the poet Maiakowsky. Now under the direction of Philippe Leroux and his delightful wife, Danièle, the hotel was been renovated and is a favorite for those seeking a convenient Montparnasse location. A pretty tiled entry with country antiques, black-and-white photos of old Paris, and Oriental rugs leads to a postage-stamp garden along the back of the hotel. Some of the rooms that overlook the garden are confining for two persons with any luggage. To avoid being cramped, request a third-floor nest. Remember though, this building is old, and spacious rooms are not its strong suit; charm and friendliness are.

ENGLISH SPOKEN: Yes

FACILITIES AND SERVICES: Direct-dial phone; elevator for main building; hair dryer; TV; room safe, no charge

NEAREST TOURIST ATTRACTIONS (LEFT BANK): Montparnasse

(8)   HÔTEL L'AIGLON ★★★
232, boulevard Raspail, 75014 (14th)
47 rooms, all with shower or bath and toilet

The Hôtel l'Aiglon is a refined choice, about a one-minute walk from the Raspail métro stop. A formal tone pervades, from the faux book-lined bar to the beautifully redecorated rooms, all of which have been planned with discretion and good taste. Don't miss seeing the original stained-glass windows over the stairway, which takes guests from the ground floor to a formal dining room with large sideboard and mahogany tables covered in starched white linen. The rooms all face outward, and many have peaceful views over the Cimetière Montparnasse. They are color-coordinated, with textured fabrics, firm mattresses, good closet and luggage space, and bathrooms with windows . . . something you rarely see in Parisian hotels. The suites are dreams come true, especially no. 55, with its soft beige walls and carpets. The sitting room is comfortably furnished with a desk, sofa bed, and easy chair, and it has a half-bath to one side. Twin beds in the bedroom, with its own balcony, and a double-sink bathroom make up the rest. No. 16 is a new room, in bright yellow and green colors that are carried out on the quilted bedspread and curtains. The gray bathroom has gold and beige accents and a floral design in the shower. If you are *tout seul,* it is a perfect choice. Now the sixth floor is completely redone. Some people may not like the rooms on this top floor because the windows are higher than normal, but I find them to be quite charming. One of my favorite choices is no. 61. I like the room itself, with a three-drawer chest, a comfortable armchair, and print fabrics, but it is the bathroom that is the real star, with two windows and a view. Motorists will appreciate the private parking, and everyone will enjoy the brand of service and hospitality provided by Jacques Rols and his staff.

TELEPHONE
01-43-20-82-42

FAX
01-43-20-98-72

INTERNET
www.paris-hotel.com/aiglon

MÉTRO
Raspail

CREDIT CARDS
AE, DC, MC, V

RATES
Single 550–620F, double 620–710F, suite (1–4 persons) 1,000–1,575F; extra bed 120F
Taxe de séjour: 6F extra per person, per day

BREAKFAST
45F extra per person

ENGLISH SPOKEN: Yes

FACILITIES AND SERVICES: Air-conditioning in rooms on the second to fourth floors; bar; direct-dial phone; elevator; hair dryer; minibar; private parking (80F, must request when reserving); TV with international reception; office safe, no charge; laundry service

NEAREST TOURIST ATTRACTIONS (LEFT BANK): Montparnasse

(9) HÔTEL LENOX MONTPARNASSE ★★★
15, rue Delambre, 75014 (14th)
36 rooms, all with shower or bath and toilet

TELEPHONE
01-43-35-34-50
FAX
01-43-20-46-64
MÉTRO
Vavin, Edgar-Quinet
CREDIT CARDS
AE, DC, MC, V
RATES
1–2 persons 550–675F, suite 990–1,300F
Taxe de séjour: 6F extra per person, per day
BREAKFAST
50F extra per person

The atmosphere is engaging and the clientele an international blend at the Lenox Montparnasse. The collection of furniture suggests Art Deco and the 1930s in both the lobby and large bar to one side. Green plants bring life to the area, and beautiful sprays of fresh orchids give it wonderful color.

Rooms are nice, with just enough personality to set them apart from other mainstream Montparnasse hotels. If you want more leg room, reserve no. 69, a big twin with a corner sitting room, a tiny fireplace, and a rooftop view. It is softly decorated in blue and light gray. The bathroom has a rolling toiletry cart and blue and green inserts of flowers set against the white tiled walls. No. 49 is a back double in yellow with good closet space and a nice bath, but not much light. No. 60 is a good-value, twin-bedded suite beautifully done in blue and white with hand-painted window shutters and an old tile heater with a marble top. Seating is nicely arranged around a sofa bed and two comfortable reading chairs. The view over a large apartment complex may remind you of *Rear Window*. The top-floor, two-room suite, with its marble fireplace, period furniture, and geometric upholstery, shows that an eclectic combination of styles and patterns can work if done correctly. Amusing etchings of French ladies of leisure with their dogs or coyly wrapped in fur—and not much else—grace the walls. The narrow bathroom has all the extras, including Roger and Gallet products.

ENGLISH SPOKEN: Yes

FACILITIES AND SERVICES: Bar; direct-dial phone; elevator; hair dryer; TV with international reception; video; office safe, no charge

NEAREST TOURIST ATTRACTIONS (LEFT BANK): Montparnasse

Fifteenth Arrondissement

(See map pages 180–181.)

The fifteenth is the biggest arrondissement and has few tourist attractions. If you enjoy seeing how the average Parisian lives, this is the perfect vantage point.

LEFT BANK
Nothing from a tourist's standpoint, but depending on the location, walking distance to La Tour Montparnasse, UNESCO, the Eiffel Tower, Champ-de-Mars

---

HOTELS IN THE FIFTEENTH ARRONDISSEMENT

OTHER OPTIONS

Residence Hotels

Private Hostel

(11) HÔTEL ARÈS ★★★
7, rue du Général-de-Larminat, 75015 (15th)
42 rooms, all with shower or bath and toilet

Jean-Pierre Seroin's Hôtel Arès is a family-owned and -run choice on a quiet street in a neighborhood of unqualified respectability. For high-scale shopping and dreaming, the Village Suisse antiques showrooms and shops are just around the corner. For dreaming of another kind, in less than ten minutes you can be in the Champ-de-Mars Park admiring the Eiffel Tower, and if you are here on the weekend, stroll through one of the best outdoor *marchés* in Paris on boulevard de Grenelle. The area is also filled with many *Cheap Eats in Paris* restaurants in all price brackets.

The public parts of the 1913 building are attractive, especially the entryway, which has the original colored tile floor intact, and the breakfast area, which is set off by a window garden filled with brightly blooming plants. Each floor features a different painter, and once you get

TELEPHONE
01-47-34-74-04

FAX
01-47-34-48-56

INTERNET
aresotel@easynet.fr

MÉTRO
La Motte-Picquet, Grenelle

CREDIT CARDS
AE, DC, MC, V

RATES
Single 470–600F, double 600–700F, triple 820F; extra bed 120F
Taxe de séjour: 6F extra per person, per day

BREAKFAST
45F extra per person

beyond the dubious color schemes of orange sorbet, bright daisy yellow, robin's egg blue, and key lime green that define the rooms, you will find them to be clean and outfitted with all the conventional comforts. The four rooms facing the street have Eiffel Tower views, as do the two top-floor rooms, which have itsy-bitsy bathrooms but are otherwise just fine. My favorite rooms are those on the corners because they have lots of natural light and more space. Quite honestly, I like everything about this hotel and its on-the-ball management except one thing . . . the square toilet paper, which should be outlawed!

ENGLISH SPOKEN: Yes, and Italian and Spanish

FACILITIES AND SERVICES: Direct-dial phone; elevator; hair dryer; minibar; parking, 90F per day; TV with international reception; room safe, no charge

NEAREST TOURIST ATTRACTIONS (LEFT BANK): Village Suisse, Champ-de-Mars, Eiffel Tower

(12) HÔTEL BEAUGRENELLE ST-CHARLES ★★
82, rue Saint-Charles, at place Saint-Charles, 75015 (15th)
51 rooms, all with shower or bath and toilet

TELEPHONE
01-45-78-61-63
FAX
01-45-79-04-38
MÉTRO
Charles-Michels
CREDIT CARDS
AE, DC, MC, V
RATES
Single 400–450F, double 430–510F; extra bed 155F
Taxe de séjour: 5F extra per person, per day
BREAKFAST
45F extra per person

This hotel is just as unassuming as its neighborhood, which offers a comfortable niche for a look at what life is really all about in Paris, once you are away from the glittery and artsy *quartiers* that draw most visitors. You can spot the hotel from the Square St-Michels . . . just look for the bright red awning and the boxwood bushes framing the entry. The lobby has Art Deco–style leather love seats and armchairs. A modern breakfast room with black laminated tables and chairs is set apart by a bank of green plants. A glassed-in walkway joins the two buildings that make up the fifty-one-room hotel. Several ground-floor rooms open onto the garden and are some of the best. Three rooms on the sixth floor have balconies and Eiffel Tower views, and one on the back, a single, also has a peek of the Eiffel Tower. All the rooms are small, but decent closet space rescues them from feeling too cramped. Light, pastel-colored fabrics and blond furniture lend a modern touch. Peace and quiet prevails when the sidewalks roll up about 9 or 10 P.M. Owner M. Colliot and his staff work hard to please their guests.

NOTE: One of the best Monoprix stores in Paris is right around the corner. See Cheap Chic, page 267, for a description of these Parisian versions of WalMart, K-Mart, and huge food supermarkets all rolled into one.

ENGLISH SPOKEN: Yes

FACILITIES AND SERVICES: Direct-dial phone; elevator in front building only; hair dryer; minibar; TV with international reception; room safe, 20F per night

NEAREST TOURIST ATTRACTIONS (LEFT BANK): Shopping at the Centre Beaugrenelle; otherwise, must use public transportation to all tourist destinations

(13) HÔTEL CHARLES QUINZE ★★
37, rue St-Charles, corner of 36, rue Rouelle, 75015 (15th)
30 rooms, all with shower or bath and toilet

To some, the Charles Quinze might be considered to be in a tourist backwater. For others, it represents a change of pace and is a safe bet for those insisting on peace in noisy Paris. I like it not only because it is well maintained and executed but because its location offers a glimpse of everyday life that you do not always see in more congested *quartiers.* In the place St-Charles, old men sit quietly under the shade of the chestnut trees reading their newspapers and talking about old times. Pretty young girls with long ribbons and smocked dresses roller-skate along the sidewalks, and matrons walk their little dogs. Hurrying housewives carrying brimming shopping baskets go from shop to shop picking just the right ingredients for their evening meal. For trips away from the hotel, a good métro line is only a ten-minute walk, and the Eiffel Tower is about twenty if you window-shop along the way.

The hotel is done simply but with great style. Blue-and-white Chinese porcelain creates an Oriental theme in the small, whitewashed lobby. Be sure to notice the framed needlepoint in the reception area. One dates from 1907, done by the owner's grandmother when she was a little girl. Another by the fireplace was done by her brother-in-law, and her son, Vincent, stitched the one hanging by the door when he was eight.

Each floor of the hotel is coordinated in a different color. The concise rooms have country-style, built-in furniture and matching draperies and bedspreads. At night you will find a chocolate on your pillow.

The hospitable owners, Claire and Martial Fournerie, also own the café/tabac next door. Drop in Monday

TELEPHONE
01-45-79-64-15

FAX
01-45-77-21-11

MÉTRO
Charles-Michels, Dupleix

CREDIT CARDS
AE, DC, MC, V

RATES
Single 425F, double 505–520F; extra bed 150F; children under 12 free
Taxe de séjour: included

BREAKFAST
45F extra per person

through Friday between noon and 2 P.M. for a typical working-class lunch and order the daily special. They are open for business from 7 A.M.–8 P.M. weekdays only, and they serve drinks and cold sandwiches when lunch is not in progress.

ENGLISH SPOKEN: Yes

FACILITIES AND SERVICES: Direct-dial phone; elevator; hair dryer; laundry service; minibar; TV with international reception; office safe, no charge

NEAREST TOURIST ATTRACTIONS (LEFT BANK): A twenty-minute walk from the Eiffel Tower, otherwise not much

(14) HÔTEL DÉLOS ★★
7, rue du Général Beuret, 75015 (15th)
43 rooms, 33 with shower or bath and toilet

TELEPHONE
01-48-28-88-32,
01-48-28-29-32

FAX
01-48-28-88-46

MÉTRO
Vaugirard, Cambronne

CREDIT CARDS
AE, DC, MC, V

RATES
Single 260–380F, double 280–430F; triple, add 100F to double rate; public showers free
Taxe de séjour: included

BREAKFAST
Continental 20F extra per person, buffet 40F extra

Thanks to a Paris pal and born tipster, I found this Cheap Sleep in Paris. Where is it? Frankly, nowhere if you demand a hot location. On the other hand, if you want to mix with the rank and file and see how the Parisian salt-of-the-earth live, you will be dead center.

The outside is neat and tidy. Inside, there is a miniature garden, a cafeteria-style breakfast room, and in the lobby, a sectional where you can sit and watch the news on a giant TV screen. Rooms are reached via a small elevator. If there are two of you, no. 11 is a serviceable choice with an open closet and a view of a green tree; no. 15 has twin beds and a window in the bathroom; and no. 16 can be for three, but it would be a tight squeeze. This is a strictly functional hotel offering unadorned, clean rooms devoid of the usual shabby chic one often finds in this price range. Okay, so the towels don't always match and the perks are few, but the prices are Cheap Sleeper friendly, and so is management. And that is what counts for most of us.

Thanks J.B., you were right on.

ENGLISH SPOKEN: Yes

FACILITIES AND SERVICES: Elevator; TV; no safe or direct-dial phone

NEAREST TOURIST ATTRACTIONS (LEFT BANK): None, must use public transportation

(15) HÔTEL FONDARY ★★
30, rue Fondary, 75015 (15th)
20 rooms, all with shower or bath and toilet

TELEPHONE
01-45-75-14-75

If you do not require much space and will not rebel at an address in a tourist desert, then the Fondary is a quiet budget choice. Were it in a more tourist-inspired setting, the hotel would command higher prices and probably be full all the time with yuppies. The surrounding neighborhood provides a glimpse into Parisian bourgeois life that can be interesting, especially on your third or fourth trip when you want to see more of the "real" Paris. On Wednesday and Sunday there is an enormous outdoor *marché* along boulevard de Grenelle, and every day along rue du Commerce you can watch daily life as shoppers crowd the stores and the open stalls that sell everything from housedresses, lampshades, and junk jewelry to food, fresh flowers, and car parts. The hotel is actually much better than outward appearances would suggest. On the main floor there is a pretty terrace off the dining room and a bar next to reception, where you can buy a soft drink or a beer. Upstairs, the rooms are decorated in white bamboo, grass cloth, and pretty fabrics. Prices match the size of the hotel: small.

ENGLISH SPOKEN: Yes

FACILITIES AND SERVICES: Bar (soft drinks and beer); direct-dial phone; elevator; minibar; TV; office safe, no charge

NEAREST TOURIST ATTRACTIONS (LEFT BANK): Twenty-five-minute walk to Eiffel Tower through interesting blue-collar neighborhood; must use métro for anything else

FAX
01-45-75-84-42

MÉTRO
Émile Zola

CREDIT CARDS
AE, MC, V

RATES
1–2 persons 400–425F
Taxe de séjour: 5F extra per person, per day

BREAKFAST
40F extra per person

(16) LE NAINVILLE HÔTEL (NO STARS)
53, rue de l'Église, entrance at 17, rue de la Rosière, 75015 (15th)
37 rooms, 5 with shower or bath and toilet

Perched over a bar and café in a pedestrian corner of the fifteenth arrondissement is the budget-lovers' Nainville. Considering the logistics, you would hardly expect it to offer the comforts it does. Let's start with breakfast, which is served in the bar below and includes orange juice and a croissant along with bread and jam. Most no-star hotels wouldn't *think* of serving breakfast, let alone providing juice as well as croissants and jam. Next, in the fancy rooms (those with a bathtub, that is) you will find a *peignoir* (a bathrobe!). Want to take a break and catch up on the news around the world? Then just flip the TV to CNN news and you have it all . . . in English (in a no-star hotel?). All right, everything isn't totally a bouquet of roses: there is no elevator, no twin beds, and the toilet paper is square. Then there is the

TELEPHONE
01-45-57-35-80

FAX
01-45-54-83-00

MÉTRO
Charles-Michels, Felix-Faure

CREDIT CARDS
None, cash only

RATES
1–2 persons 210–370F; public shower 25F
Taxe de séjour: included

BREAKFAST
38F extra per person, served only in the bar

matter of the interior decoration, which in some rooms literally screams at you with wild wallpaper and carpets that were never meant to match anything. But in the end, the good points far outweigh the bad. The semi-antique furniture is comfortably worn but not shabby. The rooms and the bathrooms—both private and those down-the-hall—are clean; rooms with private toilets and showers overlook the pretty Square Violet; the neighborhood is quiet all the time; and the owners, Mme. Dupuy and her husband, who runs the bar, are accommodating. I was interested to know that on April 10, 1938, M. Dupuy was born in the hotel in a second-floor room. It is the one that has a tree in a window box (you can see it well from Room 20). Finally, and most importantly . . . the price is right for budget-watching Cheap Sleepers in Paris. Some of the best bets include nos. 20 and 30 overlooking the park; no. 41, which looks onto a rose garden; no. 10, with a double-beveled-glass armoire; and no. 16, which is on the street, but has the best use of color. Avoid nos. 13 (too small), 14 (ugly carpet, peeling paint, no view), 23 (bad shower), and 25 (hideous furry bedspread).

NOTE: The hotel is closed from July 14 until September 1.

ENGLISH SPOKEN: No

FACILITIES AND SERVICES: Bar; direct-dial phone; no elevator or safe; TV with international reception

NEAREST TOURIST ATTRACTIONS (LEFT BANK): None; must use public transportation

(17) L'HÔTEL DU BAILLI DE SUFFREN* ★★★
149, avenue de Suffren, 75015 (15th)
25 rooms, all with shower or bath and toilet

TELEPHONE
01-47-34-58-61

FAX
01-45-67-75-82

INTERNET
www.webscapades.com/France/
Paris/suffren.htpm

MÉTRO
Ségur, Sèvres-Lecourbe

CREDIT CARDS
AE, MC, V

The hotel honors the memory of Admiral Pierre André de Suffren, who was appointed Bailli (chief magistrate) of the order of Malta and, in his wake, left a trail of adventures that ranged from Saint Tropez to the Caribbean.

The red carpet at the door suggests the type of first-class treatment you will receive at this dignified hotel owned by M. and Mme. Tardif. Tradition reigns supreme, from the downstairs living room outfitted with comfortable sofas and chairs to the mirrored garden-themed breakfast room and the fabric lined elevator, which delivers guests to the twenty-five individually decorated rooms.

Each one, warmly enhanced by undisputed good taste and harmony, displays a successful mix of reproduction furniture, lush fabrics, and thoroughly modern bathrooms. No. 304 has a ship theme, carried out in the regal colors of gold, blue, and red. The wood-paneled bathroom has a walk-in tiled shower complete with a porthole mirror and bench for those who like to sit while showering.

For families, nos. 403 and 404 can be combined into a two-room apartment. I would be happy in no. 503, a single on the front with a slightly Oriental caste suggested by the grass-cloth-covered walls and the Thai carved woodwork on the closet doors and over the bed. As with all the rooms, toiletries are excellent, towels nice, and mirrors plentiful. After a long day, it is nice to join other guests in the living room and share a glass of the hotel's own wine, which comes from vineyards in Aix-en-Provence. The wines (red, rose, and white) are also for sale by whole or half bottles.

ENGLISH SPOKEN: Yes

FACILITIES AND SERVICES: Bar; direct-dial phone; elevator; hair dryer; laundry service; minibar; room safe, no charge; room service; some trouser presses; TV with international reception; *peignoirs* for VIPs

NEAREST TOURIST ATTRACTIONS (LEFT BANK): UNESCO; fifteen-minute walk to Champ-de-Mars, Eiffel Tower, and Invalides

RATES
Single 730F, double 855F, triple 895F, suite 1,230–1,400F; ask about special rates and weekend packages
Taxe de séjour: included

BREAKFAST
65F extra per person

(18) PRACTIC HÔTEL (NO STARS)
20, rue de l'Ingénieur Robert Keller, 75015 (15th)
33 rooms, 26 with shower or bath and toilet

For the best Cheap Sleep in the fifteenth arrondissement, the Practic Hôtel, just behind the Centre Beaugrenelle shopping complex, is head and shoulders above the closest competitor. I would not want to go too far out on a limb and say it is the best no-star in Paris, but believe me, it is right up there in the top 1 percent.

While it's definitely not a candidate for those who revel in Louis XV surroundings, the hotel displays none of those depressing, exhausted, faded, and snagged interiors that plague almost every other budget dig in the city. You will be welcomed by Mme. Bihan, who has been behind the desk since 1962, and if you are lucky, by Byron, a blond cocker spaniel dog with wonderful, long, curly ears. The entry—in dull brown with industrial-strength carpeting, a vase of flowers, and old prints

TELEPHONE
01-45-77-70-58

FAX
01-40-59-43-75

MÉTRO
Charles-Michels

CREDIT CARDS
AE, MC, V

RATES
1–2 persons 260–385F, triple 460F; extra bed 80F; free public showers
Taxe de séjour: included

BREAKFAST
40F extra per person (includes juice, yogurt, and cheese)

of Paris scattered around—could use a new look. But you don't live in the entry, so just keep on going. The rooms are amazing, and spotless besides. I am a fan of no. 50, a double with soft gray and blue carpet, two desks, a view of the skyscraper apartments that line the Seine, and a beautiful bathroom with a stall shower. Double-glazed windows help to keep the noise levels down. No. 52 is just as nice and has plenty of space. No. 17, redone in blue with only a sink and bidet, is a steal at 260F for one or two people. On the fifth floor is a two-room suite (don't forget we are in a no-star here) with blond furniture. One room has twin beds, the other just one twin. The bathroom comes with soap and shampoo and shower doors . . . all for under $100. What a deal! Eight rooms have *cour* views, but they are not *too* bad. Breakfast is served in a blue-and-white first-floor dining room and includes cheese, fruit compote, juice, croissants, bread, jam, and a bonbon. Mme. Bihan is the sweetest manageress this side of heaven, and her faithful regulars know to reserve as far in advance as they can. Please do the same.

ENGLISH SPOKEN: Yes

FACILITIES AND SERVICES: Direct-dial phone; elevator; TV; no safe

NEAREST TOURIST ATTRACTIONS (LEFT BANK): None; must use public transportation; across from the Centre Beaugrenelle is one of the best Monoprix stores in Paris (see Cheap Chic, page 267)

Sixteenth Arrondissement

Known as a sedate, posh, and old-moneyed sector, the sixteenth is the home of the BCBG (*bon chic bon genre*) crowd, otherwise known as French yuppies. This is stylish territory, bordered by the Bois de Boulogne and the River Seine. Here you will see luxurious apartments and prostitutes in BMWs on the avenue Foch and fashionable shops in Passy and along the avenue Victor-Hugo. Trocadéro, directly across from the Seine and the Eiffel Tower, is the name of the gardens around the Palais de Chaillot, an imposing two-winged building that houses four museums. The spectacular view from the steps of Trocadéro at night, across the Seine to the Eiffel Tower, with the illuminated pools, fountains, and statues between, is one you must not miss.

RIGHT BANK
Avenue Foch, Bois de Boulogne, Jardin d'Acclimitation, Marmottan Museum, Musée Guimet, Passy, Palais de Chaillot, Trocadéro, shopping along avenue Victor-Hugo

HOTELS IN THE SIXTEENTH ARRONDISSEMENT

OTHER OPTIONS
Camping Out

Residence Hotels

*Indicates a Big Splurge
(†) Indicates listing not shown on map

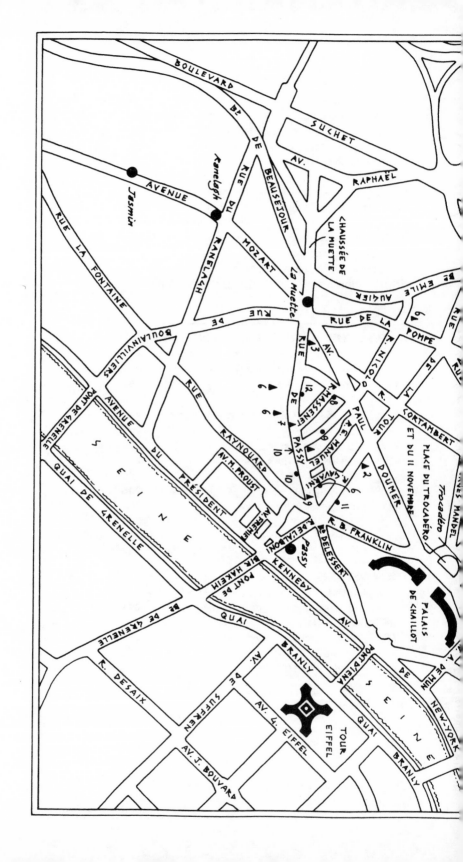

(1) AU PALAIS DE CHAILLOT HÔTEL ★★
35, avenue Raymond Poincarré, 75016 (16th)
28 rooms, all with shower or bath and toilet

TELEPHONE
01-53-70-09-09
FAX
01-53-70-09-08
MÉTRO
Trocadéro, Victor-Hugo
CREDIT CARDS
AE, DC, MC, V
RATES
Single 450F, double 520–580,
triple 680F
Taxe de Séjour: 5F extra per
person, per day
BREAKFAST
40F extra per person; free if you
show or mention
Cheap Sleeps in Paris

For up-to-the minute appeal in an area not known for budget anything, look no further than this sensational hotel. Two brothers, Cyrille and Thierry Pien, who received their masters in business administration in the United States, joined forces and completely gutted and revamped this twenty-eight room hotel, which is nicely situated between Trocadéro and the Champs-Élysées. The results are stunning, and in my opinion, the hotel is not only the best two-star in the arrondissement, but it sets the standards to which others should aspire.

From beginning to end, the hotel is a model of post-modern, casual French chic. Two potted trees frame the red awning entrance. To one side is a little summer terrace where breakfast can be served; otherwise, breakfast takes place in a marbleized yellow room with a half-mirrored wall reflecting five tables and armchairs. The bright bedrooms combine wicker with bold colors and have flashy bathrooms that include tubs and/or showers with corner shelves for shampoo and soap. All doubles face the street, and from nos. 61, 62, and 63 you can see the tip of the Eiffel Tower. There are five rooms similar to no. 34, which is on the back. I like the walk-in closet, the small sitting area with red detailing around the ceiling, and the Dufy print over the bed. These rooms also have twin beds that can be adapted to a king. In addition to the usual amenities, the hotel offers room service for drinks, laundry service, and PC compatible plugs. For the area, it is hard to imagine a better Cheap Sleep value.

ENGLISH SPOKEN: Yes

FACILITIES AND SERVICES: Direct-dial phone; elevator; hair dryer; laundry service; PC compatible plugs; room service for drinks; TV with international reception; office safe, no charge

NEAREST TOURIST ATTRACTIONS (RIGHT BANK): Palais de Chaillot, Trocadéro, shopping along avenue Victor-Hugo and in Passy, Arc de Triomphe, and Champs-Élysées

(2)   CHAMBELLAN MORGANE ★★★
6, rue Keppler, 75016 (16th)
20 rooms, all with shower or bath and toilet

In 1984, when I began writing *Cheap Sleeps in Paris,* I fell in love with a little hotel in the sixteenth arrondissement called Résidence Morgane. It was run by a *petite grand'mère* who pampered her guests beyond the call of duty. She would make an omelet at midnight, keep your messages, forward your mail, and do your laundry and ironing if asked. When I returned a year later, Madame had left and the hotel had been taken over by a gruff, noncaring owner. Five years later, on a hunch, I decided to recheck the hotel. I am so glad I did. Although Madame had not come back, new owners had masterminded a renovation that turned the hotel into the epitome of three-star elegance and classic luxury. Things have not changed since: they still do their utmost to please their international clientele.

The stage is set by the entrance and lobby, done in American Southwest colors with white enamel woodwork and beautifully upholstered Louis XV–style antiques. The only holdover from the past is the old, Morgane nameplate by the front door. Light, pumpkin-colored halls lead to stylishly outfitted bedrooms with silk wall coverings, matching quilted spreads and curtains, and efficient mirrored and marbled bathrooms. I am happy to recommend this hotel, as I did originally, for a quiet stay close to the golden triangle of the Concorde, the Eiffel Tower, and the Champs-Élysées.

ENGLISH SPOKEN: Yes

FACILITIES AND SERVICES: Bar; conference room; direct-dial phone; elevator; hair dryer; minibar; radio; room service; laundry service; TV with international reception; office safe, no charge

NEAREST TOURIST ATTRACTIONS (RIGHT BANK): Champs-Élysées, Arc de Triomphe

TELEPHONE
01-47-20-35-72

FAX
01-47-20-95-69

INTERNET
www.paris-hotel.tm.fr/fr/
chaillot.08 chambellan.html

MÉTRO
George-V, Charles-de-Gaulle-Étoile

CREDIT CARDS
AE, DC, MC, V

RATES
1–2 persons 660–900F
Taxe de séjour: included

BREAKFAST
55F extra per person

(3)   HÔTEL AMBASSADE ★★
79, rue Lauriston, at the corner of rue Cimarosa, 75016 (16th)
38 rooms, all with shower or bath and toilet

For a practical stopover near the Étoile and avenue Victor-Hugo, the Ambassade makes sense. The hotel is owned by the Mullie family, who maintain this two-star as a simple, friendly establishment that provides pleasant service and accommodations. When you walk in, you

TELEPHONE
01-45-53-41-15

FAX
01-45-53-30-80

MÉTRO
Boissiére

CREDIT CARDS
AE, DC, MC, V

RATES
Single 420–500F, double
530–600F
Taxe de séjour: 5F extra per
person, per day

BREAKFAST
50F extra per person

can't help but notice the unusual ceiling light fixture and the matching wall sconces, which date from the fifties. They dominate the entire lobby and sitting area and are quite amazing. Most of the rooms were redone in 1996. They vary in size from small to medium and are equipped with lacquered wicker furniture, soft, matching colors, and marble bathrooms. Those rooms on the ground floor have windows that open directly onto the street, creating a potential security problem, so I recommend reserving a room on a higher floor.

ENGLISH SPOKEN: Yes

FACILITIES AND SERVICES: Bar; direct-dial phone; elevator to third floor; hair dryer; TV with international reception; office safe, no charge

NEAREST TOURIST ATTRACTIONS (RIGHT BANK): Shopping on avenue Victor-Hugo, Palais de Chaillot, and Trocadéro

(4) HÔTEL DU BOIS ★★
11, rue du Dome, corner of 29, avenue Victor-Hugo, 75016 (16th)
41 rooms, all with shower or bath and toilet

TELEPHONE
01-45-00-31-96

FAX
01-45-00-90-05

E-MAIL
hoteldubois@wanadoo.fr

MÉTRO
Charles-de-Gaulle-Étoile,
Kléber

CREDIT CARDS
AE, MC, V

RATES
Single 495F, double 565–620F;
extra bed 160F;
lower off-season rates
Taxe de séjour: 5F extra per
person, per day

BREAKFAST
50F extra per person

For a stay on the exclusive avenue Victor-Hugo, just ten boutiques down from the Arc de Triomphe and place d'Étoile, consider the Hôtel du Bois, with a roster of loyal returnees who enjoy being only a few minutes' walk from the Champs-Élysées. The entrance to the hotel is in a passageway reached on foot by steep steps from the street level, or by car on an upper level through one-way streets from behind. You will recognize the hotel by the pretty planter boxes under each window. Owner David Byrne (see Hôtel Queen Mary, page 160) has shined, polished, and gradually redone the tired rooms, worn reception, and old bathrooms. The hotel is now up to speed in most areas. A host of useful information in English is also provided—everything from what to see and do to where to eat and shop in the immediate neighborhood. Rates are reasonable for this expensive area.

ENGLISH SPOKEN: Yes

FACILITIES AND SERVICES: Direct-dial phone; no elevator; minibar; TV with international reception; office safe, 10F per day

NEAREST TOURIST ATTRACTIONS (RIGHT BANK): Champs-Élysées, Arc de Triomphe, shopping along avenue Victor-Hugo

(5) HÔTEL DU ROND-POINT DE LONGCHAMP* ★★★
86, rue de Longchamp, at place de Mexico, 75016 (16th)
57 rooms, all with shower or bath and toilet

The area around the hotel dates back to the thirteenth century, when Longchamp was an austere abbey surrounded by fields and meadows belonging to a few farms. One of them was located right next to the hotel, and there is a plaque to commemorate Boileau and La Fontaine, two great French writers who came here to buy their fresh milk. Today the area is known as one of the most prestigious residential areas in the capital.

The owner of this wonderful hotel, Gerard Dumontant, served as the president of the independent hoteliers in France, so you can imagine that his hotel reflects only the best . . . and let me assure you it does. The hotel appeals to the traditionalists looking for exceptional value, classic service, and a multitude of facilities. The ground floor consists of a plant-filled lounge, a bar, and a billiards room with soft leather armchairs. Some of the rooms are decidedly Louis XIV, with four-poster beds and heavy curtains swooping from floor to ceiling. Others reflect more modern tastes. Views of the Eiffel Tower can be seen from rooms ending with the number two. Several are superbly planned for business people. These rooms double as an office and sitting room during the day and have a comfortable Murphy pull-down bed for the night. All rooms have international television reception, air-conditioning, and fabulous marble bathrooms.

ENGLISH SPOKEN: Yes

FACILITIES AND SERVICES: Air-conditioning; bar; business facilities; direct-dial phone; elevator; hair dryer; laundry services; minibar; radio; room service; TV with international reception; office safe, no charge

NEAREST TOURIST ATTRACTIONS (RIGHT BANK): Palais de Chaillot, Trocadéro, shopping on avenue Victor Hugo

TELEPHONE
01-45-05-13-63

FAX
01-47-55-12-80

MÉTRO
Trocadéro, Victor-Hugo

CREDIT CARDS
AE, DC, MC, V

RATES
Single 520–1,010F, double 750–1,520F; ask about off-season rates
Taxe de séjour: included

BREAKFAST
65F extra per person

(6) HÔTEL GAVARNI ★★
5, rue Gavarni, 75016 (16th)
30 rooms, all with shower or bath and toilet

Here is an attractive Cheap Sleep choice on a quiet street in the center of Passy, one of Paris's most sought-after residential and shopping *quartiers.* The hotel is run by the lovely Nelly Rolland, who realized her dream

TELEPHONE
01-45-24-52-82

FAX
01-40-50-16-95

MÉTRO
Passy

CREDIT CARDS
AE, DC, MC, V

RATES
Single 455F, double 480–500F;
extra bed 80F
Taxe de séjour: 5F extra per
person, per day

BREAKFAST
35F extra per person

come true when she bought this hotel from the Mornands, who owned it for years. Nelly is a graduate of the Hotel Management School in Lausanne, Switzerland. She is young and full of life and new ideas. She plans to redo the entire hotel, but she wisely started by replacing the carpet in the front rooms and adding new wall treatments in many other rooms.

Everything has been kept in top shape. The cozy singles on the back side of the hotel have corner marble fireplaces and are popular with many repeat visitors. Bathrooms are behind folding doors and are small, but functional. No. 603 is a favorite because both windows have a view of the Eiffel Tower, which is especially beautiful when lighted at night. Other rooms with various Eiffel Tower views include nos. 502, 503, 504, and 602.

ENGLISH SPOKEN: Yes

FACILITIES AND SERVICES: Direct-dial phone; elevator; TV with international reception; office safe, no charge

NEAREST TOURIST ATTRACTIONS (RIGHT BANK): Passy, Palais de Chaillot, Trocadéro

(7)   HÔTEL KEPPLER ★★
12, rue Keppler, 75016 (16th)
49 rooms, all with shower or bath and toilet

TELEPHONE
01-47-20-65-05

FAX
01-47-23-02-29

MÉTRO
George-V, Kléber

CREDIT CARDS
AE, MC, V

RATES
1–2 persons 475F; extra bed
30% of the room rate
Taxe de séjour: included

BREAKFAST
35F extra per person

For a two-star, family-run hotel, the Keppler offers much more than just a Cheap Sleep in a tony location. It has, for one thing, honest-to-goodness room service, an almost unheard-of feature in almost all three-star hotels in Paris, let alone a two-star. Since my last visit, various improvements have been made, adding even further to the overall recommendation of this hotel. The lobby shows off a pretty fireplace and a small corner bar. The large dining room has mahogany upholstered chairs, blue walls, and Levelor blinds along the streetside windows. For the price, you cannot expect luxurious rooms with deep-pile carpeting and designer fabrics. They are, however, efficiently modern with sturdy Swedish-style desks and chairs and ample closet and drawer space. Four rooms have balconies. A team of uniformed maids wearing beepers keeps everything shipshape, and management keeps an ear tuned to inappropriate noise. There are many repeat guests, and it is easy to understand their loyalty to this hidden Parisian value, where reservations and a deposit are required far, far in advance of your stay.

ENGLISH SPOKEN: Yes

FACILITIES AND SERVICES: Bar; direct-dial phone; elevator; some hair dryers; room service until 7:00 P.M.; TV with international reception; room safe, no extra charge

NEAREST TOURIST ATTRACTIONS (RIGHT BANK): Arc de Triomphe, Champs-Élysées, Guimet Museum, Palais de Chaillot, and Trocadéro

(8) HÔTEL MASSENET ★★★
5, bis rue Massenet, 75016 (16th)
41 rooms, all with shower or bath and toilet

For a beautiful stay in Paris on a tranquil street in Passy, I like the formal Massenet. The well-heeled French executive clientele appreciates the serene neighborhood close to the *bon ton* Passy shopping district, the professional services of the uniformed hotel staff—especially Thay, the courteous receptionist, who has worked the desk for almost two decades—and, above all, the prices. These travelers know that if the Massenet were in a more mainstream location, the prices would be nearly doubled.

Downstairs, the public rooms are paneled in a rich walnut. Soft seating and a small library along one wall create an appealing English intimacy. Morning croissants are served in a little alcove overlooking a colorful patio. All the comfortable rooms are well furnished and impeccably maintained. No. 70, a corner double, has its own balcony looking out to the Eiffel Tower and La Tour Montparnasse and a walk-in closet that is almost as large as some hotel rooms I have stayed in. If traveling alone, request no. 71, a top-floor single with a view terrace, or no. 51 with a small balcony, double closet with shelves, and a large bathroom. If quiet and space are top priorities, no. 25, a back twin, has a triple-drawer marble dresser, workable desk, three chairs, double luggage rack, and a bathroom with two sinks, a large tub, and oversize towels.

ENGLISH SPOKEN: Yes

FACILITIES AND SERVICES: Bar; direct-dial phone; elevator; hair dryer; minibar; TV with international reception; office safe, no charge

NEAREST TOURIST ATTRACTIONS (RIGHT BANK): Passy, twenty-minute walk to Palais de Chaillot, Trocadéro, and the Eiffel Tower

TELEPHONE
01-45-24-43-03

FAX
01-45-24-41-39

MÉTRO
Passy

CREDIT CARDS
AE, DC, MC, V

RATES
Single 555–735F, double 860F; extra bed 190F, baby bed 100F
Taxe de séjour: 6F extra per person, per day

BREAKFAST
Included; can be deducted at 40F per person

(9) HÔTEL NICOLO ★★
3, rue Nicolo, 75016 (16th)
28 rooms, all with shower or bath and toilet

TELEPHONE
01-42-88-83-40
FAX
01-42-24-45-41
MÉTRO
Passy, La Muette
CREDIT CARDS
AE, MC, V
RATES
Single 390F, double 430–450F,
triple 490F, quad 510F
Taxe de séjour: 5F extra per
person, per day
BREAKFAST
40F extra per person

Join diplomats visiting their nearby embassies, delegates to the OECD, and other smart, money-saving travelers anxious to maximize their daily travel allowances by staying at the hidden Nicolo in the center of Passy. What you save here you can spend engaging in guilt-free shopping at the discount shops on rue de la Tour (see Cheap Chic, page 258) or along rue de Passy, one of Paris's shopping meccas for traditional, well-made clothing. If shopping doesn't appeal to you, surely one of the nearby restaurants recommended in *Cheap Eats in Paris* will.

The owner of the Nicolo is an American woman who continues to gradually make changes, all with an eye to attracting more guests from the United States. Almost all rooms have a small entry, giving the feeling of spaciousness, and are free from the usual symphony of Parisian street noises. Rooms are color-friendly, and many look onto a small garden that has a lovely tree. Bathrooms are dated in terms of tile, but they are certainly spotless and serviceable. True, the hotel is old, but it has enough Gallic charm to draw many repeat guests.

ENGLISH SPOKEN: Yes

FACILITIES AND SERVICES: Direct-dial phone; elevator; TV; office safe, no charge

NEAREST TOURIST ATTRACTIONS (RIGHT BANK): Passy, twenty-minute walk to Palais de Chaillot, Trocadéro, and the Eiffel Tower

(10) HÔTEL PASSY EIFFEL ★★★
10, rue de Passy, 75016 (16th)
50 rooms, all with shower or bath and toilet

TELEPHONE
01-45-25-55-66
FAX
01-42-88-89-88
MÉTRO
Passy
CREDIT CARDS
AE, DC, MC, V
RATES
Single 580–680F, double 650–
700F, triple 850F
Taxe de séjour: 6F extra per
person, per day

The Hôtel Passy Eiffel, on the main street in Passy, provides a first-hand look at one of Paris's most exclusive neighborhoods, which has some of the best shopping you can find. The marbled foyer and lobby open onto a garden courtyard with six rooms facing it. Two salons are tucked along each side: one has a grand piano and inviting seating; the other is an airy, glass-enclosed breakfast room. Wood-beam ceilings add a sense of dimension to the variety of rooms. For the most part they are comfortable, with only a few faded overtones. All have pleasing views. I think no. 51, a suite with four windows opening onto a balcony is a good deal, as is no.

50, with soft pink damask tissue on the walls and a bathroom with corner mirrors and a large enclosed shower. From the top floor on the side street, guests can watch the elevator scale the Eiffel Tower as it takes tourists to the top. For breakfast, be sure to sample some of the honey bottled directly from the owner's beehives. During the week you can pet his dog, Volga, who holds court in the reception area.

ENGLISH SPOKEN: Yes

FACILITIES AND SERVICES: Air-conditioning in some rooms; bar; direct-dial phone; elevator to fifth floor; hair dryer; minibar; TV with international reception; office safe, no charge

NEAREST TOURIST ATTRACTIONS (RIGHT BANK): Shopping in Passy, Palais de Chaillot, Trocadéro

(11) HÔTEL REGINA DE PASSY ★★★
6, rue de la Tour, 75016 (16th)
64 rooms, all with shower or bath and toilet

Built in 1930 for the International Exhibition, this hotel is high on the Right Bank of the Seine across from the Eiffel Tower. The almost-grand lobby has a staircase framed by marvelous, signed stained-glass windows. Half of the hotel rooms have been restyled, and they are sophisticated and ultra-modern with geometric prints, chrome and leather furniture, and modern bathrooms. The older rooms are still in excellent condition and retain a benign elegance from their former glory . . . as well as lower price tags. Fifteen rooms have small balconies where you can step out and look over the Passy neighborhood with the Eiffel Tower in the distance. The two penthouse apartments with private rooftop terraces boast impressive furnishings, marble bathrooms (one with a sunken tub), small bars, fully equipped kitchens, and enough wardrobe space for most of us to unpack and stay a year. These apartments would be the answer for a small family or anyone on an extended stay. The hotel would score much better on my tally sheet were it not for the poor image created by the desk staff, most of whom need a refresher course in cordiality and customer service.

ENGLISH SPOKEN: Yes

FACILITIES AND SERVICES: Air-conditioning in one apartment; bar; direct-dial phone; elevator; hair dryer; minibar; room safe, no charge; radio; TV with international reception

BREAKFAST
40F extra per person

TELEPHONE
01-45-24-43-64

FAX
01-40-50-70-62

MÉTRO
Passy

CREDIT CARDS
AE, DC, MC, V

RATES
Single 540–830F, double 780–830F, apartments 910–1,500F; extra bed 200F
Taxe de séjour: included

BREAKFAST
Continental 55F extra per person, buffet 60F extra

NEAREST TOURIST ATTRACTIONS (RIGHT BANK): Passy, twenty-minute walk to Palais de Chaillot, Trocadéro, and the Eiffel Tower

(12) LE HAMEAU DE PASSY ★★
48, rue de Passy, 75016 (16th)
32 rooms, all with shower or bath and toilet

TELEPHONE
01-42-88-47-55
FAX
01-42-30-83-72
MÉTRO
Passy, La Muette
CREDIT CARDS
AE, DC, MC, V
RATES
Single 535F, double 590–610F, triple 690F; extra bed 80F
Taxe de séjour: 5F extra per person, per day
BREAKFAST
Included, cannot be deducted

Hidden in a garden walkway off the busy rue de Passy, the Hameau de Passy is a snappy two-star addition to this posh pocket of Paris. The owners of the Hôtel Passy Eiffel (see page 206) took this rumpled hotel and transformed it into the modern, four-building structure it is today. All the rooms face the garden and are done in the same style, with stark white walls, open closets, soft sheer curtains at the windows, and harmonizing fabrics and carpets. Ground-floor rooms lack security, so I suggest asking for something on a higher floor. If you are lucky and land in building no. 4, the elevator takes the strain out of climbing up several flights to your room. Otherwise, in buildings 1, 2, and 3, you will pay the same price and have to hike up a winding outdoor metal stairway to get to your room. If this sort of exercise does not bother you, and you want to be only a whisper away from all the great shopping in Passy, then consider this hotel.

ENGLISH SPOKEN: Yes

FACILITIES AND SERVICES: Direct-dial phone; elevator in building no. 4 only; TV with international reception; office safe, 30F per stay

NEAREST TOURIST ATTRACTIONS (RIGHT BANK): Passy, twenty-minute walk to Palais de Chaillot, Trocadéro, and the Eiffel Tower

(13) LIBERTEL ARGENTINE* ★★★
1-3, rue d'Argentine, 76016 (16th)
40 rooms, all with shower or bath and toilet

TELEPHONE
01-45-02-76-76, toll-free from the U.S., 800-44-UTELL
FAX
01-45-02-76-00
MÉTRO
Argentine
CREDIT CARDS
AE, MC, V

The Libertel Argentine, a haven of comfort and tranquillity in the fashionable district around avenue Foch and the Bois de Boulogne, commemorates the time when South America's high society occupied this prestigious quarter. For elegant living on an expanded budget, it is difficult to find higher quality and better services than this hotel offers. Although it is a bit far, the nearest métro line is direct to the Champs-Élysées, the place de la Concorde, and the Louvre. In another fifteen minutes, you can be at the Bastille seeing how the wilder half of Paris lives and plays.

The atmosphere of the Argentine is that of a gracious family home, especially in the red-and-blue sitting room and bar, whose magnificent carved ceiling is a copy of the original. The beautifully appointed rooms incorporate Pierre Frey and Laura Ashley fabrics along with rich mahogany woods and marble bathrooms with mirrored reflections of reproduction fittings. Add to this the advantage of one floor reserved exclusively for nonsmokers, mileage points given to those enrolled in the United Airlines frequent flyer program, and excellent promotional rates, and you have a Big Splurge that Cheap Sleepers in Paris appreciate for those times when the budget and occasion calls for something special.

ENGLISH SPOKEN: Yes

FACILITIES AND SERVICES: Bar; direct-dial phone; two elevators; hair dryer; laundry service; minibar; room service; TV with international reception; room safe, no charge; one floor reserved exclusively for nonsmokers

NEAREST TOURIST ATTRACTIONS (RIGHT BANK): Arc de Triomphe, Champs-Élysées, Bois de Boulogne, Palais de Congrès

RATES
Single 875F, double 950F; ask about special promotional, corporate, and low-season rates
Taxe de séjour: included

BREAKFAST
75F extra per person

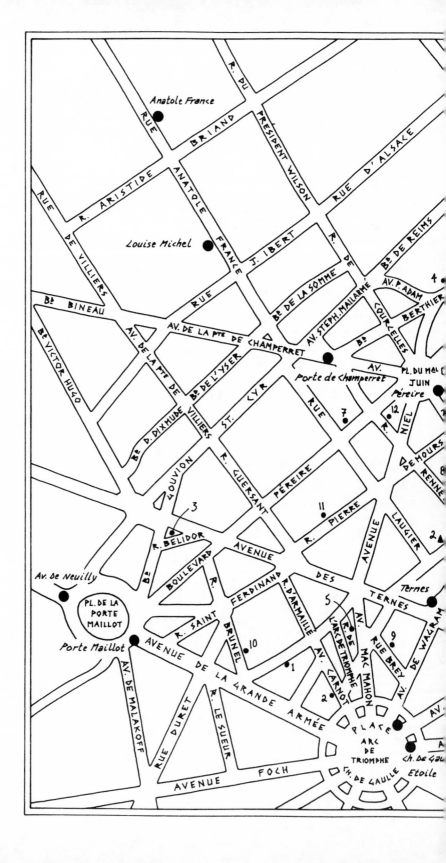

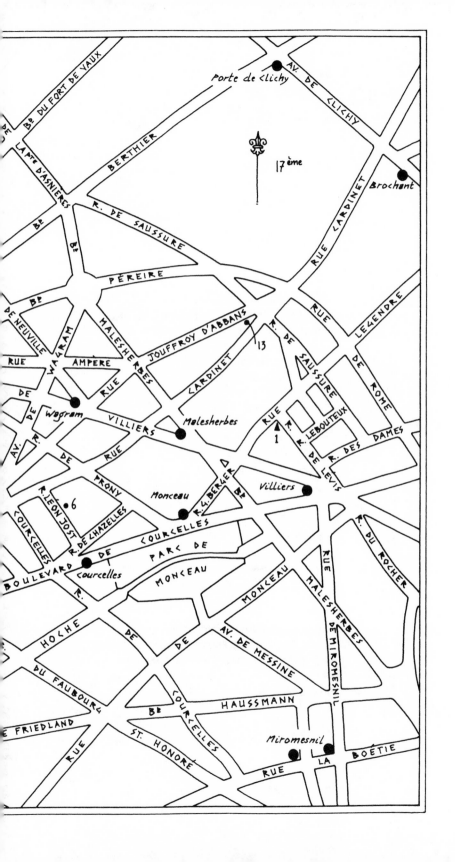

Seventeenth Arrondissement

The better half of the seventeenth arrondissement extends west from boulevard Malesherbes to the Arc de Triomphe. To the east and toward Gare St-Lazare, it is full of questionable characters dealing in the shadier side of life. This is an area to avoid. The main attraction is the Palais des Congrès, a convention center with restaurants, movie theaters, and the pick-up and drop-off point for passengers going to and from Roissy-Charles-de-Gaulle Airport. There are many fine hotels in the better section of the arrondissement, and the areas around them are safe. Bus and métro connections to more tourist-inspired parts of Paris are excellent.

HOTELS IN THE SEVENTEENTH ARRONDISSEMENT

OTHER OPTIONS
Residence Hotels

(1) CENTRE VILLE ÉTOILE ★★★
6, rue des Acacias, 75017 (17th)
16 rooms, all with shower or bath and toilet

Original, smart, and stylish are three words that adequately describe this Art Deco–inspired hotel close to the Arc de Triomphe and the Champs-Élysées. A three-story glass atrium joins the two buildings, which house only sixteen sleeping slots. An interesting collection of American cartoon prints enlivens the lobby and hallways. The small masculine rooms, which haven't a ruffle in sight, display a judicious use of space and employ hard-edge colors of red, black, blue, and white along with black lacquered furnishings. Tiled and mirrored bathrooms are modern, with shelf space for toiletries and stretch tubs for leisurely bathing. The personable staff goes beyond the call of duty in welcoming guests.

ENGLISH SPOKEN: Yes

FACILITIES AND SERVICES: Air-conditioning in all rooms; direct-dial phone; elevator; hair dryer; minibar; *peignoirs*; room service; TV with international reception; room safe, no charge

NEAREST TOURIST ATTRACTIONS (RIGHT BANK): Arc de Triomphe, Palais de Congrès

MÉTRO
Charles-de-Gaulle-Étoile, Argentine

CREDIT CARDS
AE, DC, MC, V

RATES
Single 590–800F, double 690–950F; extra bed 100F; lower off-season rates
Taxe de séjour: 6F extra per person, per day

BREAKFAST
55F extra per person

(2) HÔTEL ASTRID ★★★
27, avenue Carnot, 75017 (17th)
41 rooms, all with shower or bath and toilet

Florence Guillet heads one of the best family-run hotels in Paris. Started by her grandfather in 1937, the Hôtel Astrid provides comfortable, moderately priced accommodations in this top-drawer part of Paris. The colors throughout the hotel are cheerfully appropriate and blend well with the furnishings. Two of the nicest bedrooms have small balconies for viewing the Arc de Triomphe. The rooms are upgraded continually, and I recommend that you ask for one of the newest when reserving. No. 21, pictured on the hotel's brochure, is a nice choice because it is bigger. It has two armchairs, a marble fireplace, twin brass beds, and good closets; the bathroom has a tub, but no shower. I also like no. 25, which is done in pastels with desk and luggage space, two chairs, and a double bed. The spotless bathroom has a stall shower, hooks, and a shelf for toiletries. The hotel is only about a five-minute walk from the Air France bus stop for Roissy-Charles-de-Gaulle Airport, so if you don't have much luggage, or if you have a luggage trolley, you can save money on cab fare.

ENGLISH SPOKEN: Yes

FACILITIES AND SERVICES: Air-conditioning planned for one floor; direct-dial phone; elevator; hair dryer; TV with international reception; room safe, no charge

NEAREST TOURIST ATTRACTIONS (RIGHT BANK): Arc de Triomphe, Champs-Élysées

TELEPHONE
01-44-09-26-00

FAX
01-44-09-26-01

INTERNET
www.webscapades.com/france/paris/astrid.htm

MÉTRO
Charles-de-Gaulle-Étoile

CREDIT CARDS
AE, MC, V

RATES
Single 470–570F, double 550–740F, triple 790F, quad 900F; extra bed 100F; lower off-season rates
Taxe de séjour: included

BREAKFAST
Buffet included, cannot be deducted

(3) HÔTEL BÉLIDOR ★
5, rue Bélidor, 75017 (17th)
47 rooms, 18 with shower or bath and toilet

TELEPHONE
01-45-74-49-91
FAX
01-45-72-54-22
MÉTRO
Porte Maillot (see note)
CREDIT CARDS
None, cash only, paid in
advance
RATES
Single 200–310F, double 200–
380F; public shower 30F
Taxe de séjour: included
BREAKFAST
30F extra per person

No serious Cheap Sleeper in Paris can afford to overlook the Bélidor. It is an old-fashioned sort of hotel that has been in the same family for decades. Family furniture fills the first breakfast room, which is not only the prettiest but is nonsmoking. In the second, there is a marble and brick fireplace, an upright piano, and you can smoke, but the ambiance just isn't there. The owner is just as sweet as ever, and the room colors and patterns are just as mixed. A stay here will provide you with a clean bed in a decent area just around the corner from the Palais de Congrès. The rooms are neat as pins, and those with bathtubs are larger than many two- and three-star rooms costing twice the price. Don't let the orange chenille and nontouristy location deter you. After only a ten- or fifteen-minute métro journey, you can be standing under the new pyramid at the Louvre, floating down the Seine on a *bateau mouche,* or strolling through the most romantic streets in St-Germain-des-Prés. It is crucial to remember to plan ahead for this one because it is booked weeks in advance all during the year.

NOTE: The métro station at Porte Maillot is enormous, so look for these directions in French for the correct exit: *sorti côté Paris, bd. Gouvion-Saint-Cyr côté impair* (exit on the Paris side of the métro station, on the odd-numbered side of bd. Gouvion Saint-Cyr).

ENGLISH SPOKEN: Yes

FACILITIES AND SERVICES: Direct-dial phone; no elevator, TV, or safe

NEAREST TOURIST ATTRACTIONS (RIGHT BANK): Palais des Congrès exhibition and convention center; all other tourist attractions require public transportation

(4) HÔTEL DE BANVILLE* ★★★
166, boulevard Berthier, 75017 (17th)
39 rooms, all with shower or bath and toilet

TELEPHONE
01-42-67-70-16
FAX
01-44-40-42-77
INTERNET
www.webscapades.com//com/
france/paris/

The classic Hôtel de Banville is my idea of a wonderful, personalized Parisian hotel. It was built in 1928 by architect Jerome Bellat, who designed many of the magnificent buildings the seventeenth arrondissement is famous for. From the beautiful lobby to the rooms filled with family antiques and heirlooms, you can tell immediately that this is a hotel where the owners know and care very much about what they are doing. The hotel has developed a large following of appreciative guests who applaud the efforts of owner Mme. Lambert, her daughter, and their right-hand man, Jean-Pierre, who is also the talented artist who did all the paintings that hang throughout the hotel. A portrait of their dog, Charlie, the hotel mascot, is displayed over the reception desk. Charlie is very popular; in fact, he even receives mail from guests who have grown to love him during their repeated visits. Mme. Lambert grew up in the hotel business, and all of her family is involved in the industry in some way. Her background and expertise, combined with her impeccably good taste, are evident everywhere you look. Mme. Lambert told me, "I want this hotel to be like a private house, and I think I have realized my wish." I agree without question.

Every time I visit the hotel, I think, This is it. What more can she possibly do to improve on perfection? . . . and each time I find wonderful new additions. On my last visit, a new sitting room and piano bar featuring live music had been added next to the lobby and dining area, which displays hand-painted murals. The bedrooms are on a revolving schedule of redecorating and upgrading. All are nice and have something special to recommend them. Those on the eighth floor have sweeping views, from the Arc de Triomphe to the Tour Montparnasse. Naturally, these are in great demand. In no. 21, a small entry leads to a room papered in deep salmon and cream-colored miniature print. Twin beds have padded head-boards that complement the beige-and-white quilt pattern used on barrel chairs. The mirrored closets provide plenty of move-in space, and the back side location guarantees calm. No. 42 has a great black wrought-iron bed with an open canopy top. No. 52 is called the White Room because of its beautiful ceiling detail. It has two framed Chinese paintings on parchments that Mme. Lambert's mother brought with her from China. For one of the best bathrooms in Paris, reserve no. 61. This bathroom has a great twenties-style freestanding sink and huge mirror that was found at the Paris flea market. The room keeps pace with Canovas fabrics on the curtains and chairs, yellow-and-white stripe walls, either twins or a king-size bed, and a corner work area. Other favorites include no. 22, done in white wicker; the pink-and-white no. 24, with a brass bed and sofa that converts

MÉTRO
Péreire, Porte-de-Champerret

CREDIT CARDS
AE, MC, V

RATES
Single 735F, double 860F, triple 900F, quad 950F
Taxe de séjour: included

BREAKFAST
Continental 50F extra per person, *Dietetique* 75F extra, *Pleinform* 85F extra

into bunks for children; and either nos. 75 or 85 for singles. If romance is on your agenda, reserve no. 83, which has a view over all of Paris.

Even breakfast is special at the Banville. You can order a basic continental or the *dietetique,* which features wheat bread and yogurt, or go all out and have sausage, eggs, and fruit juice along with your croissants and coffee.

The hotel is located on a busy boulevard lined with plane trees. The métro is close, and you can take the RER to the Musée d'Orsay and St-Michel. For buses, the no. 92 puts you at Étoile and the no. 84 drops you at place de la Concorde.

ENGLISH SPOKEN: Yes

FACILITIES AND SERVICES: Air-conditioning in all rooms; bar; direct-dial phone; elevator; hair dryer; parking by reservation (75F per day); twenty-four-hour room service for light meals; TV with international reception; room safe, no charge

NEAREST TOURIST ATTRACTIONS (RIGHT BANK): None; must use public transportation

(5) HÔTEL DES DEUX ACACIAS ★★
28, rue de l'Arc-de-Triomphe, 75017 (17th)
31 rooms, all with shower or bath and toilet

TELEPHONE
01-43-80-01-85

FAX
01-40-53-94-62

MÉTRO
Charles-de-Gaulle-Étoile, Argentine

CREDIT CARDS
AE, MC, V

RATES
1–2 persons 385F, quad 460F; lower off-season rates
Taxe de séjour: 5F extra per person, per day

BREAKFAST
30F extra per person

Never mind its rather plain atmosphere—this top-pick Cheap Sleep will please visitors wanting to keep within a certain budget and still be conveniently close to the Champs-Élysées. For more than half a century, the hotel was owned and run by Mme. Delmas, who took over from her parents when they retired. Her gentle demeanor permeated the entire operation, and so did her thrift and resistance to change. I never thought I would see the day when she would leave her hotel and retire to the sunny south of France. But it has happened. The new owners are members of the Roubache family, and they have made some welcome additions. Starting with the reception area, two green tartan wing-back chairs now provide a place to sit. The breakfast room has colorful *provençal* print tablecloths and Italian flower vases. Upstairs, new paint, carpets, bedspreads, and some upgraded towels have perked up the rooms. No one could ever call this modest place modern, but with the improvements, one can certainly call it much better.

NOTE: Enclosed public parking is available across the street for motorists.

ENGLISH SPOKEN: Yes

FACILITIES AND SERVICES: Direct-dial phone; elevator; TV; office safe, no charge

NEAREST TOURIST ATTRACTIONS (RIGHT BANK): Champs-Élysées, Arc de Triomphe

(6) HÔTEL EBER ★★★
18, rue Léon-Jost, 75017 (17th)
18 rooms, all with shower or bath and toilet

Travelers longing for peace and quiet have at their disposal a group of French hotels whose owners have taken a vow of silence. The Hôtel Eber is one of the 275 members of Relais du Silence, an association of individually owned hotels dedicated to providing a silent and calm atmosphere where guests can feel at home. At the Eber, the entrance along a tiled walkway opens onto a beamed salon centered around a Henri II wooden carved fireplace. To the left of the reception desk is an inviting bar and breakfast area with comfortable armchairs. In the back is a green patio, with metal tables and chairs set out on warm days for al fresco breakfasts. The rooms tend to be small and are decorated in light beiges with good-looking art prints and posters on the walls. The family rooms feature not only two rooms, but two bathrooms. Many of the hotel clientele are from the world of fashion or entertainment, not a group known for its introverted behavior. However, owner Jean-Marc Eber says that those who want nonstop excitement should stay in St-Germain-de-Prés.

You will need public transportation for most things on a tourist agenda, but it might be interesting to walk by 25, rue de Chazelles, about two blocks away, and see where the Statue of Liberty was originally built. There is a photo of it under construction hanging by the hotel elevator. Also on display around the hotel are photos of the statue in varying stages of development and the signatures of those who attended the completion ceremonies.

ENGLISH SPOKEN: Yes

FACILITIES AND SERVICES: Bar; direct-dial phone; elevator; hair dryer; laundry service; minibar; radio; TV with international reception; office safe, no charge; room service from restaurants in the area

NEAREST TOURIST ATTRACTIONS (RIGHT BANK): Arc de Triomphe, Champs-Élysées, Parc Monceau

TELEPHONE
01-46-22-60-70

FAX
01-47-63-01-01

MÉTRO
Courcelles

CREDIT CARDS
AE, DC, MC, V

RATES
1–2 persons 610–675F, suite 1,150F
Taxe de séjour: 6F extra per person, per day

BREAKFAST
50F extra per person (served all day)

(7)   HÔTEL ÉTOILE PÉREIRE ★★
146, boulevard Péreire, 75017 (17th)
26 rooms, all with shower or bath and toilet

The Étoile Péreire, a member of the Relais du Silence (see Hôtel Eber above), is a sophisticated hotel offering modern luxury at affordable prices. Occupying a distinctive building that is hard to identify as a hotel, it benefited from a long-overdue remodeling project in 1987, when the 1900s-style rooms and claw-foot bathtubs were tossed out, and again between 1995 and 1996 when all the rooms and the lobby received face-lifts. Not lost in the changes are the tranquillity and character of the rooms and the dedicated services of the staff, headed for many years by Ferruccio Pardi and his wife, who, in her white starched apron, rigorously oversees daily room maintenance.

The crisp rooms offer guests a mixture of modern Italian furniture and country fabrics. The best selections are the two-story duplexes with both air-conditioning and ceiling fans, skylights, and soft watercolor paintings. No matter where you land, your bathroom will be modern and well supplied. M. Pardi prides himself on his breakfasts, which are served in a white-and-gray basement dining room. Diners have a choice of forty jams, jellies, or honeys to accompany their croissants and fresh orange or grapefruit juice. If you want more, ham or bacon and eggs are available.

While hardly in the tourist mainstream, the hotel is close to Porte Maillot and the Air France air terminal. A large city park with tennis courts and plenty of picnic benches is across the street, as well as several old dining favorites listed in *Cheap Eats in Paris.*

ENGLISH SPOKEN: Yes

FACILITIES AND SERVICES: Air-conditioning in four duplexes; bar; direct-dial phone; elevator; hair dryer; laundry service; minibar in all rooms except singles with showers; parking can be arranged; room service; TV with international reception; room safe, no charge

NEAREST TOURIST ATTRACTIONS (RIGHT BANK): None; must use public transportation

TELEPHONE
01-42-67-60-00
FAX
01-42-67-02-90
MÉTRO
Péreire
CREDIT CARDS
AE, DC, MC, V
RATES
Single 590–690F, double 790F, duplex 1,000F; no charge for extra bed; ask about special weekend and off-season rates *Taxe de séjour*: 6F extra per person, per day
BREAKFAST
55F extra per person

(8)   HÔTEL FLAUBERT ★★
19, rue Rennequin, 75017 (17th)
37 rooms, all with shower or bath and toilet

TELEPHONE
01-46-22-44-35

This garden hotel, designed and built by Christiane and Michel Niceron, opened its doors in January 1989.

Warm toast tones and airy bamboo furniture set the stage in the lobby and mirrored breakfast room, both filled to capacity with green houseplants. A cage of colorful parakeets adds a tropical note. All this opens onto an outdoor garden overflowing with blooming hydrangeas, impatiens, and colorful seasonal plants. It is certainly clear that the Nicerons *love* to garden. Singles or couples with scanty luggage can reserve one of the rooms opening onto this garden. For more space and better lighting, I like a top floor *chambre*. Mme. Niceron is a teacher, so she is not always at the hotel. M. Niceron *is* at the hotel full-time and works with his staff to provide pleasant stays for the guests. In addition, the rooms are perfectly clean, some new bathrooms have been added, and the Cheap Sleep prices are good for this part of Paris, which is not known for much in the budget range.

ENGLISH SPOKEN: Yes

FACILITIES AND SERVICES: Direct-dial phone; elevator; hair dryer; minibar; TV; no safe

NEAREST TOURIST ATTRACTIONS (RIGHT BANK): Ten-minute walk to Champs-Élysées and Arc de Triomphe

FAX
01-43-80-32-34
MÉTRO
Ternes
CREDIT CARDS
AE, DC, MC, V
RATES
Single 450F, double 500–550F, triple 750F; extra bed 100F
Taxe de séjour: 5F extra per person, per day
BREAKFAST
40F extra per person

(9) HÔTEL NEVA ★★★
14, rue Brey, 75017 (17th)
31 rooms, all with shower or bath and toilet

For an upmarket choice by the Champs-Élysées, the Hôtel Neva delivers comfort and convenience, especially for guests who need to be close to the Palais des Congrès conference and exhibition center. Wood-paneled walls keep the mood warm, and the interesting collection of paintings and sculpture reminds you that this is, indeed, Paris. The mother of the owner is an acclaimed artist and is responsible for the five-person metal sculpture by the front entrance and many of the other paintings that hang in the lobby, bar, and breakfast room. No one seems to know the origin of the large elephant.

The rooms are laid out in a contemporary sort of way. The largest are on the first floor. One of the best of these is no. 5, overlooking the garden. It is a large accommodation, done in gray with a painting of Provence on one wall. Closet space is good, and so is the tub and shower. No. 32 is a single on the back. Soft yellow walls give it a light look. Also on the back is no. 46, done in gray with lavender accents. In addition to being very quiet, it has a long glass-topped desk allowing plenty of work space.

TELEPHONE
01-43-80-28-26
FAX
01-47-63-00-22
MÉTRO
Charles-de-Gaulle-Étoile
CREDIT CARDS
AE, DC, MC, V
RATES
Single 600–650F, double 710–760F; extra bed 100F
Taxe de séjour: 6F extra per person, per day
BREAKFAST
45F extra per person

While there is not much to beckon the visitor in the immediate neighborhood, the Champs-Élysées is close, and from there transportation to all *quartiers* is easy.

ENGLISH SPOKEN: Yes

FACILITIES AND SERVICES: Air-conditioning; bar; direct-dial phone; elevator; hair dryer; minibar; radio; TV with international reception; room safe, no charge

NEAREST TOURIST ATTRACTIONS (RIGHT BANK): Champs-Élysées, Arc de Triomphe, Palais des Congrès

(10) HÔTEL PALMA ★★
46, rue Brunel, 75017 (17th)
37 rooms, all with shower or bath and toilet

TELEPHONE
01-45-74-74-51
FAX
01-45-74-40-90
MÉTRO
Argentine
CREDIT CARDS
AE, MC, V
RATES
1–2 persons 400–420F, triple 510F; extra bed 75F
Taxe de séjour: included
BREAKFAST
40F extra per person

If you want the most for your battered Yankee buck and don't mind being a bit far from the center of things, then the Palma is one of the best Cheap Sleep deals in the French capital. Its sensational value, coupled with the quality and quantity of service, delights its many followers, who come from all budget backgrounds. Located in the leafy precincts of the upper-crust seventeenth arrondissement, it is within an easy walk to the Palais des Congrès exhibition center, the Air France terminal at Porte Maillot, and excellent public transportation links that will whisk you anyplace you want to be in less than thirty minutes.

The best thing about this treasure besides its value and the congenial owners, M. and Mme. Couderc, is that guests will never feel like they are "budgeting" by staying here. Aside from the random use of florals, patterns, and colors, nothing is torn or tattered; no carpets are frayed; everything that should be painted is; the furnishings are exceptionally nice; and every room has a nice bathroom and color television with international reception, including CNN. The rooms in highest demand are the blissfully quiet and cozy top-floor roosts with air-conditioning, skylight views, and slanting ceilings, and the two ground-floor rooms off the lobby.

ENGLISH SPOKEN: Yes

FACILITIES AND SERVICES: Air-conditioning in rooms on the sixth floor; direct-dial phone; elevator; TV with international reception; office safe, no charge

NEAREST TOURIST ATTRACTIONS (RIGHT BANK): Arc de Triomphe, Champs-Élysées, Palais des Congrès

(11) HÔTEL REGENT'S GARDEN* ★★★
6, rue Pierre-Demours, 75017 (17th)
39 rooms, all with shower or bath and toilet

Originally built by Napoléon III for his personal physician, this building is now a refined garden hotel. Hidden behind a high brick wall, it seems a little far from the hub of activity, but in fact, rue Pierre-Demours is only a few minutes' walk from the Champs-Élysées and the Arc de Triomphe.

The cavernous, high-ceilinged rooms have crystal chandeliers, decorative moldings, marble fireplaces, brass bedsteads, floor-to-ceiling mirrors, and authentic period furnishings. Many rooms connect for convenient family use, and several have large walk-in closets with built-in shelves and shoe racks. The bathrooms are thoroughly twentieth century and luxuriously fitted with fluffy terry robes, scented bubble bath and soaps, and plenty of light and mirrors for applying makeup. Most rooms overlook the garden, which is landscaped with large trees, two gazebos, stone statues, flowering walkways, and a terrace with tables for summer breakfasts or afternoon teas. Everyone who has ever stayed here, and I include myself, loves it, and you will, too. It offers affordable elegance with an ambiance of bygone days in Paris.

ENGLISH SPOKEN: Yes

FACILITIES AND SERVICES: Air-conditioning in many rooms; bar; direct-dial phone; elevator; hair dryer; minibar; parking in front, 55F per space (first-come basis); radio; TV with international reception; office safe, no charge

NEAREST TOURIST ATTRACTIONS (RIGHT BANK): Champs-Élysées, Arc de Triomphe

TELEPHONE
01-45-74-07-30; toll-free from the U.S. and Canada, 800-528-1234 (Best Western)

FAX
01-40-55-01-42

MÉTRO
Charles-de-Gaulle-Étoile (exit rue Carnot), Ternes, Wagram

CREDIT CARDS
AE, DC, MC, V

RATES
Single 660–850F, double 710–950F
Taxe de séjour: 6F extra per person, per day

BREAKFAST
45F extra per person

(12) LIBERTEL MONCEAU* ★★★
7, rue Rennequin, 75017 (17th)
25 rooms, all with shower or bath and toilet

The Libertel hotel group is one of the best things to happen to the Paris hotel scene in some time. The group takes over run-down hotels and transforms them into smart two- and three-star winners. The Libertel Monceau is one of their best—it's certainly not short on style or charm. The theme is the Chase, or the Hunt. It is carried out with the black-and-white hunting prints hung in the bar and the deep hunter's green used in the public areas. In addition, the use of leather and brass suggests a clublike atmosphere.

TELEPHONE
01-46-63-07-52; central reservation 01-44-70-24-24

FAX
01-47-66-84-44; central fax 01-44-70-24-51

MÉTRO
Ternes

CREDIT CARDS
AE, DC, MC, V

RATES
Single 780F, double 840F;
extra bed 220F
Taxe de séjour: included
BREAKFAST
Continental 45F extra per
person, buffet 75F extra

If you want twin beds, request no. 103, with blue and maroon fabrics complementing yellow walls. The bathroom is large with sweetly framed prints of children frolicking on the moon. If a double bed is better, no. 101 on the back is quiet, with the blank view softened by the lattice work installed on the opposing gray wall. Even though you must walk up a few steps to get to it, no. 106 has a nice amount of light coming in from its two large windows, which open onto the terrace. The small sitting alcove with a desk creates a pleasant place to work.

The only blip is the windowless breakfast room, which looks like a roadside coffee stop and is stuffy besides. The hard metal chairs are certainly not conducive to a comfortable stay. Best to order breakfast sent to your room, or better yet, go out and put the hotel breakfast money toward a nice lunch or dinner. You can also save money during the happy hour in the upstairs bar, between 6:30 and 7:30 P.M., when your second drink will be free.

NOTE: As with all the Libertel hotels, the Libertel Monceau cooperates with United Air Lines and gives frequent-flyer miles.

ENGLISH SPOKEN: Yes

FACILITIES AND SERVICES: Bar; direct-dial phone; elevator; hair dryer; minibar; TV with international reception; office safe, no charge; rooms exclusively reserved for nonsmokers

NEAREST TOURIST ATTRACTIONS (RIGHT BANK): Champs-Élysées, Arc de Triomphe

Eighteenth Arrondissement

Montmartre is a rambling *quartier* full of contrasts, combining picture-postcard quaintness and razzle-dazzle. It was here that Toulouse-Lautrec drew the cancan girls dancing at the Moulin Rouge, and Picasso and Braque created cubism at the Bateau-Lavoir. The panoramic view from the steps of Sacré-Coeur at dawn or sunset, the many artists, and the intimate village atmosphere that prevails along the narrow streets—many of which are the same as when Utrillo painted them—continue to evoke the dynamic spirit and colorful past of this vibrant part of Paris. It is a must-stop for anyone wanting to absorb the spirit of Paris, both present and past.

RIGHT BANK
Montmartre, Sacré-Coeur

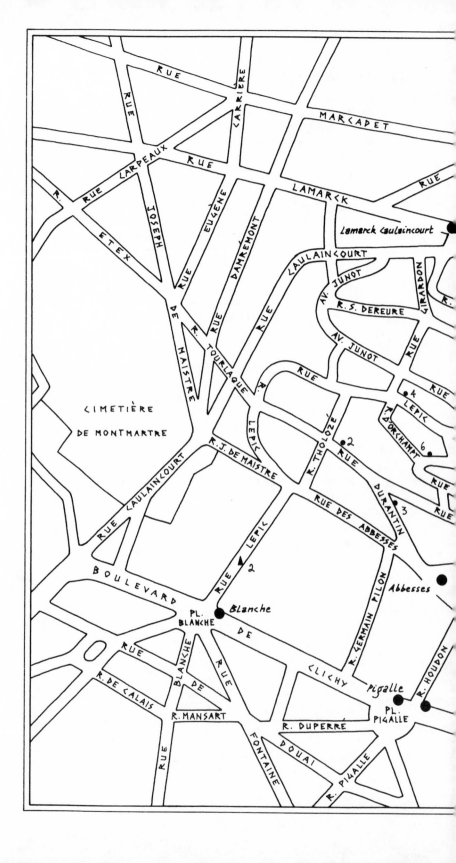

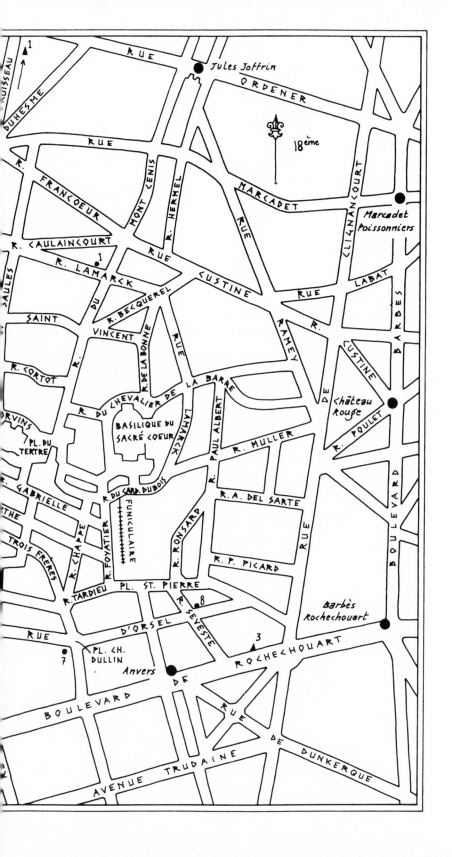

(1) ERMITAGE HÔTEL ★★
24, rue Lamarck, 75018 (18th)
12 rooms, all with shower or bath and toilet

TELEPHONE
01-42-64-79-22

FAX
01-42-64-10-33

MÉTRO
Lamarck-Caulaincourt, or bus nos. 80 or 85

CREDIT CARDS
None, cash only

RATES
Single 420F, double 490F, triple 610F, quad 710F
Taxe de séjour: included

BREAKFAST
Included, cannot be deducted

Close your eyes and imagine being in Paris and waking up in an antique-filled hotel high atop Montmartre with magical views over the entire city. Sound wonderful? It does, and it is all possible at the Ermitage, a poetic refuge run by the engaging Maggie Canipel, her husband, and now their lovely daughter, Sophie. In the late 1970s, the couple sold everything they had and bought the Ermitage. They updated the plumbing, filled the old mansion with their collection of fine furniture, and began welcoming guests, continually outdoing themselves with their boundless energy and engaging smiles to make everyone feel at home. They have succeeded beautifully and are now one of the favorite hotels for readers of *Cheap Sleeps in Paris*. So, if this sounds appealing, book the minute you know your dates for Paris.

Any one of their rooms could steal your heart, but my favorites are still nos. 6 and 10—on the top floor, with tall French windows opening onto the morning sun and views of all Paris—and nos. 11 and 12, which open onto their terrace garden. No. 2 is beautiful, with a magnificent set of nineteenth-century reproduction Louis XV bedroom furniture consisting of a carved bed, two side tables, and a mirrored armoire. A crystal chandelier completes the picture.

True, you need strong legs and lungs to walk up the hill from the métro, but once there, you will be richly rewarded not only by the warmth and hospitality of the Canipel family but by being in the center of one of the most picturesque parts of Paris. You can wander the streets once painted by Utrillo, peek into artists' ateliers, and have your portrait painted by one of the pseudo-artists lining the touristy place du Tertre. Undiscovered restaurants in all price ranges are within easy walking distance (see *Cheap Eats in Paris*).

ENGLISH SPOKEN: Yes, also German and Italian

FACILITIES AND SERVICES: Direct-dial phone; no elevator or TV; office safe, no charge

NEAREST TOURIST ATTRACTIONS (RIGHT BANK): Montmartre

(2)   HÔTEL BONSÉJOUR (NO STARS)
11, rue Burq, 75018 (18th)
34 rooms, none with shower, bath, or toilet

Attention Cheap Sleepers in Paris! If money is your first concern, this old—but very clean—hotel should be one of your first picks. Occupying a hillside corner location, it is well protected from the low life and tourist mania that plagues Montmartre and its underbelly, Pigalle.

It is run by Paul Bellart, who checks you in, and his hard-working wife, who cleans all the thirty-four rooms and hall facilities herself. The rooms appeal to a young, intellectual, and sometimes impoverished crowd of international guests, who cheerfully ignore the mishmash of furniture and do not mind using hall facilities. The cheapest rooms face walls. If you can swing just a little more money, ask for one with a balcony (nos. 23, 33, 43, or 53, which is the best because it has a nice Parisian view) or no. 51, a triple with a tiny peek of the tip of the Sacré-Coeur. The balcony rooms come with double beds. If you need twins, ask for no. 41 on the street, which also has more space and better bedspreads than some others. Breakfast is not part of the plan here, but you can save money and feel more Parisian by walking a block or two to one of the many Montmartre bakeries and cafés that line the main street.

ENGLISH SPOKEN: Yes

FACILITIES AND SERVICES: None; no elevator (five floors)

NEAREST TOURIST ATTRACTIONS (RIGHT BANK): Montmartre

TELEPHONE
01-42-54-22-53

FAX
None

MÉTRO
Abbesses, Blanche

CREDIT CARDS
None, cash only

RATES
Single 111–131F, double 172F, triple 250F; shower 10F
Taxe de séjour: included

BREAKFAST
Not served

(3)   HÔTEL LE BOUQUET DE MONTMARTRE ★★
1, rue Durantin, 75018 (18th)
36 rooms, all with shower, 22 with bath and toilet

If you are a committed Cheap Sleeper with a fondness for Montmartre, and you want to experience the fun and the village atmosphere of the area and still stay under budget, the Bouquet de Montmartre is a little honey of a hotel. Its second-floor lobby may be difficult to find, but the search is worth it.

The Gibergues family works hard to keep their Victorian hotel as nice as it is for the price. They are on duty from Monday to Saturday, 9 A.M. to 6 P.M., so when calling for reservations, bear this in mind. If you can wear blinders or dark glasses in your room, or do not mind living in a kaleidoscope of colors, then read on.

TELEPHONE
01-46-06-87-54

FAX
01-46-06-09-09

MÉTRO
Abbesses

CREDIT CARDS
MC, V

RATES
1–2 persons 350–370F, triple 420–460F, quad 490F; extra bed 10% of room rate
Taxe de séjour: 5F extra per person, per day

BREAKFAST
35F extra per person

Most of the bedrooms fall into the "cute and confusing" category. Lacy curtains, velvet chairs with plastic covers, floral rugs, and busy wallpaper march along with brightly tiled bathrooms in purple, lavender, royal blue, and aqua. All are positively spotless and tear-free. Breakfast is served in an ornate dining room with red velvet chairs, lacquered furniture, and globe lights—all of it serving to remind you that this *is* Montmartre, after all.

From the hotel you can stroll in any direction and see something interesting. You can climb up to Sacré-Coeur or crawl down the hill to Pigalle, where Paris's seedy side is on full display. For longer trips, jump on the Montmartobus, a minibus service that plies the winding streets snaking around the Butte. You can ride from the bottom at Pigalle to the end of the line at métro Jules Joffrin. Stop along the route if something intrigues you and get back on; it is one of the most pleasurable rides you can take in Paris.

ENGLISH SPOKEN: Limited

FACILITIES AND SERVICES: Direct-dial phone; office safe, no charge; no elevator or TV

NEAREST TOURIST ATTRACTIONS (RIGHT BANK): Montmartre

(4) HÔTEL PRIMA-LEPIC ★★
29, rue Lepic, 75018 (18th)
38 rooms, all with shower or bath and toilet

TELEPHONE
01-46-06-44-64
FAX
01-46-06-66-11
MÉTRO
Abbesses, Blanche
CREDIT CARDS
MC, V
RATES
Single 375F, double 420–450F, triple 525F, apartment 750F
Taxe de séjour: included
BREAKFAST
45F extra per person

The Prima-Lepic is a century-old Montmartre building that still has its ornate ceiling moldings, marble fireplaces, and a corner cherub or two for good measure. Appealing to a young, European crowd on slim budgets, the hotel is a good base for exploring Montmartre.

It looks nice from the outside—painted white with balconies overlooking the busy market street that runs the length of rue Lepic. The welcoming entry overlooks a trompe l'oeil English garden that sets the floral theme for the main floor of the hotel, including the beamed breakfast area, which has a garden mural and white scrolled metal tables and chairs. To the right of this room hangs a wonderful collection of black-and-white prints of life in Montmartre.

When reserving, request any room that faces front on the third, fourth, or fifth floor because they have balconies and more light. Nos. 15 and 55 are two of the best, and so is no. 56, done in pale lavender with an Oriental throw rug and a 1930s-style lamp as accent pieces. The country-style furniture gives it a slightly romantic flavor. These rooms all have one thing in common: noise. Better pack earplugs because Montmartre jumps all night long, especially on the weekends. The rooms on the back have more space, but less light and no view at all. These are, of course, the quieter choices. One of the nicest is no. 12, an adorable blue-and-white room with white wicker furniture and a pyramid tent over the bed. No. 35 is a cheery choice in soft blue and green with royal blue rug and an interesting fabric backdrop behind the bed. The apartments are spacious enough but not recommended, since they are dark and gloomy and have depressing views on the back side of the building.

ENGLISH SPOKEN: Yes

FACILITIES AND SERVICES: Direct-dial phone; elevator to five floors; hair dryer; TV; no safe

NEAREST TOURIST ATTRACTIONS (RIGHT BANK): Montmartre

(5) HÔTEL ROMA SACRÉ-COEUR ★★
101, rue Caulaincourt, 75018 (18th)
57 rooms all with shower or bath and toilet

Mention that you are a devoted reader of *Cheap Sleeps in Paris* and receive a 10 percent discount on the already reasonable rates at this hotel. Frankly, this place is a bit of a gamble because its location is *out* of the mainstream and does require some walking up and down hills. Still, it has cachet: Room 701 was where Georges Braque had his studio when Montmartre was in its artistic heyday in the 1920s. It is easy today to picture the artist standing on the wraparound balcony, gazing at northern Paris on the horizon, and turning out his canvases. Other rooms of note are nos. 501 and 506, with cityscape views to Sacré-Coeur, and no. 704 with a balcony. Singles do not fare well: the rooms are meager and the outlooks discouraging, so if you are a lone voyager, pay a little more and get a small double. Rooms are in nonclashing colors of soft peach, simple browns, and white. Management is agreeable, and the neighborhood is pretty in that it reflects a *real* part of Paris that is untouched by the maddening tourist crowds.

TELEPHONE
01-42-62-02-02

FAX
01-42-54-34-92

MÉTRO
Lamarck-Caulaincourt

CREDIT CARDS
AE, DC, MC, V

RATES
Single 340F, double 410–430F, triple 540F
Taxe de séjour: 5F extra per person, per day

BREAKFAST
40F extra per person

ENGLISH SPOKEN: Yes

FACILITIES AND SERVICES: Direct-dial phone; elevator to all but the top floor; hair dryer; minibar; radio; TV; office safe, no charge

NEAREST TOURIST ATTRACTIONS (RIGHT BANK): Montmartre

(6) TIMHÔTEL-MONTMARTRE ★★
11, rue Ravignan, on the place Émile-Goudeau, 75018 (18th)
60 rooms, all with shower or bath and toilet

TELEPHONE
01-42-55-74-79

FAX
01-42-55-71-01

MÉTRO
Abbesses

CREDIT CARDS
AE, DC, MC, V

RATES
Single 460F, double 560F, triple 690F
Taxe de séjour: included

BREAKFAST
50F extra per person

The hotel brochure bills the Timhôtels as the "Biggest Little Chain in Paris," which is probably close to the truth. It also states that this particular Timhôtel is close to downtown Paris and two rail stations—no, I don't think so. It is, however, quite charming, and if you are partial to Montmartre and don't mind some uphill climbs, you will be rewarded with better-than-average standard rooms in a hotel on a leafy Montmartre square. Next door is the Bateau Lavoir, where many artists including Picasso worked when they lived on this beautiful hill above Paris. Nearby is the tourist-tacky place du Tertre, Sacré-Coeur and its sweeping views over Paris, and the funicular leading down the hill to Pigalle.

Guests in the know reserve the fourth-floor rooms, which have balconies, or those on the fifth floor, which have views of either Sacré-Coeur or Paris. If you book early enough, you should be able to land no. 517, a single corner perch with three windows looking across Paris to the Eiffel Tower, Invalides, Tour Montparnasse, and of course, Sacré-Coeur. Each floor is named after a famous Montmartre artist, and a representative of their works hangs in the hallway to remind you: Renoir, Utrillo, Dali, Matisse, Monet, or Picasso. Breakfast takes place in the Toulouse-Lautrec room.

ENGLISH SPOKEN: Yes

FACILITIES AND SERVICES: Direct-dial phone; elevator; TV with international reception; office safe, 20F per day

NEAREST TOURIST ATTRACTIONS (RIGHT BANK): Montmartre

Big Splurges

The following hotels fall into the Big Splurge category. They are higher priced and included here because their location, amenities, ambiance, service, and overall appeal will suit those travelers with more demanding tastes and flexible budgets.

Other Options

If hotel life is not for you, there are other reasonable options that make Cheap Sleeping sense in Paris. For the Cheapest Sleep of all, consider a return to nature—that is, camping, which you can do just outside of Paris in the Bois de Boulogne. If you are a student, or can go the hostel route, there are many excellent Cheap Sleeps awaiting you. Other cost-saving possibilities are to stay in a residence hotel in a unit with a kitchenette, or to become truly Parisian and rent your own studio or apartment. The benefits of these last two choices are numerous, from having more space to spread out to the adventure of interacting with merchants while shopping for life's necessities in your own Parisian neighborhood.

STUDENT ACCOMMODATIONS

Apartment Rentals

If you want to live in Paris, not just be a visitor during your stay, then the best way to experience Paris *comme les Parisiens* is to rent a short-term apartment. Believe me, once you do it, you will not want to return to the confines of hotel living in the City of Light for any of your future visits. A stay in a Parisian apartment not only gives you more space than a hotel, and for less money in the long run, it allows you to become a real part of a *quartier,* which you will soon come to think of as your own.

During the years I have researched Paris apartments, I have seen just about every nightmare possible—including total dumps that were not only filthy and unattractive but in terrible areas that have absolutely nothing to offer a tourist. Many are operated by huge firms, or let by absentee owners, who are on the scene to collect your money but then vanish, leaving you high and dry when maintenance problems arise, which they generally do. Just as with all of the hotels and shops listed in this book, I have personally visited every apartment agency listed and viewed a large sampling of what they offer before I considered recommending them to you.

Even though I mention it as the number-one tip in apartment renting, it bears repeating here: If you rent an apartment, be sure you clearly understand the payment, cancellation, and refund policies. It is beyond the scope of *Cheap Sleeps in Paris* to detail the various policies you will encounter, but they are *never* in your favor. Therefore, it is absolutely essential that you purchase cancellation insurance, which is available through many state automobile associations, travel agents, and in some cases through the apartment agency itself. This small investment will pay off tenfold if you have to change dates, cancel altogether, or must suddenly cut short your stay.

CHEAP SLEEPING TIPS ON RENTING A PARIS APARTMENT

1. Most important: Know the deposit, payment, and cancellation policies, and buy cancellation insurance.

2. Get a guaranteed rate and find out about extra charges such as linens, cleaning, telephone, heating, and so on.

3. Ask for photographs of the apartment you are considering.

4. Be very specific when stating your needs: size of flat and number of occupants; stall shower versus hand-held shower nozzle in a half-tub with no shower guard or curtain; and kitchen equipment—do you need only a microwave, do you want pots and pans for major cooking events, or are you just going to drink wine and eat baguettes and French cheese at the dining room table? Don't forget to consider the beds. Will a sofa bed do, or does your back demand something better, and if so, will you require a double bed or twin beds?

5. Is a television important for you? Don't discount having one because it is a great way to improve your French comprehension. Is there a phone and how much are the calls? Can you make both local and long-distance calls? Is there an answering machine, fax, and computer hookup available?

6. How far is the apartment from *your* center of interest? Where is the nearest market, laundry

and dry cleaner, pharmacy, métro and bus stop, best café, *pâtisserie?* Ask for a good local map with your address pinpointed on it.

7. Is the apartment suitable for children? Is there a park or playground nearby?

8. Noise. Paris operates on a twenty-four-hour basis and *is* noisy. If you must have the most quiet possible, ask for an inside location *sur la cour,* where you will sacrifice view and possibly light, but gain some solitude.

9. Is there an elevator to your apartment? Many buildings in Paris do not have them. While that penthouse apartment with a dynamic view is romantically wonderful, consider carrying groceries, shopping purchases, and your luggage up and down. Think about this one carefully . . . stairs can get to be a problem, *fast.*

10. Upon arrival will someone meet you at the apartment and show you the ropes, or do you have to go to an office in Paris to get the keys? This is very important after a long international flight: dragging luggage and tired children through Paris in search of the keys to your Paris kingdom at this point is not an attractive option.

11. What other services does the apartment rental company offer? Ask about drivers; itinerary planning throughout France and in other parts of Europe; ongoing reservations; and air travel arrangements.

CHEZ VOUS
1001 Bridgeway, Suite 245
Sausalito, California 94965

TELEPHONE
415-331-2535
FAX
415-331-5296
INTERNET
www.chezvous.com
CREDIT CARDS
None, U.S. checks only
RATES
From $125 per night for 2 people (3-night minimum) and up; better rates for longer stays

Chez Vous apartments offer you a Paris address in several of the best areas of the city, not in marginal, out-of-the-way *quartiers* that some apartment owners or agencies will try and convince you are interesting. The possibilities are in the fourth, fifth, sixth, and seventh arrondissements. Each rental is lightly stocked with milk, coffee, dishwashing soap, paper products, and a bouquet of fresh flowers. Chez Vous can arrange your entire trip, including airline flights, and pick you up at the Paris airport, but that will be extra, as are linens and a cleaning fee at the end of your stay. The catalog listing the Paris properties is called *Bonjour Paris!!!,* and it not only gives you good information about their apartments but leaves nothing to chance in explaining the payment or cancellation policies. If you are venturing outside of Paris, and this type of stay appeals to you, ask about their other rental properties throughout France and in London.

ENGLISH SPOKEN: Yes

FACILITIES AND SERVICES: Varies with each location

NEAREST TOURIST ATTRACTIONS: Varies with each location

BREAKFAST
Not available

DE CIRCOURT ASSOCIATES
11, rue Royale, 75008 (8th)

De Circourt Associates was founded by Claire De Circourt to aid those people moving to Paris, either for professional reasons or for a stay of at least two months. De Circourt is a very savvy businesswoman, and she has lived and worked in New York City, so she knows the type of living accommodations most Americans want. She has computerized listings of over ten thousand apartments and homes in Paris and the suburbs, which are updated every fifteen days. Thanks to this sophisticated computerized search system, she or one of her exceptionally competent English-speaking staff will find you the place of your dreams at a price you can afford. The possibilities range from a romantic, beamed, one-bedroom walk-up on Île de la Cité, to a zany artist's studio done in black and white with a bird-shaped chair, to the to-die-for apartment occupied by Robert Altman while he was on location in Paris filming *Prêt à Porter.* It is all up to you and your budget—whatever you want, chances are excellent De Circourt Associates will have it.

ENGLISH SPOKEN: Yes

FACILITIES AND SERVICES: Varies

NEAREST TOURIST ATTRACTIONS: Varies

TELEPHONE
01-43-12-98-00
FAX
01-43-12-98-08
E-MAIL
circourt@easynet.fr
MÉTRO
Concorde
CREDIT CARDS
MC, V
RATES
From around $1,000 per month and up; minimum stay at least two months; prefer six-month or one-year lease
BREAKFAST
Not available

ERICA BERMAN AND ALEX MONY APARTMENT RENTALS
15, bis rue Cauchois, 75018 (18th)
In the U.S.: 37 Somerset Road, Lexington, Massachusetts, 02173

If you saw the Woody Allen film *Everyone Says, I Love You,* you will remember the Montmartre *pied-à-terre* he rented to impress his would-be lover, played by Julia Roberts, and the spectacular view it had of the Sacré-

TELEPHONE
France: 01-44-92-06-55, 01-42-59-37-11
U.S.: 617-862-3304

FAX
France: 01-44-92-91-17

E-MAIL
eberman95@aol.com

CREDIT CARDS
None, check in U.S. dollars or
French francs

RATES
Small studios from around
$400 per week; average price
around $1,000–$2,000 per
week; lower rates for longer
stays and in off-season

BREAKFAST
Not available

Coeur. For the film actors it was just a temporary on-site set location. For you, an apartment with the same fabulous view can be your home in Paris.

American Erica Berman and her French partner, Alex Mony, have taken several Montmartre apartments, and one right on the Palais Royale, and renovated them into smart, stylish, uncluttered accommodations that are nothing short of wonderful. Being American, Erica knows the mind-set of her compatriots and has designed the apartments to appeal to American visitors. She has used simple colors, sprinkled the rooms with antiques, and fitted the kitchens and baths to American standards and tastes. Erica and Alex live in Montmartre and are accessible to their clients. Upon arrival, they meet you on-site and provide you with the necessary details and advice you will need to feel at home during your stay. Prices are fair, and my recommendation is high.

ENGLISH SPOKEN: Yes

FACILITIES AND SERVICES: Varies with each apartment, but all are very, very nice

NEAREST TOURIST ATTRACTIONS: Montmartre and central Paris

INSIGHTFUL TRAVELERS
57 Rutland Square, #4, Boston, Massachusetts 02118

TELEPHONE
617-859-0702

FAX
617-267-4794

E-MAIL
IT@laToile.com

CREDIT CARDS
AE for some apartments,
otherwise personal checks

RATES
From 500–1,600F per day;
prices vary according to size,
location, and amenities as well
as length of stay (minimum
stay is 5 days)

BREAKFAST
Not available

Insightful Travelers, which operates out of Boston, is owned by Susan Fox and Richard Hill. This dynamic duo work with several purveyors of Paris apartments to find their clients the accommodation that is best suited to their needs, interests, tastes, and budget. They have no allegiance to any special purveyor and can therefore give clients unbiased accounts of the properties they offer. They also provide color photos whenever possible. Susan and Richard, or a staff member, make frequent trips to Paris to revise and update their inventory and to insure that the apartments they represent continue to meet their standards. Apartment choices range from the "cheap and cheerful" to "big splurge/luxurious" and can accommodate up to six. On-site Paris representatives are available to help with any emergencies. There is a minimum five-day stay.

ENGLISH SPOKEN: Yes

FACILITIES AND SERVICES: Varies with each location

NEAREST TOURIST ATTRACTIONS: Varies with each location

RENTAL DIRECTORIES INTERNATIONAL
2044 Rittenhouse Square, Philadelphia, Pennsylvania 19103

Today's travelers are more sophisticated and independent. There is a growing market of travelers interested in renting vacation apartments or homes abroad for a week to a year. Sometimes the red tape and expense, not to mention the hassle, of dealing with foreign real estate companies can take all the fun out of such a good idea. Rental Directories International, a Pennsylvania-based organization run by Helen London, has a publication providing an avenue for renting apartments, homes, and villas directly from the owners, eliminating the middleman as well as costly agency fees and commissions. The directory has over 150 different properties, with location, description, availability, price range, and information for contacting the owner directly. The directory costs $29.95 including shipping, is updated annually, and comes out in the fall.

ENGLISH SPOKEN: Yes

FACILITIES AND SERVICES: Varies with each property

NEAREST TOURIST ATTRACTIONS: Varies with each location

TELEPHONE
215-985-4001

FAX
215-985-0323

E-MAIL
Rentdirect@aol.com

CREDIT CARDS
MC, V accepted for the purchase of the directory only; all rentals in cash only

RATES
Depends on the owner

ROTHRAY
10, rue Nicolas-Flamel, 75004 (4th)

There is no longer any contest. It is an undisputed fact that RothRay apartments are the *best* in Paris. Period. This opinion is shared not only by all of their loyal and contented clients but by the rest of the competition! I absolutely agree—after one stay, I vowed to always let competent Ray Lampard and his capable partner, Roth, arrange my living accommodations anytime I am in Paris. Some short-term private apartment rentals in Paris can be potluck affairs that offer unwelcome surprises on arrival, and during a stay force you to contend with strange decor, varying amenities and levels of cleanliness, and haphazard services by the agency in charge, who shows little interest in you after they have your money . . . up front. You will find none of these problems in any apartment rented through RothRay.

Their apartments are located in interesting *quartiers,* where a stroll around a corner will put picturesque Paris at your fingertips. After a few days you will discover what fun it is to actually be a part of Paris, and you'll probably spend a good deal of your time trying to make

TELEPHONE
01-48-87-13-37

FAX
01-40-26-34-33

MÉTRO
Châtelet

CREDIT CARDS
None; cash or personal checks in your currency

RATES
From 600–1,200F per day (less by month); prices vary according to size and location as well as length of stay (minimum stay 7 days)

BREAKFAST
Not available

more permanent arrangements, or figuring out how to return again more often. It will be love at first sight when you walk into one of their tastefully furnished and beautifully equipped studios and apartments. In addition to attractive furnishings, most have cable televisions, stereo systems, washers and dryers, dishwashers, and American-style kitchens beautifully equipped with nice china, crystal, and utensils. You can only fully appreciate the quality of their kitchens if you have ever tried to prepare a meal in a French closet-style kitchen with a mish-mash of "rental" pots and pans and chipped, unmatched dishes for serving. Their own apartments are constantly being improved to meet the exacting standards of Roth, who will spend days locating just the right knobs for new kitchen cabinets. Before guests arrive, he personally inspects the apartment to make sure everything is in order, and both he and Ray are available in Paris for problem-solving. This is an important point: you are not dealing with a local representative of the person or company you rented from. With RothRay you are dealing with the two people who are the owners and who are in charge of, and responsible for, everything. Weekly maid service, linen changes, and a refrigerator stocked with fruit juices, wine, and beer are included. As one guest happily told me, "There is RothRay, and then everyone else, just trying to catch up." How very true it still is.

NOTE: RothRay Apartments are booked sometimes a year in advance. *Please* make your reservation the minute you know your dates in Paris.

ENGLISH SPOKEN: Yes

FACILITIES AND SERVICES: The best, but vary with the apartment

NEAREST TOURIST ATTRACTIONS: Varies by apartment

VILLAS INTERNATIONAL
950 Northgate Drive, Suite 206, San Rafael, California 94903

TELEPHONE
415-281-0910; toll-free 800-221-2260
FAX
415-499-9491
E-MAIL
villas@best.com
INTERNET
www.villasintl.com
CREDIT CARDS
MC, V
RATES
Vary by location, but prices generally start at $650 per week for two in a small studio

David Kendall runs Villas International, which is able to provide clients a full range of rental properties throughout Europe. Whether you need a studio in Paris, a grand apartment suitable for entertaining, a villa on the Riviera, or a simple *gîte* in the countryside, Villas International will undoubtedly have a listing. When contacting them, be sure to state your needs, dates, and budget. Office hours are Monday to Friday 9 A.M. to 6 P.M., Pacific Standard Time.

Camping Out

LES CAMPINGS DU BOIS DE BOULOGNE
Allée du Bord de l'Eau, 75016 (16th)

While Coleman stoves, tents, inflatable mattresses, and citronella candles are not on everyone's packing list for a trip to Paris, they might be on yours if you are a camper. Yes, it *is* possible to pitch a tent in Paris! Les Campings in the Bois de Boulogne is on the far edge of the park and provides the only true rustic opportunity for Cheap Sleeps in Paris. Geared to students and hearty international travelers, or those with RVs, the campground is located four kilometers away from the nearest métro, making it almost essential that you have your own set of wheels. Otherwise, there is a camp bus, but its schedule may not match yours (either going to or coming from the city) and then you'll be forced to walk. The bus service exists only from April to October, and it's free in July and August. A convenience store, money changer, hot showers, a coin-operated washer and dryer, and a restaurant are open to campers. The office is open from 7 A.M. until 10 P.M. and accepts *no* reservations for campsites, but it does accept them for mobile-home bookings and large camping groups. Everything is always on a first-come, first-served basis.

NOTE: Here are directions from the Porte-Maillot métro station, which is four kilometers from the campground. Exit the station and take bus no. 244; get off at route des Moulins, and walk down the path to the right. Do not follow misleading signs to the left on main road.

ENGLISH SPOKEN: Limited

FACILITIES AND SERVICES: Open year-round; coin-operated washing machines and dryers; convenience store; information office; money changer; free hot showers; bus service and restaurant from April to October

NEAREST TOURIST ATTRACTIONS: None

TELEPHONE
01-45-24-30-00

FAX
01-45-24-42-95

MÉTRO
Porte-Maillot, then take bus no. 244 (see note)

CREDIT CARDS
MC, V

RATES
Tent (two people) 75F per night (no electricity), 145F per night (with electricity); RV hookups 110F; mobile home 350F; lower rates Sept–June

BREAKFAST
Not available

Private Hostels

The five private hostels described below are owned by two brothers, and they appeal to travelers with youth on their side and wanderlust in their hearts. Each hostel has its own character, but all are dedicated to keeping the prices at the rock-bottom level. They are open year round, and there is no age limit (only stamina), but there is a one-week limit on length of stay. In keeping with the times, they all have guest internet hookups, but there will be a small charge for this.

ALOHA HOSTEL
1, rue Borromée, opposite 243, rue de Vaugirard, 75015 (15th)
60 beds, 8 rooms with showers, none with toilets

TELEPHONE
01-42-73-03-03
FAX
01-42-73-14-14
MÉTRO
Volontaires
CREDIT CARDS
None, cash only
RATES
100F per person per night, less by the week; showers are free; towel 5F; sheets 15F
Taxe de séjour: included
BREAKFAST
Not served

At the Aloha Hostel guests can mingle in the back-pack-laden reception area, comparing cheap travel tips gleaned from years of surviving on the edge. Rooms benefit from a redecoration project; beams were added and so were new showers. There are no singles, and your stay will be limited to a week in your dorm bunk. Everything is payable in advance by 10 P.M. the previous day. (The sign over the reception desk reads: "If you want to stay tomorrow night, please pay by 10:00 P.M. *tonight.* Please don't say, I didn't know.") The office is open from 8 A.M. to 2 A.M. without interruption: you can come by, reserve a space, and leave your luggage, but the rooms are closed and all guests must vacate the premises between 11 A.M. and 5 P.M. BYO towels and sheets, or plan on spending extra for them. Showers are free, and so is the hot plate in the communal kitchen. The working-class neighborhood is full of bakeries, supermarkets, banks, and other survival-type shopping. Otherwise, it's at least twenty minutes to tourist destinations.

ENGLISH SPOKEN: Yes

FACILITIES AND SERVICES: Safe in office, no charge; communal kitchen; internet hookup

NEAREST TOURIST ATTRACTIONS (LEFT BANK): None; must use public transportation

LE VILLAGE HOSTEL-MONTMARTRE
20, rue d'Orsel, 75018 (18th)
75 beds in rooms for 2, 3, or 4 persons, all with shower and toilet

TELEPHONE
01-42-64-22-02
FAX
01-42-64-22-04
MÉTRO
Anvers
CREDIT CARDS
MC, V
RATES
130F per person; towel 5F; sheets 15F
Taxe de séjour: included

This is the newest of the five hostels—it therefore has a lot going for it and is the most expensive. All the rooms have private facilities, and six rooms (nos. 201, 205, 302, 305, 401, and 406) have dynamite views of Sacré-Coeur and the gardens surrounding it. If these rooms are not available, you can enjoy the view from the hotel terrace. Montmartre can be fun if you don't mind the hikes around the *butte,* and you like to revel in the laid-back party atmosphere that permeates the more tourist-saturated parts of this special part of Paris. Partying can't go on forever because there is a 2 A.M. curfew. Rooms must be vacated between noon and 5 P.M., but reception is always open.

ENGLISH SPOKEN: Yes

FACILITIES AND SERVICES: Direct-dial phone; elevator; TV in lounge; office safe, no charge; kitchen privileges; internet hookup

NEAREST TOURIST ATTRACTIONS (RIGHT BANK): Montmartre

BREAKFAST
40F extra

3 DUCKS HOSTEL
6, place Étienne Pernet, 75015 (15th) (To the right side of Jean Baptiste de Grenelle Church at the end of rue de Commerce)
80 beds in shared rooms; 6 rooms have showers only, all others are without shower, bath, or toilet

This youthful hangout is not the sort of place moms and dads would check into—nor is it one you would want them to check out on your behalf. Its rugged appeal draws backpackers and other wanderers who value camaraderie along with wild and ribald fun over aesthetics or a peaceful night's rest. As in all these hostels, you must bring your own sheets and towels, or pay extra to rent sheets and buy a towel. The relaxed management requires shirts and shoes to be worn at all times and provides cooking facilities, hot showers, summer barbecues, a TV in a casual bar with cheap beer, and rooms for two, three, or four persons. Future guests should remember that there are no lockers (only a storage room), nor is there an age limit or any minimum or maximum stay. The office is open from 8 A.M. to 2 A.M.; guests must vacate rooms between 11 A.M. and 5 P.M.; and there is a strict 2 A.M. curfew.

ENGLISH SPOKEN: Yes

FACILITIES AND SERVICES: Bar with beer and soft drinks; TV in bar; office safe, no charge; kitchen privileges; internet hookup

NEAREST TOURIST ATTRACTIONS (LEFT BANK): Far from everything, must use public transportation

TELEPHONE
01-48-42-04-05
FAX
01-48-42-99-99
MÉTRO
Commerce
CREDIT CARDS
MC, V
RATES
Double 117F per person; 97F per person in a dorm room; lower rates by the week; free showers 24 hours a day; towels 5F; sheets 15F
Taxe de séjour: included
BREAKFAST
15F extra per person in winter; not provided in the summer

WOODSTOCK HOSTEL
48, rue Rodier, 75009 (9th)
62 beds in rooms with no facilities

Woodstock Hostel is about a ten-minute walk from the Gare du Nord and Gare de l'Est train stations and across the street from a pretty park where you can enjoy a

TELEPHONE/FAX
01-48-78-87-76

MÉTRO
Anvers, Poissonnière
CREDIT CARDS
MC, V
RATES
Double 100F per person; dorm
room 90F per person; towel 5F;
sheet 15F; free showers
Taxe de séjour: included
BREAKFAST
Included

picnic lunch or watch the children playing. Also close by are bakeries, a grocery, and a laundromat. Even though it is close to Pigalle and all the sleaze of that area, the hostel is in a safe pocket. Free showers are on each floor, kitchen privileges are open to all, and the cheapest beer in Paris is available at the desk. Reception is open from 8:00 A.M. to 2:00 A.M.; rooms must be vacated between 11:30 A.M. and 5:00 P.M.; and the curfew is at 2:00 A.M.

ENGLISH SPOKEN: Yes

FACILITIES AND SERVICES: Office safe, no charge; kitchen privileges; internet hookup; luggage storage room

NEAREST TOURIST ATTRACTIONS (RIGHT BANK): Not much, must use public transportation

YOUNG & HAPPY HOSTEL (Y & H HOSTEL)
80, rue Mouffetard, 75005 (5th)
75 beds, none with private shower, bath, or toilet

TELEPHONE
01-45-35-09-53
FAX
01-47-07-22-24
MÉTRO
Monge, Censier-Daubenton
CREDIT CARDS
MC, V
RATES
Double 117F per person; dorm
room 97F per person; showers
are free; towel 5F; sheets 15F
Taxe de séjour: included
BREAKFAST
Included

The Young & Happy Hostel is so named because it's friendly and everyone who stays here has such a good time. It is located on rue Mouffetard, a famous *marché* street with loads of Cheap Eats—everything from crêpes and croissants to pizza slices and dripping Greek sandwiches. Reception is open daily from 8 A.M. to 2 A.M. Showers and breakfast are included in the rate. You can reserve with a one-night advance deposit, or arrive when they open and hope for the best. There is no age limit, but you can stay only one week. There is a room lockout from 11 A.M. to 5 P.M. and a 2 A.M. curfew.

ENGLISH SPOKEN: Yes

FACILITIES AND SERVICES: Office safe, no charge; TV in lounge with international reception; internet hookup

NEAREST TOURIST ATTRACTIONS (LEFT BANK): Rue Mouffetard, Jardin des Plantes

Residence Hotels

CITADINES

The Citadines residence hotels are large, modern, and somewhat impersonal, but they offer all the comforts of living in a city apartment as well as the advantages of hotel services. There are several types of accommodations, ranging from a studette to an apartment. Frankly, the studettes are just too minuscule for any degree of long-term comfort. If you go in the off-season, or stay longer than a week or two, the prices drop. The group has almost a dozen Paris locations, in addition to others in major European capitals. In Paris, I like the three listed here because of their proximity to more on a tourist's agenda. The others tend to be far from much on my list, but their off-beat locations may appeal to some. For information and locations of Citadine residence hotels in other parts of Paris and in European cities, contact the main office at (telephone) 01-41-05-79-79 or (fax) 01-47-59-04-70.

CITADINES PARIS RASPAIL MONTPARNASSE ★★★
121, boulevard du Montparnasse, 75006 (6th)
52 apartments, all with fitted kitchen, shower or bath, and toilet

For affordable quality in a Montparnasse residence hotel, this polished Citadines choice is just steps away from a kir or an espresso at Le Dôme and a leisurely stroll to many recommended Cheap Eats in Paris. Once inside there is a vaguely Philippe Starck look to its minimalistic lobby and sleek, chrome-furnished breakfast room. The apartments offer the latest in soft lighting, excellent space execution, and top-of-the-line marble baths. You won't be inspired to cook a Thanksgiving dinner here, but the kitchenettes, with two burners and a microwave, will allow you to shop with purpose at any of Paris's colorful outdoor *marchés*. Best sites are those on the back or overlooking the inner courtyard garden. Prices are quoted by the day, but reductions for long-term stays are always negotiable.

ENGLISH SPOKEN: Yes

FACILITIES AND SERVICES: Air-conditioning; bar; baby beds; conference room; direct-dial phone; elevators; hair dryers; fitted kitchens; no laundromat, but a laundry and cleaning service; TV with international reception; safe in office, 90F per week; two studios for the handicapped; daily maid service for linens, weekly for cleaning

NEAREST TOURIST ATTRACTIONS (LEFT BANK): Montparnasse, Luxembourg Gardens

TELEPHONE
01-43-35-46-35

FAX
01-40-47-43-01

MÉTRO
Vavin

CREDIT CARDS
AE, DC, MC, V

RATES
Studettes, studios, one- and two-bedroom units from 600–1,225F per day; lower rates in off-season and for longer stays; dogs, 40F per day
Taxe de séjour: 6.30F extra per day, per person

BREAKFAST
60F extra per person

CITADINES TROCADÉRO ★★★
29, bis rue Saint-Didier, 75016 (16th)
97 accommodations, ranging from studettes to full-size apartments, all with shower, bath, and toilet

At Citadines Trocadéro, the best deals are the studios in the new wing, which integrate Art Deco design with the latest in bathrooms and room layout. All the facilities are furnished with equipped kitchens, a full bath

TELEPHONE
01-44-34-73-73

FAX
01-47-04-50-07

with shelf space, a color TV with international reception, weekly linen changes, and a direct-dial telephone. You must do your own housekeeping, unless you opt for a maid, which is extra. Baby beds, an iron and ironing board, and a vacuum cleaner are provided free of charge. There is a coin-operated washing machine and dryer in the basement. Enclosed, private parking is also available. Stays can range from a night to several months, but the longer the stay, the lower the price, especially during the off-season. Just a block away is one of the best indoor supermarket complexes in Paris. After one trip through the aisles of this market, you will be inspired to use your kitchen.

ENGLISH SPOKEN: Yes

FACILITIES AND SERVICES: Direct-dial phone; dishwasher in all but studettes; baby bed; coin-operated washer and dryer; elevator; iron and ironing board; TV with international reception; vacuum cleaner; enclosed private parking, 50F per day; office safe, 90F per week; weekly linen and maid service

NEAREST TOURIST ATTRACTIONS (RIGHT BANK): Shopping on avenue Victor-Hugo, Arc de Triomphe, Champs-Élysées

CITADINES VOLTAIRE/RÉPUBLIQUE ★★★
75, bis avenue Parmentier, at rue Oberkamph, 75011 (11th)
75 apartments, all with fitted kitchenettes, shower or bath, and toilet

The Voltaire/République Citadine is included because of its reasonable price, with a caveat about its location. True, it is not in the center of Paris as most think of it, but it is in the heart of the rapidly developing eleventh arrondissement. It isn't too far from the Marais, the Picasso Museum, and all the pulsating night life near the Bastille. Perhaps more of its appeal lies in the fact that this is a typical Parisian neighborhood where you can really mix with the locals in their daily life by frequenting corner cafés, shopping in the street *marchés*, and discovering little restaurants you would otherwise have missed. The units have all the perks found in the rest of the chain, but the cost is less, which should appeal to Cheap Sleepers in Paris looking for this sort of stay.

ENGLISH SPOKEN: Yes

FACILITIES AND SERVICES: Direct-dial phone; baby beds; coin-operated laundromat and dryer; elevator; fitted kitchens; parking, 45F per day, 250F per week, 750F per month; office safe, 20F day, 90F week, 200F month; TV with international reception; solarium; weekly linen change; weekly maid service, 90F per hour extra unless stay one month, then it is free; vacuum and iron available

NEAREST TOURIST ATTRACTIONS (RIGHT BANK): Bastille, Marais

FAMILY HÔTEL (NO STARS)
23, rue Fondary, 75015 (15th)
21 studios all with kitchenette, shower, and toilet

These new plain-as-a-pin studios in the middle of the working-class fifteenth arrondissement put the B on Basic. The twenty-one sites are geared for those Cheap Sleepers in Paris in for the long haul who want *only* a place to cook, eat, sleep, and take a shower. Nothing more. Fifteen have a TV; some have sofa beds; and some have proper double or twin beds. The low-maintenance floors are white tile, bathrooms are reminiscent of train compartments, and the closets are designed for those who travel light and never shop. Since it is new, colors match and so does the simple furniture. Kitchens are stocked with the barest essentials you will need to do simple cooking. The units are kept clean, thanks to the maids who swoop through three times a week. The operation is run by the Pacific Hôtel just down the street, and from what I could see, the staff is available only to check people in and out and render crisis management.

NOTE: All reservations and check-ins are handled through the Pacific Hôtel at the telephone and fax given in the sidebar. Please don't mistake the two establishments: make sure you check in to the Family Hôtel, *not* the Pacific Hôtel.

ENGLISH SPOKEN: Yes

FACILITIES AND SERVICES: Direct-dial phone with separate line for each studio; elevator; kitchenettes; maid service three times a week; TV in fifteen rooms; office safe at Pacific Hôtel, no charge

NEAREST TOURIST ATTRACTION (LEFT BANK): Eiffel Tower, Seine; otherwise, must use public transportation

TELEPHONE
01-45-75-20-49

FAX
01-45-77-70-73

MÉTRO
Émile-Zola

CREDIT CARDS
MC, V

RATES
1–2 persons, 220–400F; lower prices for longer stays: 7 nights for 20% discount, 15 or more nights for 30% discount
Taxe de séjour: included

BREAKFAST
Not available

HOME PLAZZA RÉSIDENCE HÔTELS: BASTILLE AND SAINT-ANTOINE

Home Plazza Bastille

TELEPHONE
Central reservations 01- 40-21-
22-23; reception at hotel 01-
40-21-22-00

FAX
01-47-00-82-40

MÉTRO
St-Sebastien-Froissart

CREDIT CARDS
AE, DC, MC, V

RATES
Residence plan: from 780F (for
one person) to 2,180F (for 6
persons) per day; hoteliere plan:
from 870F (for one) to 2,280F
(for 6 persons) per day; rates in
both plans vary with length of
stay and time of year
Taxe de séjour: 7F extra per day,
per person

BREAKFAST
65F extra per person

Home Plazza Saint-Antoine

TELEPHONE
01-40-09-40-00

FAX
01-40-09-11-55

E-MAIL
hplaza@isp.fr

MÉTRO
Nation

CREDIT CARDS
AE, DC, MC, V

RATES
Residence plan: from 780F (for
one person) to 2,180F (for 6
persons) per day; hoteliere plan:
from 840F (for one) to 2,280F
(for 6 persons) per day; both
plans have varying rates
according to length of stay
Taxe de séjour: 7F extra per
person, per day

BREAKFAST
65F extra per person

The two Home Plazza residences are located in a part of Paris that until a few years ago was considered a tourist wilderness. Now they are close to the thick of things in the eleventh arrondissement. The two residence hotels offer equipped studios and flats furnished in a modern style that holds up well under hard use. There are two plans: the Résidence Plan, with cleaning and linen changed once a week, or the Hôtelière Plan, where there is daily cleaning and towel change, but the bed linens are changed every three days. In both plans, the longer you stay, the less you pay. One of the benefits of staying here is all the extras available to the guest. While the Bastille résidence has the edge on location and amenities offered, the Saint-Antoine site seems less impersonal.

HOME PLAZZA BASTILLE ★★★
74, rue Amelot, 75011 (11th)
289 studios and apartments, fully furnished with equipped kitchens

ENGLISH SPOKEN: Yes

FACILITIES AND SERVICES: Bar; conference room; direct-dial phone; elevator; hair dryer; iron; laundry and cleaning service; parking, 100F per day; room safe, 5F per day; TV with international reception; restaurant

NEAREST TOURIST ATTRACTIONS (RIGHT BANK): Marais, Bastille

HOME PLAZZA SAINT-ANTOINE ★★★
289, bis rue de Faubourg St-Antoine, 75011 (11th)
90 studios and apartments, fully furnished with equipped kitchens

NOTE: From a security standpoint, I would avoid the rooms on the garden level.

ENGLISH SPOKEN: Yes

FACILITIES AND SERVICES: Conference room; direct-dial phone; elevator; hair dryer; iron; laundry and cleaning service; parking, 100F per day; room safe, 5F per day; radio; TV with international reception

NEAREST TOURIST ATTRACTIONS (RIGHT BANK): Nothing; must use public transportation

PIERRE & VACANCES: RÉSIDENCE CHARLES DULLIN ★★★

10, place Charles-Dullin, 75018 (18th)
76 studios and apartments with equipped kitchens, shower or bath, and toilet

During two extended stays in Paris, the Résidence Charles Dullin was my *pied à terre.* I continue to recommend it as a home-away-from-home for those who want to explore Paris from a typical neighborhood. This part of Montmartre is full of contrasts. By day, it is interesting for its many colorful local characters who wander the streets and sit and reminisce in the cafés. In the evening, the atmosphere changes and it becomes young and alive until the wee hours, with Parisians and tourists eating and drinking in the many bistros and restaurants, which offer every kind of cuisine from African couscous to health burgers and Spanish tapas.

From a practical standpoint, everything you will need to set up short- or long-term housekeeping is within an easy five- or ten-minute walk: small supermarkets, banks, a main post office, pharmacies, dry cleaners, a shoe repair shop, a photo store, pungent cheese shops, tempting *boulangeries,* colorful fish and meat markets, *charcuteries* brimming with beautiful, ready-made food (if you don't care to cook), and finally, one of the best shopping streets in this part of Paris, rue Lepic.

The seventy-six studios and apartments are for the most part spacious and livable. All have kitchens and a uniformity of services and facilities. Weekly maid service *is* included, as are linen and towel changes twice weekly. If you want more frequent maid service, there is an hourly rate. The best part is, the longer you stay, the lower the price, especially in the low season.

ENGLISH SPOKEN: Yes

FACILITIES AND SERVICES: Direct-dial phone; dishwasher in most units; dry cleaning service; elevator; parking, 100F per day; TV with international reception; office safe, no charge

NEAREST TOURIST ATTRACTIONS (RIGHT BANK): Montmartre

TELEPHONE
01-42-57-14-55

FAX
01-42-54-48-87

MÉTRO
Abbesses, Anvers

CREDIT CARDS
AE, DC, MC, V

RATES
From 575F for a studio in low season to 1,275F per night for a 3-room apartment sleeping 6; weekly, monthly, and seasonal rates available
Taxe de séjour: 6F extra per person, per day

BREAKFAST
50F extra per person

RÉSIDENCE HÔTELIÈRE TROUSSEAU ★★
13, rue Trousseau, 75011 (11th)
66 studios and suites, all with fully fitted kitchens, bath, shower, and toilet

TELEPHONE
01-48-05-55-55

FAX
01-48-05-83-97

MÉTRO
Ledru-Rollin

CREDIT CARDS
AE, MC, V

RATES
Hotel plan: from 580F for a studio to 1,575F per night for an apartment sleeping 5–6; daily cleaning and linen change; sheets changed every two days. *Residence plan (3-night minimum):* from 550F for a studio to 1,420F for an apartment sleeping 5–6; weekly maid service and change of sheets and towels, otherwise maid service 90F per day; in both plans prices vary according to the season and length of stay. *Taxe de séjour:* included

BREAKFAST
50F extra per person

To tell you the truth, I never expected to find such a nice residence hotel a fifteen-minute walk *east* of the Bastille. If it was almost anyplace else in Paris, it would be almost twice the price and jam-packed year round. It is part of a small chain that deals mainly in four-star addresses in Paris and along the French Riviera, so demanding, exacting guests are nothing new to management. The sixty-six studio flats and duplex suites have fully equipped kitchens with microwaves and satellite television reception. Disciples of Sister Parish and Billy Baldwin were not called upon to be decorating consultants, but the no-surprise rooms have excellent bathrooms with lots of shelf space, a medicine cabinet, and a drying rack. No. 710 is a large, two-story duplex with a mezzanine bedroom. The theme is that of a ship, carried out with photos of yachts on the walls and in the bathrooms, or "Captain's Quarters," port-hole mirrors and wooden slat shower floors. Just so you know, in the studios the sofa doubles as the bed, the closets have no doors, and some floors are tiled, not carpeted. The overall popularity of this selection is due in no small measure to the list of amenities offered: private car parking, conference room, office space, fax capabilities, a golf practice cage— no kidding!—along with coin-operated laundries and shopping carts in the garage to help you lug your loot.

The proprietors own wineries in Bordeaux and sell their wines at this hotel. To go with your bottle of wine, you can order a light meal almost any time of day.

ENGLISH SPOKEN: Yes

FACILITIES AND SERVICES: Bar; conference room; office rooms; fax services; direct-dial phone; elevator; hair dryer; fitted kitchen; private parking, 90F per day; TV with international reception; office safe, no charge; coin-operated laundry; golf range, 20F per hour; weekly or daily maid service, depending on accommodation; light meals served (mostly frozen)

NEAREST TOURIST ATTRACTIONS (RIGHT BANK): None; must use public transportation

RÉSIDENCE MALESHERBES HÔTEL (NO STARS)
129, rue Cardinet, 75017 (17th)
21 studios, all with equipped kitchens, shower or bath, and toilet

There is something about living in an apartment during your stay in Paris that makes you feel less frantic about seeing and doing absolutely everything. You are caught up instead with the fun and adventure of exploring and getting to know your own Paris neighborhood and feeling rather Parisian in the process.

These twenty-one soundproofed studios have been decorated with provincial prints, quilted spreads, and antiqued furniture. Kitchenettes are mini in size and scope—not geared for preparing banquets or experimenting with Julia Child's most complicated recipes—but they are big enough to prepare something purchased from the tempting outdoor *marché* held along rue Levis, just a few minutes' walk from here. There is also no getting around the small bathrooms and limited drawer space, but the showers are good and everything works. Maid service is included once a week.

ENGLISH SPOKEN: Limited

FACILITIES AND SERVICES: Private telephone line for each studio; elevator; equipped kitchenettes; hair dryer; parking 75F per day; laundry and cleaning service; baby bed; dogs accepted; TV; office safe, no charge

NEAREST TOURIST ATTRACTIONS (RIGHT BANK): None, must use public transportation

TELEPHONE
01-44-15-85-00

FAX
01-44-15-85-29

MÉTRO
Malesherbes

CREDIT CARDS
AE, MC, V

RATES
Studio from 430–580F per day, lower rates for longer stays; baby bed 25F extra per day; dogs 35F extra per day *Taxe de séjour*: 3F extra per person, per day

BREAKFAST
Not available

Student Accommodations

There are more than ten thousand student beds in Paris. The following list of both public and private sources offers youthful Cheap Sleepers in Paris help in finding low-cost accommodations year round. Where applicable, only main reservation offices are listed. Most sites have a minimum stay in the summer, and curfews are not uncommon. All will give you the rules of the road *before* you get your bed, so there will be no excuses for improper conduct or pleading ignorance. It is critically important to remember that often *only* cash is accepted and that sometimes you must either be an enrolled student, within a certain age bracket, or belong to a group to qualify (such as a youth hostel).

Any student can take advantage of the French government–run and/or subsidized student lodgings in

Paris. To do so, you will be required to show proof of full-time student status, in addition to your university or college ID, or if you are not a student, prove you are between the ages of twelve and twenty-five. The best way to show this additional proof is with the International Student Identity Card, known as the ISIC, or with the Go-25 card if you are between twelve and twenty-five years old and for some reason not a student. Both cards entitle you to savings on selected museum entry fees, transportation costs, meals at certain student dining halls, and, of course, lodgings. If you purchase your ISIC or Go-25 card in the United States, you will also receive medical, accident, and hospital insurance. Teachers can get some of the same discounts and all of the benefits by purchasing the International Teacher Identity Card (ITIC). All cards cost $20. For more information about these important bargains, contact the Council on International Education Exchange (CIEE), 205 East 42nd Street, 16th floor, New York, NY 10017; telephone 212-661-1414, 800-438-2643, or 888-COUNCIL; fax 212-822-2699; or via e-mail at info@ciee.org. Office hours are Monday to Friday from 9:30 A.M. to 5 P.M. EST. You can also buy the cards in Paris, but you won't receive the medical benefits. Go to 119, rue St-Martin (4th); métro, Rambuteau; open Monday to Friday from 9:30 A.M. to 6 P.M.

Another option for cash-strapped Cheap Sleepers, regardless of age or student status, is to be a member of Hosteling International. These simple, sometimes spartan, sleeping dormitories, which range from barracks to restored castles, are a great deal for hard-core Cheap Sleepers because the price is right and the camaraderie that hosteling fosters is great. To make life easier on the road, become a member of the American Hosteling organization *before* you leave. If you show up at a hostel without a membership card, there will be a supplement per night for six nights, then you will be a member. For more information, write or call the American Youth Hostel at P.O. Box 37163, Washington, DC 20013; telephone 202-783-6161.

Finally, if none of the above work, try the Office du Tourisme at 127, Champs-Élysées, 75008; métro, Charles-de-Gaulle-Étoile; 01-47-23-61-72. It's open daily from 9 A.M. to 6 P.M. Lines are long and selections not always the cheapest. Count on paying a supplement for the reservation service.

There are also private hostels, which I think are usually suspect in terms of cleanliness and security. Those listed below have higher standards than most and can be recommended as clean, safe choices in the Cheap Sleeping game in Paris.

ACCUEIL DES JEUNES EN FRANCE (AJF)
119, rue St-Martin, 75004 (4th)

Located across the square from the Centre Pompidou, the AJF provides discount travel help and information on accommodations and many other related items of interest to anyone aged eighteen to thirty. It can also do same-day reservations for youth hostels and other budget options for a small additional booking fee. For best results do not telephone, but arrive in person before 10 A.M. especially during the summer. Office hours are Monday to Saturday from 9 A.M. to 6 P.M. If you are traveling elsewhere in France, ask for their thick book detailing a multitude of student accommodations throughout the country.

ENGLISH SPOKEN: Yes

FACILITIES AND SERVICES: Varies with each location

NEAREST TOURIST ATTRACTIONS: Varies with each location

TELEPHONE
01-42-77-87-80

FAX
None

MÉTRO
Rambuteau

CREDIT CARDS
Depends on location; plan on cash

RATES
Depends on location
Taxe de séjour: included

BREAKFAST
Depends on location

ASSOCIATION DES ÉTUDIENTS PROTESTANTS DE PARIS (AEPP)
46, rue de Vaugirard, 75006 (6th)
45 dormitory beds, no private facilities

Centrally located by the Luxembourg Gardens, the facility is open to students between eighteen and twenty-six years old. Maximum stay is five weeks in dormitory-style accommodations, which must be paid for in advance. From June through August there are a few rooms for one or two. There is a café for breakfast (which is included in the daily rate) and dinner (which is extra). Cooking facilities are also available. On arrival, a refundable key deposit and a one-year 10F membership fee will be charged.

Office hours are Monday to Friday from 8:45 A.M. to noon, 3 to 7 P.M. in winter and from 5 to 7 P.M. in summer; Saturday from 8:45 A.M. to noon, 6 to 8 P.M.; and Sunday from 10 A.M. to noon.

ENGLISH SPOKEN: Limited

FACILITIES AND SERVICES: Café and cooking privileges; office safe, no charge; TV downstairs

TELEPHONE
01-43-54-31-49,
01-46-33-23-30

FAX
01-46-34-27-09

E-MAIL
aepp@worldnet.fr

MÉTRO
Mabillon, St-Sulpice

RATES
Single 100F, double 90F per person; dorm room (4 to 8 persons) 80F per person
Taxe de séjour: included

BREAKFAST
Included

NEAREST TOURIST ATTRACTIONS (LEFT BANK): Luxembourg Gardens, St-Michel, St-Germain-des-Prés, Montparnasse

BUREAU DES VOYAGES DE LA JEUNESSE (BVJ)
Paris/Louvre Location: 20, rue Jean-Jacques Rousseau, 75001 (1st)
204 beds, none with shower, bath, or toilet
Quartier Latin Location: 44, rue des Bernardins, 75005 (5th)
158 beds, none with shower, bath, or toilet

TELEPHONE
Paris/Louvre: 01-42-36-88-18,
01-40-26-66-43,
01-42-33-82-10
Quartier Latin: 01-42-29-34-80

FAX
Both locations: 01-42-33-40-53

MÉTRO
Paris/Louvre: Les Halles
Quartier Latin: Maubert-Mutualité

CREDIT CARDS
MC, V for groups, cash only for individuals

RATES
Single 130F, double or dorm 120F
Taxe de séjour: included

BREAKFAST
Included; can be deducted at 20F per person

There are 362 beds for young people (ages eighteen to thirty-five) available in the heart of Paris, either on the Right Bank near the Louvre (called Paris/Louvre) or on the Left Bank in the Latin Quarter (at Quartier Latin). Most of the clientele, who travel light with only a backpack, don't mind sharing dorm rooms with up to seven other weary travelers. The good news is the prices are reasonable, and there are some single and double accommodations in addition to the shared dorm rooms for up to eight. The key is to land in a room with as few roommates as possible. No towels or soap are provided with the free showers; lockers cost only 10F and are worth it; there is no daytime lockout; and at the Louvre location, there is a subsidized restaurant. Individual travelers usually need a two- or three-day advance reservation, but groups should reserve sooner.

ENGLISH SPOKEN: Yes

FACILITIES AND SERVICES: Lockers for 10F; meals are 65F for lunch or dinner; no towels or soap provided; no daytime lockout

NEAREST TOURIST ATTRACTIONS: Paris/Louvre location (Right Bank): Louvre, Palais Royal, Centre Pompidou; Quartier Latin location (Left Bank): St-Michel, Seine, Île de la Cité, Île St-Louis

CITÉ UNIVERSITAIRE
15, boulevard Jourdan, 74014 (14th)

TELEPHONE
01-45-89-35-79

MÉTRO
Cité Universitaire

The Cité Universitaire is a vast maze of forty international student residences located on the edge of the city next to the Parc Montsouris. Both advance- and short-notice reservations are possible, depending on the residence. Foreign students and teachers are accepted from July 1 to September 30. Minimum stay is seven to fifteen days, depending on the residence. There are more than forty-five hundred rooms, so getting something should not be difficult, if you don't mind the outskirts location. Office is open Monday to Friday from 8 A.M. to 7 P.M.

CROUS ACADÉMIE DE PARIS
39, avenue Georges-Bernanos, 75005 (5th)

CROUS is mainly known for providing students with inexpensive meals in its Restos-U (see *Cheap Eats in Paris*). It also is in charge of all university student accommodations in Paris, and it has beds available during French university vacations. It is also a source of cheap trips and discount tickets for theater and cultural events. The ISIC card is accepted for discounts. The address above is the main office where you should start your search, whether it be for meal tickets, a bed for your stay, or a trip outside of Paris. Hours are Monday to Friday from 9 A.M. to 5 P.M.

ENGLISH SPOKEN: Usually

TELEPHONE
01-40-51-36-00

MÉTRO
RER Port-Royal

HOSTELING INTERNATIONAL
La Centrale de Réservations (FUAJ-HI)
4, boulevard Jules Ferry, 75011 (11th)

La Centrale de Reservations (FUAJ-HI), run by Hosteling International, is the best place to get a cheap student bed in Paris. Membership in Hosteling International is required. You can acquire it in the United States or pay a daily supplement. (To acquire an HI membership, contact the American Youth Hostel, P.O. Box 37163, Washington, DC 20013; telephone 202-703-6161.) A trip to their Paris office will provide you with a same-day reservation in any of their affiliated hostels or budget hotels. Not only can you book a bed, but you can make on-going travel arrangements by bus, boat, or air; book tours to other parts of the world; or nail down an excursion in Paris. There will be a reservation fee, payable at the time of booking, but it is deducted from the cost of your bed. The office is open daily from 8 A.M. to 10 P.M.

ENGLISH SPOKEN: Yes

FACILITIES AND SERVICES: Reservations for other hostels and travel arrangements

NEAREST TOURIST ATTRACTIONS: Varies with each location

TELEPHONE
01-43-57-02-60

FAX
Fax reservations taken for groups of 10 or more: 01-40-21-79-92

E-MAIL
auberge@micronet.fr

INTERNET
www.fuaj.fr

MÉTRO
République

CREDIT CARDS
MC, V

RATES
Double 120F per person; 110F per person in dorm (4 to 6 beds); showers are free; towels 15F; paper sheets 14F; must be an HI member or pay 20F nightly supplement. *Taxe de séjour*: included

BREAKFAST
Included, cannot be deducted

MAISON INTERNATIONALE DES JEUNES (MIJCP)
4, rue Titon, 75011 (11th)
170 beds, no private facilities

TELEPHONE
01-43-71-99-21

FAX
01-43-71-78-58

MÉTRO
Faidherbe-Chaligny

CREDIT CARDS
None, cash only

RATES
120F per person, per day; free shower; sheets and pillow 15F
Taxe de séjour: included

BREAKFAST
Included

Open to people from eighteen to thirty (older if with a group), the MIJCP offers clean rooms with three to eight basic bunks and not much else. Breakfast and a free shower are included in the daily rate; everything else is extra. Facilities are nil: no safes, lockers, laundry, TV, or even bed lights, and it's buy your own soap and towels. There is a 2 A.M. curfew and a daily cleaning lockout from 10 A.M. until 5 P.M. The office is open from 8 A.M. to 1 A.M. This is one to keep in mind when all else fails.

ENGLISH SPOKEN: Yes

FACILITIES AND SERVICES: None

NEAREST TOURIST ATTRACTIONS (RIGHT BANK): Bastille, long walk

MAISON INTERNATIONALE DE LA JEUNESSE ET DES ÉTUDIANTS (MIJE)
6, rue de Fourcy, 75004 (4th)

TELEPHONE
01-42-74-23-45

FAX
01-40-27-81-64

MÉTRO
St-Paul

CREDIT CARDS
None, cash only

RATES
Single 170F, double 150F per person, dorm (for 3 to 8 people) 125F per person
Taxe de séjour: included

BREAKFAST
Included

For my student Cheap Sleeping Franc, MIJE offers some of the best student beds in Paris. The MIJE has converted three historic mansions in the Marais, and each room holds from three to eight people; all rooms have a sink and shower. The address given above (Le Fourcy) is also the main office where all reservations are made. There is also a dining room here, which is open to anyone staying in the three hostels. The maximum stay is seven nights, and there is a room lockout from noon to 3 P.M. Advanced reservations by telephone or fax are accepted from 7 A.M. to 9 P.M. daily. Do it! These are very popular accommodations.

NOTE: The other two locations are Le Fauconnier, 11, rue Fauconnier (4th), métro St-Paul and Maubuisson; and 12, rue des Barres (4th), métro Hôtel-de-Ville.

ENGLISH SPOKEN: Yes

FACILITIES AND SERVICES: None, but the locations are tops

NEAREST TOURIST ATTRACTIONS (RIGHT BANK): Marais, Bastille, the islands, St-Michel, St-Germain-des-Prés

UNION DES CENTRES DES RENCONTRES INTERNATIONALES DE FRANCE (UCRIF)
72, rue Rambuteau, 75001 (1st)

UCRIF has several lodgings in Paris, with no age limit. For the complete listing, contact the Maison de L'UCRIF at the above address (telephone 01-40-26-57-64). Office hours are Monday to Friday from 9 A.M. to 6 P.M.; métro Chatelet.

Shopping: Cheap Chic

Paris is wrenchingly beautiful, and so are many of its people. If you use your eyes and take in everything, you can learn more about true style in a weekend than in a lifetime's perusal of fashion magazines.
—*Lucia Van der Post*

A museum is a museum, but a bargain is forever . . .
—*Suzy K. Gershman*, Born to Shop Paris

Paris is a shopper's dream world. Even those who claim to dislike shopping are bound to be attracted by the unending selection of shops with beautiful window displays. The *haute couture*, open air *marchés* overflowing with beautiful foods, extravagant toy shops, and the dazzling displays of jewelry, antiques, and collectibles tempt everyone from the serious buyer to the casual browser. There has always been something very stylish about the French. Just the addition of the word *French* to everyday objects such as jeans, silk, perfume, bread, wine, cheese, and toast lifts them out of the ordinary. For many of us, going to Paris is a dream come true, but it isn't quite enough . . . we want to bring something of Paris home with us. However, a recent study showed Paris to be the most expensive city in Europe for buying clothes and shoes. What are we to do—those of us who cannot afford to pay the astronomically high prices that come with such glorious merchandise? The answer is: Become a Parisian smart shopper.

After you have been in Paris for a day or so, you will realize that style counts: the French do not just get dressed, they get turned out. You will no doubt wonder how a modest shop clerk manages to look so elegant, considering his or her low wages and the high price tags on clothing. The answer is simple: savvy Parisian shoppers know where to go for the best quality and value, and they *never* pay full price.

As a life-long, dedicated discount shopper with a black belt in the art, I know that bargain shopping can be both frustrating and exhausting—until you find that fabulous designer suit in your size and favorite color for half price. This type of discount shopping in Paris takes a good eye, limitless patience, endurance, and comfortable shoes. In Paris, of all places, it should be more than just a quest to track down the cheapest items available . . . it should be fun. Finding something *très a la mode* at below retail in Paris is not that difficult once you know how. The trick is in knowing when and where to shop to get the most for your money. That is what Cheap Chic will help you to do: transform your T-shirt into a significant outfit, with just the right pair of pants, a sassy jacket, and perfect accessories for the moment—all for reduced prices and, more importantly, for less than you would pay at home.

With all discount shopping, the selections will vary from day to day and season to season. Shops also come and go. What is here today and very "in" may be gone tomorrow. Not all shops take credit cards, so be prepared with extra francs. The comfort of the customer is seldom a top priority. As a result, many places do not have proper dressing rooms, most are jammed with merchandise, there is limited individual attention, and in many cases only fragmented English is spoken. And never mind the icy salesperson who has an innate knack for sizing you up and pricing everything you are wearing in one glance. Believe me, it is all worth it because nothing is more satisfying than being clad in designer labels at knockdown prices. Armed with Cheap Chic, you are bound to find great buys, save money, and come home with things your friends will die over. *Bonne chance!* And please, if you discover something wonderful, let me know.

Cheap Chic Shopping Tips

1. Know the prices at home so you will be able to spot a bargain when you see it in Paris.

2. To get a rough idea of how much something costs, double the francs and move the decimal (100F = $20.00; 80F = $16.00). To be precise, carry a calculator.

3. If you like something, can get it home, and can afford it, buy it when you see it. If you wait until later, it probably will not be there when you go back, or you will see it later or when you get home for twice the price.

4. Look for these signs in the windows—they mean lower prices:
Soldes	a sale in progress (see page 262 for Parisian sales)
Fin de Séries	end of collection
Dégriffés	labels cut out
Stock	overstock
Dépot Vente	resale
Fripes	used clothing

5. Nothing is returnable. Be sure when you buy something that it does not have flaws and that it fits.

6. *Never* change money at a shop. The rate will not be in your favor. Go instead to a bank or use a credit card.

7. If you are shopping at one of the flea markets, be sure to bargain. The asking price is *not* the price you are expected to pay. You should be able to bargain the price down by 15 to 30 percent. Also, bring cash: plastic is not part of a bargaining discussion, and most sellers do not take credit cards of any type.

8. Pharmacies marked with a green cross on a white background are upscale and expensive. They are the places to go if you need a prescription filled or advice on cold remedies. Buy toiletries, cosmetics, and basic over-the-counter drugs in supermarkets or at Monoprix or Prisunic. Pharmacy prices are at least double.

9. Pack an empty, soft-folding suitcase in your luggage so you can transport your treasures without the extra hassle and expense of mailing. An extra bag on an airline (over the limit of two, plus a carry-on) will cost around a hundred dollars, and that will be less than you will have to pay at the store or at the post office to have it sent.

10. Take the time to do all the *détaxe,* and remember to turn it into the customs officials at the airport *before* you relinquish your luggage or go through customs or passport control (see Tax Refund: *Détaxe,* page 260).

11. When returning to the United States, remember these points when going through customs:

   • You and every member of your family, regardless of age, can bring back $400 worth of purchases duty-free. Family members can pool their duty-free purchases (see Customs, page 261, for further pointers).

   • Don't cheat, don't smuggle, and above all, don't do drugs.

   • Be nice.

12. Generally speaking, shop hours are Monday through Saturday from 10 A.M. to 7 P.M. Large department stores are open one night a week. Small shops often close Monday morning, for lunch, and often for all or part of August. Except for shops in the heavy tourist areas, everything is closed on Sunday and holidays.

13. When you enter a store, you will be greeted with "Bonjour Madame" (or "Monsieur"), and when you leave, "Au revoir Madame" (or "Monsieur"). Please respond in kind, with "Bonjour Mademoiselle," and so on. It is considered extremely bad form not to acknowledge the salespeople when entering or leaving a store.

Tax Refund: *Détaxe*

Every tourist visiting France is entitled to a *détaxe* (tax rebate) for purchases totaling 2,000F or more in one store. The refund averages about 13 percent. If shopping with a friend, combine your purchases to reach the total and share the proceeds when they arrive. The simple paperwork is filled out by you and the store. You will need to have your passport available for identification. On the *détaxe* form, you will be asked to state whether you want the refund mailed to you in a French-franc check (not recommended because it is hard to deal with in the United

States and getting it can take forever), or to have it credited to your credit card. This last option is the best because your credit card company will credit the refund to you in U.S. dollars. Expect a delay of two to three months. For items shipped directly from the store, the *détaxe* is automatically deducted without any paperwork. At your point of exit from France, a customs official will stamp your documents, which you then mail back to the store in the self-addressed, stamped envelope the store will give you at the time of purchase. That's it. Sometimes an eager official will ask to see your purchases, so keep them handy just in case. At the airport, look for the window that says *douane de détaxe* and allow an extra half hour to accomplish the mission. Generally, you must *ask* for the *détaxe* forms because most smaller shopkeepers do not volunteer the information. In the large department stores there are special offices that take care of the paperwork. Yes, it all does take some extra time and effort, but the savings do add up, so persevere.

NOTE: The *détaxe* does *not* apply for food, drink, medicine, unset gems, antiques, works of art, automobiles or their parts, or commercial purchases.

Customs

Each United States citizen, even a week-old baby, is entitled to bring back $400 worth of duty-free goods acquired abroad. Families can pool their duty-free purchases, so *you* can use what your spouse and children do not. After the $400 point, there will be a 10 percent charge on the next $1,000, and more as the amount increases. Have your receipts ready and make sure they coincide with what you filled out on the landing card. Don't cheat or lie, as you will invariably be caught. You and your luggage will undergo exhaustive searches, and that will just be for openers. Any purchase worth *less* than $50 can be shipped back to the States as an unsolicited gift and is considered duty-free, and it *does not* count in your $400 limit. You can send as many of these unsolicited gifts as you wish, but only one unsolicited gift per person for each mailing, and don't mail anything to yourself. If your package worth exceeds $50, you will pay duty.

Antiques must be one hundred years old to be duty-free.

A work of art is duty-free, and it does not matter when it was created or who the artist was.

If you have expensive cameras, piles of imported luggage, fancy watches, or valuable jewelry, carry the receipts for them, or you could be questioned about them and even end up paying duty on them.

Finally, people who look like hippies get stopped and have their bags searched. So do bejeweled and bedecked women wrapped in full-length furs, carrying expensive designer luggage. For more information on U.S. Customs rules and regulations, send for the free brochure "Know Before You Go," available from the U.S. Customs Service, Box 7407, Washington, DC 20044; telephone 202-927-6724.

Sales: *Soldes*

During most of the year, when you venture into one of the designer shops, they are quiet enough for you to hear the rustle of money being spent by wealthy customers. However, we less-affluent mortals also have a chance in these stores. For the first three weeks in January and July, Paris is *on sale.* In addition, Galeries Lafayette and Au Printemps have sales in March and October. During the January and July sales, the crowds of shoppers move with dizzying swiftness, all zeroing in on the considerable savings. If you can brave these shopping pros, this is the time to go to the designer boutiques and pick up a little number for about one-third the U.S. retail price. In October, Hèrmes has its once-yearly sale. The line forms the night before, with shoppers eager to pay 50 percent less for the famous signature scarves (currently retailing for over $200), ties, leather goods, and conservative line of clothing. Again, if you do not mind standing in line and fighting crowds packed in ten-deep, then this sale is a must for Hèrmes fans.

Consignment Shops: Dépôts-Ventes

Consignment shops sell previously owned items at a fraction of original cost. It might be hard to consider wearing "used" clothing, but please try to. You would be surprised at the number of very sophisticated and well-known fellow bargain-inspired shoppers you may recognize standing next to you searching the racks for just the perfect outfit.

AMÉLIE
17, rue Amélie, 75007 (7th)
Smaller than most, but worth a look if you are nearby. Owner Marie Hubert stocks quality clothing, including such names as Hermès and Chanel.

TELEPHONE: 01-47-05-90-11
MÉTRO: Latour-Maubourg
CREDIT CARDS: AE, MC, V
HOURS: Tues–Fri 11 A.M.–2 P.M., 3–7 P.M., Sat 11 A.M.–1 P.M., 4–7 P.M.; closed July 15 to the end of Aug

DÉPÔT-VENTE DE PASSY
14–16, rue de la Tour, 75016 (16th) (Women)
25, rue de la Tour, 75016 (16th) (Men)
This is one of the best, offering a super selection of clothing in mint condition featuring all the biggies for women, from Chanel to Yves St-Laurent to Cardin and Ricci. It has a nice staff, fair prices of about 40 percent off regular retail (only 20 percent for Chanel), and good dressing rooms. This is one of the favorites of smart French discount denizens. The

men's shop stocks both new (without labels) and used. It is all mixed together, but except for the shoes, it is hard to tell the old from the new.

TELEPHONE: 01-45-20-95-21 (women's shop), 01-45-27-11-46 (men's shop)

MÉTRO: Passy

CREDIT CARDS: AE, MC, V

HOURS: Mon 2–7 P.M., Tues–Sat 10 A.M.–7 P.M.; closed Aug

L'OCASSERIE
19, rue de la Pompe, 75016 (16th)
30, rue de la Pompe, 75016 (16th)
14, rue Jean Bologne, 75016 (16th)
16 & 21, rue de l'Annonciation, 75016 (16th)

At these four locations in the upmarket sixteenth arrondissement, men and women can find gently worn designer togs, furs, accessories, and shoes for less. The shops are all within easy walking distance of each other, but none stocks children's wear.

TELEPHONE: 01-45-03-17-99, 01-45-03-16-56, 01-45-27-32-40, 01-45-25-11-38

MÉTRO: Passy

CREDIT CARDS: MC, V

HOURS: Mon–Sat 11 A.M.–7 P.M.; not all the shops observe these hours, but you will find at least one or two open; Aug closing varies with each shop

RÉCIPROQUE
89, 92, 93, 95, 97, 103, 123, rue de la Pompe, 75016 (16th)

The grande dame of formerly worn designer duds for a fraction of their original retail price, this is the largest consignment shop in Paris and has everything from gifts and antiques to estate jewelry, shoes, bags, clothes, furs, evening wear, and men's wear. The sheer volume is staggering, so allow plenty of time if this type of *haute* thrift shopping is your forte. Sales are held from January 1 to February 15. The staff is helpful.

TELEPHONE: 01-47-04-30-28

MÉTRO: Pompe

CREDIT CARDS: AE, MC, V

HOURS: Tues–Sat 11 A.M.–7:30 P.M.; closed Sun and Mon and last week of July to last week of Aug

Cosmetics and Perfumes

CATHERINE PERFUMES AND COSMETICS
6, rue de Castiglione, 75001 (1st)
7, rue de Castiglione, 75001 (1st) (across the street)

Jacques Levy, his wife, and their two daughters run these two boutiques on rue de Castiglione, where they offer an excellent selection of
perfumes, cosmetics, scarves, hair ornaments, jewelry, and ties. They
speak English, and don't employ "hard sell" tactics. You will receive a
tax-free price of 20 percent off if you purchase 1,600F or more worth of
merchandise, which translates into a savings of up to 35 percent. If you
buy less than 1,600F, you will get a 20- to 30-percent discount, but you
will pay the 15-percent tax. For mail orders, which you can do by fax, the
same discounts are offered.

TELEPHONE: 01-42-61-02-89, 01-42-60-48-17
FAX: 01-42-61-02-35
MÉTRO: Tuileries
CREDIT CARDS: AE, DC, MC, V
HOURS: Mon–Sat 9:30 A.M.–7 P.M.; closed 15 days in Aug, dates vary

FREDDY
3, rue Scribe, around the corner from American Express,
75009 (9th)

Freddy specializes in perfumes, but also stocks scarves, ties, cosmetics,
and costume jewelry. Forty percent is taken off if you spend 1,200F; if
you spend less, you will get a 30-percent discount. Prices are marked *with*
the discount already taken off.

TELEPHONE: 01-47-42-63-41
MÉTRO: Opéra
CREDIT CARDS: AE, DC, MC, V
HOURS: Mon–Sat 9 A.M.–7 P.M.

L'OCCITANE
55, rue St-Louis-en-l'Île, 75004 (4th)

For the best in natural, vegetable-based cosmetics, go to l'Occitane.
All the products are from Aix-en-Provence and include soaps, creams,
perfumes, and bath accessories. It is worth a trip to the shop just to smell
the aromas and admire the beautiful displays. This and the shop on the
place des Vosges are two of my favorites, but there are branches all over
Paris.

TELEPHONE: 01-40-46-81-71
MÉTRO: Pont Marie
CREDIT CARDS: MC, V
HOURS: Mon 2:30–7 P.M., Tues–Sun 10:30 A.M.–7 P.M.

SEPHORA
70, avenue des Champs-Élysées, 75008 (8th)

An absolutely mind-boggling collection of cosmetics, perfumes, and miscellaneous accessories. They carry all the lines, including Bourjois. No *détaxe*, but competitive prices make them worth a look. No air-conditioning in the rue de Passy store, so avoid on hot days.

OTHER LOCATIONS: 66, rue Chausée-d'Antin, 75009 (9th); métro: Chausée-d'Antin; 50, rue de Passy, 75016 (16th), métro: Passy; and Forum des Halles, 75001 (1st), métro: Les Halles.

TELEPHONE: 01-53-93-22-50

FAX: 01-53-93-22-51

INTERNET: www.sephora.com

MÉTRO: George-V

CREDIT CARDS: AE, MC, C

HOURS: Mon–Sat 10 A.M.–midnight, Sun noon–9 P.M. (Champs-Élysées store only); all others, Mon–Sat 10 A.M.–8 P.M.

Department Stores

Cheap Chic Shopping Note: At most of the department stores listed below, if you go to the store's Welcome Desk you will be issued a 10-percent discount shopping card upon presentation of your passport. The exceptions are Tati, Monoprix, Prisunic, and Marks & Spencer.

AU PRINTEMPS
64, boulevard Haussmann, 75009 (9th)

This is known as "The Most Parisian Department Store." Famous designer boutiques, a separate men's store, and an excellent leather and cosmetic department are on the ground floor. Don't miss the beautiful views of Paris from a window perch in the cafeteria or outdoor terrace. Have a coffee if you must, but don't waste time or money on the dismal food.

TELEPHONE: 01-42-82-50-00

MÉTRO: Havre-Caumartin

CREDIT CARDS: AE, DC, MC, V

HOURS: Mon–Sat 9:35 A.M.–7 P.M.

BAZAR DE L'HÔTEL DE VILLE (BHV)
52, rue de Rivoli, 75004 (4th)

This is a shopping experience no do-it-yourselfer should miss, except on Saturday when an estimated twenty-five thousand shoppers stream through the store. Famous for its basement hardware department, which is a Parisian experience in itself, they have vast kitchen and automotive sections, not to mention paints, electrical goods, furnishings, and even clothes and accessories.

TELEPHONE: 01-42-74-90-00
MÉTRO: Hôtel-de-Ville
CREDIT CARDS: AE, MC, V
HOURS: Mon–Sat 9:30 A.M.–7 P.M.

FRANCK ET FILS
80, rue de Passy, 75016 (16th)

This small, elegant department store caters primarily to the women of Passy, one of Paris's most expensive neighborhoods. They sell clothing and accessories only, with super sales in January and July. They also have rooftop branch of the famous *pâtisserie* Ladurée (see *Cheap Eats in Paris*).

TELEPHONE: 01-44-14-38-00
MÉTRO: Muette
CREDIT CARDS: MC, V
HOURS: Mon–Sat 10 A.M.–7 P.M.

GALERIES LAFAYETTE
40, boulevard Haussmann, 75009 (9th)

They carry the top names in fashion, featuring seventy-five thousand brand names, including their own label. Everything else you can imagine is also here, including a one-hour photo service, *bureau de change*, car park, restaurants, travel and theater agencies, and a watch and shoe repair department. Gourmets and gourmands will want to visit their grocery department, which borders on the inspirational: its dazzling array of delicacies features everything a gastronome could possibly want, including food stations where you can stop for a plate of just-made pasta, a sampling of sushi, a quick cappuccino, or a pastry (see *Cheap Eats in Paris*). Even dedicated noncooks will want to see this beautiful section of Galeries Lafayette.

OTHER LOCATION: Centre Commercial Montparnasse, Tour Montparnasse Complex, 212, rue du Départ, 75014 (14th); métro: Montparnasse.
TELEPHONE: 01-42-82-36-40
MÉTRO: Chausée-d'Antin
CREDIT CARDS: AE, MC, V
HOURS: Mon–Sat 9:30 A.M.–6:30 P.M.

LA SAMARITAINE
19, rue de la Monnaie, 75001 (1st)

The panoramic view of Paris from the top floor of building two is justly famous (take the elevator to the ninth floor and then stairs to the terrace). Five buildings make up this store, which has the biggest toy department in Paris at Christmas. During the rest of the year it is a good place to buy Parisian-style work clothes as worn by waiters, chefs, butchers, and so on.

TELEPHONE: 01-40-41-20-20

MÉTRO: Pont Neuf
CREDIT CARDS: AE, DC, MC, V
HOURS: Mon–Sat 9:30 A.M.–7 P.M.

LE BON MARCHÉ
38, rue de Sèvres, at rue du Bac, 75007 (7th)

The first department store in Paris, and still my favorite, this show-place store has balustrades and balconies designed by Gustave Eiffel. It combines the elegant and the practical. Be sure and see their excellent grocery and fresh food stores—a fairyland for the gourmet.

TELEPHONE: 01-44-39-80-00
MÉTRO: Sèvres-Babylone
CREDIT CARDS: AE, DC, MC, V
HOURS: Mon–Sat 9:30 A.M.–7 P.M.

MARKS & SPENCER
35, boulevard Haussmann, 75009 (9th)

This is the Parisian branch of the London standby, which has a good selection of basic clothes that are *not* in the trendy fast track. The silk lingerie is well priced. The food hall in the basement is a good place to buy prepared snacks or a jar of real English bitter marmalade.

OTHER LOCATION: 88, rue de Rivoli, 75001 (1st); métro: Hôtel-de-Ville, Châtelet.
TELEPHONE: 01-47-42-49-91
MÉTRO: Havre-Caumartin
CREDIT CARDS: MC, V
HOURS: Mon–Sat 9:30 A.M.–8 P.M.

MONOPRIX
Boulevard Haussmann, between Au Printemps and Galeries Lafayette, 75009 (9th)

This chain is ever-present in Paris, and it's a notch or two above Prisunic. This is one of their biggest stores. The grocery departments are very good places to find jars of fancy mustard, jams, jellies, and good cheap wine. It is also a good place to stock up on your Bourjois cosmetics (which all savvy Cheap Chic shoppers know is the prototype for Chanel) at a fraction of the designer name-brand cost. You probably won't consider either Prisunic or Monoprix for your seasonal wardrobe, but they do have cute outfits that are "fashionably correct" at reasonable prices. If you are a Target or WalMart shopper, you will become a Monoprix regular.

TELEPHONE: 01-42-61-78-08
MÉTRO: Havre-Caumartin
CREDIT CARDS: MC, V
HOURS: Mon–Sat 9:30 A.M.–6:30 P.M.

PRISUNIC
52, avenue des Champs-Élysées, at rue La Boétie, 75008 (8th)

Similar to Target and K-Mart, this chain of low-priced stores is good to keep in mind for quick-fix cosmetic buys (including Bourjois, the prototype for Chanel), children's clothes, cotton underwear, fashion accessories of the moment, and housewares. At the Champs-Élysées address above, there is a tourist souvenir corner and a basement complete with a *boulangerie* selling Poilâne bread, a *charcuterie*, and a wine department. There are other Prisunic stores in Paris, but this is the one most visitors will see. This link in the chain serves an impressive nine thousand tourists and locals each day. Because of the inadequate ratio of cash registers to shoppers, you may feel as if you are in line behind all nine thousand.

TELEPHONE: 01-42-25-27-60
MÉTRO: Franklin-D-Roosevelt
CREDIT CARDS: V
HOURS: Daily 9:45 A.M.–midnight; other stores close earlier

TATI DEPARTMENT STORES
4–30, boulevard Rouchechouart, 75018 (18th)

If you love swap meets, garage sales, and basement fire sales, then Tati is for you. The crowds are impossible, especially on Saturday, but for truly amazing bargains hidden among some real junk, join the diverse crowd at a Tati. Prices defy the competition on stock that ranges from bridal wear to linen slacks, cheap silk shirts, cheaper shoes, baby gear, and kitchen equipment. Be sure to check each item carefully because quality control is not a priority when this much volume is concerned.

Warning: Watch out for pickpockets, especially children, at the boulevard Rouchechouart store. If this is a new sort of shopping trip for you, your best initiation will be at the Tati on rue de Rennes.

OTHER LOCATIONS: 140, rue de Rennes, 75006 (6th), métro: Montparnasse, St-Placide; 13, place de la République, 75003 (3rd), métro: République; and their jewelry store, Tati Or, is at 19, rue de la Paix, 74002 (2nd), métro: Opéra (see Tati Or, page 285).

TELEPHONE: 01-42-55-13-09
MÉTRO: Anvers
CREDIT CARDS: V
HOURS: Mon–Sat 10 A.M.–6 P.M.

Discount Shopping Stores

The following stores sell their stock well below the retail prices you will pay elsewhere in Paris for exactly the same items. In the case of the designer discount boutiques, you will be looking at last season's collections.

ADECTA . . . ACCESSORIES DE MODE
(sign over door says: Manufacture de Chapeaux)
6–8, rue du Grenier-Saint-Lazare, 75003 (3rd)

This is really a wholesale operation featuring children's accessories, hats for every member of the family, scarves, belts, umbrellas, and ties (including the snap-on variety). If you are tactful and don't ask questions, and spend around 150F, they will let you buy. You can find baby hats here for 15F to 20F that sell for three and four times the price in baby shops.

TELEPHONE: 01-42-71-79-88, 01-42-77-31-33
MÉTRO: Rambuteau (exit rue du Grenier-St-Lazare)
CREDIT CARDS: V
HOURS: Mon–Fri 8 A.M.–1 P.M., 2–6 P.M.; closed Sat–Sun, holidays, mid-July to mid-Aug

ANNA LOWE
104, rue du Faubourg du St-Honorè, 75008 (8th)

Anna Lowe is one of the best. The location is great, next door to the famous Hôtel Bristol, and in the midst of many top fashion houses and designers. You will find all the top-name French and Italian designers, including Chanel, and a fabulous selection of evening wear at reduced prices. All labels are left in. Sensational July and mid-December sales and fast alterations.

TELEPHONE: 01-42-66-11-32
MÉTRO: Miromesnil, St-Phillippe-de-Roule
CREDIT CARDS: AE, DC, MC, V
HOURS: Mon–Sat 10 A.M.–7 P.M.

ANNEXE DES CRÉATEURS
19, rue Godot-de-Mauroy, 75009 (9th)

No Chanel or Yves St-Laurent, but last season's clothes from French, Italian, and Japanese manufacturers. Labels are left in, and quality varies. There are two shops next to each other, one for dressy, the other for sportswear and separates. They also have hats, jewelry, coats, bags, and wedding gowns. Sales are in January and July.

TELEPHONE: 01-42-65-46-40
MÉTRO: Madeleine
CREDIT CARDS: AE, MC, V
HOURS: Mon–Sat 10:30 A.M.–7 P.M.

BETTY
10, place d'Aligre, 75012 (12th)

Probably the best time to check Betty is early Sunday morning; combine it with a trip to the flea market at place d'Aligre. Betty is not worth a separate journey, but it is worth a quick look. Upstairs they say they have designer labels, but not many on most top-ten lists. The prices are low, and if you want something *French* and don't care about famous designer labels, this could be interesting.

TELEPHONE: 01-43-07-40-64

MÉTRO: Ledru-Rollin

CREDIT CARDS: None, cash only

HOURS: Tues–Sun 9 A.M.–12:30 P.M., Thur and Sat 2:30–7 P.M.; closed Mon

DEJAC
13, rue du Mail, 75002 (2nd)

To find Dejac, go into the courtyard and take the elevator or stairs to the first floor. Once this far, you will find the showrooms on the right after you pass the office and reception area. The merchandise, all displayed on racks, is of good quality. Look for coats, dresses, slacks, suits, and blouses. Prices may seem a bit high, but not if you can hit it during the May and November sales. The staff do not speak much English, but it is all very easy to handle even if you don't speak a word of French.

TELEPHONE: 01-42-97-40-63

MÉTRO: Sentier

CREDIT CARDS: None, cash only

HOURS: Mon–Fri 9 A.M.–12:30 P.M., Mon–Thur 1:30–6 P.M., Fri 1:30–5 P.M.; closed Sat, July

FRANCHI CHAUSSEURS
15, rue de la Pépinière, 75008 (8th)

They have lots of Charles Jourdan shoes at half price, but the styles are a bit dated (such as pointed toes, stiletto heels). They also have end-of-series shoes and Italian designs at good prices, but there's no place to really sit to try on unless you count the one stool by the door. Remember, this is discount and comfort is not part of the price you are paying.

OTHER LOCATION: 10, rue de Rome, 75008 (8th); telephone 01-43-87-42-59; métro: Saint-Lazare; same hours, but closed in July.

TELEPHONE: 01-42-94-28-88

MÉTRO: Saint-Augustin, Saint-Lazare

CREDIT CARDS: AE, DC, MC, V

HOURS: Mon–Fri 10:30 A.M.–7 P.M.; closed Sat and Aug, but the branch on rue de Rome is open in Aug, closed July

JEAN-LOUIS SCHERRER STOCK
29, avenue Ledru-Rollin, 75012 (12th)

Two rooms of *haute couture* by Scherrer for the classy, elegant look of old money. The well-displayed selection is good and easy to go through, and someone on the staff will speak English. Sales, held at the end of May and November, are *not* at this location. Call about three weeks ahead to get the address, and mark the dates on the calendar. Other times, prices are about half.

TELEPHONE: 01-46-28-39-27
MÉTRO: Gare de Lyon
CREDIT CARDS: AE, V
HOURS: Mon–Fri 10 A.M.–6 P.M.; Oct–Mar also open Sat 10 A.M.–6 P.M.; closed Aug

LA BOUTIQUE DE LISAA
5, rue Dupin, 75006 (6th)

A cooperative of the collections of thirty up-and-coming young fashion designers on the cutting edge of what is new and exciting. Some of the creations are marvelous, others just plain awful. The stock of hats, accessories, clothing, and housewares changes often, with sales held in January, February, and September.

TELEPHONE: 01-42-22-36-39
MÉTRO: Sèvres-Babylone
CREDIT CARDS: AE, MC, V
HOURS: Tues–Sat 10:30 A.M.–7 P.M.; closed Mon and Aug

LE MOUTON À CINQ PATTES
8, 10, 18, 19, 48, and 130 rue Saint-Placide, 75006 (6th)

With numerous addresses in Paris, these bargain-bin stores have the corner on the discount shopping market. Fellow shoppers are ferocious and the places are messy. I also think the overall quality is poor and the service almost nonexistent. So, why bother? Well, for real discount diggers who are near one of the locations, it is worth a quick look for the once-in-a-blue-moon find.

OTHER LOCATIONS: 15, rue Vieille-du-Temple, 75004 (4th), tel: 01-42-71-86-30, métro: Filles-du-Calvaire, Hôtel-de-Ville; 19, rue Grégoire-de-Tours, 75006 (6th), tel: 01-43-29-73-56, métro: Odéon; 130, avenue Victor-Hugo, at rue de la Pompe, 75016 (16th), tel: 01-47-55-42-25, métro: Victor-Hugo. All stores have the same hours as the rue Saint-Placide location.

TELEPHONE: 01-45-48-86-26
MÉTRO: Saint-Placide, Sèvres-Babylone
CREDIT CARDS: AE, MC, V
HOURS: Mon–Fri 10:30 A.M.–7:30 P.M., Sat 10:30 A.M.–8 P.M.; some of the stores close between 1–2 P.M., but it is not consistent

MENDÈS-YSL (YVES ST-LAURENT)
65, rue Montmartre, 75002 (2nd)

Mendès sells Yves St-Laurent variations (first floor) and Rive Gauche lines (second floor) one season out of date and at bargain prices for this designer. Collections arrive in July and January, and in December and June they have a sale and take off an additional 20 to 30 percent. There are no dressing rooms, so you must change in public. Do not expect help from the ice maiden *venduses*. If you hit this one right, it is a gold mine.

TELEPHONE: 01-45-08-52-62, 01-42-36-83-32
MÉTRO: Sentier
CREDIT CARDS: AE (after 3,000F), MC, V (any amount)
HOURS: Mon–Fri 10 A.M.–6:30 P.M., Sat 10 A.M.–5:30 P.M.; closed Sat in Aug

M.G.S.
10, rue du Pont-aux-Choux, 75003 (3rd)

The street has lots of men's and women's shops, none very *haute*, but wearably conservative. M.G.S. sells cut-rate designer clothing for men. Many names most Americans will not recognize, but they do have Dior.

TELEPHONE: 01-42-78-09-27
MÉTRO: St-Sébastien-Froissart
CREDIT CARDS: MC, V
HOURS: Mon–Sat 9 A.M.–7 P.M.

MISS "GRIFFE'S"
19, rue de Penthièvre, 75008 (8th)

The shop has been in business for more than a half century, and it is now run by its third owner, Madame Vincent, who has been here for almost twenty years. I think it is one of the best in the discount hunt for women's clothing, shoes, handbags, and accessories from all the top names, including Chanel and Valentino. Also available are prototype collections of last season's models, a few of Madame Vincent's own designs, and wonderful custom-made blazers. Free alterations are ready in two days. A 10-percent discount will be given to readers who show her *Cheap Sleeps in Paris.*

TELEPHONE: 01-42-65-10-00
MÉTRO: Miromesnil
CREDIT CARDS: AE, DC, MC, V
HOURS: Mon–Fri 11 A.M.–7 P.M., Sat 3–7 P.M.; closed middle two weeks in Aug

OLIVER B
21, rue Pierre Lescot, 75001 (1st)

Oliver B is omnipresent in Paris. This is one of their biggest and best shops, with bargains galore. You will find inexpensive separates that are easy to wear and cheap enough to toss out after a season or two. Lots of small sizes and nothing too far out.

TELEPHONE: 01-40-26-26-26
MÉTRO: Étienne-Marcel, Les Halles
CREDIT CARDS: MC, V
HOURS: Mon–Sat 10:30 A.M.–7 P.M., Sun 2–7 P.M.

PWS (PRICES WITHOUT SURPRISE)
13, rue de Sévigné, 75004 (4th)

Owner Claude Windisch got the idea for his men's discount store after visiting the United States and seeing all the cut-price stores. He stocks everything for men from top-name to no-name designer clothing. Prices are 30 percent off *this* season's clothing.

OTHER LOCATION: 1, rue de Penthiévre, 75008 (8th); telephone 01-47-42-64-30; métro: Miromesnil.
TELEPHONE: 01-42-72-98-96
MÉTRO: St-Paul
CREDIT CARDS: V
HOURS: Tues–Sat 10 A.M.–7 P.M.

SOLDE TROIS
3, rue de Vienne, 75008 (8th)

Well worth the safari to the edge of things to check out the impressive selection of Lavin clothing and accessories for women that have not sold in the very high-priced boutique on rue St-Honoré. The quality is excellent and the prices are at least 50 percent less than in the boutique. If you shop during January or June, the sale bargains, at an additional 20 to 50 percent off the already discounted prices, are even more exciting.

TELEPHONE: 01-42-94-93-34
MÉTRO: Europe, St-Lazare
CREDIT CARDS: MC, V
HOURS: Mon–Fri 10:30 A.M.–1:30 P.M., 2:30–6 P.M.; Sat 10:30 A.M.–3:30 P.M.; closed Aug

STUDIO LOLITA
2, bis rue des Rosiers, 75004 (4th)

Left-overs from the popular Lolita store at 3, bis rue des Rosiers. Definitely an acquired taste.

TELEPHONE: 01-48-87-09-67
MÉTRO: St-Paul
CREDIT CARDS: AE, MC, V
HOURS: Tues–Sat 10:30 A.M.–1 P.M., 2–7 P.M.; closed Mon and three weeks in Aug

SULMACO
13, rue de Trévise, 75009 (9th)

English-speaking owner Philippe Madar offers an excellent selection of designer men's fashions and accessories at below retail. In addition to off-the-rack clothing, it is possible to order custom-made clothes. The detail in the double-lined tailor-made suits is superb. Ready-made suits start around 2,700F, and tailor-made, with your initials inside, begin around 5,000F. These are marvelous prices when you consider you can deduct the $17\frac{1}{2}$-percent *détaxe* after spending only 1,200F. A master tailor is also employed to do alterations, which are included in the price of the garment except during sales. Tailor-made suits are guaranteed ready in twenty days for a first fitting, and delivery in the next three days. If a Frenk tailor-made suit appeals to you, make Sulmaco your first shopping stop in Paris. Sales are held at the end of December and during the first part of July.

OTHER LOCATION: 68, rue de La Boétie, 75008 (8th); telephone 01-45-63-19-03; métro: St-Augustin.

TELEPHONE: 01-48-24-89-00

MÉTRO: Montmartre

CREDIT CARDS: AE, DC, MC, V

HOURS: Mon–Sat 10 A.M.–7 P.M.; Aug noon–6:30 P.M.; closed middle 10 days of Aug

SYLVIE DEGUY CRÉATIONS
8, rue du Grenier-St-Lazare, 75003 (3rd)

Wholesale plus the current *taxe* is what you pay at this treasure trove of children's wear. One of my shopping assignments on my last trip to Paris was to buy a "French" bathing suit for the two-year-old daughter of one of my very good friends. Sounded easy to me, and, of course, it would have been if I had been willing to pay prices that *started* at fifty dollars and went up! And that is just for the bottom half of the bikini, which is made out of a tiny square of material! After days of searching, I had all but given up until I found this remarkable shop. I couldn't believe my luck—here were dozens of adorable bathing suits with hats, bags, and hair bows to match. I was so thrilled I bought two ensembles for less than half of what I would have paid for only a bikini bottom anywhere else in Paris. Boys are not left out. There are just as many irresistible items for the young man on your list. In addition to swimwear, there are appealing hats and other accessories. If you have anyone under six on your shopping list, this is a required stop.

TELEPHONE: Not available

MÉTRO: Étienne-Marcel, Rambuteau (exit rue du Grenier-St-Lazare)

CREDIT CARDS: None, cash only

HOURS: Mon–Fri 9:30 A.M.–1 P.M., 2–6 P.M.; Aug closing varies, call to check

TEA & TATTERED PAGES
24, rue Mayet, 75006 (6th)

Run by vivacious expatriate Kristi Chavane, Tea & Tattered Pages promises hours of contented browsing through an enormous sea of used English-language books. If you need a little sustenance, tea, coffee, and light snacks are served. Kristi and her staff are friendly and plugged into the English-speaking Paris scene, and I guarantee you will not regret a visit to her two-level shop.

TELEPHONE: 01-40-65-94-35
MÉTRO: Falguière, Duroc
CREDIT CARDS: None, cash only
HOURS: Daily 11 A.M.–7 P.M.

TIZIANO
7, rue Notre-Dame-des-Champs, 75006 (6th)

Last year's collection of Italian shoes for men and women, at 30 percent off and more. It can be one of the best selections of wearable footwear in Paris. Despite uninterested salespeople, who seem rarely in the mood to be at all helpful, I never miss shopping here on every trip to Paris, and I have yet to come away empty-handed. They also have a few handbags, but you are here for the shoes.

TELEPHONE: 01-42-22-74-20
MÉTRO: St-Placide
CREDIT CARDS: MC, V
HOURS: Mon 1:30–7 P.M., Tues–Sat 10:30 A.M.–7:30 P.M.

Discount Shopping Streets

Just as Paris has its high-priced shopping streets, it also has its discount shopping streets. No certified Cheap Chic shopper will want to miss a trip to one of these streets where, if you are lucky, you will bring home something marvelous that your friends would kill for . . . even at three times the price *you* paid.

RUE D'ALÉSIA, 75014 (14th)

Both sides of rue d'Alésia are home to an assortment of outlet shops carrying last season's lines of designers, some you have heard of and some you never will. The best line of attack is to go up one side and down the other to get an overview, then come back to those that seem promising. Worse time to go is on Saturday. Some of the better shops are the following: Carré d'As, No. 62; SR (Sonya Rykiel), No. 64; Evolutif, No. 72; Dorothée Bis, No. 74; Stock & Stock II, Nos. 92–94; Stock System, Nos. 110–112; Kookai, No. 111; Cacharel, No. 114; Daniel Hechter, Nos. 116–118; Philippe Salvert, No. 122; Alésia Discounts, No. 139.

MÉTRO: Alésia

CREDIT CARDS: Varies by shop

HOURS: Generally shops are open Mon afternoon, Tues–Sat 10 A.M.–7 P.M.

RUE MESLAY, 75003 (3rd)

One entire street devoted to shoes—one store after the other—with everything from clodhoppers to four-inch red-satin sling pumps. Prices are good. The best advice is to browse first, then go back and do serious buying. Finding the perfect pair of shoes takes time and energy, not to say patience. Don't try to squeeze this one in . . . allow time and leave nonshopping pals at the hotel. If all else fails here, you can run by Tati at 13, place de la République (see page 268).

MÉTRO: République

CREDIT CARDS: Varies with each shop

RUE SAINT-PLACIDE, 75006 (6th)

Bargain fever has hit Paris in a cluster of boutiques along the rue Saint-Placide. Start at Bon Marché department store and work both sides of the street. This is hard work if the crowds are out in force, especially at lunchtime when the office workers surge through and on Saturday when housewives leave *les enfants* at home and make the pilgrimage. Best buys are in casual sportswear and teenage "must-haves" of the moment. There are a limited number of top-name designers, but everything is *au courant*. Windows are often more appealing than the stuffy, cramped interiors. Sharpen your elbows for this.

MÉTRO: Sèvres-Babylone

CREDIT CARDS: Varies with each shop

HOURS: Usually closed until 2 P.M. on Mon; open Mon afternoon until 7 P.M., Tues–Sat 10 A.M.–7 P.M.

RUE ST-DOMINIQUE, 75007 (7th)

From avenue Bosquet to boulevard de Latour-Maubourg, shops sell clothing for men, women, and children from designer *dégriffés* (labels cut out) to bins of last season's T-shirts. Affordable.

MÉTRO: Latour-Maubourg

CREDIT CARDS: Varies with each shop

HOURS: Some shops closed until 2 P.M. on Mon and in August; Mon afternoon 2–7 P.M., Tues–Sat 10 P.M.–7 P.M.

RUE DE PARADIS, 75010 (10th)

This is the best area in Paris for china and crystal, in one crowded shop after another. Be sure to look at the magnificent Baccarat crystal store, and check their back table with the red dots on end of the line designs that sell for up to half regular price. Baccarat is at 32, rue de Paradis; it's open Monday to Friday from 9 A.M. to 6 P.M., Saturday from 10 A.M. to noon and 2 to 5 P.M. Another excellent choice is Limoges-Unic at 12, rue de Paradis; same hours as Baccarat. Staff at both shops speak English; the *détaxe* is available after spending 2,000F, and they ship.

MÉTRO: Château-d'Eau

CREDIT CARDS: Varies with each shop

Flea Markets: Les Marchés aux Puces

What to do on a Saturday or Sunday morning? Go early to the flea market. Wear old clothes and comfortable shoes, beware of pickpockets, and bring cash. You will have a good time even if you don't buy a thing. The days of finding a fabulous antique for a few *centimes* are gone, but you will probably find a keepsake or two. If you have nothing special on your list, just people-watch; the wildlife at the *puces* beats that at the zoo.

MARCHÉ D'ALIGRE
Place d'Aligre (12th)

This is a small, daily food and flea *marché*, good for little objects, antique buttons, bric-a-brac, and tacky clothes. The quality is often low, but so are the prices. Fashion shoppers might want to swing through Betty, a designer discount shop that at times has something interesting (see Betty, page 270).

MÉTRO: Ledru-Rollin

HOURS: Tues-Sun until 1 P.M.

MARCHÉ DE CLIGNANCOURT
Avenue Michelet, at rue des Rosiers (18th)

Clignancourt is the largest flea market in the world—too big to conquer in only a day. Once you get past the piles of jeans and the Indians selling cheap beads, head for the Marché Biron on the corner of rue des Rossiers. It has the most expensive sellers, but also the most serious. The Paul Bert Marché, 16, rue Paul Bert, has an unusual collection of Art Deco pieces and antiques from the late 1890s. The Marché Jules-Valles, 17, rue Jules-Valles, has the least expensive items. For vintage clothing, the Marché Malik at 60, rue Jules-Valles, is the place.

MÉTRO: Porte de Clignancourt

HOURS: Sat between 8–9 A.M. and 6 P.M., Sun and Mon from 10–11 A.M. to 6 P.M.

MARCHÉ DE MONTREUIL
Porte de Montreuil (20th)

The huge market begins once you get through the long line of vendors hawking cheap trash on the bridge. It is not worth a special trip unless you happen to be in Paris on Ascension Day in May or Toussaint Day, on November 1, when hundreds of flea market dealers hold a one-day *grand déballage.*

MÉTRO: Porte de Montreuil
HOURS: Sat–Mon 9 A.M.–5 P.M.

MARCHÉ DE VANVES
Avenue Georges-Lafenestre (14th)

It is a good place for small antiques and collectibles that tuck easily into a suitcase. Start by walking along avenue Marc-Sangier, and in a morning you will be able to browse and bargain your way through it and come away with a treasure or two. The locals know to come way before noon, when most of the serious sellers fold up their stalls. Every Sunday morning from March to October, the Square George-Lafenestre is an open-air art gallery where you can buy directly from the artists.

MÉTRO: Porte-de-Vanves
HOURS: Sat and Sun 7:30 A.M.–6 P.M.

Food Shopping Streets and Outdoor Roving Markets

MARKETS

There are two types of markets in Paris (in addition to the growing number of *supermarchés*): *rue commerçantes*—stationary indoor/outdoor markets open six days a week, including Sunday morning, but not on Monday—and the *marchés volants*—roving markets of independent merchants who move from one neighborhood to another on Tuesday to Sunday mornings only, never in the afternoon. A visit to one of these markets provides a real look at an old, unchanging way of daily Paris life. When you go, take your camera, don't touch the merchandise, and watch your wallet. I guarantee you that a trip or two to a Paris market will spoil you for your hometown supermarket. In Paris markets, fruits and vegetables of every variety are arranged with the skill and precision usually reserved for fine jewelry store windows. Equal care and attention is given to the displays of meats, fish, cheese, and fresh flowers. Everyone has a favorite vendor for each item on their shopping list, and vendors respond with very personal service. It is not unusual for a fruit seller to ask you not only what day you want to eat your melon or peaches, but at what time, and to select the fruit accordingly. A few favorites are listed here. To locate the ones closest to your hotel, ask at the desk.

FOOD SHOPPING STREETS—*RUES COMMERÇANTES*

Generally, these are open Tuesday to Sunday 8 A.M.–1 P.M. and 4:30–7 P.M.; closed Monday all day and Sunday afternoon.

RUE MONTORGUEIL (1st)
MÉTRO: Étienne-Marcel

RUE MOUFFETARD (5th)
MÉTRO: Censier-Daubenton, Monge

RUE DE SEINE & RUE DE BUCI (6th)
MÉTRO: Odéon

RUE CLER (7th)
MÉTRO: École-Militaire

RUE DAGUERRE (14th)
MÉTRO: Denfert-Rochereau

RUE DU COMMERCE (15th)
MÉTRO: Commerce, La Motte-Picquet Grenelle

RUE DE LÉVIS (17th)
MÉTRO: Villiers

RUE PONCELET (17th)
MÉTRO: Ternes

RUE LEPIC (18th)
MÉTRO: Abbesses, Blanche

OUTDOOR ROVING FOOD MARKETS—*MARCHÉS VOLANTS*
These are open on the days listed from 7:30 A.M. to 1:30 P.M. only.

CARMES (5th)
Place Maubert

MÉTRO: Maubert-Mutualité
Tuesday, Thursday, Saturday

MONGE (5th)
Place Monge

MÉTRO: Monge
Wednesday, Friday, Sunday

RASPAIL (6th)
Boulevard Raspail, between rue du Cherche-Midi and rue de Rennes

MÉTRO: Rennes, Sèvres-Babylone
Tuesday, Friday, and Sunday (organic)
NOTE: On Sunday this is an organic market. At time of printing, there was some question of whether this organic market would move, so before going, check to see if there is a new location for it.

RICHARD-LENOIR (11th)
Boulevard Richard-Lenoir, at rue Amelot
> **MÉTRO:** Bastille, Richard-Lenoir
> Thursday, Sunday

DUPLEIX (15th)
Boulevard du Grenelle, between rue Lourmel and rue de Commerce
> **MÉTRO:** Dupleix, La Motte-Piquet-Grenelle
> Wednesday, Sunday

COURS DE LA REINE (16th)
Avenue Président Wilson
> **MÉTRO:** Alma Marceau, Iéna
> Wednesday, Saturday

Miscellaneous Cheap Chic Finds

Flowers

LE MONDE DES ORCHIDÉES
65, avenue Bosquet, 75007 (7th)

If you need a thank-you gift for someone in Paris, or just want to surprise the love of your life with a beautiful French orchid, Jacqueline Augnet's orchid boutique is the place to go. You can buy one large bloom in a clear transparent bag for under ten dollars. It is a striking gift that will last for several weeks. Also available are orchid potted plants, orchid jewelry, and books in French about orchids.

> **TELEPHONE:** 01-45-56-08-75
> **MÉTRO:** École Militaire
> **HOURS:** Mon 3:30–8 P.M., Tues–Sat 10:30 A.M.–8 P.M.; closed 3 weeks in Aug

Gifts and Handicrafts

BAÏKAL
24, rue St-Paul, 75004 (4th)

After seven years on a quiet and tourist-free square in the eleventh arrondissement, Michael Monlaü and his partner, Thierry de la Salmoniere, have moved their unique gift shop to a more central location along the antique laden rue St-Paul, which runs off the River Seine to the Marais. Their new location has had an interesting past. For almost seventy years it was a local bar run by the same woman, and by her parents before that. When Michael and Thierry took it over, they saved and restored the old bar and countertop, which had stood in the same place for a century. Today it stands in the middle of the shop, where for all those years the locals spent part of their lives, and left part of their souls, standing against it, tossing down their daily quotas. The bar is not for sale, but everything else is. The stock is made up of one-of-a-kind gifts you will want for friends and yourself. I love the black-and-white Limoges plates, the limited editions of French cars (even Colombo's 1957 Peugeot), and the Raku pottery made in the Alps using a thirteenth-century technique that still seems contemporary. For small, tuck-in gifts to take home, look at the Parisian perfume bottles, collection of boxes, and their own line of batiks, designed in Paris and made in Indonesia. When I visited shortly after they had opened in this location, Michael told me that the last customer to visit their old shop was a reader of *Cheap Sleeps in Paris*. I hope many more will go to his new location. Michael loves Americans, speaks perfect English, and is willing to take the time to help you select just the right item. Prices are within all budgets.

TELEPHONE: 01-42-74-73-39
FAX: 01-42-74-73-35
MÉTRO: St-Paul
CREDIT CARDS: AE, MC, V
HOURS: Tues 2–7 P.M., Wed–Sun 10:30 A.M.–7 P.M.; closed Mon, one week mid-Aug

LA BOUTIQUE DE L'ARTISANAT MONASTIQUE
68, bis avenue Denfert-Rochereau, 75014 (14th)

Doting *grand'mères*, beware! What a find for adorable children's clothing (including christening outfits that are destined to become family heirlooms), layettes, handicrafts, embroidered linens, cosmetics, food products, and beautiful robes and nightgowns . . . all made by French priests and nuns in monasteries throughout France. The quality is beautiful, and whatever you buy will show the name of the monastery where it was made. A volunteer staff of sweet, gray-haired ladies will graciously assist you, wrap your purchase, and take your money. Even if you only buy a candle or a bar of soap, it is worth a visit.

TELEPHONE: 01-43-35-15-76
MÉTRO: Denfert-Rochereau, RER-Port Royal
CREDIT CARDS: V
HOURS: Mon–Fri noon–6:30 P.M., Sat 2–7 P.M.; closed holidays and Aug

LA DAME BLANCHE
186, rue de Rivoli, 75001 (1st)

You will soon become dizzy and confused walking along the tourist trail that leads from place de la Concorde down rue de Rivoli. The area has one of the highest concentrations of tourist merchandise in the city.

You know the type: plastic Eiffel Towers, T-shirts with the Mona Lisa and a smart saying, gaudy scarves, and wild ties your husband will blush wearing. However, dedicated shophounds know that with a little digging, treasures are here. Where? At Michael and Suzanne's La Dame Blanche, which was started by their mother in 1969 as a small glove boutique. The windows of their side-by-side shops are jam-packed with Limoges boxes that collectors will go mad over, leather gloves, authentic French berets, silk scarves, small and large tapestries, and more. Do not let this confusing clutter deter you from exploring the best shop along this stretch. Not only is the selection the best, so are the prices. If you want a special Limoges box, ask Michael and he can have it made for you. Both Michael and his sister Suzanne speak English, offer excellent service, and are delightful besides. They give a 15-percent discount if you spend 1,600F or more, and they ship all over the world.

TELEPHONE: 01-42-96-31-56
FAX: 01-42-96-02-11
MÉTRO: Palais-Royal
CREDIT CARDS: AE, DC, MC, V
HOURS: Mon–Sat 10 A.M.–6:30 P.M.

RICOCHET
15, rue Bréa, 75006 (6th)

From camera bags to weekend duffels, backpacks, dressy handbags in washable suede, or a simple shopping bag, chances are great that you will find something affordable here. Many of the heavy-duty items are trimmed in bright florescent colors, which is an especially good idea on a backpack. There is much, much more you will find, such as whimsical glass fish you can float in a bowl, funny plastic items to delight the child in all of us, and silk flowers. Both the owners speak English, and the shop is open on Sunday, except for the first two weeks in August.

TELEPHONE: 01-44-07-34-91
MÉTRO: Vavin
CREDIT CARDS: MC, V
HOURS: Mon 3–7:30 P.M., Tues–Sun 11 A.M.–7:30 P.M.; closed on Sun during the first two weeks of Aug

Hairdresser

FRANCK FANN COIFFEUR (FOR MEN AND WOMEN)
5, rue d'Ormesson, 75004 (4th)

Where to get your hair cut? It is always a problem in a strange city, especially if you cannot communicate very well. Relax, now you have Franck to do your hair. He is wonderful at cutting both men's and women's hair, and he speaks English. In fact, he has given me the best hair cuts I have *ever* had. I only wish I could convince him to move to the

States so I could go to him on a regular basis. I haven't had any of the other operators, so my advice is to stick with Franck and tell him I sent you. In French salons, all services are individually priced, from the shampoo to the blow dry. At Franck's, it should run around 200F, and that is very reasonable. Appointments are not necessary, but it doesn't hurt to call ahead to let him know you are coming.

TELEPHONE: 01-48-04-50-62
MÉTRO: St-Paul
CREDIT CARDS: MC, V
HOURS: Mon–Sat 10 A.M.–7 P.M.

Handbags

31 FÉVRIER
2, rue du Pélican, 75001 (1st)

Wonderfully whimsical handbags and shopping carts straight from fantasyland. Just think how envious your friends and neighbors will be of your Parisian shopping cart covered in aqua-colored feathers. If aqua is not one of your colors, the designers at 31 Février can make you one in any feather color you choose, or bedeck one for you in sequins or fake fur. Their handbags must be seen to be believed. Starting from the top of the line, the Fabergé egg handbag will set you back only 33,000F. Of course, it is gold plated and covered with hand-set crystal. For something slightly more practical, yet still not too down to earth, there are lace bags in twenty different colors, made in velvet, with grosgrain ribbon, leather, or goosefeathers. Hélène Nepomiatzi and Marc Gourmelen are the two talented designers, and their wildly creative designs have been featured in fashion magazines around the world.

TELEPHONE: 01-40-26-39-51
FAX: 01-40-26-39-41
MÉTRO: Palais-Royal
CREDIT CARDS: MC, V
HOURS: Mon–Fri 11 A.M.–1 P.M., 2–7 P.M.

Hats

MARIE MERCIÉ
56, rue Tiquetonne, 75002 (2nd)

Hats off to these fabulous *chapeaux!* I love hats and wear them often, especially when traveling. The hats at Marie Mercié's two shops run the gamut from frankly fanciful to downright sane and sensible. I like her summer Panama hats you can roll up in your suitcase; they just pop back into shape when ready to wear. If you need a hat for any occasion, or are like I am and just like wearing—or admiring—them, please make a point of seeing some of the best hats in Paris.

OTHER LOCATION: 23, rue Saint-Sulpice, 75006 (6th); telephone 01-43-26-45-83; métro: Odéon. All other information the same.
TELEPHONE: 01-40-26-60-68
MÉTRO: Etienne-Marcel
CREDIT CARDS: AE, DC, MC, V
HOURS: Mon–Sat 11 A.M.–7 P.M.; closed middle of Aug

Herbalist

HERBORISTERIE DU PALAIS ROYAL
11, rue des Petits-Champs, 75001 (1st)

The shop stocks between five and six hundred types of herbal teas and makes their own plant-based cosmetics (try the carrot face oil) and soaps. They also sell nutritionally correct cereals, cookies, bottled juices, honey, essential oils, and vitamins. But you had better know what you want, since you can't count on too much English.
TELEPHONE: 01-42-97-54-68
MÉTRO: Bourse
CREDIT CARDS: V
HOURS: Mon–Fri 8:30 A.M.–7 P.M., Sat 10:30 A.M.–6:30 P.M.

Jewelry

ALLIX
6, rue de Surène, 75008 (8th)

The two owners make simple, well-priced handbags and unusual jewelry, which is sold throughout the world at three or four times the prices you will pay here. The merchandise is very well displayed, and English is spoken.
TELEPHONE: 01-42-65-10-79
MÉTRO: Madeleine
CREDIT CARDS: MC, V
HOURS: Mon–Fri 11 A.M.–2:30 P.M., 3:30–6:30 P.M.; closed Sat–Sun and Aug

MATIÈRE PREMIERE
12, rue de Sévigné, 75004 (4th)

Baubles, bangles, and beads—either assemble your own or buy ready-made necklaces, earrings, and pins at decent prices. No English is spoken, and they're not much help either, but if you like this sort of thing, you will enjoy looking at this shop.
TELEPHONE: 01-42-78-40-87
MÉTRO: St-Paul
CREDIT CARDS: MC, V
HOURS: Mon–Sat 10 A.M.–7 P.M.

TATI OR
19, rue de la Paix, 75002 (2nd)

What!? A Tati jewelry store four doors down from Cartier and only a block or two from the Place Vendôme, home of Van Cleef & Arpels and the Ritz Hotel!! *Quelle horreur.* The Tati stores, the biggest and lowest-priced retail stores in Paris, are known for promoting volume, never quality (see page 268 for more on these Cheap Chic wonders). If Cartier and the like are beyond your budget, now you have Tati Or, a ninety-square-meter boutique selling discount gold jewelry, with prices starting around 30F for a little gold heart, 125F for a wedding band, and up to 9,000F for an ostentatious bauble set with precious stones. The chairman of Bucheron jewelers was quoted as saying, "You have Lasserre and Taillevent restaurants, but there is also McDonald's." This is definitely the McDonald's of jewelry stores. Obviously owner Fabien Ouaki thinks the store will do well. He has signed a lease requiring a monthly rent of 1.5F million, which translates to more than $30,000. That means selling lots of gold hearts.

TELEPHONE: Not available
MÉTRO: Opéra
CREDIT CARDS: MC, V
HOURS: Mon–Sat 10 A.M.–6 P.M.

Kitchenware/Cooking Utensils

A. SIMON
36, rue Etienne-Marcel, 75002 (2nd)
33 & 38 rue Montmartre, 75002 (2nd)

Calling all past, present, or budding chefs, gourmets, and gourmands—and anyone else with a love of cooking and good food—A. Simon is your shop of choice. With its vast inventory of cooking utensils of every known type and variety and its fascinating array of tableware, this is the Rolls Royce in its field. Prices are geared for the volume buyer, but anyone is welcome, and you will be graciously treated whether you outfit a restaurant or buy a tiny *pichet* for your *vin du table.*

TELEPHONE: 01-42-33-71-65
FAX: 01-42-33-68-25
MÉTRO: Etienne-Marcel
CREDIT CARDS: AE, MC, V
HOURS: Mon–Sat 8:30 A.M.–6:30 P.M.

Renting an Outfit

L'AFFAIR D'UN SOIR
147, rue de la Pompe, 75016 (16th)

The shop is located in one of the poshest neighborhoods of Paris, so this tells you another secret of the well-dressed French woman—maybe she leases! If you have been invited to the Élysée Palace and "haven't a thing to wear," don't worry, call l'Affair d'Un Soir for your dress rental appointment. For women *soirée*-goers, silk dresses, ball gowns, hats, and elegant accessories are available. For the men, tuxedos and everything to go with them are also here. Sophie de Mestier designs two original collections each year that she rents to her elegant clientele. Many customers rent an outfit and cannot bear to part with it, so they end up buying it. Prices for rentals start from 750F to 900F. To rent something, you must make an appointment.

TELEPHONE: 01-47-27-37-50, 01-47-27-37-60
MÉTRO: Victor-Hugo
CREDIT CARDS: AE, MC, V
HOURS: Tues–Sat 10:30 A.M.–7 P.M.

Silk

GIANNI D'ARNO PUR RÉVE DE SOIE
17, rue St-Marc, 75002 (2nd)

Come here for the best-priced washable silk blouses in Paris in a rainbow of colors, patterns, and styles. No Chinese imitation imports . . . all are French or Italian silk. Scarves by Erre, the same quality as Hermès, but for much less money.

TELEPHONE: 01-42-36-98-73
MÉTRO: Richelieu-Drouot, Bourse
CREDIT CARDS: V
HOURS: Mon–Fri 9:30 A.M.–6:30 P.M., Sat 10 A.M.–6:30 P.M.

Spas

LES BAINS DU MARAIS
31-33, rue des Blancs-Manteaux, 75004 (4th)

Les Bains du Marais is billed as a "haven of beauty in the heart of the Marais." It is true. This is a welcome oasis where you can escape the hustle and bustle of Paris. Indulge in a dozen or more beauty treatments, including sauna, massage, manicure, pedicure, facials, hair dressing, peelings, and waxings. There is also a tearoom and small restaurant serving healthy snacks. Monday to Wednesday is reserved for women; Thursday to Saturday is for the men; and on Sunday it is mixed. It is all beautiful, clean, and oh, so relaxing—a well-spent hour or two out of your Paris stay that will revive you immeasurably. Prices vary with each service, packages are available, and appointments are required for the special one-on-one services and strongly suggested for all other spa services.

TELEPHONE: 01-44-61-02-02
MÉTRO: Rambuteau
CREDIT CARDS: AE, MC, V

HOURS: Women only: Mon 11 A.M.–8 P.M., Tues 10 A.M.–11 P.M., Wed 10 A.M.–7 P.M. Men only: Thur 10 A.M.–11 P.M., Fri–Sat 10 A.M.–7 P.M. Mixed: Sun 11 A.M.–8 P.M.

Sweaters

PIERRE VIVEZ
6, rue des Sausaies, 75008 (8th)

A large collection of traditional, lightweight, pure wool sweaters in every classic design imaginable, plus seasonal outfits and cotton T-shirts for women and sweaters for men. Everything is guaranteed washable.

TELEPHONE: 01-42-65-26-54
MÉTRO: Champs-Élysées, Miromesnil
CREDIT CARDS: AE, MC, V
HOURS: Mon–Sat 10 A.M.–7 P.M.

Watches

CAPION
9, rue Auber, 75009 (9th)

Watches for everyone on your list at prices starting at 80F. Several locations throughout Paris.

TELEPHONE: Not available
MÉTRO: Opéra
CREDIT CARDS: AE, MC, V
HOURS: Mon–Sat 10 A.M.–7 P.M.

Wines

LA DERNIÈR GOUTTE
6, rue de Bourbon-le-Château, 75006 (6th)

"I'm single, a great chef, and I also sing and tap dance," said Juan Sanchez, the multidimensional American owner of this wine shop near the St-Germain-des-Prés Church and the famous Les Deux Magots café. Juan also knows his wines, and he features in his shop lesser known estate-bottled regional wines at prices that are 30 to 40 percent less than you would pay elsewhere. Tastings are usually held on Saturday, and often the winemaker is present to talk about his wines. If you are close by, stop in, have a taste, and you will probably leave with several bottles to sample in Paris or to take home.

TELEPHONE: 01-43-29-11-62
FAX: 01-40-46-84-47
MÉTRO: St-Germain-des-Prés
CREDIT CARDS: AE, MC, V
HOURS: Mon 4–9 P.M., Tues–Fri 9:30 A.M.–1:30 P.M., 4–9 P.M., Sat 9:30 A.M.–9 P.M., Sun 10:30 A.M.–2 P.M., 3–6:30 P.M.; wine tastings: Sat 11 A.M.–1:30 P.M., 4–9 P.M.

Passages

Long before anyone heard of shopping malls, Paris had *galeries* and *passages*—skylighted, decorated, tiled, and beautiful. Tucked away off major commercial streets, mainly in the second and ninth arrondissements, they are easy to miss if you are not looking for them. Unfortunately, in a few commercialism has taken over and there are some low-end shops. Fortunately, the occupants of the spaces come and go, so it is still fun to stroll through one or two if only to see a sampling of the old-fashioned shops still selling handmade dolls, fancy pipes, old books, 78-rpm records, model trains, and toys.

GALERIE COLBERT
6, rue des Petits-Champs, 75002 (2nd)

MÉTRO: Bourse

Next to the Biblioteque Nationale and restored to all of its nineteenth-century glory.

GALERIE VIVIENNE
4, rue des Petits-Champs, 75002 (2nd)

MÉTRO: Bourse

The most beautiful *passage* of all.

PASSAGE JOUFFROY
12, boulevard Montmartre, 75009 (9th)

MÉTRO: Montmartre

The oldest *passage*, opened in 1800. In the *passage* is the Hôtel Chopin (see page 163) and the Musée Grevin, the hundred-year-old Paris wax museum inspired by Madame Tussaud's in London.

PASSAGE DES PANORAMAS
11, boulevard Montmartre, 75009 (9th)

MÉTRO: Montmartre

The name is taken from the panoramas of Rome, Jerusalem, London, Athens, and other world capitals.

PASSAGE VERDEAU
31, bis rue du Faubourg-Montmartre, 75009 (9th)

MÉTRO: Montmartre

Shops feature collectibles: books, records, and more.

Premier Shopping Areas: Cost Is Not an Object

AVENUE GEORGE-V, AVENUE MARCEAU, AVENUE MONTAIGNE, RUE DU FAUBOURG ST-HONORÉ, AND RUE FRANÇOIS 1ᴱᴿ (8th)

For window-shopping and dreaming of the highest order, these five premier shopping streets are to designer fashion and *haute couture* as the Louvre is to priceless art. The boutiques and shops are not to be missed, even if you only stroll by the elegant window displays.

LE FORUM DES HALLES (1st)

When it first opened, the ultramodern, multilevel complex on the site of the old Les Halles market and the shops around it attracted more than 40 million visitors per year. Even though the area has lost some of its original luster and allure, the youthful—in mind, body, and spirit—still come to this covered shopping wonderland to cruise the shops displaying the latest fashion fads, eat in the fast-food joints, and try the hair salons offering sculpted cuts or dye jobs in glowing green or blue. The largest métro station in the world lies under it, but it is not considered by Parisians to be safe at night, so please be careful.

MARAIS (3rd and 4th)

The kosher food shops along rue des Rosiers, the trendy boutiques along rue Francs Bourgeois, and the avant-garde designers make shopping in the Marais an excellent off-beat adventure. Be sure to include a stroll by the lovely place des Vosges and sit in one of the cafés (see *Cheap Eats in Paris*).

PLACES DES VICTOIRES (1st)

This is a smart shopping section nestled behind Palais-Royal. After going around the place des Victoires, branch out down the side streets. This is an area of many fashion innovators and well worth serious time just to see what you will be wearing two years from now. The prices are not in the bargain department, unless you happen to hit a sale.

ST-GERMAIN-DES-PRÉS (6th and 7th)

Sensational shopping can be found on the rue de Sèvres, rue Bonaparte, rue de Four, rue St-Sulpice, rue Jacob, and the rue de Seine, to mention only a few of the streets that line this *quartier*, which is literally packed with fashion boutiques, antique shops, art galleries, and bookshops. In fact, if you have only a short time to devote to shopping and browsing, this is where you should go.

CHAMPS-ÉLYSÉES (8th)

The day has passed when the Champs-Élysées was considered the finest address a retailer could have. Today there are waves of tourists flowing up one side and down the other. Movie theaters, airline offices, banks, car dealers, fast-food outlets, mini-malls, and outdoor cafés—all charging top francs for everything—line each side of the famous avenue. Pickpockets also work both sides of the street and are pros . . . watch out! Reserve your time on the Champs-Élysées for sipping an afternoon drink at a café and for fascinating people-watching. Do your shopping elsewhere.

RUE DE PASSY AND AVENUE VICTOR-HUGO (16th)

Walking down either of these streets in the sixteenth arrondissement will give you an idea of what it is like to be in the upper-middle-class and live in Paris. You will see few tourists, no razor-shaved haircuts, and certainly no hawkers waving T-shirts or plastic replicas of the Eiffel Tower. This is the land of the BCBGs (French yuppies), old money, and tradition. There are several cafés if someone in your party would rather sit and have a beer while watching the world wander by.

Shopping Malls

Indoor shopping complexes are popping up all over Paris. They are not my favorite shopping venues, but if you need several items and only have a short time to shop, they are useful. Here are three.

FORUM DES HALLES
Main entry: rue Pierre Lescott or rue Rambuteau, 75001 (1st)

This is the result of filling the hole left after the wholesale food market Les Halles was moved to Rungis. The Forum des Halles is the largest commercial project in France and has the largest métro station beneath it. The shops sell fashions of the moment, aimed at a hip, slim crowd, all under thirty . . . at least in spirit. If you don't feel like shopping, you can watch a film, grab a snack or meal, or just hang out. Warning: This is not considered a safe place to be late at night. For more details, see page 289.

TELEPHONE: 01-40-39-38-74
MÉTRO: Les Halles
CREDIT CARDS: Depends on each shop
HOURS: Mon–Sat 10:30 A.M.–7:30 P.M. for the shops

PASSY PLAZA
Corner rue Jean Bologne and rue de Passy, 75016 (16th)

This has middle-of-the-road boutiques with lots of clothes for the junior set or for something to knock around in and still feel fashionable. Also a very good supermarket.

TELEPHONE: Not available
MÉTRO: Passy
CREDIT CARDS: Varies with each shop

HOURS: Shops: Mon–Sat 10 A.M.–7:30 P.M.; Supermarché: Mon–Sat 8:30 A.M.–8 P.M.

LES TROIS QUARTIERS
23, boulevard de la Madeleine, 75008 (8th)

Here you'll find seventy-five boutiques including Kenzo, Yves St-Laurent, Dorothée Bis, and Givenchy. Prices are high, but stroll through anyway to get an idea of how much you will save by shopping at the Cheap Chic shops listed in this book. The quality is better than at Forum des Halles, but the spirit is really dead.

TELEPHONE: 01-42-97-80-12
MÉTRO: Madeleine
CREDIT CARDS: Depends on the boutique
HOURS: Mon–Sat 10 A.M.–7 P.M.

Special Recommendations

This section covers some very special people I have met in Paris who provide unique services. In addition to being multilingual, extremely talented, and very well qualified, they are passionate about what they do. All of them possess an intimate, detailed knowledge of Paris, a city they have come to love and call their own through many years of living and working here. Time spent with any one of them will enhance your trip in ways you never would imagine, and as you bid them farewell, you will know you have made a wonderful friend in Paris you will be eager to see again and again.

FRENCH LINKS: RACHEL KAPLAN
29, rue Patrice de la Tour du Pin, 75020 (20th)

Rachel Kaplan never stops developing and perfecting her personalized tours of Paris. Whatever your needs, interests, or requirements, Rachel will be up to the challenge. A day spent with her will reveal the hidden treasures of this sophisticated city, whether it be on one of her tours covering Paris Gardens, Literary Paris, Children's Paris, Jewish Paris, Discount/Upscale Shopping (including tickets to fashion shows), or Women's History of Paris—just to mention a few. In addition to her tours, she is a recognized authority on the little-known museums in and around Paris and has written a book on the subject. If you need help with transportation, finding a gym to work off those buttery croissants, planning for a handicapped person, or purchasing advance tickets, Rachel is the person to call.

TELEPHONE/FAX: 01-44-64-76-26
E-MAIL: kaplan@club-internet.fr.
CREDIT CARDS: None, cash only
PRICES: Depends on your agenda and specific needs, but a full day will be around 1,500F, and worth it

PARIS WALKING TOURS: PETER AND ORIEL CAINE
10, rue Samson, St Denis, 93200

If you are fluent in French, finding an interesting walking tour in Paris is easy. Just look in the weekly issue of *Pariscope* and you will find several possibilities every day of the week. For those whose French is limited, a walking tour, in English, with British expatriates Oriel and Peter Caine is the solution. The Caines are licensed "blue badge" guides in France. They and a small group of assistants have put together a series of well-researched walking tours through parts of Paris the casual visitor is likely to miss. Their comments are both educational and entertaining, filled with little-known tidbits that humanize the particular area covered. The tours are given year round, last approximately an hour and a half, and all you have to do is to show up at the appointed time and place wearing comfortable shoes and be ready to learn and enjoy. For a schedule, contact them at the numbers listed below.

TELEPHONE: 01-48-09-21-40
FAX: 01-42-43-75-15
CREDIT CARDS: None, cash only
PRICE: 60F per person, collected at the beginning of the walk

PAULE CAILLAT
118, boulevard Richard Lenoir, 75011 (11th)

It doesn't matter who you are—everyone from gourmet chefs to fledgling novices will learn something from this dynamic Parisian chef, whose love of cooking and family heritage of fine food transforms everything she touches. Paule gives private and group cooking lessons in Paris, but I can assure you they are a quantum leap from the ordinary, stilted classes I have often attended. Cooking with Paule means hands on from the get-go: shopping at the market right through enjoying what you have prepared and cleaning up afterward. On the trip to the outdoor market, you will learn how to recognize the best ingredients, discern the different types of bread and cheese, detect a French apricot from one imported from Israel and know which one to buy, select the perfect meats and fish, and avoid anything that is not absolutely fresh. Through her knowledge of food you will also be able to place the products you buy into their historical and geographical context in France.

Cooking lessons are not the half of Paule and her enthusiasm about food. She also leads small groups on excursions to areas in France that are specifically known for their exceptional food products. The trips include train travel, all meals and accommodations, and visits to points of interest.

Paule is a delightful, dynamic, knowledgeable woman. If you love food and cooking, please treat yourself to one of her cooking lessons or trips. You won't regret it for a minute.

TELEPHONE: 01-43-14-00-80
FAX: 01-43-14-95-01

CREDIT CARDS: None, cash only

PRICES: Vary with specific class or trip

TRAVEL Á LA CARTE: MOIRA JOHNSON
5, rue Marie Pape Carpentier, 75006 (6th)

Paris-based Moira Johnson uses her twenty years of experience in travel and the arts to prepare original travel itineraries, tailored to your personal interests, travel dates, and budgets. It can be something as simple as planning a Parisian vacation for a couple or family who simply do not have the time or knowledge to do it well on their own to orchestrating your own personalized trip through several major cities and the countrysides of France and Italy. With Moira helping you, you will have the expert help you need to make your trip a dream vacation come true.

TELEPHONE: 01-42-84-01-88

FAX: 01-42-84-19-60

E-MAIL: majohnson@compuserve.com

CREDIT CARDS: None, cash only

PRICES: Based on amount of work involved with your particular request

Size Conversion Charts: French and American Clothing Sizes

Many French off-the-rack manufacturers have their own cuts, and sizes are not always uniform. Whenever possible it is important to try on your purchase. Because that is not always possible, bring measurements and carry a tape measure with both inches and centimeters. Be careful with men's shirt sleeves, as the length is not always given; be prepared to measure. Table and bed linen sizes are also different from those in the States.

Women's dresses: To change French dress sizes to U.S. sizes, subtract 28 from the French dress size.

To change U.S. dress size to French, add 28 to the U.S. dress size.

French	32	34	36	38	40	42	44
U.S.	4	6	8	10	12	14	16

Women's sweaters and blouses: To change French sizes to U.S., subtract 8 from the French blouse or sweater size.

To change U.S. sizes to French sweater or blouse sizes, add 8 to the U.S. blouse or sweater size.

French	38	40	42	44	46	48	50
U.S.	30	32	34	36	38	40	42

Men's suits: To change French suit size to U.S. sizes, subtract 10 from the French suit size.

To change U.S. suit size to French, add 10 to the U.S. size.

French	46	48	50	52	54	56	58
U.S.	36	38	40	42	44	46	48

Men's shirts: To change French shirt size to U.S. shirt size, subtract 8 from the French size and divide by 2.

To change U.S. shirt size to French, multiply the U.S. size by 2 and add 8.

French	36	37	38	39	40	41	42	43
U.S.	14	14.5	15	15.5	16	16.5	17	17.5

Shoes: To change French shoe size to U.S., subtract 32 from the French size.

To change U.S. shoe size to French shoe size, add 32 to the U.S. shoe size.

French	36	37	38	39	40	41	42	43	44
U.S.	4	5	6	7	8	9	10	11	12

Children's clothing: French children's clothes are sized according to the age of the child: 2m means 2 months, 16m means 16 months, and so on. 2a means 2 years, 6a means 6 years (*a* stands for *ans,* which in French means *years*).

Cheap Chic Shopping Vocabulary

affiche	poster
à la mode	in style
atelier	workshop
bas	stockings
bleus de travail	blue cotton worker's uniform
bricoleurs	do-it-yourselfers
brocanteur	second-hand dealer
caleçons	boxer shorts
Carte Bleu	VISA charge card
ceinture	belt
chaussures	shoes
cravate	tie
dégriffés	labels cut out
dépôt vente	resale shop
détaxe	tax refund
duvet	down comforter
écharpe	scarf

espèces	cash
Eurocard	MasterCard charge card
faience	hand-painted pottery
fermé	closed
fin de series	end of the collection
fripes	second-hand clothes (à la thrift shops)
gant	glove
grand magasin	large department store
haute couture	expensive custom-made designer clothing
jupe	skirt
magasin	large department store
manteau	coat
marché	market
marché aux puces	flea market
ouvert	open
pantalons	pants
parfumerie	perfume store
peignoir	dressing gown, robe
premier étage	first floor above ground (second floor in U.S.)
prêt-a-porter	ready to wear
pull	sweater
rez-de-chausée	ground floor (we call it the first floor)
sac	purse
stock	overstock
tablier	apron
taille	size
Ça coute combien?	How much does this cost?
Acceptez-vous les cartes de credit?	Do you accept credit cards?

Index of Cheap Chic by Arrondissement

Readers' Comments

While every effort has been taken to provide accurate information in this guide, the publisher and author cannot be held responsible for changes in any of the listings due to rate increases, inflation, the rise and fall of the dollar, the passage of time, or management changes.

Cheap Sleeps in Paris is updated and revised on a regular basis. If you find a change before I do, make an important discovery you want to pass along to me, or just want to tell me about your trip to Paris, please send me a note stating the name and address of the hotel or shop, the date of your visit, and a description of your findings. Your comments are very important to me. I answer every letter personally, and I follow through on the comments and suggestions I receive. Thank you very much for taking the time to write.

Send your letters to Sandra A. Gustafson (*Cheap Sleeps in Paris*), c/o Chronicle Books, 85 Second Street, Sixth floor, San Francisco, CA 94105.

Index of Accommodations